The police, the publ

THE POLICE, THE PUBLIC, AND THE PURSUIT OF TRUST

A cross-national, dynamic study of trust in the police and police trust-building strategies

DORIAN SCHAAP

Eleven International Publishing
Den Haag
2018

Published, sold and distributed by Eleven International Publishing
P.O. Box 85576
2508 CG The Hague
The Netherlands
Tel.: +31 70 33 070 33
Fax: +31 70 33 070 30
e-mail: sales@budh.nl
www.elevenpub.com

Sold and distributed in USA and Canada
International Specialized Book Services
920 NE 58th Avenue, Suite 300
Portland, OR 97213-3786, USA
Tel.: 1-800-944-6190 (toll-free)
Fax: +1-503-280-8832
orders@isbs.com
www.isbs.com

Eleven International Publishing is an imprint of Boom uitgevers Den Haag.

ISBN 978-94-6236-845-3
ISBN 978-94-6274-850-7 (e-book)

© 2018 Dorian Schaap | Eleven International Publishing

Cover image by Jaanus Jagomägi; http://jaanus.cc

Printed in The Netherlands

PREFACE

It is often so *'that within a given case, when we try to track down the origins of an idea or proposal, we become involved in an infinite regress'* (Kingdon, 1995: 72-73). Taking that into account, I would still argue that this project must have commenced sometime in early 2010. The starting point was a paper I wrote for Crime & Security Policy, a subject I attended as part of a minor to my sociology bachelor's education at Radboud University Nijmegen. In spare hours I had as a student-assistant at the Criminal Law & Criminology department, I delved deeper into the subject and decided to make it my research master thesis topic. An application for a Ph.D. grant to the Netherlands Organization for Scientific Research (NWO) was honored in 2012. As such, I gained a Ph.D. position at Criminal Law & Criminology under supervision of prof. dr. ir. Jan Terpstra and prof. dr. Peer Scheepers; both of whom had been involved with my master thesis as well.

Ideas and projects change over time. This holds for ideas about policing—as we will see throughout this book—but also for this research project itself. It grew a wider scope, gained more dimensions, added questions, theories and methods. Departing initially from the question how meaningful differences in trust in the police between countries are (and how to explain those differences), soon a synchronic perspective was adopted by tracing developments in trust over time. Most importantly, however, realization dawned that all studies of levels of trust in the police tend to be one-sided: police trust-building strategies needed to be taken into account, lest we remain half-blind in our understanding of trust in the police.

The resulting contribution attempts to provide a more complete image of trust in the police, dispelling some common myths about the subject in the process. It is explicitly cross-national in nature, albeit primarily focused on the European context. Moreover, it takes a dynamic perspective, taking account of change in different ways. Finally, by including quantitative analyses of levels of trust as well as qualitative examinations of how the police themselves relate to the problem of trust, two sides of the medal are illuminated. Without one, I would argue that knowledge of the other will be only of limited use. It is my hope that including both perspectives, that of the police and that of the public, will be to the benefit of all.

There are those who consider themselves to be self-made men and women; people who do not owe anything to anyone, who have only themselves to thank for their achievements. These people clearly never wrote a Ph.D. dissertation. Often cast as the ultimate solitary activity, producing a dissertation is, in fact, a deeply social process.

Finishing a project like this is a humbling experience, much more so than starting it. In the beginning, one is full of optimism, fresh ideas, a revolutionary attitude. The end is, strangely, a much more introspective phase. Over the past year, my thoughts wandered more and more often to all who made this book possible. Where can I begin to express my gratitude to everyone who contributed? This doubt becomes even more embarrassing when I realize that many of these people may have forgotten all about me—after all, for them, I must have been just a foreign researcher doing some interviews, an observer, almost a ghost. For others, a friend or family member who tends to disappear behind stacks of books and has occasional troubles keeping in touch. And for yet different people, a colleague rather less reliable than they might have wished. I am grateful to all of them.

Some individuals in particular are worthy of thanks. My supervisors, Jan Terpstra and Peer Scheepers, have seen my work evolve (or escalate) from a minor study project, to a master thesis, to a Ph.D. dissertation. Both of them have had a powerful influence on who I am as a professional. Jan once told me he only employs people who are as headstrong as he is (his words, not mine!). Meanwhile, I can only admire the patient and rock-solid way he guided this particular headstrong candidate towards completion of his book. I am more than grateful for all the opportunities he has given me. Peer deserves the highest praise and appreciation for his rigorous approach towards structure and methods, for his occasional directness when I was in need of a wake-up call and for his support and positive attitude during times when I doubted my work.

It is hard for me to properly convey my gratitude to Barry Loveday and Lars Holmberg, both of whom went above and beyond the line of duty to help a young foreign researcher find his way. I am looking forward to buying them a well-deserved beer or two during a future ESC conference. To the members of my manuscript committee, Piet Hein van Kempen, Taco Brandsen and Els Enhus, I am deeply indebted for their time, effort and constructively critical attitude. I would like to thank NWO for funding this project, as well as the Faculty of Law of Radboud University. Geoff Palmer is not just a good friend; he has been an extremely dedicated and thorough editor, too. I feel that his contribution vastly improved this book. Any remaining errors are obviously my own.

I would also like to use this opportunity to thank all the people who proved willing to be interviewed, from small-town police officers to eminent scholars, and those who otherwise contributed.

There is a remarkable list of former office mates who put up with me throughout the years: Caroline, Mirjam, Jelle, Teun, Ruben, Joeri, Jeroen and Elco. Every single one of them taught me something. Especially Jelle and Teun left their mark on my time as a Ph.D. candidate: Jelle because of the many good conversations and beers, Teun because he is likely to remain the only colleague I ever shared a Siberian banja with.

There is a host of other colleagues I would like to thank. I will limit myself to mentioning the people from criminal law, new and veteran, who have proven to be engaging and fun colleagues—no matter how different our perspectives occasionally are. Most of my fellow criminologists have been mentioned in one way or another, but here I would like to thank Bas and Renze in particular. Working with them has been and will remain a pleasure. Similarly, collaborating with Bart, Daniela and Gesa, my Ph.D. colleagues in the University Works Council, has meant two years of fun, hard work, shared frustrations and surprising achievements.

There are too many friends who have contributed one way or another to mention here. Thanks to anyone who has been with me for part of the ride; you know who you are—and if you don't, then at least I do. Jarno and Anouk, having you as *paranymphs* means that the festivities are in capable hands. I know you got my back.

Pa en ma, veel dank voor jullie warmte, toewijding en geduld in de afgelopen jaren. Het is niet waar dat ik mezelf heb opgevoed, zoals jullie altijd zeggen. Ik heb van jullie geleerd dat nieuwsgierigheid en doorzettingsvermogen heel goed samen kunnen gaan. Pa, sorry voor het gebrek aan draken in dit boek. Ma, ik zal niet naast mijn schoenen gaan lopen. Danja, Raymond en Robin: ik hoop jullie de komende tijd vaker op te kunnen zoeken. Hou me daaraan. My dear Dina, how funny life can be! Not too long ago, I couldn't have dreamed of this. Σ' αγαπώ; të dua; in these languages and all others.

Table of Contents

Tables and figures

Figures

PART I

INTRODUCTION AND THEORIES

1 | INTRODUCTION AND RESEARCH QUESTIONS

1.1   TRUST AND THE POLICE AS REPRESENTATIVES OF SOCIETAL ORDER[1]

By the time I conducted my field research in Denmark in early 2015, it seemed to me as if all of Western Europe was holding its breath. To some extent, such a perception is deeply personal. However, most social scientists would probably agree that there was a sense of disquiet in society, a kind of insecurity that was hard to attribute to any concrete event or problem in particular. The European Union (EU) was in a state of uncertainty, with cracks showing between the north and the south. Recovery from the 2008 economic crisis was progressing at a grindingly slow pace. The conflict in Syria and its magnetic effect on foreign jihadists had increased the risk of terrorist attacks across the continent to levels not seen in at least 10 years and there was a fear of more to come.[2] Citizens appeared to be profoundly dissatisfied with their governments, while state authorities grappled with public shows of distrust and the rise of populist political movements. It was hard to find solutions, as even a convincing diagnosis of what was wrong was still lacking. Yet to a large extent, this is what was expected from the police more than from any other actor.

For one neighborhood police officer, despite the fact that he was working in one of Denmark's more difficult and least trusting neighborhoods, these were merely challenges to overcome, rather than cause for despair. A former member of the military, he applied his experience from his time abroad to his local police work back in Denmark. In his view, policing suburban Denmark was fundamentally no different from being a soldier in Iraq. *'It's very easy to take a whole country by force,'* he told me, *'but much more difficult to take the heart and soul.'* Similarly, *'it's easy for the police to patrol the city and to show force at some stage, but the next step is to actually have people believe.'* It was his goal, his mission even, to gain the trust of a skeptical public and then to be able to make a difference in their lives.

---

1.   Small segments from this introduction have, in an altered form, been previously published in Schaap and Scheepers (2014).

2.   Indeed, the evening before my departure from Denmark, a former convict in Copenhagen killed a film director and a synagogue security volunteer in the name of the Islamic State terrorist group.

On that gray day in early February, as this police officer showed me around his neighborhood and introduced me to people in his area, I realized that he, like thousands of other officers at that very same moment, was building public trust. In his neighborhood's complex web of local associations, preconceptions, relationships, and expectations, he was attempting to convince citizens that he was a trustworthy representative of legitimate, fundamentally benign, state authority. This was the basis. He worked on the foundations of societal order—those very foundations that appeared at that time to be more vulnerable than ever.

Western societies strive for internal harmony in one way or another. That a government or a state wields mere dominion over its citizens is not enough; a monopoly on the use of force too banal to fully legitimize its authority in a modern society (Beetham, 1991a). Thus, in many countries, there is a continuous endeavor on the part of the state to accomplish something more encompassing, more meaningful than that. It is the duty of the police, arguably over and above any other institution, to represent this fundamental strife for legitimate order both in a symbolic and in a very practical way. In order to fulfill this task, however, the police need a certain measure of support on the part of the public. They need to be trusted.

In recent decades, democratic governments all over the Western world have been concerned with a loss of trust on the part of the public and a decrease in perceived legitimacy. The idea of a crisis of confidence is widespread and intensifying, determining political and societal discourse (Van de Walle, Van Roosbroek, & Bouckaert, 2008). This seems to hold for parliament, government, and other democratic institutions (Chanley, Rudolph, & Rahn, 2000; Dalton, 2005; Newton & Norris, 2000; Wilkes, 2015), the armed forces (Newton & Norris, 2000), civil servants (Houston et al., 2016), and the police (Bradford, 2011a; Jackson et al., 2009; Loader & Mulcahy, 2003; Myhill & Quinton, 2010; Reiner, 2010; Terpstra & Trommel, 2009; Tyler & Huo, 2002). For some institutions, such as the judiciary, there has been no clear evidence for a decrease in trust (Gibson, 2007) and for most of the other institutions mentioned above, empirical evidence gathered so far has actually been mixed (Norris, 2011). The perceived trend, however, seems to be one of governmental institutions gradually being trusted less. On a rhetorical level, this is a notion that has permeated public debate. An exception to this trend is Eastern Europe, where institutional trust is said to have remained at a more or less constant (low) level ever since the fall of communism (Mishler & Rose, 2001; Thomassen, 2013). Such a lack of confidence in governmental institutions is problematic, since democratic governments need to be trusted in order to function (Chambliss & Seidman, 1971; Hetherington, 1998; O'Neill, 2002).

The police are thought to be among the primary victims of these supposed falling trust rates (Bradford, 2011a; Reiner, 2010). Terpstra and Van der Vijver (2006), in the context of the Netherlands, stated that the emergence of public safety as one of the central pillars of societal debate during the early 1990s caused citizens to—seemingly paradoxically—nurse higher expectations of the police as well as have less trust than before. In contemporary society, the police are expected to symbolize the difference between 'good' and 'evil,' bestowing upon the police an important symbolic power for many citizens (Loader & Mulcahy, 2003; Mawby, 2002). This is closely related to the increased needs of the public for protection against risks, danger, and insecurity (Boutellier, 2004). However, police officers on the beat perceive that they command ever less respect, which complicates their work (Loader & Mulcahy, 2003; Terpstra & Schaap, 2011, 2013; Terpstra & Trommel, 2009). For the police, the entire matter of maintaining or building trust therefore appears to have become considerably more difficult than it was several decades ago.

It is essential for the police to be trusted by the public. A range of studies have found that trust in the police increases citizens' compliance with the rule of law, is related to the willingness to cooperate with the police and report crime, improves the readiness of citizens to intervene in cases of minor problems of social disorder in their neighborhood, and is an important precondition for overall police effectiveness (FitzGerald, 2010; Goudriaan, Wittebrood, & Nieuwbeerta, 2006; Jackson & Bradford, 2010; Koster, 2017; Sunshine & Tyler, 2003; Tyler, 2004). Trusting the police, then, furthers citizens' willingness to engage in more trusting, risk-taking behavior (Goldsmith & Harris, 2012). Skogan (2009) found, additionally, that trust in the police increases feelings of security. This implies that high rates of trust in the police are beneficial for the public as well as the police. While seldom emphasized, we should note that the opposite also holds true: public mistrust will be accompanied by a multitude of harmful or negative effects. Moreover, mistrust risks leading to behavior that will further more mistrust, becoming self-fulfilling (Gambetta, 1988).

The importance of citizens' attitudes toward the police is, however, even more encompassing. When studying the relationship between citizens and their government, the standing of the police amongst the public is quite a central issue. Since the police are the main actor in maintaining societal order, the police are often considered to be the most visible representation of the authority of the state in general (Bittner, 1980; Fleming & McLaughlin, 2010, 2012). As such, they are actively steered by the state (Brodeur, 2010; Manning, 2003, 2012)—although the intensity with which this occurs arguably depends on the nation involved (Manning, 2005).[3] This makes public trust in the police also an important indicator of the legitimacy of governmental institutions in general. But while there is always a relationship between government, or the state as a whole, and the police, they should not be mistaken for the same thing. The police have their own priorities, their own ways of thinking, their own culture, their traditional role, and their historical function.

---

3. England & Wales has, for example, a tradition of weaker ties between (central) government and police than many of the more centralized continental European countries. In some ways, a more decentralized structure tends to diffuse the power of national governments over their police organizations (Mawby, 2003).

Many factors other than government policy affect the police, on the operational, the tactical, and the strategic levels. Therefore, studies delving into the relationship between the police and the public need to have some conceptual understanding of what the police do and why they do it.

Based on the above, we may conclude that a study of citizens' trust in the police involves at least three relevant actors: citizens, police, and the state. However, there are more factors of relevance. First, an international perspective is crucial in understanding the causes and consequences of trust in the police: we may learn from positive experiences in some countries and utter failures in others, and we could discern similarities as well as differences concerning trust in the police and the factors affecting it between countries. In an age of globalization in general and of policing specifically, international comparative studies in criminal justice research have therefore simply become a necessity (De Maillard & Roché, 2016; Nelken, 2010; Pakes, 2010). But not only is an international comparative perspective required: a longitudinal, dynamic approach can also prove to be of great value in order to study changes in the relationship between citizens and the police. Such a diachronic scope might additionally yield more profound insights into the societal mechanisms that underlie the shaping of trust in the police.

Knowledge about public trust in the police, taking all these factors into account, could have important policy implications: if we know what influences trust, it might be possible to address these factors through policy measures and thus attempt to improve the standing of the police with the public. Since the police encounter similar—although by no means equal—problems in the field of trust and perceived legitimacy in many different countries, such knowledge could prove to be of international benefit. Although the goal of the present study is not to provide a guidebook-like 'how to' or a collection of best practices that promote public trust, it may help us to improve our understanding of trust and the directions that we may take to influence it in a broader sense. After all, '*the best practice for 'us' to learn from may not always be the best practice as such, but rather that which stretches our imagination about what is possible*' (Nelken, 2010: 23).

1.2   GAPS IN OUR KNOWLEDGE

Much excellent work has been done in the field of police legitimacy and citizens' trust in this institution. In fact, one of the perks of writing a book such as this is becoming acquainted with a body of knowledge consisting of so many high-quality contributions. Nevertheless, I wish to argue that the existing field is still found wanting in several respects. These relative weaknesses can be summarized as follows: most studies have a limited scope concerning their theoretical approach, as well as the temporal and geographic range taken into consideration. As a result, they may do insufficient justice to various methodological and conceptual issues. They also tend to take either a qualitative or a quantitative approach. While understandable, this has the undesirable side effect that insights drawn from the other research tradition are ignored or, occasionally, misunderstood. This study aims to improve upon previous literature on these elements by including multiple perspectives and methods. Let me briefly dwell upon each of the main presently existing weaknesses.

First of all, previous studies have often concentrated on a single theoretical approach when explaining or understanding public attitudes toward the police. It is important to note, however, that there are multiple ways of thinking about what factors determine trust and what strategies the police should follow to gain public trust. Studies that include only one of these perspectives refrain from formulating rival hypotheses or accounting for possible confounding factors on the level of individuals, neighborhoods, regions, or nations. Similarly, by viewing the police organization and the problem of trust through a single theoretical lens, scholars of police strategies, actions, or culture may omit alternative views on the same phenomenon. In the present study, I aim to let different theoretical lenses compete by centering my analyses around three scientific police perspectives or paradigms— each with their own implications on what affects trust in the police and on how police-related factors themselves can improve or decrease trust. Not only does this competition enable us to more adequately test the central assertions of each theory, but it also helps us to better understand their relationship with one another and more critically evaluate their merits and weaknesses. It will provide us with insight on what characteristics and assumptions they share, in which respects they differ, and in what way each of them is a response to perceived shortcomings of the others.

A second main contribution that I aim to make concerns the dynamics of trust. It is important to note that only a very small number of existing studies cover developments in citizens' attitudes toward the police over the years, just as only a select few have studied changes within police organizations and strategies over time. As stated earlier in this chapter, trust in the police and government is argued to have declined all over Western Europe since the 1980s (Reiner, 2010). Rising crime rates, various violent conflicts between protest or minority groups and the police, and increasing egalitarianism in Western societies are thought to be causes of less trust in and respect for the police (Loader & Mulcahy, 2003; Reiner, 1995, 2010; Terpstra & Trommel, 2009). Given the domination in the public discourse of the presumption that trust is steadily declining, one would expect firm empirical support for a decrease in trust in the police across the Western world over time. This support, however, is scant. Longitudinal studies focusing on developments of public attitudes toward the police are almost exclusively of British origin and are often drawn from the same data source (Bradford, 2011a; Hough, 2003; Jansson,

2008; Myhill & Quinton, 2010).[4] Information on developments in other European countries is, although usually available in one way or another, unsystematic in nature, including widely different time frames, and occasionally of questionable quality. Thus far, scholars of the relationship between the police and the public have not concentrated on developments over time from a European perspective. Whether the decline in trust as reported in British studies, for instance, holds across the rest of the continent hence remains to be seen.

This lacuna does not only affect analyses of trust in the police; it also concerns the police themselves: societal change takes place not only on the level of individual citizens, but also on that of institutional dynamics. Qualitative studies providing in-depth analysis of developments and shifts within police organizations and the dynamics of how they relate to citizens over time are, unfortunately, similarly rare (Bottoms & Tankebe, 2012). Systematic, comparative analyses regarding the question of how the police have responded over the years to a perceived lack of or decrease in public trust are altogether absent. This lack of a dynamic perspective adversely affects both our understanding of trust in the police and of how the police relate to the problem of trust. This scarcity of diachronic, rather than synchronic, approaches is a second shortcoming of extant research in both the quantitative and in qualitative research traditions. The present study will adopt a dynamic perspective on trust.

Third, the vast majority of prior contributions have focused on one country, while the aim of this work is explicitly to include a cross-national perspective. As was noted before (Alalehto & Larsson, 2016; Goldsmith, 2005; Hough et al., 2010; Jang, Joo, & Zhao, 2010; Kääriäinen, 2007; Lambert et al., 2010), there is a lack of theory-based comparative research on citizen's trust in the police. This is despite considerable differences in the level of trust between, for example, European countries (Alalehto & Larsson, 2016; Kääriäinen, 2007). Such comparative studies are of the essence for understanding social phenomena such as the subject of the present contribution. Assume, for instance, that in terms of trust, citizens in country A award the police on average with a 6 on a 0-10 scale. What does that tell us? Is it high, or rather low? Saying anything definite on this matter is likely to require some kind of comparison. Similarly, we may only adequately understand or even perceive the peculiarities of our own police organization in terms of its relationship with citizens through comparisons with other countries. This was already noted over 50 years ago by Banton, who wrote that '*the extent to which the British police are regarded, and regard themselves, as different from other institutions is not fully apparent to anyone who knows only the position in Britain and has nothing with which to compare it. I*

---

4.   An extremely worthwhile exception would be the study by Loader and Mulcahy (2003), who used retrospective group interviews to reconstruct the development of public images of the police and of the role of the police institution in public cultural identity, as well as developments within the police organization and society as a whole. Nevertheless, its astonishing depth by necessity also implies that it remains an exclusively British study.

came to feel that the police were a sacred sort of institution in British social life only after experiencing the very different situation in the United States' (Banton, 1964: 236).

While the number of comparative, especially quantitative, studies on public attitudes toward the police has been steadily on the increase as of late,[5] there is still plenty of ground to cover: most of these contributions have admirably and insight-fully explored public attitudes in different countries, yet very few have managed to shed much light on the police themselves while doing so. Most importantly, too few scholars have followed in the tradition of Banton (1964), providing insight into how police organizations perceive and define their own role vis-à-vis the public and the problem of trust in different countries (but see Cassan, 2010; De Maillard et al., 2016). The police's understanding and definition of the issue of trust, in particu-lar, as well as the ensuing processes of building trust in various differing national and cultural contexts, are issues of great scientific as well as societal importance that have gone largely unaddressed (Goldsmith, 2005).

1.3   Research questions

The subject of police–public relationships as briefly introduced in the first section entails a field of complex, dynamic, and interrelated concepts such as trust, confi-dence, legitimacy, satisfaction, and consent. There are various actors involved, who influence one another, interact, and respond to each other's actions or attitudes. These actors include, but are not limited to, citizens as individuals or in groups, police officers and managers, policy-makers, governments, journalists, private agencies, nongovernmental organizations (NGOs), and civil servants. They all operate on various levels, such as the global, the national, the regional, and the local; they do so in vastly different contexts, in terms of cultural areas, countries, or periods of time. These are the central assertions of the present study.

Taking these fundamentals into account, it appears wildly inadequate to study such a complicated phenomenon through the lens of only one actor or agency at a single moment in time. The outline of a study aiming to understand public trust in the police should hence, at the very least, include perspectives from the public realm as well as from the police—shedding light on the attitudes and perceptions of citizens and on the characteristics and dynamics of the police institution as rela-ted to trust. It is not too outlandish an assumption to state that these two will con-tinuously affect and shape one another. This ambiguity, this drive to illuminate both sides of the same coin, will guide the present contribution.

How can we do justice to the complexities briefly outlined above? Obviously, we cannot—at least, not in one single book. To fully cover these subjects would be

---

5.   Notable more or less recent studies taking this approach, in chronological order, include Cao and Zhao (2005), Sung (2006), Kääriäinen (2007), Kutnjak Ivković (2008), Jang et al. (2010), Cao, Lai, and Zhao (2012), Thomassen (2013), Jang, Lee, and Gibbs (2015), Morris (2015), Alalehto and Lars-son (2016), and Boateng (2017).

a hugely ambitious endeavor that would require more time, resources, and talent than I possess. But what we can do is address each of the three main knowledge gaps that I have described in the previous section. This at least ought to advance our understanding of the issue. Hence, in two separate yet interconnected empirical parts of this book, we will study both the citizens' side as well as the police side of public trust in the police. In both respects, this is to be done through the application of the same three theoretical lenses, and by taking an international comparative approach as well as a dynamic, diachronic perspective.

Focusing on the public, several questions arise that we will address in the first empirical part of this book. The first of these problems is that we need to ensure that we actually have sufficiently accurate, valid information regarding public trust in the police in as many European countries as we can: we need to do justice to the comparative approach that we aim to take. Will the sources of empirical information available to the researcher pass critical methodological scrutiny? Only if that is the case can we continue to answer the following questions. The second question, then, is descriptive and is both comparative and diachronic in nature: for those countries where we have evidence for cross-national comparative validity as determined by the answer to the first research question, we will assess differences between, as well as developments in, levels of public trust in the police. Finally, the third question concerning public trust in the police deals with explanations for these differences in trust between countries. For this question, it is essential to be guided by a thorough theoretical framework, consisting of various theoretical lenses. This framework will help us narrow down the factors of interest in finding the main determinants, on the individual and national level, of public trust in the police. The research questions we shall answer in the first empirical part of this book, focusing on public attitudes toward the police, are the following:

> Research Question 1: *To what extent are measures of citizens' trust in the police empirically comparable across European countries?*

> Research Question 2: *What are the differences between European countries in terms of citizens' trust in the police, and how has trust in the police developed across Europe over the past few decades?*

> Research Question 3: *What factors on the national and on the individual level explain differences between countries in terms of citizens' trust in the police?*

When these questions are answered, we will have addressed each of the three main knowledge gaps as far as citizens are concerned: applying multiple theoretical approaches as well as having a cross-national and a dynamic perspective. These questions are presumed to yield information on the comparability of trust in the police between contexts, on how levels of trust have developed over time, what differences there are in these terms between countries, and why the police are trusted or distrusted in different contexts. This also aims to provide us with tentative leads as to how trust might be improved or how harm to trust may best be avoided.

After answering these three research questions, we will switch focus. In the second empirical part of this book, we shall concentrate on the police rather than on the public. This is closely connected with what Bottoms and Tankebe (2012: 159) call *'the dialogic character of legitimacy,'* meaning that there is both power-holder legitimacy (the claim on legitimacy by the police) and audience legitimacy (public perceptions of legitimacy), and that they interact. This dual view on legitimacy implies that public trust in the police and police views on trust both matter if we wish to gain a richer understanding of trust. The authors argue that taking both perspectives on legitimacy into account will yield information on congruence—when assessments of legitimacy by the power-holder and the audience align—and incongruence—when they conflict. Taking these two perspectives into account, we can shed light on the consequences of incongruence, on the actions and reactions that ensue when there is a discrepancy between public trust and police views on trust. It is in this dialogic character between two sides of legitimacy that police trust-building strategies become relevant.

While plenty of research both past and present has attempted to explain citizens' attitudes toward the police, very few if any scholars have indeed explicitly studied how the police themselves think about their relationship with the public, how they view the subject of public trust, and how they act on it. This is a serious lacuna. This is why Bottoms and Tankebe (2012: 160) argue that there is *'an urgent need to develop studies of power-holder legitimacy.'* After all, a good police service, as emphasized by Braithwaite (1992) and Goldsmith and Harris (2012), seeks to build the confidence of the community. This implies that studies of trust in the police and of police attitudes toward trust belong together.

Implicitly agreeing with this assessment, many studies on citizens' attitudes toward the police, including my own, do provide leads for police organizations to improve their relationship with the public. But it is curious to see that the police themselves, in terms of how they perceive the problem of trust and the best way to deal with it, are to a large extent terra incognita to scholars. After all, the police are the main driver of public attitudes toward the police (Gourley, 1954). History, in many different countries, has taught us that it is often a perceived slight on the part of the police that drives public protest and criticism; that sets off a crisis of trust.[6] Similarly, it is that very same police who often come up with new, innovative strat-

---

6.   Examples of this can no doubt can be found in most European countries, but some poignant (and diverse) discussions of this matter over recent decades include the following: Balvig, Holmberg, and Nielsen (2011) in Denmark; Newburn et al. (2016) and Scarman (1982) in England & Wales; Body-Gendrot (2013, 2016) in France; Xenakis and Cheliotis (2016) in Greece; Heijink et al. (1977) in the Netherlands; Zernova (2012) in Russia; and Hörnqvist (2016) in Sweden.

egies to (re)gain trust, authority, or legitimacy. Of interest is not only whether these strategies are objectively effective, but also how they come into being in the first place. What are the motivations for the police in a specific country at a specific moment in time to accept and implement a certain method for gaining public trust? What are the assumptions, problem definitions, and expectations underlying those methods? How and why do they change over time?

Without knowledge about these factors, devoid of awareness of the context in which our well-intended advice ends up—in a police organization that may or may not itself perceive a problem with trust, that may or may not already have formulated strategies to deal with such a problem, and that consequently may or may not align with our own propositions and suggestions—such advice might be ineffective or even counterproductive. This is why we need to gain a better understanding of this most central actor in determining citizens' trust in the police: the police themselves. The police stand to gain from this too, as their collective, institutional memory tends to be selective or skewed, framed by their current perspective or historical dogma. An analysis of the processes, developments, and origins of certain ideas and strategies could help the police to learn from their past and be more self-aware. Moreover, they also stand to gain from more insight into the choices and paths followed in shaping strategies to increase public trust in other countries.

I have argued, following Bottoms and Tankebe (2012), that we require a change in research object. In parallel with this shift also comes a different methodology, one that is qualitatively oriented and geared toward understanding societal and institutional mechanisms rather than quantitative and concentrated on explanatory models. If our aim is to increase our knowledge of how the social, cultural, and political realities in different societal contexts affect the way the police deal with the public, quantitative methods are found wanting. Note that this different approach also implies, for reasons explicated later, that we can no longer take most of Europe into account but, rather, we have to limit ourselves to a smaller selection of contexts to study (see also Nelken, 2010).

In spite of all this, it is important to note that we shall let the same principles guide us as in the first empirical part. While changing our object of study from citizens to the police will necessarily require adjustments to our mode of inquiry, the research approach in the second empirical part of this book will still apply the same theoretical lenses as before and will also have a comparative as well as a dynamic perspective. Similarly, the key concept will remain public trust in the police, but changing our point of view also means altering our approach to trust. Rather than looking at levels and determinants of trust, we will study police perspectives on the problem of trust, and, of vital importance, the ensuing police trust-building strategies in three Western European countries. We shall ask questions about how the police view citizens, their relationship with citizens, and what they do to improve it.[7] This reflects the 'dialogic approach' discussed by Bottoms and Tankebe (2012). Without knowledge on the role of local context and history on the way in which the police and their management view their relationship with the public, information on the determinants of citizens' trust may very well pass by unnoticed, unapplied. Discovering the factors that affect public trust and confidence is, in itself, simply not sufficient to understand the relationship between the police and the public. The pursuit of trust requires knowledge of trust, as perceived and acted upon by all relevant sides. What are the reasons, rationalities, and assumptions behind policies aiming to address police–public relationships? How has police thinking about the public changed? What have societal and political developments meant for changes in police–public relationships?

Since we will return to the idea of trust-building strategies at length in Chapter 7, a brief account of what they entail will suffice for now. Police trust-building strategies can be summarized as ways to address the problem of *'how institutional arrangements and practices associated with policing can be reshaped so as to make them more deserving of public trust'* (Goldsmith, 2005: 457). While Goldsmith (2005) concentrates on developing and non-Western countries, there is no reason to assume that this question is not equally salient in Western contexts—although the challenges involved obviously differ.

The invention and application of trust-building strategies naturally comes with some requirements. First and foremost is the recognition of a need to work on trust; the realization that, in fact, *'institutional arrangements and practices associated with policing'* actually need to *'be reshaped so as to make them more deserving of public trust.'* This can only take place once the problem of trust has been defined and accepted as such. The timing and manner of this problem definition will be of great consequence to the trust-building strategies eventually applied in a specific country. And since the definition of a problem is not a static concept, it is also commendable to trace this conceptualization over time. This problem definition and how it has evolved is what the fourth research question of this study aims to address.

For the fifth question, we then turn to the strategies that were designed and applied to deal with the problem of trust in a selection of different European countries. In what different ways have the various actors involved attempted to build trust between the police and the public in different European countries? Finally, the sixth question aims to further our understanding of cross-national differences in trust-building strategies, as it seeks to single out the main mechanisms behind and explanations for the differences we have found between countries in terms of these strategies.

---

7. That is not to say that quantitative research shedding light on this matter is altogether absent. See, for example, Kääriäinen and Sirén (2012), who conducted an international comparative study on police trust in citizens, rather than the other way around.

Research Question 4: *When and how was citizens' trust in the police defined as a problem in different European countries, and how did it evolve?*

Research Question 5: *Since that time, what strategies and 'solutions' have been adopted by whom to address the problem of trust in these countries, and to improve police–public relationships in general?*

Research Question 6: *How can we understand the differences that we find between and within countries in terms of problem definition and trust-building strategies?*

In answering these three questions, we will have addressed the knowledge gaps we previously discerned (limited theoretical, geographic, and temporal scope) as far as the police and trust-building strategies are concerned.

1.4   OUTLINE OF THE STUDY

Before we commence with addressing these six research questions, however, we need to take several additional steps. In the rest of this study, I will first attempt to determine and define several central concepts in Chapter 2, thus narrowing down the subject of study and clarifying what it does and does not entail. Then, in Chapter 3, I will proceed to the description and elaboration of three different scientific theoretical perspectives on policing and their implications for citizens' trust in the police. That will bring our introductory Part I to a close.

In Part II, we shall endeavor to answer Research Questions 1, 2, and 3. This part of the book is devoted to public trust in the police, focusing on the perceptions of citizens in different European countries over recent decades. In Chapter 4, we apply the theoretical perspectives described in the preceding chapter to formulate expectations and hypotheses aiming to explain trust in the police. The research design and methodology for the rest of Part II is also introduced. In Chapter 5, we continue with the description of differences between and developments within different European countries, after rigorously testing for the cross-country and within-country measurement equivalence of our available data. Chapter 6 then displays the results of our explanatory analyses regarding factors affecting public trust in the police in different European countries. All in all, Chapters 4-6 tell us to what extent we can empirically compare trust between countries and within countries over time (Research Question 1), what differences between and developments within levels of trust in different European countries are (Research Question 2), and how we can explain these differences (Research Question 3).

We then continue with Part III, where we answer Research Questions 4, 5, and 6. In this part of the present study, we will concentrate on the police organizations of three northwestern European countries and how they perceive and deal with the problem of trust—looking at both the present and the past. Chapter 7 will contain a theoretical framework, using the same theoretical approaches as in Part II, but applied differently and geared toward processes of trust-building rather than explaining trust. Moreover, this chapter will address the methodology and case selection. Chapter 8 concentrates on the first case study: thinking about the problem of trust and police trust-building strategies in England & Wales. Chapter 9 does the same for the second case study, Denmark, while Chapter 10 concentrates on the Netherlands, the third case study. Finally, this part of the study will conclude with a systematic comparison of the three case studies in Chapter 11. Here, we will compare definitions of the problem of trust in the three countries (Research Question 4), and the strategies and solutions adopted and applied in these countries at different moments in time (Research Question 5), and we will attempt to reach an understanding of the mechanisms behind the differences that we find between our cases with regard to these matters (Research Question 6).

Part IV is the final part of this contribution, consisting of a single chapter: Chapter 12. It is here that we will briefly summarize our main findings and conclusions, drawing together the evidence of both our quantitative public-oriented Part II and our qualitative police-oriented Part III. We shall continue to take an extensive look at the practical implications of the research findings, aiming to provide leads for police organizations and governments. Moreover, we will wish to reflect on the contribution to the research field that we have achieved throughout this study. We will evaluate the limitations of this research, the novel questions it raises, and let both of these inspire us in an attempt to formulate a future research agenda.

2 | Central concepts

2.1   Introduction

In this chapter, I will address the nature of some concepts aimed at describing the attitudes and beliefs of the public toward the police—and sometimes vice versa. The relationships between these concepts, phrases which are all often used and appear to be just as often confused, remain vague and demand due clarification. Especially in an international comparative context, at least a working definition is required. The words most often used when dealing with citizens' attitudes toward the police are trust, confidence, and legitimacy. Let us first consider trust and confidence, before we proceed to legitimacy. Finally, I will briefly discuss some other terms and phrases used to describe the relationship between the public and the police and how they relate to issues in the current study.

2.2   Trust and confidence

To the average user of the English language, trust and confidence are probably practically synonymous. Scientific literature, on the other hand, sometimes discerns between the two (Cao, 2015; Gilmour, 2008; Luhmann, 1988; Seligman, 1997; Sztompka, 1999), although there does not appear to be a consensus about the nature of the presumed difference in meaning and about their proper application. Many authors in the field of public attitudes toward the police—and other institutions—tend to circumvent possible misunderstandings by either using trust and confidence together as a single phrase, or as separate but largely interchangeable words (Goldsmith, 2005; Hohl, Bradford, & Stanko, 2010; Jackson & Sunshine, 2007; MacQueen & Bradford, 2015; Mishler & Rose, 1997; Tyler, 2001). Others are careful to consistently speak of either trust (Hawdon, 2008; Kääriäinen, 2007; Saarikkomäki, 2016) or confidence (Cao, Frank, & Cullen, 1996; Goudriaan et al., 2006; Jang et al., 2010; Morris, 2015), but often without providing more than a cursory rationale for choosing one or the other. Let us take a look at some of the literature dealing with the relationship between trust and confidence, and subsequently consider to what extent a differentiation between trust and confidence could potentially prove valuable in the context of an international study of public attitudes toward the police. In the final part of this section, we will then move toward a provisional definition of trust in the police.

Several authors have differentiated between trust and confidence, albeit with varying rationales. It is worth examining the most influential of these approaches to inform us about the nature of trust and of confidence. One of the more elaborate arguments on the difference between trust and confidence is made by Luhmann (1988). In his work, both confidence and trust—as well as distrust—are tools or mechanisms to reduce complexity (Luhmann, 1979).[1] This occurs because they yield expectations, generally about the behavior of others, that help structure our world. Such expectations, it should be noted, can be confounded. In the case of confidence, there is no perceived alternative to these expectations: they are essential to prevent one living in constant uncertainty, or what Giddens (1990) refers to as 'ontological insecurity.' Absence of confidence might lead to a state of utter anxiety and permanent doubt, hence making life very complicated and ultimately unpleasant. When, for example, we have an important appointment on the 27th floor of a skyscraper, most of us would not even consider taking the (emergency) stairs. We will instead have confidence that the elevator will take us there in good order, rather than refusing to open its doors, failing to take us to the correct floor, or even falling down the shaft. Being stuck for an hour in a broken elevator would admittedly be a highly frustrating experience and a breakdown in our confidence, but we would still hardly perceive any *choice* in the kind of transportation we use. The next time our presence is required on the 27th floor, we might feel extremely uncomfortable: due to our past experience, our confidence may have been seriously damaged. But since we do not perceive a realistic alternative, we will still proceed to take the elevator regardless. Confidence therefore falls *'within the discourse of fate'* (Sztompka, 1999: 25). Important in the understanding of confidence is that, in this situation, we will tend to blame the elevator rather than ourselves; this is what Luhmann (1988) calls 'external attribution.'

In the case of trust, this is different. Trust implies taking a risk that is willingly accepted (Luhmann, 1988): trust means that we expose our vulnerability but expect the other party not to take advantage (Montgomery, Jordens, & Little, 2008). Taking the risk of trusting someone might hence result in bitter disappointment, but it could also yield some form of profit. The possible damage, however, will be larger than the profit we are aiming for, and we will regret our choice to trust if our trust is betrayed. Since we blame ourselves, this is a matter of 'internal attribution' (Luhmann, 1988). When trust is betrayed, we can opt not to trust in the future. Trust

---

1.   In a previous essay, translated from German, Luhmann (1979) distinguishes not between trust and confidence but between 'personal trust' and 'system trust.' It is unclear to what extent this reflects his evolving views or, rather, illustrates a useful property of the English language that German appears to lack. To a high degree, however, his earlier idea of personal trust appears to overlap with his later understanding of trust, while system trust appears to refer to what he was to call confidence.

therefore implies a form of agency that confidence lacks: it has the properties of a gamble (Sztompka, 1999). In this sense, profit, agency, and risk are words associated with trust, whereas confidence is related to reliability, fate, and danger. Similarly, Misztal (1996: 16) views trust as a matter of individual determination that involves choosing between alternatives, whereas confidence refers more to habitual expectations that require rather less conscious effort.

Such a distinction is not clear-cut when we talk about the police. While we cannot opt out of the police in general (we can still be arrested after committing a crime, and part of our taxes will be used to fund the police), we can choose not to cooperate with the police by not reporting a crime, refusing to provide them with information, or ignoring their requests. The police therefore have characteristics of both a system-level institution with a certain degree of reliability, but also of individual agency, implying risk and choice when interacting with police officers. This is a key ambiguity in the very nature of the police (and a select few other institutions): the police have individual or social characteristics as well as institutional ones. The police are an organization composed of many individuals. What makes the police different from many other institutions is that police officers have a large number of day-to-day interactions with citizens in which they have considerable discretionary autonomy (Bittner, 1980; Muir, 1977). However, they also represent a unique state institution with a particular, peculiar place in public consciousness. As such, they have an important societal, symbolic role (Loader & Mulcahy, 2003). We can trust or distrust police officers, and we can trust or distrust the police institution. In this sense, both confidence and trust are terms applicable to the police if we follow Luhmann's categorization. This fundamental ambiguity between the police as an institution and as a collection of individuals interacting with citizens is a recurring theme in police science, and will be relevant throughout this dissertation.

Seligman (1997, 1998) makes a somewhat different distinction between confidence and trust. In his view, the role of confidence in social interactions is based on the assumption that the interaction is either set within a social system that will impose sanctions when an agreement is broken or in a context where the 'other' is familiar. In both cases, there is a high degree of—perceived—predictability in the actions of the other due to the clear presence of role expectations (Seligman, 1997). Trust comes into play when there is no basis for confidence; in the absence of a system with sanctions and when the other is unfamiliar. There is no particularly strong predictability, we acknowledge the other's agency and individuality—and thus that the other may harm us—and despite all that we trust. Trust hence comes at the system's limit, in '*that metaphorical space between roles, that area where roles are open to negotiation and interpretation*' (Seligman, 1997: 27). While confidence is, according to Seligman, typically associated with the public domain, trust is more related to the private domain.

What the explanations of Luhmann and Seligman have in common is a greater emphasis on agency when talking about trust than in the case of confidence, which is more related to predictability and reliability. The difference between the two, however, explains why some police scholars tend to speak of trust when discussing attitudes of citizens toward the police, while others prefer to use the term confidence. In the interpretation of Luhmann (1988), depending on the circumstances, either trust or confidence could apply. Putting one's faith in the police often involves a risk that is willingly accepted. For instance, the decision to report a crime might lead to the police making a serious effort to solve the crime, but it also poses the risk of being derided or, in the worst case, even being abused by bad officers. Whether or not to report hence relies on trust: it is a risk, not a danger. Confidence, in this interpretation, could apply when we think about the core functions of the police institution; the ones we cannot opt out of. Those following Seligman's reasoning are more likely to use confidence consistently, as police-citizen relationships are part of the public realm and a system of rules and sanctions is in play. In most instances, the police have a clearly defined role in such a situation: it is clear what the law expects of them, or what is socially acceptable.

Many authors using both trust and confidence when addressing police-citizen relationships seem to attempt to find a middle road. Writing specifically about the police, Bradford et al. (2008) focus on Seligman's interpretation of confidence as related to the public realm and trust as based in private interactions:[2] they describe confidence as public attitudes toward the police as an institution, a global assessment of the extent to which the police as a whole fulfill their role (Bradford et al., 2008) or do their job (Bradford & Jackson, 2010). Trust, in their view, can be found in interactions between individual police officers and citizens: in encounters, cooperation, and compliance. They share with Luhmann the acceptance that trust deals with concrete risk-taking and decision-making, while confidence deals more with factors one cannot affect—an assessment also shared by Cao (2015).

Gilmour (2008) has a similar view of trust in the police being rooted in individual interactions and confidence being more general, arguing that this also implies that trust precedes confidence. Whereas trust is the belief that something that ought (not) to be done will (not) be done despite uncertainty, confidence holds when such belief is based on prior experiences and knowledge. Instances and events during which citizens trust the police and are not disappointed hence form the foundation for a broader state of confidence (Gilmour, 2008: 58).

To summarize, although differences exist in interpretation and hierarchy of confidence and trust, there tend to be some common denominators: while both confidence and trust deal with expectations that can be confounded, confidence is seen as a more generalized, system-based measure of expectations founded in previous

---

2.   Although they, somewhat surprisingly given the commonalities, do not refer to Seligman's work.

experience and predictability, while trust is considered more particular and indi-
vidualistic, playing a role in unpredictable, risky, and unique situations.

That these authors at least have some common ground in their understanding
of the difference between trust and confidence does not necessarily mean that others would agree with their assessment. Other lines of reasoning are imaginable.
Giddens (1990, 1991), for example, like the earlier work of Luhmann (1979), cir-
cumvents the use of the word confidence, referring rather to 'trust in persons' and
'trust in systems' as the central distinction between the particular and individual
on the one hand and the general and collective on the other. Moreover, even fundamental ontological security, defined by Luhmann (1988) as the result of confidence, is in Giddens' (1990: 99-100) terms determined by 'basic trust' instead. This
is not because Giddens would reject the notion of confidence as irrelevant, but
because his interpretation of trust is that of being a specific type of confidence—a
type where one lacks access to complete information (Giddens, 1990: 32-34[3]). While
possibly less elegant, there is the undeniable appeal of conceptual clarity in omitting the notion of confidence entirely and only referring to various forms of trust
instead.

Acknowledging the differences in interpretation and theorizing of the subtleties
surrounding trust and confidence, we may wonder whether the categorizations as
described above are actually salient in a cross-national context. After all, the nuances and differences in meaning as studied by Luhmann (1988), Seligman (1998),
Sztompka (1999), Bradford et al. (2008), or Gilmour (2008) are only applicable in an
international context if other languages make similar distinctions between their
particular equivalents of trust and confidence in the police. There may be a relatively simple way to find out whether this is the case.

In large-scale, cross-national surveys, great efforts are usually made to ensure
comparability and equivalence of translated questions (Harkness, 2003; Jowell,
1998). For each question, the best possible translation is required; one that retains
the meaning and implications of the core question as completely as possible. We
can hence assume that well-known cross-national surveys have gone to great
lengths to accurately translate questions about trust or confidence into various different languages. Let us compare two geographically overlapping international
surveys: one including questions about confidence in the English-language core
questionnaire, and the other about trust. If other languages make a similar distinction between trust and confidence, this should show in their translations of these
questions. Fortunately, two well-known surveys are suitable for our purposes: the
fourth wave of the European Values Study (EVS) and the fifth wave of the European Social Survey (ESS), conducted in 2008 and 2010, respectively. These studies

---

3.   Although Giddens' (1990: 34) eventual definition of trust as '*confidence in the reliability of a person or
     system, regarding a given set of outcomes or events, where that confidence expresses a faith in the probity or
     love of another, or in the correctness of abstract principles (technical knowledge)*' for our current purpo-
     ses does more to obscure the concept than to clarify it.

share many surveyed countries and both ask questions measuring public attitudes toward various institutions such as the police. While the core questionnaire of the EVS contains an item asking about confidence, the ESS asks about trust in institutions instead. Note that the ESS includes trust as a verb (yet at the end of the question also as a noun), while the confidence measure in the EVS is only phrased as a noun; something that might cause minor differences in translation even if the words are conceptually equivalent.

– ESS 2010: Using this card, please tell me on a score of 0–10 how much you personally **trust** each of the institutions I read out. 0 means you do not **trust** an institution at all, and 10 means you have complete **trust**.
– EVS 2008: Please look at this card and tell me, for each item listed, how much **confidence** you have in them: is it a great deal, quite a lot, not very much, or none at all?

In Table 2.1, I compare translations of these questions between 12 different European languages with a large geographic and linguistic spread. We can observe that there are remarkably few differences between the two surveys in the words used, although the grammatical structure of the question (and whether the reference to trust or confidence is made in the form of a verb or a noun) varies substantially between countries.

Table 2.1   Translations of trust or confidence in the police in the ESS and EVS

	ESS 2010	EVS 2008	Type	Meaning
Czech	důvěřujete	důvěru	(1) verb, (2) noun	same
Danish	tillid	tillid	(1) noun, (2) noun	same
Dutch	vertrouwen	vertrouwen	(1) noun, (2) noun	same
English	**trust**	**confidence**	**(1) verb, (2) noun**	**different**
Finnish	luotatte	luotat	(1) verb, (2) verb	same
French	confiance	confiance	(1) noun, (2) noun	same
Greek	εμπιστεύεστε	εμπιστοσύνη	(1) verb, (2) noun	same
Hungarian	bízik	bizalma	(1) verb, (2) noun	same
Lithuanian	pasitikite	pasitikite	(1) verb, (2) verb	same
Russian	доверяете	доверяете	(1) verb, (2) verb	same
Slovenian	zaupate	zaupanje	(1) verb, (2) noun	same
Spanish	confía	confianza	(1) verb, (2) noun	same

As we can observe, the English distinction between trust and confidence is made in no other language included here. The differences that we can see between the two surveys are merely grammatical: the origins are the same word or stem every time.

Apparently the difference between trust and confidence, which is often made in English-language literature, does not exist in other languages. This sheds quite a different light on the existing studies dealing with differences between the words; it appears to be an exclusive English-language problem. In an international comparative context, we must conclude that the concepts are best treated as being synonymous. On the one hand, this implies that results from international studies concentrating on confidence are likely to be more or less applicable to trust and vice versa. On the other hand, it also means that a nuanced difference, as is present in English, cannot be made in an international study. Taking this into account, I would suggest that it is generally best not to make a distinction between trust and confidence when studying citizens' attitudes toward institutions in a cross-national context.

How, then, do we interpret trust or confidence in the police in such an international context? Due to differences between the two concepts in English and possible variations in meaning in different countries, we will have to rely on a common, not too specific definition of trust/confidence. If we are to accept that there may be differences in meaning between trust and confidence in English, we need a working definition to comprise both, in order to prevent comparability problems in the English but also in the international context. Let us, for example, consider the difference between the French and the Dutch translations. The French *confiance* is clearly linguistically more closely related to the English *confidence* (both originating from Latin) than to *trust*. In Dutch, this is the other way around: *vertrouwen* shares a common linguistic origin (proto-Germanic) with *trust*, but not with *confidence*. Could these historical roots mean that the Dutch *vertrouwen* has conceptually slightly different implications, more related to individual evaluations and interactions, than the French *confiance*? Let us err on the side of caution and assume that translations of trust or confidence may in fact have somewhat different associations in different countries.

We require a definition of trust/confidence that is applicable to the police. Doing so requires several steps. First, the previously discussed ambiguous nature of the police—a state institution with a central, highly symbolic function, and yet at the same time also comprising a large number of individuals who have many daily interactions with citizens—needs to be acknowledged in a working definition of trust. The second issue that arises when attempting to formulate a working definition of trust in the police specifically flows from the first. It has implications for trust in different institutions, but particularly with regard to the police. Hetherington (1998: 791), for instance, defined '*political trust as a basic evaluative orientation toward the government founded on how well the government is operating according to people's normative expectations.*' The ambiguous nature of the police as both an institution and a collective of individuals means that trust concerns expectations about future behavior, but is at the same time also rooted in evaluations and images of the police, operating institutionally as well as interacting personally. Interestingly, these evaluations rely not merely on personal experience with the police (as is the case with interpersonal trust), but also draw from reputation, image, and hearsay.

More than an evaluation, these can actually be understood to entail belief. Trust in the police, having aspects of individual as well as institutional trust, is therefore related to beliefs as well as to expectations (Hetherington, 1998; Rothstein, 2005).

We have now established that trust/confidence in the police refers to beliefs and/or expectations regarding the police, either individually or as an institution. But what kind of beliefs and expectations? Many definitions of trust rely on the expectation that another actor will not do us harm or will yield us profit (Gambetta, 1988; Luhmann, 1988; Rothstein, 2005; Sztompka, 1999). Montgomery et al. (2008) employed a more careful phrasing, emphasizing that trust in public services and care providers refers to expectations that the other will not take advantage of vulnerability. However, such a definition encounters serious problems when we try to apply it to the police. It suggests a very rational, calculating interpretation of trust—one that is probably insufficient to explain, let alone understand, the concept of trust (Rothstein, 2005). Misztal (1996: 22), acknowledging this, notes that trust has *'emotional, cognitive and instrumental'* aspects. A definition of trust in the police should not ignore their symbolic, emotional, and moral significance, which goes to emphasize the importance of adding the notion of 'belief' to the definition. Nor should such a definition neglect the societal function of the police.

It is in this function that we find another problem with the common definition of trust as first formulated by Luhmann (1988). The police, by the nature of their function, have to provide negative outcomes for citizens. Under certain conditions, such negative outcomes will be perfectly acceptable to citizens and need not violate the definition of trust. On the contrary, sometimes a certain, measured degree of harm will be preferable to citizens, as it affirms to them that the police are adhering to their societal duty. Citizens who trust the police trust that the police will act in a negative, harmful way toward them if they commit a blatant crime in full view. A central aspect of common definitions of trust (acting in a way beneficial, or at least not harmful, to the self) is hence not applicable in the context of trust in the police. That being said, many other types of harm or hurt could definitely cause us to mistrust the police. So where do we draw the line?

The key here, I would suggest, lies in the function of the police. Fining, correcting, arresting, or constraining citizens, while all dealing us some form of harm, could well align with the function we ascribe to the police. We know, of course, that this function itself is hard to define and narrow down (Bittner, 1980). Moreover, opinions on what this is or should be could differ radically between different people and countries. We should hence not attempt to specify the police function here. For our working definition of trust in the police, it suffices to refer to people's views. As long as the police fulfill their function, in the eyes of the public, well (whatever 'well' might mean for the individual citizen), they are trusted—even if citizens themselves are harmed in the process.

The preceding considerations lead to the following definition of trust and confidence in the police: trust and confidence, in this study, entail ***the belief and expect-***

ation that the police, either as individuals or as an institution, fulfill their func-
tion 'well.'

This working definition of trust and confidence specifies trust in the police as a concept that is different from trust in many other people or organizations. Moreover, it allows plenty of room for different interpretations and associations in different languages and between different countries, individuals, and circumstances. And while such a provisional definition of trust and confidence inevitably invites further debate, it should suffice for the purposes of the present study.

2.3   LEGITIMACY

Legitimacy is an issue no less complicated than trust or confidence and equally popular in use (Ashforth & Gibbs, 1990). As Suchman (1995: 573) justly notes, many researchers employ the term 'legitimacy,' but few actually define it. This threatens to make it a highly confusing concept. Let us briefly address some of the main thoughts on what legitimacy entails and how it can be defined, before we proceed to discussing its relevance in the study of citizens' trust in the police.

While my working definition of trust may be applied to people as well as institutions, legitimacy is a characteristic of the institutional level (Hawdon, 2008; Suchman, 1995; Tyler, 1990): the police as an institution have a certain level of legitimacy.

Max Weber is seen as the principal author on the subject of legitimacy. He defined legitimacy as the belief in the rightfulness of a certain authority (Weber, 1980)—although the word 'authority' may not be the appropriate translation of Weber's 'Herrschaft,' because the former is argued to already imply a degree of legitimacy (Beetham, 1991a),[4] whereas the latter can also include decidedly illegitimate dictatorships. In the work of Weber, there are three possible principles through which an authority or *Herrschaft* can claim legitimacy, which in reality are often combined and interwoven. The authority can derive its legitimacy from legal rules established by formal, impersonal procedures, from established (patrimonial and patriarchal) traditional norms, and from charismatic leadership (Weber, 1980). Beetham (1991a) argues that this distinction is flawed, and that Weber tends to account only for juridical aspects in defining legitimacy, while labeling all else as 'charismatic.' Charisma, however, is insufficient to explain the legitimacy of an institution: it is an individual characteristic that obscures the nature of legitimacy rather than helping us to understand it. Describing all nonlegalistic forms of legitimacy as charismatic neglects citizens' values and nonformal norms. Weatherford (1992) and Terpstra (2011) hence describe the Weberian interpretation of legitimacy as 'legitimacy from above.' Beetham (1991b) proposes a categorization that

---

4.   Beetham (1991a: 35) laments the *'unusual inadequacy of the English language'* in translating Weber's *'Herrschaft'* and hence continues using Weber's term. When I use the word 'authority' throughout this section, it is to be interpreted in the sense of *'Herrschaft.'*

attempts to do justice to both the legal and the social aspects of legitimacy, entail-ing three elements. If each of these criteria is met, an authority actually *is* legitimate —as opposed to Weber's assumption that the *Herrschaft* can only be *perceived* as legitimate. These three requirements are juridical legitimacy or legality, normative legitimacy or justifiability, and express consent. In this view, an authority or insti-tution such as the police can be considered legitimate if its rights and responsibili-ties in society are defined by the law, acknowledged through shared popular belief and norms, and accepted and supported by according actions on the part of the public. Such an interpretation adds an important Durkheimian element to the tra-ditionally Weberian perspective of legitimacy (Terpstra, 2011).

Terpstra (2011) additionally argues that the definition of the Weberian sense of legitimacy as posed by Beetham (1991a) is too narrow and that this interpretation is not only to include laws but other (democratic) rules and norms as well. This corresponds with the distinction made by Weatherford (1992) between a tradi-tional, system-level interpretation of legitimacy on the one hand and a micro-level interpretation related to public orientations and expectations on the other. In this way, we could separate formal from informal legitimacy, reflecting a Weberian and a Durkheimian view, respectively, rather than making a distinction between legal and normative legitimacy as included in the work of Beetham. There are several advantages to making such a categorization. First, it yields comparative conceptual simplicity: separating legitimacy along the lines of two theoretical traditions can hopefully result in us doing justice to both. Second, it emphasizes that legitimacy is a different concept for institutions than it is for the citizens who are subject to them. Formal legitimacy is then a characteristic of institutions, whereas informal legitimacy is what citizens bestow on them.

Formal legitimacy consists of system-level frameworks of legal and social rules and norms, hence including both legality and wider norm conformation. In a police context this would, for instance, imply that the four criteria formulated by Bayley (2006) in describing democratic policing—service responsiveness to citi-zens, adherence to the rule of law, observance of human rights, and transparency and external accountability[5]—are conditions for this formal, Weberian interpreta-tion of legitimacy. These can be characteristics of the police institution: it follows such principles to a certain degree.

The informal, Durkheimian interpretation of legitimacy includes citizens' understanding and acceptance of police authority (Terpstra, 2011). It is in this informal interpretation that we can find concepts such as citizens' cooperation and compliance with the police (Tyler, 1990), but also confidence or trust: trust can hence be considered a vital component of—informal—legitimacy (Tyler, 2004; Rei-sig, Bratton, & Gertz, 2007; Sunshine & Tyler, 2003). Without trust—the expectation

---

5.   This appears to be a specification of Weatherford's (1992: 150) description of system-level legiti-macy as consisting of accountability, efficiency, procedural fairness, and distributive fairness, as applied to the police.

that the police will act in a way that is beneficial, or at least not harmful, to the self
—citizens are unlikely to accept police authority and consider this authority as just.
The police hence possess legitimacy if and only if they adhere to formal principles
and (sometimes unwritten) rules as present in a democratic society, if they are trusted by the public, and if the public accept that they have to obey the authority of
the police even if they personally disagree. It should be noted that the concept of
authority is a bit ambiguous here. On the one hand, police authority is a clear element of formal legitimacy, being derived from legal as well as nonlegal norms. On
the other hand, authority is also something bestowed upon the police and other
institutional actors by virtue of citizens' beliefs and morality (Jackson et al., 2013:
151-152). This also firmly posits authority in the territory of informal legitimacy.

Obviously, there is a link between these different aspects of legitimacy: it seems
credible to assume that a police organization possessing formal legitimacy is more
likely to also have informal legitimacy than one that does not. But despite such a
likely correlation between formal and informal legitimacy, it is still quite possible
that the police are on the one hand trusted, but on the other hand not fully legitimate—for instance, if police work is not enshrined in a democratically established
framework of rules or regulations. However, regardless of good intentions and
watertight democratic rules, the police will most definitely suffer a legitimacy deficit if they are not trusted. Since the police are often viewed as representatives of the
state (Fleming & McLaughlin, 2012; Sung, 2006), it can be argued that citizens' trust
in the police eventually affects the legitimacy of governmental authority as a
whole. Eventually, this might lead to a situation in which *sustained low trust ultimately challenges regime legitimacy*' (Hetherington, 1998: 792). Citizens' trust in the
police therefore may be considered an essential condition for police legitimacy.

Fortunately, it can be said, this is not a one-way mechanism from citizens
toward the state. According to Beetham (1991a), all systems of power and authority
strive for some form of legitimation. While this could be subject to debate in the
case of violent dictatorships—authorities without legitimacy—this principle does
hold even for actors whose very function relies on coercion and incapacitation,
such as prison guards (Sparks & Bottoms, 1995), or, indeed, the police. Police
organizations attempt to reinforce and construct their own legitimacy through
their actions (Mawby, 2002). For them, in a democratic society, it is even more
important to do so than for many other actors, as they deal with nonnegotiable
coercive force (Bittner, 1980). Such power is simultaneously particularly capable of
breaching all forms of legitimacy and, because its use is so contentious, in urgent
need of legitimation (Beetham, 1991a: 40). Besides, legitimacy contributes to volun-
tary compliance with an authority such as the police and saves massive amounts of
resources that would otherwise need to be expended on enforcing obedience
(Tyler, 1990: 4; Van Reenen & Verton, 1974), meaning that police organizations
have much to gain from being legitimate. These authorities attempt to '*establish and
maintain conditions that lead the public generally to accept their decisions and policies*'

(Tyler, 1990: 19): hence they actively try to build informal legitimacy. One can imagine that a framework of fair, democratically established laws, procedures, and rules can contribute to people's sense of legitimacy and compliance. As a consequence, this study will also delve into the ways in which aspects of police formal legitimacy are used to shape their degree of informal legitimacy (and hence trust). Indeed, as we will see throughout this book, such forms of self-legitimation are the foundation of many a police trust-building strategy.

2.4   OTHER NOTIONS

In discussing the relationship between the public and the police, terms and phrases other than trust/confidence or legitimacy are often applied. Here, I will briefly explore some of these: *satisfaction, consent*, and *authority*. It is worth emphasizing that they will be discussed in greater depth throughout this study where they are relevant. This is because their popularity or applicability often depends on specific circumstances: country or cultural context, moment or period in time, or type of research. For each of these concepts, it is important to note that their usefulness in understanding the relationship between the police and the public is more limited than that of trust/confidence or legitimacy.

Satisfaction is less of a theoretically contested concept than are trust/confidence and legitimacy. In fact, it sometimes seems so self-explanatory that many authors do not feel the need to make its meaning explicit (e.g. Reisig & Parks, 2000; Weitzer & Tuch, 2005). However, in the context of a study of trust, such a closely related but nonidentical notion does demand some conceptual clarification. Occasionally, for example, satisfaction is understood as citizens' assessment of how good a job the police are doing (Sampson & Jeglum Bartusch, 1998), while this is more commonly perceived to be an element or an approximation of trust or confidence (Stanko & Bradford, 2009). This implies that there is a degree of overlap, or a gray zone, between satisfaction and trust: both arguably deal with attitudes toward as well as an evaluation of the police. However, contrary to trust (or, for that matter, legitimacy), satisfaction tends to be internally oriented toward the state of mind of the individual. It is based on more or less concrete examples and experiences, and describes the state of an individual after having received something (Cao, 2015). A certain degree of (dis)satisfaction is then typically the outcome of a concrete interaction between the police and the public (Brandl et al., 1994; Keenan, 2009) or experiences with the police in a more general sense (Reisig & Parks, 2000). This gives it more of a consumerist-oriented ring than confidence or trust, and it tends to be associated with a more managerialist type of language in general. Hence, satisfaction is a term commonly used in the context of 'public satisfaction with police *services*' (Hinds & Murphy, 2007) or with 'police *performance*' (Skogan, 1978). This satisfaction is then hypothesized to affect trust or legitimacy (Tyler, 1990), a notion to which we will return later in this study.

Consent and *authority* are two other relevant concepts that come into play in the relationship between the police and the public. The public consent, in the form of willing obedience, to being governed in some way by the police. As discussed before, this makes consent an essential part of (informal) legitimacy: the police draw their legitimacy from public consent. It has, however, a particular connotation in the context of British policing, where it is an essential element of the historically *'almost mystical process of identification* [of the police] *with the British people'* (Reiner, 2010: 74). This will be discussed in greater depth in Chapter 8, when we deal with British trust-building strategies: the strategy of democratic accountability implies a special function and interpretation of consent (Brogden, 1982; Jones, Newburn, & Smith, 1996).

Authority, not unlike consent, has internationally accepted uses but also has particularly intense connotations in some specific cultural contexts—as we shall see in Chapter 10, especially in the Netherlands. It has already been discussed in the section on legitimacy as a pragmatic yet somewhat unsatisfactory translation of Weber's *Herrschaft*. However, as a concept it is often used in its own right, and occasionally confusingly so, since it has multiple meanings. The police after all, *are* an authority, since they are an institution of power. However, they also *have* authority. This can be legal authority (part of formal legitimacy) as well as moral or social authority (which would be part of informal legitimacy). Finally, there are also authorities *over* the police, such as the former Police Authority bodies in England & Wales, or mayors and public prosecutors in the Netherlands. This refers to agencies with power over the police institution. Authority therefore has several different uses and interpretations that sometimes overlap but can also be quite distinct. This complex of meanings will recur throughout this study.

3 | An introduction to the three theoretical perspectives

3.1 Understanding trust in the police

If we wish to achieve some kind of fundamental understanding of public trust in the police, it is first of all relevant to acknowledge that there are two main actors involved: the public and the police. As with any type of relationship, to understand it we need to grasp some basic aspects and properties of both parties. While this is not a particularly new idea, its implications are quite important, since it guides us toward our questions of interest. First, it means that we need to understand what characteristics of citizens will affect their trust in the police, *regardless* of police actions or strategies. Keeping police-related properties constant, which citizens have more trust and which ones have less? Second, we need to take a look at the police: a prerequisite is that we need to comprehend police organizations—what they are, what they do, and how they came to evolve into the organizations that they are.

While these two matters should provide us with some insight, they are not nearly sufficient to understand the relationship between the police and the public. A third aspect is that we need to know what citizens want and expect from the police. What police actions and strategies will improve trust, and what will hurt it? The fourth and final matter is that there is a need to learn more about how the police deal with citizens. How do the police see citizens, and how do they think they should relate to them? What strategies do the police apply to gain public trust, and why do they choose these strategies over others?

These final two problems, emphasizing mutual expectations, interactions, and treatment, have been the subject of interest of scholars and policy-makers alike. Looking at the literature as well as at concrete policies, there appear to be several leading schools of thought concerning this relationship. In this chapter, we will examine the content of these different schools. Throughout the rest of this study, we shall continue to apply their conceptual frameworks and theoretical expectations to promote an understanding of the relationship between the police and the public.

3.2   Three paradigms of thinking about trust and trust-building

Before we explore the different theoretical schools in the study of public trust in the police, we should note that they have a common point of departure. This is the notion that the interaction between the police and the public is not merely an individual matter, dependent on choices of isolated street-level officers on the basis of personal ethics, examples of colleagues, or direct orders from superiors (Muir, 1977). Interactions can also affected by broader mechanisms, both intentional and unintentional, that can, for instance, be organization- or society-wide.

It is in terms of these mechanisms that the three paradigmatic schools of thought have their different expectations and strategies: there are supposed to be specific means for police officers and organizations to make the public view them in a more positive way. Since the very start of police–public relations studies in various countries, recommendations have been made to change policies, improve training and education, and to alter police priorities—for instance, Gourley (1954) in the United States (U.S.), the Home Office (1962) in England & Wales, or Rijksen (1946) in the Netherlands. In recent decades, such recommendations and considerations have only become more popular as policing in many countries has gone through several rounds of significant reforms. Police forces have adapted to new circumstances and demands, as societies have changed and developed technologically as well as socioeconomically. New views on the role of the police in society have been articulated, systematic approaches toward police organization and education have developed, and awareness of the relevance of police–public relationships has grown. The formulation of systematic approaches toward improving the relationship between the police and citizens is therefore thought to be essential.

Decades of research and policy-making on the subject have given rise to manifold ways of thinking about what citizens want from the police and what the police should do to improve public trust. There are, however, three theoretical schools that dominate and hence have become the focus of this study. They are, to the best of my knowledge, reflected at least in some form in most European countries' public and scientific debate. I dub them the *proximity policing, instrumentalist*, and *procedural justice* schools. It should be noted that these theoretical perspectives, although they have many properties of unique, separate paradigms, are not mutually exclusive; nor do they cover all possible ways of understanding citizens' trust in the police. There is also no reason to assume that these very schools of thought—instead of any others—were predestined to become dominant. This is because processes of policy transfer or the diffusion of ideas and concepts could have contributed to the spread of these particular theoretical schools and their central notions, ideas, logic, and typical hypotheses across contexts. This means that the emergence of these three particular perspectives as central to the present study may to some extent be coincidental in origin. The fact is, however, that the three of them have grown to become the most important schools of thought regarding police–public relationships and should be treated as such.

Despite these preceding notes of caution, it is important to accept that the theoretical paradigms I discern are not only the dominant schools of thought concerning police–public relationships, but we shall see that they also possess various analytically useful properties that make them particularly applicable to the present study.

Over the following sections, we will first become acquainted with views on police–public relationships before any of these three schools was developed. Then, I will introduce each of the theoretical approaches that have since come to dominate our thinking about trust. The aims are to familiarize the reader with the origins and roots of these schools, to elucidate their central tenets and core concepts, and to introduce some of their principal authors and contributions. Finally, I shall examine how each of these paradigms could contribute to our understanding of trust in the present study.

3.2.1   *Proto-trust-building: Professional policing*

Proximity policing, instrumentalism, and procedural justice-based policing all were preceded by earlier ways of thinking about the relationship between the police and the public, and how to gain or preserve public trust. The most important of those was the paradigm of professional policing—which is relevant to this day because (a) it was a strategy, or group of strategies, from which other strategies could derive some notions, (b) it was at the same time a trust-building strategy against which others would later agitate, and (c) we can still see its influence, in altered and evolved form, in current-day policing practices.

The precise moment when it was first realized that the police needed public trust, and that public trust was an issue that needed to be worked on, is unclear. As always, tracing the invention of a concept or idea back to its roots tends to devolve into infinite regress (Kingdon, 1995: 72-73). Let it, for now, suffice to say that the conception of public trust in the police as a relevant issue probably occurred in different contexts, at different moments in time, phrased by different actors, who formulated and understood it in different terms. Moreover, it is likely that various individuals first picked this up well before it had any organization-wide effect. That being said, there is no denying that the need for a certain form of public approval or support has been a recurring theme in policing for a long time. It was arguably the foundation, at least on a rhetorical level, of one of the most iconic police organizations: London's Metropolitan Police (Emsley, 1992; Lyman, 1964; Reiner, 2010; Smith, 1985).

The first institutional responses to the problem of trust shared similar central ideas across many Western countries. During the 19th century and parts of the 20th, the state of policing in Anglo-American societies, particularly the U.S., was

described as one of dominion by politics; of corrupt, often unmotivated police officers with low salaries, education, and social status, whose main interest was the
protection of their (local) political patrons rather than crime control or the provision of services to the public (Walker, 1984). On the European continent, the situation was a bit different in the sense that police loyalty tended to rest more with
central than with local authorities, but it still meant that continental policing was
deeply political (Brodeur, 2010). Let us also note that there were substantial differences between countries and regions in the means, goals, and legitimization of
police forces and their activities.[1] In spite of all this, several elements tended to
recur in many countries. The police derived their legitimacy mostly from their
political command (Walker, 1984), and their relationship with the public, especially
the lower social classes, was often antagonistic in nature (Fielding, 2005; Gourley,
1954; Reiner, 2010). This had various negative consequences, as corruption and a
hostile relationship with parts of the population went at the expense of police
effectiveness and societal order. Throughout the first half of the 20th century,
therefore, various countries underwent different forms of professionalization of
their police forces. In terms of police–public relationships, three countries perhaps
deserve some particular attention: Germany, the U.S., and the United Kingdom
(U.K.).

An early, notable wave of police professionalization took place in interbellum
Germany (Besel, 1991), influencing the neighboring Netherlands (Fijnaut, 2007;
Meershoek, 2007: 178-181) and Denmark (Kruize & Jochoms, 2013: 72). Weimar
Germany, which lacked a substantial army after the signing of the Versailles Treaty
in 1918, had to rely entirely on its police organization to maintain peace and order
in a time of great civil unrest. Somewhat ironically, out of sheer necessity, the vulnerable and unstable Weimar Republic hence became a breeding ground for innovative policing methods, and of rationalization of technologies and strategy. Professionalization had, as part of its aims, the improvement of legitimacy and trust.
Police organizational architect Wilhelm Abegg stated in 1925 that '*in today's world
all means must be employed to overcome public hostility towards the police and to bring
about general recognition that the modern police is not only the authorized defender of the
existing state structure but also the ever-ready helper and protector of the public*' (as quoted in Besel, 1991: 187). Professionalization of the German police emphasized '*the
importance of technology and expertise in modern policing, and the need to cultivate and
preserve a positive and cooperative relationship with the population at large*' (Besel, 1991:
188). This was an ideologically quite revolutionary idea, influenced by the dominance of social democrats in politics. Additionally, police legal and technological
education rapidly evolved in training schools across the country. However, the
German police of the 1920s also maintained a militaristic outlook and brutally

---

1.   Contrast, for example, Brodeur (2010) and Smith (2007) on (the origin of) police forces in France,
      Canada, and the U.S. with Loader and Mulcahy (2003) and Reiner (2010) in England & Wales.

repressed communist protests. The eventual fate of the Weimar Republic was, as is well known, not a happy one. The professionalized police were remarkably easily absorbed into the national-socialist system during the 1930s. Meershoek (1999) noted a similar vulnerability of the Dutch police in Amsterdam during Nazi occupation—as Besel (1991: 205) reasoned, professional policing is not necessarily wedded to the idea of democracy.

A second wave of police professionalization emerged in somewhat different, but related, shapes in the U.S. and the U.K. during the postwar period. In the U.S., the influential work of O. W. Wilson (1950) was pivotal in the gradual substitution of political policing by professional (or reform) policing (Hoover, 2005; Manning, 2008). In the U.K., the main drive for reform was a more general preference for innovation. At the core of the Anglo-American professional policing model lies an instrumental notion of efficient, effective police administration (Bittner, 1980; Hoover, 2005). A professional police force was to have a centralized, top-down structure and be increasingly focused on motorized patrol, rapid response to calls for service, and investigation of crimes (Alderson, 1979). Taking these aspects into account, the professional model's emphasis on technology and a formal, bureaucratic structure meant that it was an attempt to achieve a rational-legal model of policing (Manning, 2008).

Particularly in the U.S., this meant a drive to reject the arbitrary style of policing that was heavily affected by local and national politics and prone to corruption and excessive police violence (Westley, 1970): professional policing emphasized a distance from politics as well as the public, strong internal discipline (Gourley, 1950), and a definition of good police practice in a relatively narrow, instrumental sense (Wilson & Kelling, 1982). This was thought to turn the police into a professional and efficient crime-fighting force rather than a corrupt, unreliable political tool (Manning, 2008; Stone & Travis, 2011). The role of citizens in crime control was ideally thought to be minimal, limited to reporting crime or acting as witnesses (Kelling & Moore, 1988). Public attitudes toward the police were, in the U.S. model, not considered to be particularly relevant; police management generally assumed that for the police to gain public approval, professional techniques and equipment would suffice. Studies of public opinions about the police were rare, as police interest amongst the general public was low (Gourley, 1954).

In the U.K., professionalism had somewhat different connotations. Contrasting the U.S. to Great Britain, Banton noted that the British police as an institution had characteristics of the 'sacred'; perceived by the public to be intrinsically both good and dangerous (Banton, 1964: 237). In this sense, the late 1940s and the 1950s, in particular, were considered to be a 'golden age of policing' (Reiner, 2010). The police felt that they had ample public support and were considered (or at least considered themselves) to be an example for the world (Emsley, 1992; Loader & Mulcahy, 2003). Increasing professionalism was hence not required to gain more public trust and support, but it was necessary to deal with the growing crime rate and its

changing nature (Mawby, 2002; Reiner, 2010). Technological developments, over
the course of the postwar decades, both increased opportunities for crime and
improved police methods to deal with it. The British police were quick to integrate
new technology, such as patrol cars and personal radios, in their working styles.
The adoption of unit beat policing, with its emphasis on motorized patrol, made
the police far more mobile and quick to respond (Loader & Mulcahy, 2003; Sherman, 1983), but also went at the expense of nonconflict, personal interaction
between the police and the public (Ackroyd, 1993; Alderson, 1979). The British and
American waves of professionalization had a substantial influence on policing in
other Western countries, as would other strategies from those same contexts, in
later years.

The professional model of policing slowly lost its appeal in the U.S. and the
U.K. over the course of the 1960s and 1970s. The decline of the professional policing paradigm was marked by a number of events and social processes, as well as
by publications and research results that did not sit well with the professional
school of thought. Refuting the professional interpretation of police practice as consisting of a limited number of core activities such as car patrol and post hoc rapid
response, several scholars first of all proved convincingly that, in practice, police
roles and daily work prove much more encompassing than merely fighting crime
(Bittner, 1980; Cain, 1973; Muir, 1977; Reiss, 1971).[2] In an oft-quoted phrase, Bittner
described the vast number of activities that fall into the police domain as entailing
all instances that featured *'something that ought not to be happening and about which
someone had better do something now!'* (Bittner, 1980: 132). And not only was the
actual work of police officers found to be much broader than merely effectively
fighting crime; they appeared not even to be particularly capable of reducing crime
(Manning, 1977). Bittner (1980), as well as Manning (1977), argued that it was in the
interest of the police to maintain an air of control and success in their crime-fighting ability, but that this did not reflect reality all that well.

During the decades of professional policing dominance, crime rates increased
explosively across the Western world. Rapid response to calls, previously thought
to be essential for apprehending criminals, was, despite its high costs, found to
have little effect on the number of arrests (Spelman & Brown, 1984). In the U.K.
and the U.S., as well as in many other Western countries, this was combined with
bouts of civil unrest, strikes, and urban riots in different constellations, starting in
the 1960s. The police response was often violent and repressive, particularly when
dealing with minorities (Scarman, 1982). The ideally professional model was hence

---

2.   This was not an entirely new finding. Even some authors firmly entrenched in the professional
     model noted that the image of the police as crime-fighting organization did not always corre-
     spond with police daily practice. See, for example, Gourley (1954: 136): *'The greatest number of
     police contacts today is not with the criminal element of society, but rather with the 'good' citizens of a com-
     munity. It has been estimated that at least 90 per cent of all police business is not of a strictly criminal
     nature.'*

often not applied in a very professional fashion, and proved not only to be ineffective in reducing crime, but also in dealing with civil disorder (Goldstein, 1977; Loader & Mulcahy, 2003; Stone & Travis, 2011; Waddington, 1992; Zhao, Lovrich, & Thurman, 1999). Eventually, this meant that the professional paradigm was in serious trouble: nothing the police did appeared to work (Hoover, 2005).

It was for these reasons that, during the late 1970s, an alternative model of policing and of dealing with the public began to emerge. A series of publications in different countries—including Goldstein (1979) and Wilson & Kelling (1982) in the U.S., Alderson (1979) and Scarman (1982) in the U.K., and Heijink et al. (1977) in the Netherlands—indicated a gradual paradigm shift. This alternative model, although highly diverse by nature, has certain core characteristics—properties that have a strong degree of similarity in most contexts. This is why we can speak of a new school of thought: that of proximity policing.

3.3   THE EMERGENCE OF PROXIMITY POLICING APPROACHES

The proximity policing perspective is a policing paradigm that has had a major influence on the way in which police forces across the globe operate. The term 'proximity policing' is seldom used in the Anglo-American literature, but is common in many translations on the European continent (for example, the French *police de proximité*, the Danish and Norwegian *nærpolitiet*, or the Dutch *gebiedsgebonden politiewerk*). Several models of police practice can be argued to fit into the category of proximity policing, but the most well-known model is community-oriented policing. These two concepts—proximity policing and community-oriented policing—could in fact be argued to be one and the same thing (Holmberg, 2002), but for the purposes of the present study I make a distinction. I use the term 'proximity policing' when referring to the police *science* perspective, a theoretical construct, whereas I consider 'community policing' to be a police *practice* strategy; the application of proximity policing as interpreted by police organizations in large parts of the Western world, but especially in the U.S. and the U.K. Hence, it is one of the strategies derived from the broader proximity policing school of thought.

It is hard to define proximity policing on an international scale, since this perspective's most central tenet is arguably that the police need to adapt to local communities and contexts (Holmberg, 2002). This could very well be one of the reasons why attempts to implement the Anglo-American style of community-oriented policing appear to be doomed to fail in many developing countries (Brogden, 2005).[3] Still, all interpretations of the proximity policing perspective share some

---

3. A police force or society in general must also meet several basic demands of professionalization before one can even start to consider implementing principles of proximity policing. Goldstein (1979: 239) argued that '*Without a minimum level of order and accountability, an agency cannot be redirected.*' Proximity policing reforms will most likely fail in countries that have historically only known political policing—or worse.

basic premises. Clearly, it means a rejection of the professional model: while proximity policing does accept that a basic level of professionalism is required for
police officers, it argues against the narrow definition of good police work in terms
of effectiveness and efficiency. The emerging proximity policing school of thought
criticized the professional model for the loss of nonconflict interactions between
the police and the public (Alderson, 1979: 41-42), for being rigidly bureaucratic
(Manning, 1984), for enforcing the law in a literal, means-over-ends way (Goldstein, 1979), for having too narrow a focus on crime, rather than on broader disorder (Skogan, 1990), for targeting ethnic minorities in a discriminatory fashion
(Scarman, 1982; Skogan & Hartnett, 1997), and for being insufficiently prepared to
adjust to a changing society (Alderson, 1979; Heijink et al., 1977).

To compensate for the perceived damage being done by the adverse effects of
professional policing, the proximity policing school of thought holds that the relationship between the police and the public needs to be improved. The police
should decrease their distance from citizens by being approachable and visible,
focusing on addressing a broad range of (social) neighborhood problems such as
disorder and feelings of insecurity, collaborating with partners, and being proactive in the battle against crime and disorder by involving the community and
exchanging information with the public (Goldstein, 1987; Herbert, 2006; Skogan,
1990; Skogan & Hartnett, 1997; Terpstra, 2010; Trojanowicz & Bucqueroux, 1990).
This is realized in practice by decentralizing the police command structure,
increasing the discretionary autonomy of street-level officers, increasing the geographic dispersal and number of police stations or storefront offices, increasing
involvement in local networks, and by moving the focus of police training and
education from merely enforcing criminal law toward problem-solving and
addressing a wide range of issues (Oliver & Bartgis, 1998; Rosenbaum, 1988; Skolnick & Bayley, 1988).

Proximity policing understands police work in a much wider sense than professional policing did, and embraces a diversity in police tasks and duties. This does
not mean that reducing crime is out of the picture, but in this paradigm the purpose of policing is often perceived to be more than just crime-related: it should also
attempt to repair or improve the social fabric of local communities (Alderson, 1979;
Heijink et al., 1977; Herbert, 2006). Policing should not merely concern the uphold-
ing of individuals' rights, but should most of all protect communities (Wilson &
Kelling, 1982). In order to achieve this goal, citizen involvement and participation
in neighborhood security are vital elements of proximity policing. Next to other
beneficial effects, this reduced distance between the police and citizens is expected
to improve citizens' views of the police (Tilley, 2003), and hence their trust and
police informal legitimacy.

Although highly popular in recent decades, the proximity policing school of
thought is not uncontroversial and is problematic in several respects. The first
problem is that it proves difficult to successfully implement in practice. Part of the

value and appeal of ideas related to proximity policing appears to lie on the rhetorical level (Manning, 1984; Seagrave, 1996), even causing Klockars (1988) to imply that the concept is hardly more than a rhetorical tool. Additionally, there is often a large divide between 'management cops' (Reuss-Ianni, 1983) on the one hand, who might wish to apply the ideas provided by proximity policing, and the extent to which these ideas are then actually implemented by 'street cops,' who are often deemed conservative and resistant to change (Loftus, 2010; Reiner, 2010). The daily, street-level application of these ideas in the form of community policing is often something of a 'black box' (Terpstra, 2010). This holds particularly for countries and contexts that are not as intensively studied by scholars as the U.S. or the U.K. And it is not only on the police side that the application of proximity policing ideas can suffer setbacks: citizens themselves are often unwilling to become—and remain—involved in community partnerships and projects with the police (Grinc, 1994; Herbert, 2006; Skogan & Hartnett, 1997).

Another problem when dealing with proximity policing, briefly addressed above, is in its vague definition, or perhaps even the absence of any definition at all (Seagrave, 1996; Skogan & Hartnett, 1997; Skolnick & Bayley, 1988; Stone & Travis, 2011). This has led to the blossoming of a myriad of different interpretations, elaborations, and adaptations of the ideas offered by the proximity policing perspective. Next to community-oriented policing, there are related models such as problem-oriented policing (Eck & Spelman, 1987; Goldstein, 1979; Tilley, 2003), intelligence-based policing (Maguire, 2000; Tilley, 2003), and reassurance policing (Innes, 2004, 2005; Peterson, 2010), as well as—somewhat further removed from the proximity policing school of thought—hot spot policing (Braga, 2005; Sherman & Weisburd, 1995) and the politically influential *broken windows*-inspired zero-tolerance or order-maintenance policing (Bayley & Shearing, 1996; Dixon, 2000; Kelling & Bratton, 1998).

Despite these problems, however, there is empirical evidence that the application of proximity policing principles at least has the potential to achieve positive results and improve public trust in neighborhoods and towns in different countries,[4] indicating that Klockars' (1988) view may be too negative. Unfortunately, systematic international comparisons on the subject of proximity policing are thus far absent.

Policing modes inspired by proximity policing have become leading police paradigms in most Western countries over recent decades, at the very least on a rhetorical level (Bayley & Shearing, 1996; Stone & Travis, 2011; Terpstra, 2010).

4.   A small, by no means exhaustive, selection of contributions offering varying degrees of empirical support is as follows: Adams, Rohe, and Arcury (2005), Gill et al. (2014); Rosenbaum (1986, 1996), Skogan (2006b), and Skogan and Hartnett (1997), all in the U.S.; Millie and Herrington (2004) and Tuffin, Morris, and Poole (2006) in England & Wales; Dunn et al. (2016) in Australia; Holmberg (2002) and Balvig and Holmberg (2004) in Denmark; Broer, Schreuder, and Van der Vijver (1987) and Terpstra (2008, 2010) in the Netherlands; Mackenzie and Henry (2009) in Scotland.

Still, it seems likely that there are differences between nations in the extent to which they have actually managed to realize the principles of proximity policing in their street-level police practice. This could partially be due to the aforementioned difficulties in implementing them. Besides, there are differences in terminology. In Norway, for example, the local *lensmann*, or sheriff, has been responsible for many of the main tasks associated with proximity policing (closeness to citizens, cooperation with local agencies, and focusing on a wide range of issues) for centuries, but these tasks are not labeled as community policing or a related police practice paradigm, and are thus not accepted as such (Larsson, 2010). This means that, if we wish to study the effects of proximity policing practice on trust in the police, it is important to concentrate on the implementation of specific elements that are dominant in proximity policing thinking, regardless of the way these elements have been labeled.

3.4   INSTRUMENTALISM

While the 1990s were characterized by large-scale experimentation with, and implementation of, proximity policing principles across the Western world, we can also discern the rise of an almost opposite movement in thinking about the police that commenced during that period. Originating in the U.K. and the U.S., it spread like wildfire across the Western world. I dub that movement *instrumentalism*. Instrumentalism was an institutional response to the continually rising crime rates; its assertion was that growing crime and falling public support for the police could at least partially be attributed to failings of the police (Loveday, 1994). Ever-increasing amounts of money were spent on policing, yet there was little evidence for police effectiveness in crime control (Ackroyd, 1993). As a response to this perceived problem, instrumentalism was a marriage of effectiveness-centered core elements of professional policing and influences from the emerging New Public Management (NPM) school of thought (Hood, 1991; Osborne & Gaebler, 1992; Pollitt & Bouckaert, 2000).

The instrumental model, on the one hand, retains the professional ideal of the police as effective fighters of crime but, on the other hand, is also heavily influenced by the rise of NPM views on the importance of measurable output in shaping legitimacy of and trust in public institutions. These two elements prove to be highly compatible, although it proved necessary to discard some elements of the professional model in the merging process.

Instrumentalism, like professionalism, considers rationalization of processes and police practices to be key in gaining public support, legitimacy, and trust. Unlike professionalism, however, this rationality is based on achieving demonstrable efficiency and effectiveness rather than on a bureaucratic logic that depends on, and is derived from, legal codes (Ackroyd, 1993; Manning, 2008). This is where the influence of the NPM model shows. The NPM is an umbrella term for different ideas about introducing private-sector principles into the public sector: it aims to make government operate more like a business (Hood, 1991). When the police publicly advertise their adoption of NPM principles, they *'suggest having a market orientation to clientele rather than being a distant coercive force'* (Manning, 2008: 32-33). This occurred in many Western countries over the course of the 1990s, where governments, and with them the entire public sector, adopted a 'value-for-money' rationality (Savage, 2007). The purpose of these reforms was to regain trust and legitimacy, although evidence is mixed concerning the extent to which this was actually achieved (Van de Walle, 2011).

The value-for-money mantra, as applied to the police, meant that they should provide evidence for their effectiveness: they needed to prove that they were worth the money the taxpayer contributed (Loveday, 1994; Mawby, 2002). This criterion of accountability is where the professional policing model again provided a source of inspiration: crime control forms the most logical measure of police effectiveness, and definitely the easiest one to document (Bittner, 1980: 124; Kirby, 2013). Crime has also been at the center of attention in politics and in mass media in Western countries over recent decades (Loader, 2006; Mawby, 2002; Oliver & Bartgis, 1998; Reiner, 2010; Terpstra & Van der Vijver, 2006), supporting the idea that it is also highly important to the public. Following this logic, instrumentalism can be blind to challenges and criticisms of its central assumptions; for instance, that crime is near impossible to measure objectively (Kirby, 2013).

Different from the professional policing paradigm, where citizens were at most of auxiliary importance, in instrumental thinking the public is quite central. Following in the footsteps of the NPM model, instrumentalism considers public satisfaction to be key to a successful public institution. But contrary to the community-oriented school of thought, where citizens' emotions and feelings of connectedness are central concepts, instrumentalism tends to assume that citizens are mostly rational beings who primarily judge the police by their performance, and that even emotions such as fear of crime are firmly rooted in rational considerations or calculations of the likelihood of victimization. Trust, in this view, is determined by performance—specifically, performance in crime-fighting. According to this interpretation, a well-performing police organization is one that reduces crime and catches criminals. Such an organization is worth its money and worthy of public trust. A poorly performing organization, on the other hand, is considered unreliable, maybe even untrustworthy.

Those who share the view on police–public relationships as implied by the NPM model will find themselves strongly attracted to professional model ideas in their focus on crime, criminal law, and a limited number of relevant police activities—those that are measurable. In the instrumental perspective, the police will gain public trust if they fight crime effectively and efficiently and are able to prove to the public that they are doing so. This notion has become dominant in England & Wales during the 1990s and 2000s (Loader & Mulcahy, 2003). It has led to the introduction of policing by objectives, target setting, endeavors to redefine police work in a narrower, more crime-related sense, attempts to discard police activities that are not associated with a select few 'core tasks,' and a range of related reforms in police forces (Hough, 2007).

Instrumentalist views of police–public relationships spread rapidly to other contexts from the late 1990s onward. We can, for example, clearly see these influences in the police organizations of Denmark, Norway, and Sweden (Andersson & Tengblad, 2009; Holmberg, 2014; Holmberg & Balvig, 2013), as well as in Germany (Frevel & Kuschewski, 2013), Ireland (Mulcahy, 2007), and the Netherlands (Terpstra & Trommel, 2009). Occasionally, attempts have been made to combine this instrumentalist rationality with proximity policing ideas (see Andersson & Tengblad, 2009), but usually the two movements are considered to be hard to reconcile, as they have fundamentally different core definitions of what comprises good police work: a narrow focus on crime-fighting and effectiveness as opposed to solving a wide range of problems. As a consequence, we shall see throughout the rest of this study that these notions tend to compete rather than complement each other.

3.5   PROCEDURAL JUSTICE THEORY AND FAIR TREATMENT

One issue with the perspectives described above is that they have a primary focus on the organizational level of the police—not exclusively so, but predominantly. Proximity policing has the strongest focus on the level of neighborhoods and communities. While this certainly has implications for individuals and for whole societies, proximity policing's main area of interest tends to lie on the organizational level of cities and neighborhoods. Instrumentalism is particularly engaged with outcomes on the national level, or (sometimes but not always synonymous) on the level of police organizations. This clearly has implications for individuals and for departments, but in its policies there is a focus on the highest possible level of abstraction.

Less central in proximity-related and instrumentalist analyses of police–public relationships, albeit never completely absent, are the individual interactions between police officers and citizens. This is in some ways peculiar, since most of the classic policing literature involving police-citizen relationships did focus on police officers as individual, more or less autonomous, decision-makers with substantial discretionary autonomy, whose actions strongly depend on the context of the interaction and the individuals involved (Banton, 1964; Bittner, 1980; Cain, 1973; Muir, 1977; Reiss, 1971; Skolnick, 1966; Westley, 1970). While few of these authors consistently focused on trust (their scope tended to be wider and their focus targeted on somewhat different issues), it is possible to distill some foundations of a third paradigm of thinking about public trust in the police out of their contributions.

One particularly worthwhile nudge toward what would later become the procedural justice paradigm was made by Banton, who stated that *'the sociologist will emphasize that the public in Britain are able to trust the police because the actions of individual officers follow a common pattern so that the subject knows what to expect'* (Banton, 1964: 167). This reflects an important aspect of procedural justice: predictability. Another early contribution with consequences for the procedural justice paradigm was made by Wiley and Hudik (1974), who found that public cooperation with police officers after a stop becomes much more extensive when an explanation for that stop is provided.

Contrary to the two other perspectives, which were both firmly rooted in police practice and experience and included active involvement and contributions of police chiefs and management, the procedural justice perspective is predominantly academic in its origin and nature. Effectiveness and reducing crime, which are dominant in instrumentalism, are not key values in the procedural justice school of thought; nor are closeness and cooperation, which are so vital in proximity policing.

As a coherent school, the procedural justice perspective is historically linked to court (informal) legitimacy and psychological studies of citizens' compliance with courtroom decisions in common-law countries rather than to trust and the police. In recent years, it has increasingly (indeed, almost exponentially) been applied to trust and to the police force. Tyler (1988, 1990) was the first to combine elements of individual-level research on determinants of public trust in the police such as conducted by Gourley (1954) and Jacob (1971) with social-psychological studies of the legitimacy of law and courts (Lind, 1982; Thibaut & Walker, 1975). This marriage yielded a theory of procedural justice for law enforcement—although it has been argued that procedural justice theory can also be applied to other street-level bureaucrats (Tyler & Huo, 2002), or indeed to virtually any type of organization (Greenberg, 1986, 1990). While this may be true, I will argue in this section that procedural justice theory needs to be reformulated in at least one important way in order to be successfully applicable to the police.

Procedural justice theory concentrates on the psychological processes that determine trust, perceived legitimacy, and compliance. Tyler (1990) discerns two stages in which an organization may act beneficially or harmfully in its interaction with the individual: the process and the outcome. As discussed in Chapter 2, law enforcement agencies such as the police or the courts are in the unique position that they structurally need to deliver outcomes that are harmful and unsatisfactory to citizens. Together, police and courts threaten, arrest, fine, and incarcerate citizens (Goldstein, 1977; Tyler & Huo, 2002). And even when no particularly negative outcome or harm is delivered, the result may still not be beneficial to the public— for example, when the police or courts cannot offer a satisfactory solution to citizens' problems. Hence, police and courts have very limited possibilities of increasing public satisfaction and trust through providing desirable outcomes. Besides,

Tyler (1990) and Tyler and Huo (2002) found that favorability of outcomes only determines a very small part of trust in the police or the courts. This implies that any gains in terms of promoting public trust will have to be made during the process, which is where procedural justice-based policing enters the stage. Procedural justice theory entails, at its core, that individuals need to be treated fairly and equally and must not be harmed more than absolutely necessary during the process of interacting. Procedural justice-based policing entails, in the words of Tyler (1988), various elements: opportunity of representation for the citizen to make his case and consistency, impartiality, quality of decision, correctability, and ethicality on the part of the police officer. When the police show respect, let citizens explain their views on situations, and show their commitment to making informed decisions, citizens will comply more often (McCluskey, 2003: 91), will have more confidence in the police (Jackson & Sunshine, 2007), and will hold more favorable attitudes toward the police in general (Frank, Smith, & Novak, 2005). Sunshine and Tyler (2003) found that elements of perceived police procedural justice have a larger influence on public attitudes toward the police than instrumental concerns about crime rates.

Following the procedural justice logic, we can conclude that individual police officers together have the possibility to shape public trust in a positive sense by making use of their discretionary autonomy. Procedural justice-based policing is a strategy that attempts to educate and steer police officers in this direction; for instance, through training, instruction, encouragement, or by other stimuli. There are convincing empirical indications—for instance, through randomized field trials —that there is something to these assertions (Mazerolle et al., 2013a,b; Sargeant et al., 2016).

However, while procedural justice as applied in policing is thought to have a positive impact on police–public relationships, we also need to take a look at the flip side. The minimization of harm during the interaction process must be a key goal. Police violence and evidence of corruption, generally being rather the opposite of fair treatment, will have an inverse effect on public perceptions of the police (Banton, 1964; Semukhina, 2016; Sunshine & Tyler, 2003). Negative interactions are usually found to have a larger potential to harm trust in the police than that of positive interactions to increase it (Bradford, Jackson, & Stanko, 2009; Skogan, 2006a; Tyler & Huo, 2002), but it is an asymmetry of undefined size and unclear cross-cultural salience.[5]

For the police, this is a serious problem. Bittner (1980) famously defined the unique property of police competence as the capacity to use nonnegotiable coercive force, coupled with the principle of applying the minimum amount of force required. But, in the tradition of Weber, he also noted that this use of force is by

---

5.   See, for instance, Broekhuizen et al. (2015) and Lammers (2004), who confirm this asymmetry in
     the Netherlands, while Kääriäinen (2008) and Van Damme (2017) find largely different results in
     Finland and Belgium, respectively.

definition apt to spiral out of control even in a liberal, functioning democracy with a modern police force (Bittner/Brodeur, 2007; see also Westley, 1970). Moreover, Punch (2009) argued that the police as an institution are intrinsically exceptionally vulnerable to pervasive forms of corruption. It appears that a tendency to violate procedural justice principles is inherent in the police function. The police possess both the power and the opportunity to harm citizens through corruption and violence during the process of interaction. They differ in this respect from most street-level bureaucrats, who may have the opportunity to do so due to their large degree of individual autonomy, but not the power: they lack the capacity to use coercive force. They are also distinct from the military, which has the power to do harm, but seldom the opportunity—due to a lower likelihood for contact with citizens and because soldiers possess virtually no individual street-level autonomy.

The unique police capacity to use force or otherwise do harm comes particularly strongly into focus when analyzing specific elements of police culture. Police culture may shape police attitudes and behavior toward citizens in a negative fashion (Muir, 1977; Reiner, 2010; Skolnick, 1966). Despite the fact that police cultural characteristics are not ingrained in the same way across countries or individuals (Terpstra & Schaap, 2013), and that the discrepancy between talk and action in police culture might generally not be appreciated sufficiently (Waddington, 1999), there are some cultural characteristics that appear to be present in most police forces. Among other characteristics, police officers are thought to be cynical and distrusting toward the public, to show strong internal solidarity, and to be susceptible to machismo and racism (Reiner, 2010). At least in the U.K., these characteristics appear to be more or less constantly present over time (Foster, 2003; Loftus, 2009). All of these elements, when displayed in contacts between police and public, may negatively affect procedural justice and lead to public distrust of the police.

Taking this line of thought into account, the focus should, specifically in the case of the police, perhaps lie on preventing blatant procedural *injustice* rather than on promoting procedural *justice*. Throughout this study, we will, in the analysis of procedural justice-based policing as trust-building strategy, include aspects of procedural justice as well as (the attempted prevention of) injustice.

3.6 CONCLUDING REMARKS

We have now achieved a basic understanding of the three main schools of thought about police–public relationships. Each of these schools operates on a different analytical level, and each has different origins, proponents, core assumptions, favored vocabulary, and proposed measures. Their main similarities are that all three of them accept that public trust in the police is important, that the police have a responsibility in stimulating this trust, and that they can—strategically—work on this issue. The relationship between these different paradigms, or their compatibility, is not immediately clear. This is partially due to the aforementioned differences: to a large extent, each school forms a closed circuit and people deeply involved in one often have serious difficulty understanding the logic of the other. On an academic level, as was discussed in Chapter 1, it is also because few analyses have managed to include all three of them. In the present contribution, we will take all three into account, and leave additional room for other perspectives or possible viewpoints when they arise.

In an internationally comparative study with a dynamic perspective, we should note that we require an equally dynamic approach toward these three paradigms. Because they have such completely different central assumptions and implications, they can—inadvertently and without anyone immediately noticing—interact to affect one another. This becomes particularly salient when discussing trust-building in an international context, and we shall see, over the following chapters, that strategies derived from these paradigms can compete with or suppress each other.

When does one perspective advance to have its central tenets become dominant in policy and practice, as opposed to another? When and why do shifts occur in which perspective and strategy are dominant? Do these changes emerge from within the police organization or from elsewhere, and why? What are the consequences of such changes and developments in the long run? It is through these more complex interpretations that we shall approach the three paradigms in Part III of the study, when comparing police trust-building strategies in England & Wales, Denmark, and the Netherlands.

Part II

Public trust in the police

4 | RESEARCH DESIGN AND HYPOTHESES

4.1   INTRODUCTION

There are many ways to go about gauging public trust in the police, and even more challenges that arise when doing so. Obviously, this means that we need to be quite focused in our approach. In this chapter, I will construct a research strategy that aims to do justice to the many questions and problems involved. Its core elements, as discussed before, are that a thorough examination of public trust in the police ought to take a cross-national, dynamic, and theoretically versatile approach.

In Chapter 1, three research questions were formulated that will guide this part of the study. Given the many pitfalls that can be encountered in this type of research, it is with good reason that Research Question 1—'*To what extent are meas**ures of citizens' trust in the police empirically comparable across European countries?*—is a methodological one. In Section 4.2, we will examine a previously underused method to determine the comparative validity of cross-national survey data on public attitudes toward the police: multi-group measurement equivalence tests.

Applying the outcomes of this primary examination as a foundation, it becomes possible to proceed with describing developments within and differences between countries in terms of trust; Section 4.3 expounds on the rationale behind understanding differences and developments in levels of trust across those countries that were found to be empirically comparable in our equivalence tests. This relates to Research Question 2: '*What are the differences between European countries in terms of citizens' trust in the police, and how has trust in the police developed across Europe over the past few decades?*'

Once we have established a strategy to properly measure differences and developments, and have assessed trajectories of change, it is possible to continue with explaining differences in levels of trust between countries. In Section 4.4, I will reexamine the three main theoretical perspectives and how they relate to the problem of trust and its determinants. A range of hypotheses will be distilled regarding factors on the national and on the individual level that these theoretical perspectives suggest promote or diminish trust. This framework helps us to answer Research Question 3: '*What factors on the national and on the individual level explain differences between countries in terms of citizens' trust in the police?'* These hypotheses, taken together, form an explanatory model of trust in the police—a model that will be rigorously tested in Chapter 6.

4.2   THE PROBLEM OF MEASUREMENT EQUIVALENCE[1]

The problem of measurement equivalence is most salient in quantitative studies of a particular kind: synchronic international studies and diachronic single-country research. Both types of research involve comparing different 'groups' (either countries or years); the former type being more common than the latter in the field of research on public attitudes toward the police, I will concentrate especially on cross-national contributions when discussing the problem. The problem of measurement equivalence challenges the validity of descriptive as well as explanatory research.

Cross-sectional, synchronic international comparative research on the subject of trust or confidence in the police, mostly based on survey data, has recently gained much traction. Presumably, this is due to improved statistical technology and because of an increased availability of cross-national data. While cross-national research in general is becoming more common, this holds particularly for comparative studies of public trust in the police. A steady stream of publications have concentrated on public attitudes toward the police in different countries from a quantitative, explanatory perspective. Some of these have included countries from all over the globe (Cao et al., 2012; Jang et al., 2010, 2015; Morris, 2015; Sung, 2006; Thomassen, 2013), and some have focused on specific continents or regions such as Latin America (Cao & Zhao, 2005), Europe (Alalehto & Larsson, 2016; Kääriäinen, 2007; Kutnjak Ivković, 2008), or Africa (Boateng, 2017). Still, these are merely the publications that compare a relatively large number of countries—those comparing two or three countries are even more numerous. Similarly, there is a growing number of contributions comparing trust in institutions other than the police (Clausen, Kraay, & Nyiri, 2011; Hakhverdian & Mayne, 2012; Norris, 2011). This latter, parallel body of work will be referred to when relevant for the purposes of the present study.

International comparative research is never without its weaknesses, and as the authors themselves are often well aware, the studies mentioned above are no exception. Most of them list a number of shortcomings, such as the—perceived—relatively small amount of cases included (between nine and 60 countries), which limits the statistical power of the analyses (Jang et al., 2010), and their nonrandom sampling (Boateng, 2017; Cao et al., 2012). Most studies also reflect on the simplicity of their measures of attitudes toward the police, which in many cases have con-

---

1.   Condensed parts from Section 4.2 have previously been published by this author with co-author Professor Peer Scheepers, in the *International Criminal Justice Review* (Schaap & Scheepers, 2014).

sisted of a single indicator (Cao et al., 2012; Jang et al., 2010; Kääriäinen, 2007; Tho-massen, 2013), or on the absence of some possibly relevant control variables such as past victimization (Cao et al., 2012). But although some of these are genuine issues that have potentially affected the results of these studies—most notably the nonrandom sampling—they are not my primary concern here. Let us, for example, note that most social scientists would not consider over 50 countries to be a small sample at all; quite the opposite. I will therefore argue that these comparative stud-ies are more fundamentally flawed: it is their cross-national comparative validity, and more specifically their measurement equivalence, that is at risk. The rationality here is that while internationally designed surveys can provide valuable informa-tion, their mere supposed international character is in itself insufficient for actual cross-cultural comparisons (Van de Vijver, 2003).

Remarkably similar criticism on international comparisons of attitudes toward criminal justice comes from two very different research traditions, although differ-ent terminology is used and different aspects of the issue are emphasized. Never-theless, these two groups, qualitative researchers and rigorously quantitatively ori-ented ones, touch on the same issue. Roughly, we can formulate this problem, the problem of equivalence, as the question about whether a specific concept has the same meaning to citizens in different countries or regions, or at different points in time (Chan, 1998; Davidov et al., 2014). Indeed, criminal justice researchers from very different traditions have asked to what extent trust in the police has the same meaning to citizens in different countries (Hough, 2012: 339; Nelken, 1994: 238). When studying citizens' trust in and attitudes toward justice institutions, we must '*know whether we are comparing like with like*' (Nelken, 2012: 144). We therefore need at least some *basic* empirical evidence that it is justified to compare these countries in terms of trust in the police. Measurement equivalence issues may occur when-ever a survey instrument is compared across two or more groups (Vandenberg & Lance, 2000); in this particular case consisting of countries (or, in a longitudinal interpretation, several moments in time within the same country). A certain amount of difference in the meaning that people attach to the concepts of inquiry, between countries or moments in time, will reflect upon survey data when we attempt to measure trust in the police. This negatively affects the validity of the comparison and may lead us to faulty conclusions.

In this particular context, there are many aspects that could endanger equiva-lence: functional, structural, and cultural as well as linguistic differences in societ-ies might cause the meaning and interpretation of trust in the police as asked in a questionnaire to differ. This can render comparisons invalid. When measurement equivalence of survey data has not been tested for, cross-cultural comparisons risk becoming '*meaningless*' (De Beuckelaer, Lievens, & Swinnen, 2007): potentially, entirely different concepts and relationships are being compared. Even if we have empirical indications in favor of equivalence, however, this does not actually guar-antee that trust in the police has the same meaning to citizens across countries; we merely know that our particular measurement instrument does not detect substantial differences in meaning. Still, without any empirical evidence of measurement equivalence whatsoever, we are certainly guilty of *'occidental'* thinking—in the interpretation of Cain (2000)—the assumption that key cultural and institutional characteristics are the same across Western and non-Western countries, whereas they are possibly not.[2] Manning (2005) reached the conclusion that much American and to a lesser extent British police research is, in this sense, *'ethnocentric, narrow and parochial'* (Manning, 2005: 32).

Although previous studies in the field of attitudes toward the police considered it a strength when more countries (Cao et al., 2012; Morris, 2015) and more diverse countries (Jang et al., 2010) were included in statistical analyses, problems with measurement equivalence also have the potential to grow more daunting whenever more countries are analyzed, and more serious if more diverse countries are taken into account. Let me showcase several ways in which cross-national equivalence could be endangered when studying citizens' attitudes toward the police.

4.2.1   *The researcher: Translation and understanding*

In international surveys, translation issues are often central. The reaching of accurate, valid translations of a survey instrument into (many) often fundamentally different languages is an art in itself (Harkness, 2003; Jowell, 1998). Nevertheless, straightforward human mistakes are sometimes made.[3]

Aside from such clear-cut examples, the majority of translation issues have to do with genuine linguistic difficulties—aspects that often reflect profound elements of local or national history and culture. Remember the translations of 'trust' and 'confidence' as discussed in Chapter 2. The English distinction between these two words was made in none of the other languages; they were consistently translated into the same word or different conjugations of the same word. Logically, if we are to accept that there is some conceptual difference between the two words in English, we must conclude that this difference has been lost in translation. It is possible that this slight discrepancy is entirely inconsequential. However, it *could* also have implications for the answers that respondents give on questions regarding trust/confidence in the police, so that differences we find in their answers to such questions reflect linguistic and cultural discrepancies rather than substantive differences in attitudes. Hence, cross-national comparability is potentially compromised.

---

2.   Cain's interpretation differs from the dominant discourse on occidentalism in anthropological literature, in which it refers to stylized images and renderings of the West—either by 'alien' societies or by the West itself (Carrier, 1992).

3.   Rother (2005: 123) provided an example of an international survey including questions on what criteria foreign immigrants should meet, where the original English word 'wealthy' was misread and the word 'healthy' was translated into Italian instead. Obviously, this led to invalid comparisons between the English and the Italian respondents on this particular question.

4.2.2   *The police: Function, structure, and culture*

We know that the police have widely different organizational structures,[4] control mechanisms, functions, tasks, and goals in different societies (Bayley, 1979, 1985; Mawby, 1992, 2003). Taking this to an extreme, one may even state that *'police practice ranges from social work to torture and murder'* (Pakes, 2010: 42), obviously rather depending on the country, the moment in time, and the specific situation. But in some societies, especially those facing serious internal or external threats, the police may to a larger extent need to resort to political and secret *'high policing'* (Brodeur, 1983) as opposed to mundane and visible *'low policing.'* Examples in this sense might be Israel, where the police have sizeable antiterrorism responsibilities (Brodeur, 2007; Jonathan, 2010), or Russia, where the police tend to prioritize protecting the regime rather than providing security to the public (Beck & Robertson, 2009). Hence, when comparing the police in different countries, we may be discussing completely different things. Will trust in the police mean the same thing under these differing circumstances?

The problem here becomes apparent when we look at the previously listed large-scale comparisons. The study by Jang et al. (2010) compared citizens' confidence in the police in, among other countries, Spain and Kyrgyzstan. I am no expert in the field of policing in Kyrgyzstan, but it is probably safe to expect that policing a partially nomadic former Soviet republic, plagued by poverty, corruption, political instability, authoritarian rule, and violent ethnic conflict (Marat, 2010), is a completely different thing altogether than policing a developed Western country such as Spain. There are probably more discrepancies than similarities between the police in these countries, making a valid comparison practically impossible even at face value. When we are comparing 'the police' between these countries, we are comparing institutions—in very different states—that probably have little in common but their name. But less radical dissimilarities between countries, such as differences in legal or enforcement culture, may also complicate comparisons when studying public attitudes toward the police (Nelken, 1994, 2009). Terpstra and Schaap (2013) found, for instance, that the typology of (British and American) police culture as formulated by Reiner (2010) proved to be only partially applicable in the Dutch context. Again, this implies that the police are not the same across countries; and if the police themselves are different, public perceptions of the police may not be validly compared.

---

4.   Kutnjak Ivković (2008) and Morris (2015) statistically controlled for several elements of organizational structure; characteristics of each country's own police force. The addition of such control variables, while laudable, is insufficient for problems related to measurement equivalence: they account for substantive differences in the construct, but not for measurement artifacts.

4.2.3   The public: Expectations and fears

Not only can citizens' judgments diverge due to the different natures of the police forces, but also their expectations of the police, their desires, and their wishes. Citizens and society as a whole can therefore also affect measurement equivalence. For citizens, the police have an important symbolic power related to their hopes, fears, and fantasies, to feelings of belonging and identity (Loader & Mulcahy, 2003; Muir, 1977: 4). The particular emotional connections that citizens have with the police are deeply ingrained in national culture and history and will therefore probably differ strongly across countries (Loader & Mulcahy, 2003: 53-54; Manning, 2012).

An interesting case in this sense is made by a study of Davis et al. (2004). In a comparative analysis of urban citizens' attitudes toward the police in the U.S. and Russia, the researchers found that there are no substantial differences between the American and the Russian samples in their perceptions of police use of excessive physical force. This result is rather unexpected considering a range of other studies that have painted an image of the Russian police as exceptionally violent and corrupt (Beck & Robertson, 2009; Semukhina & Reynolds, 2014; Shlapentokh, 2006), referring to Russian police practice as *'pathological'* (Zernova, 2012) or even *'predatory'* (Gerber & Mendelson, 2008). The counterintuitive absence of a substantial difference in public attitudes between the U.S. and Russia found by Davis et al. (2004) could be caused, as the authors suggest, by larger media attention to cases of police misconduct in the U.S. than in Russia. But in a broader cultural sense, Russian citizens may also have entirely different expectations of their police officers, different associations with the notion of policing, and other definitions of what exactly 'excessive' force entails as compared to Americans. This chimes with the discussion in Chapter 2, when we formulated a working definition of trust; trust in the police depends on the understanding of their function. When the Russian police are not expected by their citizens to adhere to the principle of minimum use of force, which was argued to be the basic foundation of the police function in the U.S. (Bittner, 1980), citizens will have an entirely different view on police behavior. The police may then not be seen as representing the authority of the (essentially benign) state operating from a minimal force paradigm (Brodeur, 2010: 107), but as a predatory institution that is fully expected to mistreat its citizens (Gerber & Mendelson, 2008; Semukhina, 2016). As a result, excessive physical force on the part of the police may be defined quite differently in the two countries. Although it has not explicitly been tested for, this case has all the makings of a serious equivalence problem. It would therefore be a mistake to just compare citizens' reported perceptions of excessive police violence between the two nations and be done with it: the observed similar values are probably a result of profoundly different societal mechanisms and, as Davis et al. (2004) duly note, need to be interpreted with great care.

Let me add a final caveat. Social desirability is a problem common to many social science studies, be they cross-national or not (Johnson & Van de Vijver, 2003). But if there are differences in social desirability between respondents in different countries, we will face not only a biased reflection of the population's true opinions within a country, but also a bias in comparing nations. Braun (2003) and Cao and Burton (2006) reasoned, for instance, that there are likely to be differences in terms of social desirability between collectivist and individualist cultures, possibly leading to nonequivalent measurements of trust in the police in cross-national surveys. When asking questions about opinions of the police in countries with authoritarian or totalitarian regimes, the term 'social desirability' even becomes an understatement. Rather, we are risking completely nonsensical answers rooted in fear of persecution (Lai, Cao, & Zhao, 2010). In a comparison of confidence in the police in Taiwan and China, the researchers noted that the validity of their survey data was likely to have been affected by China's authoritarianism (Lai et al., 2010: 940). It would therefore not be commendable to compare opinions of the police in countries with authoritarian regimes (Cao & Burton, 2006): not only do the police have a completely different function and status than in democratic societies, but even more serious is the fact that answers to survey questions cannot be trusted to reflect the population's true opinion. Unfortunately, this seems to exclude substantial parts of the world from further analysis. However, this is still preferable to drawing misleading inferences from invalid comparisons.

4.2.4   *Measurement equivalence in previous research*

None of the previous large-scale international comparative studies of citizens' attitudes toward the police have dealt sufficiently with issues related to measurement equivalence, although some authors have indicated that they were aware of the problem. Most outspoken in this sense are Cao et al. (2012: 41), who repeated Cao and Burton (2006) in stating that the measurement of public opinion on subjects such as attitudes toward the police is inaccurate in authoritarian nations. But despite this statement and the fact that they titled their study 'Shades of blue,' because '*beneath the superficial similarity, the shades of blue differ and police differ fundamentally in their organizational priorities and in their means to achieve the priorities*' (Cao et al., 2012: 47), they still compared democratic as well as authoritarian countries without evidence of measurement equivalence. Kääriäinen (2007) probably implicitly attempted to circumvent comparability issues when selecting only EU Member States.[5] But this is still lacking. Tests for measurement equivalence in the field of public attitudes toward the police are nearly absent, but one study that has been

---

5.   Alalehto and Larsson (2016) even did so explicitly, referring to our earlier contribution (Schaap & Scheepers, 2014).

conducted (Jackson et al., 2010) indicates that equivalence can be problematic even within Europe and the EU.

More common are cross-national measurement equivalence tests focusing on other forms of trust. These include political or broader institutional trust (Marien, 2011; Schneider, 2017) or social trust (Van der Veld & Saris, 2011). The results from such studies might provide us with some tentative leads in terms of how serious we can expect measurement equivalence problems to be in a cross-national comparative study of trust in the police. The same holds for assessments of longitudinal measurement equivalence, although they are thus far extremely rare (Poznyak et al., 2014), and of equivalence of measures in different linguistic regions within the same country (Freitag & Bauer, 2013). What most of these studies have in common, though, is that they have found at least some evidence of nonequivalence and therefore of comparability issues. These include problems in a single indicator of an extensive construct as measured over time (Poznyak et al., 2014) and between different European countries (Jackson et al., 2010; Marien, 2011; Van der Veld & Saris, 2011). When comparing a sample of European and Central Asian countries in terms of institutional trust, including trust in the police, Schneider (2017) also finds serious indications of nonequivalence, challenging the validity of cross-national comparisons of institutional trust particularly outside of the EU. Thus, it seems reasonable to conclude that measurement equivalence should not be taken for granted.

To summarize, regardless of the superficial face validity of the country sample, cross-country measurement equivalence of trust in the police needs to be adequately tested for, or we run a serious risk of drawing invalid conclusions. Regarding attitudes toward the police, I have shown that these risks are to be taken seriously, for theoretical as well as empirical reasons: there are good a priori reasons to expect comparability issues, and there is substantial evidence that these issues do indeed arise. Before we can move to any type of comparison of trust between countries, it is hence necessary to conduct empirical tests so as to ascertain measurement equivalence.

4.2.5   *Testing for measurement equivalence in the present study*

Taking previous contributions in the field of measurement equivalence of trust-related measures into account, as well as more theoretically oriented work regarding the position of the police in democratic societies, it is possible to distill a strategy for testing for measurement equivalence in the present study. The one study that has concentrated on testing for measurement equivalence of trust in the police (Jackson et al., 2010) included various measures of trust in the police, assuming that nonequivalence of one of those measures as compared to the others meant an indication of an invalid comparison. This method of assessing measurement equivalence, however, was geared toward the specific aims of their study: to test whether measures of various sub-dimensions of trust in the police held across different cultures. The interest of this study is less specific: our present interest is whether measurements of trust in the police *in general* are cross-nationally and diachronically equivalent.

When we look at trust in the police institution as a whole, it is most suitable to position it in the broader constellation of institutional trust. The police are not an isolated agency, but are—in a Weberian tradition—an essential part of the state. Indeed, they are the most visible representatives of state authority (Bittner, 1980; Brodeur, 2010; Fleming & McLaughlin, 2012). Let us recall the previously included words of Banton that *'the extent to which the British police are regarded, and regard themselves, as different from other institutions is not fully apparent to anyone who knows only the position in Britain and has nothing with which to compare it'* (Banton, 1964: 236). It stresses not only the relevance of studying the police cross-nationally, but also the importance of doing so in a broader state context; the cross-national and diachronic comparability of citizens' trust in the police depends to a large extent on the position of the police in the framework of governmental institutions. It is in this constellation that differing police structure, function, and culture, as well as diverging public expectations and fears—meaning those factors likely to affect equivalence—will most clearly be reflected. If public trust in the police proves to be nonequivalent in a certain country as compared to others, measured in a broader institutional context, it is problematic to validly compare across nations. Similarly, if multiple measurements within the same country over time yield nonequivalent results for trust in the police in this same institutional context, validly tracing developments in trust over time becomes questionable.

To conclude, this study will test for measurement equivalence of public trust in the police in a cross-national European as well as a diachronic within-country perspective, seen in the context of broader institutional trust. These tests are essential for the comparative quantitative survey data that we have. With the aid of measurement equivalence tests, we can preserve the advantages of large-scale comparative data while correcting for one of their main weaknesses.

If trust in the police passes the measurement equivalence tests, we have some indication that we can validly conduct different types of comparative analyses: that of mean levels of trust between and within countries at different moments in time, and of relationships between trust in the police and other variables in these different contexts.

4.3   PERSPECTIVES ON DIFFERENCES AND DEVELOPMENTS IN TRUST IN DIFFERENT
        COUNTRIES

After establishing evidence for valid cross-national and diachronic comparisons in our measurement equivalence tests, we can use those countries and years that have passed the tests for further analysis. Research Question 2 aims to examine differences and developments in levels of trust in the police between different European countries. Where is trust low, and where is it high? What countries have seen remarkable developments in trust in the police? This descriptive analysis will, of course, concentrate on those countries and years of measurement that have been found equivalent.

In terms of differences between countries in levels of trust in the police, we are not exactly without points of reference. Quite a few comparative studies have compared mean levels of trust in (or other assessments of) the police between European countries, based on the European Social Survey (Kääriäinen, 2007), the International Crime Victimization Survey (Kutnjak Ivković, 2008), or the World Values Survey (Thomassen, 2013), among other data sources. Nevertheless, what is still lacking is a dynamic, diachronic perspective. The aforementioned studies have taught us that trust in the police across Europe tends to be highest in the Nordic countries, and lowest in the former Soviet Union. Other northwestern European countries generally have a relatively high level of trust, whereas Eastern and Southern European countries, on average, feature medium to low levels of trust. But our knowledge of how these trust rates have developed over time is, as yet, extremely limited. This is quite remarkable, as trends are at least as interesting as synchronic differences.

The questions, then, are what kind of trajectories of trust we should expect and why. As discussed in Chapter 1, public discourse tends to emphasize a fall in levels of trust across Europe over recent decades—not just regarding the police, but concerning the entire public sector. Empirically, support for this assertion has so far remained thin. It has been argued that *'the debate on citizens' trust in the public sector is dominated by […] a lack of historical perspective'* (Van de Walle et al., 2008: 48). The information we do have is inconclusive and the few high-quality contributions that have so far been made have a different focus than the present study. Twenge, Campbell, and Carter (2014) found a strong decline in institutional and interpersonal trust in the U.S. between 1972 and 2012, whereas Van de Walle et al. (2008) reported no evidence for a cross-national decline in trust in the civil service in Western societies over recent decades, and mixed results in terms of trust in government. In a European context, although covering only a limited period of time, Marien (2011) argued that there were few strong developments in institutional trust across the continent as a whole. Nevertheless, on average, the data that she presented did suggest declining rather than improving trust in various institutions —including the police.

Not only is empirical support for a decrease in trust in the police quite thin so far, but a coherent theoretical argument to expect a cross-national fall in public trust in the police has not been constructed either. With firm theoretical underpinnings, it is mainly English-dominated police research that has stressed a steady decline of police authority and legitimacy (Loader & Mulcahy, 2003; Reiner, 1995, 2010). This has been partially supported by survey results (Bradford, 2011a;

Hough, 2003; Jansson, 2008). A similar finding of gradually falling trust has been reported in the Netherlands by Terpstra and Trommel (2009). For the rest of Europe, theoretically rigorous research on the subject is scant. However, it requires a stretch of the imagination to assume that explanations and expectations of the English decline in trust will simply hold across all of Europe. The current state of affairs is that, in many countries, we simply do not know whether trust in the police is on the increase or on the decrease. When present, existing inquiries are often unsystematic or atheoretical, and occasionally of unclear methodology.

4.3.1   Understanding change

Two things of note arise when discussing changes in trust in the police over time. The first may provide an explanation for the curious absence of diachronic studies in the field of trust in the police: it concerns the near impossibility—given the serious deficiencies in available data—of testing explanatory models addressing the causes of developments in trust in the police. To view this as a reason not to conduct any diachronic research on the subject at all, however, risks throwing out the baby with the bathwater. Existing data, as of yet, simply lack the quality and quantity for a rigorous examination of cause and effect; we should, for now, simply accept that this is out of reach. This also means that the theoretical models that we constructed previously regarding factors determining trust in the police cannot be tested diachronically. In spite of this, fortunately, a more elaborate study than has been done before still seems to be within our range of possibilities; many cross-national European surveys have by now been conducted in several waves, often running for many years. Provided that the comparative, diachronic data pass our equivalence tests, we can at least describe trends in trust in the police across Europe over recent decades. Even such a bare description is an improvement over the current absence of any systematic information whatsoever.

As argued before, it will not be possible to present hard conclusions on the causes or main drivers of these developments. Nevertheless, it may be worthwhile to examine some of the main possible mechanisms that potentially affect trends in trust, and that have shaped public as well as political and scientific discourse on the subject. This is where the second note arises in understanding change. The mechanisms examined to study the dynamics of trust are not synonymous—although they overlap—with the three theoretical perspectives introduced before. While this appears counterintuitive, the point is that developments over time require additional explanations to comparisons at a fixed moment in time: the three theoretical perspectives will not be rendered useless in this phase of the study but, rather, will be supplemented by additional notions. When we examine trust in the police cross-nationally and diachronically, the lens through which we study change will include a broader scope than the one applied to cross-national comparisons. The dynamic nature of diachronic research points us in the direction of explanations involving societal developments, including action and reaction, policy transfer, imitation, and learning processes.

Not all of these types of explanation can be properly assessed with our available data. We will return to notions of policy transfer and learning processes in depth in Part III of this study. Instead, in the dynamic analyses, we will concentrate on four different popular ideas about developments in trust in the police. These popular ideas, in their assumptions and logic, have some commonalities with the three theoretical perspectives used to explain differences between countries in levels of trust. Nevertheless, as discussed before, they do not fully correspond with them as their logic is different. This is due to both the different quality of available data for these two types of analysis and because of the fundamentally different nature of change as opposed to difference.

The four popular ideas regarding developments in trust in the police are of a broader nature than the theoretical perspectives. They often concern not only the police, but also other law enforcement agencies or even all institutions. All of the four ideas suggest certain descriptive trends in trust and the explanations behind those trends. They mostly stress a decrease (or continuous low level) of trust, but what makes them suitable for inclusion in this study is also that they propose certain patterns of developments—expected trajectories of change that can be matched with the actual data. If reality matches the expected trends, the explanatory logic of these popular ideas will be attributed with more credibility.

These popular ideas can be labeled the *desacralization* thesis, the *safety utopia* thesis, the *post-authoritarian paradox* thesis, and the *socioeconomic crisis* problem. While they tend to have a pessimistic approach toward developments in trust, they differ in their theoretical assumptions and the geographic and temporal domains on which they focus, which makes it worthwhile to examine them separately.

Since there is, as yet, no satisfactory way to rigorously test the mechanisms behind developments in trust, I will refrain from formulating hypotheses. The purpose of this examination is hence merely to assess the preliminary plausibility of some popular ideas about (perceived or assumed!) trends in public attitudes toward the police. By studying the trajectories of trust in relation to the societal processes thought to shape those trajectories, we can at least assess whether such explanations share a common basis with empirical reality. We must be careful, though, not to mold this loose examination into a rigid framework of cause-effect expectations.

4.3.2 *The desacralization thesis*

The desacralization thesis, as a phrase, has been derived from Loader and Mulcahy (2003). Reiner (2010) and Loader and Mulcahy (2003) offered what is to date the most elaborate argument for a decline in public trust, albeit focused exclusively on the English (and possibly applicable to the Welsh and Scottish) situation. It has also been influential outside this limited sphere, and is therefore worth discussing. They describe a mythical *'golden age'* of postwar policing in the 1950s, when the image of the benevolent 'bobby on the beat,' in its heyday, was constructed and optimally nurtured. The police, in this view, had a *'sacred'* status (Banton, 1964). Brogden (1982) refers to this construction as part of a discourse of consent—an ideological tool for police self-legitimation. All of these authors fully acknowledge that police behavior did not always chime with their reputation: it was the rhetorical, cultural construction of the police image (Mawby, 2002) that shaped the golden age.

After this period, a gradual decline in police legitimacy commenced. Economic, political, and sociocultural changes in society were argued to have permanently desacralized the police as an institution (Loader & Mulcahy, 2003). Societal pluralization from the 1960s onward featured the rise of multiple social strata that had a fundamentally difficult relationship with the police, including various youth movements and ethnic minorities (Reiner, 2010)—even though it could be argued that the lower social classes had always had an antagonistic relationship with the police (Brogden, 1982). This in itself was already problematic, since it implied the structural presence of groups of citizens with low trust in the police. Societal developments, however, made these groups more visible and more vocal. Heavy-handed police responses against ethnic minorities and labor unions during demonstrations and riots from the 1960s until the 1980s exacerbated problems, leading to a loss of legitimacy in the eyes of the general public (Loader & Mulcahy, 2003). Moreover, the political position of the police weakened as the rise of the NPM model during the 1990s meant that police performance came to be scrutinized like that of any other institution (Reiner, 2010). The police were increasingly perceived as a profane institution, as eligible a target for criticism as any other. Public disillusionment with the police might even mean that the police were more eligible for criticism than other, previously less revered, institutions, due to the large discrepancy between their past image and their current status.

To conclude, the desacralization thesis suggests that in places where the police used to have a 'sacred' cultural status, processes of 'secularization' or demystification may have caused the police to be more subject to criticism than other institutions. To what extent this holds outside of England (and Wales, and possibly Scotland) remains to be seen. Translated to rates of public trust in the police, the desacralization thesis emphasizes gradually falling levels of trust over a long period of time, and the finding of such a pattern in our data would provide some support for this thesis.

4.3.3   *The safety utopia thesis*

The desacralization thesis, although compelling, is not sufficient in itself to explain changing trajectories of police legitimacy and public trust even in England (Loader

& Mulcahy, 2003). The societal position of the police is much more ambivalent than that of a formerly sacred institution experiencing a fall from grace. Indeed, Manning (1977) described how the police contain features and undertake activities that are both sacred *and* profane. This is part of why, while acknowledging a shift in the public image of the police from the sacred to the profane, the safety utopia thesis argues that citizens actually continue to attach a near-sacred meaning to the police. The importance of crime and safety in the public and political discourse has greatly increased. For a multitude of reasons, crime rates skyrocketed in many Western societies from the 1960s or 1970s until at least about the turn of the century—something the media were quick to stress (Brodeur, 2010; Mawby, 2002). However, not only are the police considered to be at least partially responsible for developments in crime, but they are also looked to as the institution that should do something about it (Loader & Mulcahy, 2003). In a notion derived from Garland's (2001) '*culture of control*,' citizens desire a '*safety utopia*' (Boutellier, 2004): a guarantee of security. This leads to the paradoxical situation that the police are both heavily criticized and, ideally, seen as the solution to a myriad of problems. The role of the media is typical in this sense: on the one hand, there are dozens of television series that have the police glorified as tireless crime fighters protecting us from evil; yet, on the other hand, these very same media are also quick to pick up on miscarriages of justice or 'soft' police responses to crime (Mawby, 2002). More than before, the media watch the every step that the police take. As such, police mistakes or scandals are bound to receive a lot of (negative) attention (Terpstra & Fyfe, 2013). In this view, the issue with the police is not that they have been demystified—looking to the police as solvers of all problems implies a certain mystique as well.

It is this very mystique that poses a problem for police legitimacy (Terpstra & Trommel, 2009): it is impossible for the police to meet an expectation of perfect security. The police lack manpower, information, and the ability to sufficiently coordinate and regulate the social sphere to create the desired level of safety. Worse, the state is often unable or unwilling to recognize its own deficiency in this respect. This is what Loader and Walker (2007) called the view of the state as an idiot—emphasizing the state's ignorance of the limits on its own power. Promises or guarantees will be given that cannot possibly be kept, inevitably leading to the feeling that trust was betrayed. This effect may be expected for many Western European countries.

Nevertheless, in order to attach such heavy moral significance to the police and maintain high public expectations, citizens must also have a certain basic level of trust—referring, after all, to expectations. Reiner (2010: 67) labeled the police a '*Teflon service*,' surviving scandal and controversy while remaining an institutional force to be reckoned with, while Loader and Mulcahy (2003) employed the very idea of societal fragmentation to argue that there is still a substantial group of '*defenders of the faith*': a solid core of citizens who continue to support the police. The desacralization and safety utopia theses hence may explain why attitudes in high-trust societies are growing more negative, but do not tell us much about contexts where a basic level of police legitimacy was never achieved.

4.3.4   *The post-authoritarian paradox thesis*

There are two reasons to expect a decline in trust even in societies where trust was already not too high to begin with. Let us address the first of those, the *post-authoritarian paradox*, here. This is most relevant for formerly communist Central and Eastern Europe, where authoritarian regimes were replaced with more democratic ones during the late 1980s and early 1990s. These revolutionary changes could, on the one hand, be expected to vastly improve public trust in various state institutions—including the police. After all, a repressive, totalitarian state was replaced with a democratic style of governance: democratic elections brought governments to power that, at least nominally, reflected the public will. The communist state apparatus was reformed using liberal Western examples. The police, in many countries, no longer operated as the strong arm of a totalitarian regime.

   While this could increase trust in institutions, including the police, there are also good reasons to expect the exact opposite. Describing trajectories in confidence in parliament and the civil service in a number of Central and Eastern European countries, Catterberg and Moreno (2006: 45-46) found a '*post-honeymoon trend of political disaffection*': falling levels of confidence in institutions after the end of communism. The authors suggested that this was due to newly democratic governments failing to curb corruption and improve the well-being of their citizens in the period of transition. This brings us to the post-authoritarian paradox: the finding that newly democratic states experience a fall in institutional trust, rather than the rise that would more intuitively be expected.

   The paradox entails that the era of post-communism, while arguably in many ways more democratic than that of communism, also ushered in a multitude of problems. For many post-communist countries, the 1990s saw falling standards of living (Sapsford & Abbott, 2006), exploding (official) crime rates (Caparini & Marenin, 2005; Gilinskiy, 2006; Gruszczynska, 2004; Kerezsi & Lévay, 2008; Lappi-Seppälä & Lehti, 2014), and disintegration of communities and familiar social bonds (Laitin, 1998; Pridemore & Kim, 2006). Moreover, the post-communist state system offered more opportunities for corruption and abuse of power (Sajó, 1998)—not to mention sheer incompetence. In the words of one Ukrainian observer, contemporary administrative institutions in his country, notably including the police, are '*a reincarnation of [the] Soviet bureaucratic pyramid—minus the Soviet restraints*' (Makarov, 2013). While the strict communist system would, albeit in an arbitrary fashion, reign in the worst excesses of corruption and self-advancement through strict social and political control, such controls were absent or severely weakened in the post-communist system (Dzhekova, Gounev, & Bezlov, 2013; Krastev, 2005). Elaborating on this logic, Krastev (2005) described a transition in Eastern Europe from 'do me a favor' societies to 'give me a bribe' societies. This marked a shift from particularistic governing, meaning the provision of services in exchange for other services, to outright bribery and extortion (Mikkelsen, 2013): monetary in nature, more visible, and much more offensive to social norms (Krastev, 2005). Such a development might not always be reflected in corruption data such as Transparency International's Corruption Perceptions Index, but the altered nature of corruption can severely impact trust.

How would this post-authoritarian paradox impact trust in the police specifically? Let us briefly recall the debate on procedural injustice discussed in the previous chapter. The police are known to be among the institutions most vulnerable to corruption (Punch, 2009), since they have both the autonomy and the opportunity to abuse their power in such a way. Accountability and transparency, always contentious issues in policing, are often particularly weak in states undergoing a radical transformation. A decrease of citizens' trust in the police in post-communist countries is therefore to be expected. This is why Szikinger (1993), briefly after the end of communism, warned not to invest any more proactive power in the Hungarian police organization until it was fundamentally reformed. And from an instrumental perspective, rising crime rates too may have negatively affected trust in the police.

These are clear reasons to expect falling levels of trust in the police in post-communist or other post-authoritarian societies. However, since most of these countries have by now seen at least 25 years of different developments since the process of transition commenced, it is particularly interesting to observe more recent changes in trust in the police. The 1990s are history and much has changed since those tumultuous years. The post-authoritarian paradox thesis gives us very little information about what to expect *after* the initial shock has passed.

4.3.5   *The socioeconomic crisis problem*

If we take into account more recent developments, we find an additional theoretical reason to expect a decline in public trust in the police across significant segments of Europe: the *socioeconomic crisis* problem. This refers to the impact of the financial crisis and the ensuing social unrest that commenced in 2008 on attitudes toward the police and other institutions. It differs from the other three theses in that it has received scant attention in the policing literature. It is for this reason that we are not yet entirely sure what its effect is and how, if at all, the impact of the socioeconomic crisis differed for the police as compared to other institutions. This means that we will speak of a problem rather than a thesis.

Much of Europe has been struck by the economic downturn and its social consequences, although the economic and societal impact varies by country. Roth (2009) surprisingly reported a short-term increase in levels of citizens' trust in their governments across Europe during the first months of the economic crisis, which he attributed to a rally-around-the-flag effect: citizens supporting their leadership during a time of national crisis. Several years later, however, Torcal (2014) compared European developments in political distrust between 2008 and 2012 and, rather, found evidence of a serious decline over this period. The short-term boost in institutional trust hence appeared to have turned into a longer-term fall.

That political institutions were confronted with rising distrust in the wake of the socioeconomic crisis, once the effects of that crisis were felt, can hardly be called surprising. Governments requiring financial bailouts and/or facing a perceived necessity to radically cut expenses understandably have to answer to dissatisfied citizens. But what of the police? Expectations may vary. For police services across Europe, the economic crisis has had strong—albeit heterogeneous—effects. In some countries, it has led to severe budget cuts likely to negatively affect police–public relationships (Sindall & Sturgis, 2013; White, 2014). As the most visible representatives of the state, and as an agency that occasionally clashes fiercely with protesters—particularly in countries with a strong protest movement, such as Greece (Karakatsanis, 2016; Simiti, 2016)—the police could very well bear the brunt of the crisis. In this case, one would expect trust in the police to decrease more drastically than trust in other institutions. However, another possibility is that the police, being hardly the instigators of the crisis, will not be held as strongly accountable as more political institutions. This would imply a weaker decline of trust in the police than in other institutions. Finally, the chances are that times of economic and political crisis actually have a positive effect on public trust in the police: as an order maintenance service, the police could be seen as a beacon of stability in the stormy waters of the crisis.

Whichever of these mechanisms seems most plausible, what appears hard to accept on the face of it is that the crisis has absolutely no connection with public trust in the police. Rather, the question is which of the possible effects is strongest. In times of swift, sometimes radical, social change, the police as frontline service are always likely to be affected in *some* way. The socioeconomic crisis problem thus entails that the crisis probably has had an impact on public trust in the police, but it does not specify what, precisely, this impact is: this is what we aim to find out. As we currently have no firm evidence either way, it is worth investigating how trust in the police developed in times of economic crisis, particularly in the countries that were most severely impacted.

4.4   Perspectives on explaining differences between countries

As discussed before, the data we currently have at our disposal are not of sufficient quality to empirically determine the causes of developments over time in trust in the police. They are designed for cross-national comparisons. While tracing developments over time should give us important information about the state of public trust in the police in Europe, our understanding of those developments remains limited to matching them with general, societal processes over recent decades and observing whether they correspond with what one would expect based on those processes. However, as we will soon see, trends in trust in the police are actually not straightforward or easy to interpret. Another way to understand trust is then to compare levels between countries and attempt to explain the differences at a specific moment in time. This can add a level of depth to the analyses that is currently impossible in longitudinal analyses.

Describing differences and developments in levels of trust in the police is one thing; explaining and properly understanding those differences is quite another. In the previous section, I argued that establishing cause-effect mechanisms in developments in trust is, given the currently available data, practically impossible. But while such diachronic explanations are out of reach, the same cannot be said for synchronic analyses. In this section, we will attempt to flesh out a theoretical framework of hypotheses on factors determining trust, explaining differences between individuals and countries in terms of trust in the police at a fixed moment in time. Guided by the three theoretical perspectives introduced in the previous chapter, this section will formulate expectations on the main determinants of trust in the police.

4.4.1   Proximity policing

To what extent can proximity policing explain public trust in the police? As an umbrella paradigm stressing police proximity to citizens, their involvement in local neighborhoods and communities, and proactive approaches toward not only crime but also a wider range of social problems, it is worth testing whether police adherence to such principles can explain differences between individuals and countries in public trust in the police. In other words: what evidence is there that proximity policing improves trust?

A word of caution: that proximity policing is the hardest of the three theoretical paradigms to mold into concrete, measurable determinants—in general, and in our specific data source in particular. This is due to the loose, often vague definition of proximity-related initiatives and because of the absence of cross-nationally agreed-upon indicators. This is not a criticism of police practice—nor of our existing empirical information—but, rather, reflects the flexible, at times elusive, nature of the paradigm. Fortunately, as long as we take into account that any cross-national examination of the relationship between proximity policing and public trust in the police can only yield a rough approximation of a far more complex reality, we still have several possibilities.

These possibilities exist on the national and on the individual level. This is a necessity, since we are aiming to explain and understand trust in the police on both of these levels as well. Hence, we need national-level indicators on the extent to which the police adhere to proximity policing principles. Moreover, we are looking for individual-level indicators on the extent to which individual citizens perceive police officers to adhere to these principles.

As, to the best of my knowledge, thorough indicators of proximity policing on the national level do not yet exist, we will need an alternative approach. Previous research has seldom included international comparisons of proximity policing. A few studies have attempted to assess factors that approximated some aspects of the paradigm. For instance, Morris (2015) controlled in her analyses for whether or not the police organization was centralized. As proximity policing emphasizes a decentralized police structure, one could argue that there is some degree of overlap here. However, as an assessment of proximity policing, centralization is only a partial indicator at best—certainly if it is included as a rough yes/no variable. Hence, this approach is clearly insufficient for our present purposes. Other aspects of police organizations that are sometimes included, such as whether the country has a gendarmerie-style or a civil police organization (Kutnjak Ivković, 2008; Morris, 2015), or whether there are multiple types of police operating in the country (Morris, 2015), are potentially relevant as such—and yet are only marginally related, if at all, to proximity policing principles.

Given the absence of reliable and valid data on the prevalence of proximity policing in different European countries,[6] we have no option other than attempt to collect such data ourselves. Hence, I sent out a brief questionnaire to policing experts and scholars across Europe, inquiring about the extent to which the police in their country adhered to the central tenets of proximity or community policing. Due to the difficulty in objectively measuring policing priorities and practices, expert surveys are a useful tool in research on proximity policing (Zhao et al., 2003). The survey consisted of 10 indicators of different aspects of proximity policing and inquired about additional English-language literature on the subject in the country. These 10 indicators were used to construct an index of the degree to which the police in that country were seen to adhere to principles of proximity policing; I will hence refer to this scale as the proximity policing index. For the methodology and more detailed information on the survey and the construction of the index, see Appendix F. A positive rating on this index is expected to affect public trust in the police positively: countries where the police adhere to a higher degree to proximity policing principles are expected to have higher levels of public trust in the police.

---

6.   In the US, various efforts have been undertaken to systematically assess local police organizations' adoption of community policing principles, through expert surveys (Zhao, He, & Lovrich, 2003) or through amalgamations of existing data sources (De Guzman & Kim, 2017; Wells & Falcone, 2005), resulting in similar indices of the degree in which police organizations within the U.S. adhere to proximity policing. European collections that touch on aspects of proximity policing in different European countries lack a rigorous systematically comparative element (e.g., AEPC, 2001f; Bayerl et al., 2017; Donnelly, 2013; Fyfe, Terpstra, & Tops, 2013; Haberfeld & Cerrah, 2007; Meško et al., 2013).

Hypothesis 1a. In countries that adhere to a higher extent to proximity policing principles, citizens have more trust in the police.

The proximity policing index yields a useful indicator on the national level of the extent to which the police adhere to proximity policing principles. Nevertheless, for a proper examination of the paradigm, it would be preferable to also have an individual-level indicator. Preferably, this indicator would reflect on an individual level several aspects of the national-level proximity policing index. However, despite the popularity of proximity policing-inspired strategies across Europe, no cross-national survey so far has aimed to include aspects that would measure people's attitudes toward these strategies. This is remarkable, as highly diverse questions about public attitudes toward and trust in the police are rather common in such surveys. Nevertheless, without indicators on how citizens perceive proximity policing, an important part of the puzzle of trust is missing.

One indicator that is available in our data concerns the extent to which the police are perceived to be effective at preventing crime.[7] Evidently, this is not a complete assessment of proximity policing, but there is a considerable degree of overlap. An emphasis on police prevention is a core element of all proximity-based strategies. We need to acknowledge that it is also a possible characteristic of some strategies that are *not* rooted in proximity policing, yet the connection between prevention and proximity is, historically, extremely strong. Hence, while this item offers only a partial indicator of citizens' perception of proximity policing, it does appear to be the most promising lead we have for studying the role of proximity policing in shaping public attitudes toward the police.

Assuming that our newly constructed proximity policing index does indeed yield an adequate approximation of the extent to which the police adhere to proximity policing principles, and also assuming that perceived police successes in preventing crime reflect the workings of proximity policing on the ground, we first expect a positive relationship between proximity policing on the national level and perceived police preventive successes. That is, a higher score on the proximity policing index is expected to yield more positive perceptions of police preventive efforts. Second, when citizens perceive the police to be more successful in preventing crimes, they are then expected to also have more trust in the police.

Hypothesis 1b. In countries that adhere to a higher extent to proximity policing principles, citizens perceive the police to be more successful in preventing crime.

Hypothesis 1c. Citizens who perceive the police to be more successful in preventing crime have more trust in the police.

---

7.   The full question in the source questionnaire being '*Based on what you have heard or your own experience how successful do you think the police are at preventing crimes in [country] where violence is used or threatened?*'

To summarize, proximity policing has a direct effect on trust in the police (Hypothesis 1a) as well as an indirect effect, through the intermediary factor of perceived police preventive successes (Hypotheses 1b and 1c).

4.4.2   Instrumentalism

The second theoretical paradigm, that of instrumentalism, has seen quite a few different operationalizations in the past, being included in quantitative models far more often than proximity policing. Some of these past studies have even been cross-nationally comparative in nature (Alalehto & Larsson, 2016; Jang et al., 2010; Sung, 2006). This is not to say that it is an easy paradigm to subject to tests; rather, it means that there are multiple potentially acceptable and interesting ways of doing so.

   The purpose of this section is to formulate hypotheses regarding the viability of the central assumptions underlying instrumentalism, which entails that demonstrable police effectiveness positively affects trust, since the public are expected to hold the police to account. In this logic, as argued in Chapter 3, the role of crime control is that of the key indicator of police performance. Good police performance in terms of reducing crime leads to more trust; bad performance to less trust. So, if the core assumptions of instrumentalism hold, there should be a connection between crime rates and public trust in the police.

   In a broader interpretation of the term, instrumentalist logic often acknowledges that there may be a discrepancy between actual crime rates or police performance and public perceptions thereof (Bottomley & Coleman, 1980). Realizing that citizens may not be aware of or even interested in crime statistics, many instrumentalist-leaning police managers and politicians emphasize good communication with media and public. As a consequence, they will often also invest in professional public relations (PR) departments (Mawby, 2002). In this view, it is not as much the actual performance of the police that counts, but how citizens perceive it. What influences trust is then not the substantive crime rate per se, but public perceptions of police effectiveness (Alalehto & Larsson, 2016; Bradford et al., 2014; Ellison, Pino, & Shirlow, 2013; Jackson et al., 2014; Sampson & Jeglum Bartusch, 1998). This gives rise to police presentational strategies: police effectiveness is as much a rhetorical tool as it is an empirical matter (Terpstra & Trommel, 2009). Interestingly, a time-series analysis by Sindall, Sturgis, and Jennings (2012) provides support for both interpretations, concluding that changes in both actual property crime rates and perceptions of crime rates affect confidence in the police.

   If we accept this division of the instrumentalist paradigm in actual crime figures as a measurable indicator of police effectiveness on the one hand and of public perceptions of police effectiveness on the other, it appears appropriate to take both interpretations into account in our analyses. This is where we encounter several challenges. First, the question arises of how to define or understand actual crime levels (particularly in an internationally comparative context). Second, we need to specify how crime levels are expected to relate not only to trust, but also to public perceptions of police effectiveness. After all, if we do not find a connection between the occurrence of crime and citizens' perceptions of how well the police are doing, a core tenet of instrumentalism—that the public hold the police accountable for their performance—is rejected. Third, we should clarify what is meant by public perceptions of police effectiveness. What does it entail, and what does it not include?

To address the first issue, there are multiple possibilities for assessing actual occurrence of crime. However, we should also be aware of the fact that crime rates are notoriously difficult to compare cross-nationally (Stamatel, 2006). Even for homicide, a crime that is, on the face of it, reasonably clear-cut in its definition and registration, this remains a serious challenge (Liem et al., 2013; Neapolitan, 1999; Smit, De Jong, & Bijleveld, 2011). Taking this into consideration, we may look for data sources that provide a solid, basic impression of crime rates, and yet are not reliant on the recording of criminal justice agencies—these are the most vulnerable to comparability issues.

As a first indicator of instrumentalism on the national level, this means that we will include homicide rates. While fortunately a relatively rare occurrence in most contexts, homicide is a crime with a great impact and even a single murder, when well-publicized, can sometimes signal serious police failures to the general public. This renders it quite central to instrumentalist thinking. Additionally, it is relatively straightforward in definition, certainly in Western contexts—although see Smit et al. (2011). Moreover, it is an indicator used in multiple preceding studies (Cao et al., 2012; Jang et al., 2010; Stack, Cao, & Adamzyck, 2007; Twenge et al., 2014), which makes it interesting to contrast the present findings with previous ones. While correlations between the different ways of registering homicide are generally high, I deem doctors' cause of death registrations collected by the World Health Organization (WHO) to be more reliable than most other forms of data. This is because the WHO collects this information by counting victims, not perpetrators or convictions, thus reducing the dark number—the discrepancy between the number of crimes that actually occurred and the number that has been recorded. The WHO also works with a uniform definition of homicide across countries (Smit et al., 2011). Finally, I expect physicians' institutional interests to be somewhat less likely to affect the data than those of criminal justice agencies or other organs of state.[8] While this approach does not entirely exclude the possibility of differences between countries, it should aid in substantially reducing them, making these data particularly useful for the purposes of the present study.

---

8.   Although we should note that Douglas (1967: 163-231) already extensively analyzed ways in which institutional interests and cultural dimensions could influence doctors' decisions to register a death as a case of suicide or not; similarly, we should not blindly accept WHO homicide registrations as perfectly valid either.

Despite the usefulness of homicide as an internationally comparable type of crime, it remains somewhat lacking as an indicator of police effectiveness. Fortunately, it is a relatively rare crime and most citizens will remain unaffected by it. Hence, it is somewhat questionable whether it plays a strong role in public assessments of the police. Because of this, an alternative operationalization of crime occurrence is commendable; a more general indicator of victimization (Boateng, 2017). As the same limitations will hold as before—police registration being rather deficient for the purposes of an international comparison—we are left looking for other sources of information on crime rates: either (potential) victim or (potential) offender surveys. Fortunately, our survey contains information on citizens' victimization of burglaries and (threatened) assault within the 2 years preceding the interview. If we aggregate this information to the level of nations, a procedure also followed by Visser, Scholte, and Scheepers (2013) in their cross-national examination of fear of crime, we are left with a country-level victimization rate of burglaries and (threatened) assault. These crimes are far more common than homicides, and can still be expected to considerably affect people's lives. The instrumentalist assertion that people judge the police by their performance in reducing crime may very well be applicable in this sense.

To summarize, our actual crime levels will be measured in two terms: that of homicide rates and that of victimization rates of burglaries and (threatened) assault. This leads to the following hypothesis:

Hypothesis 2a. In countries with lower homicide rates and with lower victimization rates of burglaries and assault, citizens have more trust in the police.

But, as was previously argued, instrumentalism does not always purely concentrate on objective crime rates; it is also concerned with subjective police performance in terms of efficiency and effectiveness. Measures of subjective police performance have been used in the form of expert surveys conducted on the national level, composing a country-level index of subjective police performance (Sung, 2006), but mostly tend to focus on individual citizens' assessments (Alalehto & Larsson, 2016; Bradford et al., 2014; Sindall et al., 2012). The latter has the advantage of allowing us to test whether the auxiliary instrumentalist assertion holds that actual crime rates affect citizens' assessments of police effectiveness.

How, then, would citizens' assessments of police performance and effectiveness best be defined? Because of the centrality of crime-fighting to the instrumentalist paradigm, a measure of how citizens judge the police in their capacity to do so is essential (but not sufficient by itself). Alalehto and Larsson (2016) include three measures of police effectiveness in their analysis of determinants of trust in the police, described by the authors as aspects of 'police efficiency and competence.' Following Jackson et al. (2011), they construct a scale consisting of perceived police effectiveness in catching house burglars, police rapid response to calls, and police successfulness in preventing crime. However, while all of these three aspects measure some sort of police performance, they are conceptually and theoretically quite distinct and only in one case indicate police crime-fighting. As I argued in Section 4.4.1, the police capacity to prevent crime is more an indicator of their proximity-oriented approach than of effectiveness: instrumentalism is more concerned with catching criminals than with prevention-oriented activities—efforts that often require close proximity and cooperation. Police rapid response to calls, while certainly a measure of police efficiency and effectiveness and hence fitting well in the instrumental paradigm (Cihan, Zhang, & Hoover, 2012), is not necessarily connected to fighting crime. It provides more information on the service orientation of the police and on their general efficiency than on their pure crime-fighting ability—inclusion of this indicator broadens the instrumental perspective. As such, rapid response to calls is expected to be important for citizens and their trust in the police from a wider instrumental perspective than that of crime-fighting (Hoover, 2010).

This leads us to the conclusion that of those three aspects included by Alalehto and Larsson (2016) and Jackson et al. (2011), two can contribute to an instrumentalist model of trust in the police: one as an indicator of their effectiveness in fighting crime (catching burglars[9]) and the other of their response to calls (rapid response[10]). However, as they probe different aspects of instrumentalism, it is conceptually the richer choice to include them separately rather than as a composite scale. This results in two country-level indicators of more or less objective police performance in terms of crime-fighting (homicide rates and victimization rates of burglary and assault), and two individual-level indicators of subjective police performance in terms of crime-fighting and broader police effectiveness (perceived successfulness in catching burglars and perceived quickness in responding to calls for help).

Following from this, in examining the supposed mechanisms behind the instrumental logic, we will additionally need to assess whether there is a connection between actual crime rates on the one hand and public perceptions of police effectiveness on the other. The expectation here is that higher crime rates will go hand in hand with diminished perceptions of police effectiveness, since the police are perceived to fail in their 'core task' of reducing crime. If there is no such connection, then the notion that the public hold the police accountable for their performance appears problematic.

---

9.   The full question in the source questionnaire being '*How successful do you think the police are at catching people who commit house burglaries in [country]?*', measured on an 11-point scale ranging from 0 (extremely unsuccessful) to 10 (extremely successful).
10.   The full question in the source questionnaire being '*If a violent crime were to occur near to where you live and the police were called, how slowly or quickly do you think they would arrive at the scene?*', measured on an 11-point scale ranging from 0 (extremely slowly) to 10 (extremely quickly).

Hypothesis 2b. In countries with lower homicide rates and lower victimization rates of burglaries and assault, citizens perceive the police to be more successful in catching criminals and to respond more rapidly to reports of crime.

The final link in the instrumentalist theoretical mechanism of trust in the police is that between perceived police effectiveness and public trust in the police. Instrumentalism holds that citizens deem police effectiveness to be the main criterion in gauging their trustworthiness. This would suggest a strong positive relationship between perceived police effectiveness and trust.

Hypothesis 2c. Citizens who perceive the police to be more successful in catching criminals and respond more rapidly to reports of crime have more trust in the police.

4.4.3   Procedural justice

The third theoretical paradigm is that of procedural justice. Emphasizing procedural justice-based policing rather than effectiveness or proximity, this line of thought has grown over recent decades and its development has accelerated in recent years (see Ariel et al., 2016; Hough et al., 2010; Macqueen & Bradford, 2015; Mazerolle et al., 2013a; Sargeant et al., 2016; Wolfe et al., 2016). Often, procedural justice ideas have been contrasted with or tested against aspects derived from instrumentalism (Bradford et al., 2014; Ellison et al., 2013; Koster, 2017; Van Damme, 2017). The popularity of procedural justice scholarship means that our angle of inquiry requires some novelty to add to the existing, considerable, and often high-quality body of knowledge.

Like the previous theoretical schools, the procedural justice one will be tested on the macro and on the micro level. Since procedural justice and its application in policing centers around fair treatment, and as fair treatment shows mostly in personal interaction, it is also on the micro level that it has most often been studied. However, it is also possible to examine aspects of procedural justice on the national level. Additionally, as discussed in the preceding chapter, procedural justice is often most clearly visible by its absence; when principles of procedural justice are violated, the hurt has consistently been shown to be more severe than any potential benefit of actually following these principles (Bradford et al., 2009; Skogan, 2006a; Tyler & Huo, 2002). This means that a thorough assessment of the procedural justice school of thought requires the inclusion of both positive and negative indicators.

A phenomenon that has been well studied empirically but under-appreciated theoretically by the procedural justice school is corruption. The pervasiveness of corruption in a country has often been related to attitudes toward the police (Alalehto & Larsson, 2016; Boateng, 2017; Jang et al., 2010; Kääriäinen, 2007; Kutnjak Ivković, 2005; Morris, 2015; Thomassen, 2013), but has usually been considered separately from procedural justice concerns. This is, presumably, because corrupt practices are diametrically opposed to procedurally just ones. This link between the two is hence, as discussed in the previous chapter, a negative one: the more corrupt a police organization becomes, the less able it will be to treat citizens fairly, honestly, and equally. This also means that the connection, while negative, is conceptually strong. In this sense, corruption can be considered the antithesis to procedural justice—eroding, rather than improving, trust. Likewise, scandal (notably including corruption) and the often spiraling intensity of media coverage and official inquiries have a corrosive effect on the legitimacy of the regulatory state as a whole (Greer & McLaughlin, 2017).

Corruption has been found harmful to the legitimacy of, and confidence in, various public institutions (Anderson & Tverdova, 2003; Clausen et al., 2011; Houston et al., 2016; Van der Meer & Dekker, 2011). Compound that with the fact that the police are among institutions that are most vulnerable to corruption (Punch, 2009), and it becomes clear that corruption is a potentially revealing negative indicator of procedural justice principles in policing practice on the national level. Pervasive corruption in a country is expected to hurt public trust in the police: the police are considered a fundamentally unfair institution, with representatives who deal out justice arbitrarily, behave unpredictably, and are primarily motivated by personal gain rather than by concerns of lawfulness and fairness. Transparency International (2010a) provides the most often used national indicator of corruption: the Corruption Perceptions Index (CPI). The CPI is a composition of different independent expert and business surveys on corruption (Transparency International, 2010b); the wide range and quality of the data sources included makes the CPI possibly the most valid cross-national indicator of corruption available.

This brings us to the first procedural justice-shaped hypothesis: the expectation that more corruption goes hand in hand with lower trust, or, formulated in reverse:

> *Hypothesis 3a. In countries with less corruption, citizens have more trust in the police.*

In addition to this national-level negative indicator of procedural justice, which will inform us about the extent to which the level of corruption in a country affects the level of trust in the police, an individual-level indicator of corruption is required. Corruption is a phenomenon that is salient (in various forms) on different levels, and a thorough examination should include both individual- and country-level assessments of corruption (Clausen et al., 2011). Moreover, the inclusion of the micro level will shed light on the relationship between individual perceptions of police corruption and trust in the police institution. For the connection between corruption and trust in the police to be credible, we will also need indications that corruption on the national level indeed influences individual-level perceptions of police corruption.

Fortunately, our data contain information on public perceptions of police corruption. Conceptually the most valid indicator is the extent to which the police are perceived to take bribes.[11] Although this is clearly not the only shape corruption can take, it is a visible, well known, and low-level type of corruption that most people have some inkling about. Such individual-level assessments of police corruption and bribes are, like the national-level indicators, quite popular in research on public attitudes toward the police (Jackson et al., 2014; Semukhina & Reynolds, 2014; Tankebe, 2010). Similarly, in the present study we are particularly interested in the relationship between perceived police bribe-taking and citizens' trust in the police.

The preceding sections have given us indicators probing police procedural justice on the national and on the individual level. However, while violations of procedural justice principles give us important information, operationalizing a paradigm only negatively is an approach that will fall short. So, in addition to corruption on the national level and perceived police bribe-taking on the individual level, we shall also include the perceived extent to which the police adhere to procedural justice principles. Again, our data, being designed to test procedural justice assertions (Jackson et al., 2010, 2011), offer us excellent possibilities in this regard. As part of their 'conceptual road map' to understanding trust and legitimacy, the research consortium developing measurements for the 2010 wave of the European Social Survey included a set of indicators measuring perceived police procedural justice (Jackson et al., 2010). These indicators consist of three items measuring perceived police respectful treatment of citizens, their fairness and impartiality, and their willingness to explain their actions when asked to.[12] These three questions cover a substantial part of what can be considered procedural justice-based policing and hence conceptually reflect the procedural justice paradigm very well. The

---

11.   The full question in the source questionnaire being '*How often would you say that the police in [country] take bribes?*', measured on an 11-point scale ranging from 0 (never) to 10 (always).

12.   The full questions being as follows:

1.   *'Based on what you have heard or your own experience how often would you say the police generally treat people in [country] with respect?*

2.   *About how often would you say that the police make fair, impartial decisions in the cases they deal with?*

3.   *And when dealing with people in [country], how often would you say the police generally explain their decisions and actions when asked to do so?'*

All these questions are measured on the same scale, ranging from 1 to 4, where 1 is 'not at all often,' 2 is 'not very often,' 3 is 'often,' and 4 'very often.' In the case of the third question, an additional option was given, entailing "no one ever asks the police to explain their decisions and actions.' I interpreted this as being equal to 1 ('not at all often').

exploratory factor analysis and reliability analysis that I have conducted indicate
that the three items empirically form a satisfactory scale.[13]

With these individual-level determinants defined, we can move on to formulating more procedural justice-influenced hypotheses. First, if the assertion holds that
corruption indeed has a close, negative connection to procedural justice, we should
expect a relationship between corruption on the country level and individual perceptions of police adherence to procedural justice principles.

> *Hypothesis 3b. In countries with less corruption, citizens perceive the police to act in
> a more procedurally just fashion and be less likely to take bribes.*

In addition to that, we will, of course, also expect a relationship on the individual
level between perceived police bribe-taking and perceived police adherence to procedural justice principles on the one hand and trust in the police on the other,
which brings us to the final hypothesis:

> *Hypothesis 3c. Citizens who perceive the police to act in a more procedurally just
> fashion and be less likely to take bribes have more trust in the police.*

To summarize, we have three different indicators of procedural justice: country-
level corruption, individual-level perceived police bribe-taking, and individual-
level perceived police adherence to procedural justice principles. We expect a negative relationship between corruption on the national level and public trust in the
police (Hypothesis 3a). The expectation is also that country-level corruption affects
individual perceptions of police bribe-taking and of police adherence to procedural
justice principles (Hypothesis 3b). Finally, we expect a negative relationship
between perceived police bribe-taking and trust, and a positive connection
between perceived police procedural justice and trust (Hypothesis 3c).

---

13. Exploratory factor analyses tested whether these indicators could be said to measure a single
underlying construct in our data. The KMO test yielded a value of .677 (the minimum should be
around .5 for factor analysis to be appropriate) and Bartlett's test was highly significant (indicating that factor analysis was appropriate). Item communalities were found to be between .360
and .637 (the value should be above .2 to indicate that items have some degree of overlap), while
factor extraction yielded a single underlying construct. Factor loadings on this single underlying
construct were between .600 and .798 (the value should be above roughly .4 for each item to indicate that they are sufficiently related to the construct). Finally, an additional reliability test of the
newly formed factor 'procedural justice' yielded a Cronbach's alpha of 0.755, which is satisfactory
(as a rule of thumb, this should be above .7 to form a reliable measurement scale). Results did not
differ substantially when the analyses were split along countries, with the exception of western
Germany. Here, communality and factor loading of the third indicator (whether the police explain
their actions) had values below the recommended thresholds. However, this being the single
exception, I did not deem this violation problematic enough to take action. Similarly, in some
countries the reliability (Cronbach's alpha) value dipped below .7. However, considering the low
number of indicators and the 4-point scale on which they were measured, this is unlikely to reflect
serious issues.

4.4.4   *Other determinants and control variables*

In explanatory analyses, it is often important to control for alternative explanations so that we do not mistakenly attribute an effect to a hypothesized mechanism, when there is in fact an alternative process that could equally well account for the results. Hence, our analyses will include a variety of control variables on the national and individual levels. In order to select potentially relevant determinants, it appears the better course of action to draw from previous studies.

On the national level, there are a few national factors that could be of relevance to better understand trust. Two oft-included factors of potential importance are key societal aspects: economic inequality and level of democracy. These variables both are related to societal factors that may shape public attitudes toward the police—and trust in other institutions. Including them in the analyses may help to specify the origins of trust or mistrust in the police.

First, *income inequality*, often measured by the Gini coefficient, reflects the distribution of economic resources across a society. It has been argued that in more unequal societies, the police could be perceived to represent the interests of the wealthy and powerful more than of anyone else (Jang et al., 2010). Some studies have suggested a negative relationship between income inequality and institutional trust, as rising inequality indicates a failure from the part of the state, in the eyes of the public, to successfully redistribute resources (Twenge et al., 2014; Uslaner, 2011). While, specifically, this notion has not found much empirical support in previous worldwide comparative studies on trust in the police (Cao et al., 2012; Jang et al., 2010), it has some intuitive appeal and has not been tested in a merely European context. Hence, as a macro-economic indicator, it holds potential value as a control variable. In our analysis, we will therefore include the Gini coefficient of every country as indicator of income inequality (UNU-WIDER, 2011a,b).

Second, a country's *level of democracy* might well be expected to affect trust in the police (as in other institutions, but possibly even more so). In nondemocratic countries and countries that have recently transitioned to democratic forms of government, the police may well still be considered tools of a repressive, authoritarian state (Cao & Zhao, 2005; Caparini & Marenin, 2005; Schaap & Scheepers, 2014). The fact that the police are considered, for historical reasons, part of a nondemocratic system can, regardless of their actual behavior, then negatively affect trust in the police. Either the present level of democracy or a country's democratic history can be applied to gauge this assertion. The level of democracy or the democratic history has so far shown inconsistent results in terms of influence on different types of institutional trust.[14]

14.   Contrast the negative results of Anderson and Tverdova (2003) with the mixed results of Norris (2011) and the positive connection with trust in parliament found by Van der Meer and Dekker (2011).

For attitudes toward the police, the results have also been mixed. Jang et al. (2010) found a positive relationship between level of democracy and trust in the police, but Jang et al. (2015) and Morris (2015) then saw this effect disappear after other factors were taken into consideration. Cao et al. (2012) and Sung (2006) shed light on these inconclusive findings, arguing that there was a 'convex curvilinear' relationship between democracy and confidence in the police (Cao et al., 2012) or their perceived effectiveness (Sung, 2006). They found that reported attitudes toward the police were rather positive in full democracies, but also in deeply authoritarian countries. The middle-range countries performed most poorly, suggesting a U-shaped relationship between democracy and confidence in the police. However, we should question the ultimate validity of the conclusion that authoritarian countries have a high level of trust in the police. Rather, the likely explanation is that respondents there refuse to answer survey questions truthfully—as already discussed in Section 4.2.3. The alternative interpretation of these results is hence that the level of trust tends to be higher in full democracies, lower in flawed democracies or mixed models of government, and impossible to measure properly —and possibly theoretically irrelevant—in authoritarian contexts.

We will see, in the following chapters, that the countries that we can empirically compare in terms of public trust in the police are all at least nominally democratic. From a democratic perspective, the most meaningful differences between these countries are in terms of their level of democracy; the extent to which they adhere to democratic principles. So, while no nondemocratic countries are included, the ones that are included still differ in how flawed their democratic systems are.

On the individual level, an additional range of control variables ought to be included. This helps to account for differences between individuals as well as— since countries are aggregations of their individual citizens—between countries. Most of the control variables have been included in a multitude of previous studies of trust in the police and for brevity's sake need no further explanation: *gender, age, education, income, marital status*, main *occupation, urbanization* of the respondent's home, and the frequency of their *religious attendance*—if any. These characteristics have previously been found to determine people's attitudes toward the police to some extent and should hence be accounted for. Importantly, these are also all factors where the supposed causality is relatively uncontroversial: if, for instance, a significant relationship between a respondent's age and their level of trust in the police is found, we can safely assume that age influences trust in the police and not the other way around. This also implies that, differing from some previous studies, I have chosen not to include individual-level control variables where the causality of a relationship is likely spurious or reverse in nature. This holds for attitudinal variables such as generalized social trust, political orientation, trust in government, or fear of crime.[15] The reasoning is not only that including them could lead us to causally erroneous logic, but also that including the effects of such variables in multiple regression analyses would likely unjustifiably diminish the estimated effects of other, more relevant, variables.

Some individual-level control variables require a bit of clarification and theorizing. The first of those is prior *victimization* of the respondent. This is a matter of considerable relevance, since the police often have to deal with victims—requiring their cooperation, too, and hence their trust (Koster, 2017). The experience of becoming a victim of a crime, however, can logically be expected to have a negative impact on one's trust in the police. The police, after all, are expected to attempt to prevent crimes from happening and adequately investigate them when they do occur. As is well known, clearance rates of most crimes are quite low: the majority of crimes go unsolved. This unpleasant experience, often coupled with the inability of the police to make a difference, could well diminish public trust in the police.

While early, American, studies did not find a substantial relationship between victimization of various types of crime and citizens' trust in the police (Biderman et al., 1967; Smith & Hawkins, 1973), more thorough examinations (Garofalo, 1977) and contributions from other countries (Koenig, 1980) did find a negative connection between victimization and trust. These days, the negative effect of victimization on trust in the police is well established and in itself hardly needs more testing (Bradford, 2011b; Myhill & Bradford, 2012; Payne & Gainey, 2007; Van Dijk, 2001). Nevertheless, it is relevant to control for.

One other reason why it is important to investigate victimization is the interaction with the police that often follows. Myhill and Bradford (2012), in a longitudinal study, concluded that while victimization tends to have a considerable negative effect on trust in the police, people evaluating the process of reporting crime to the police positively gain more trust. This touches on another key question of police–public relationships: the impact of individual interactions. As was discussed in Section 4.4.3 on procedural justice, interactions between citizens and police officers have been found to have more potential to do harm to trust than to benefit it (Bradford et al., 2009; Broekhuizen et al., 2015; Lammers, 2004; Skogan, 2006a; Tyler & Huo, 2002). However, as some of these studies concluded that satisfactory contact does have the potential to improve trust in the police (Bradford et al., 2009; Broekhuizen et al., 2015), it will be of great interest to observe these possible effects in a cross-national examination by including not only the question of whether or not people have had contact with the police, but also how they evaluated it.

A final control variable that we should take into account is membership of an ethnic minority. Do respondents consider themselves to be part of an ethnic minority or not? As an international comparative study, the present contribution will not

---

15.   Fear of crime in particular has often been included as a determinant of trust in the police, yet one longitudinal examination has indicated that the causality is mostly reverse: public confidence in the police affects concern about crime more than the other way around (Skogan, 2009).

be able to make a more nuanced distinction into, for instance, different ethnic minority groups, or between immigrants and nonimmigrants, or between different generations of immigrants—all possibly relevant aspects to discern. However, even when we just split the population into ethnic majority members and ethnic minority ones, the results might be surprising. Much previous research on the relationship between ethnicity and attitudes toward the police originates from the US. Early studies indicated that ethnic minorities and blacks especially had lower trust in the police (Bayley & Mendelsohn, 1969; Biderman et al., 1967; Jacob, 1971; Skogan, 1978; Smith & Hawkins, 1973). While these findings were later argued to be more reliant on neighborhood socialization than on ethnicity per se (Cao et al., 1996; Kusow, Wilson, & Martin, 1997), more recent American contributions have time and again noted that ethnic minority members continue to harbor more negative attitudes toward the police than whites (Sharp & Johnson, 2009; Weitzer, 2014; Wolfe et al., 2016; Wu, Lake, & Cao, 2015).

These, however, are all studies pertaining to the U.S. Things may be completely different in other countries. Kautt (2011), for instance, noted that self-defined ethnic minority members in the U.K. tended to have more trust in the police than those who considered themselves to be ethnic majority. This runs counter to most American studies. Kautt and Tankebe (2011) found that such assessments also strongly differ depending on the specific ethnic minority. Results from Belgium (Van Craen, 2013), the Netherlands (Goudriaan et al., 2006), and France (Oberwittler & Roché, 2013) suggest that ethnic minorities have less trust in the police in these countries than the majority. However, research on Germany (Oberwittler & Roché, 2013; Sato, Haverkamp, & Hough, 2016) suggests that there is no difference between ethnic groups. Hence, while it is plausible that ethnicity plays an important role in determining trust in the police, it is rather unclear what this effect will be from an international perspective.

As a result of this ambiguity regarding the relationship between minority membership and trust in the police in studies from different countries, it makes sense to not only present a full model of trust in the police in Europe, but also to split these analyses by country. This aims to shed light on the possibility of divergent effects in different countries—not only where ethnic minorities are concerned, but also for other determinants for which such issues may arise.

4.4.5   *An explanatory model of trust in the police*

The preceding sections result in a full model of trust in the police. In this model, the arrows portray the expected explanatory mechanisms; from the country-level indicators derived from the three theoretical perspectives, directly and through the individual-level intermediary variables, to public trust in the police. Control variables on the country level and and individual level are taken into account both for the dependent variable trust in the police and the intermediary variables.

Where appropriate, each arrow has an accompanying number to indicate the hypothesis that it tests. Hypothesis 1a assumes a direct positive relationship between proximity policing and trust in the police. Hypothesis 1b tests the effect of proximity policing on citizens' evaluations of police preventive success, whereas Hypothesis 1c examines the connection between perceived police prevention and trust in the police—in both cases expected to be positive relationships. These hypotheses all test the proximity policing school of thought.

Moving on to instrumentalism, we can see two mechanisms testing Hypothesis 2a: the supposed negative effect of homicide rates on trust in the police, and that of victimization rates. Similarly, Hypothesis 2b gets tested by two different arrows: from these same country-level determinants to the intermediary variables of perceived police successfulness in catching criminals and their rapid response. Again, the relationships are expected to be negative. Finally, Hypothesis 2c examines the supposedly positive effect of these two intermediary variables on trust in the police.

Finally, procedural justice theory first sees Hypothesis 3a investigating the expected negative influence of country-level corruption on trust in the police. Hypothesis 3b supposes effects of corruption both on perceived police adherence to procedural justice principles (positive) and on perceived police bribe-taking— their corruptibility (negative). Finally, we anticipate procedural justice and perceived police corruption to be directly related to trust in the police, albeit positively in case of the former and negatively in the case of the latter variable.

Figure 4.1   A hypothetical framework of trust in the police

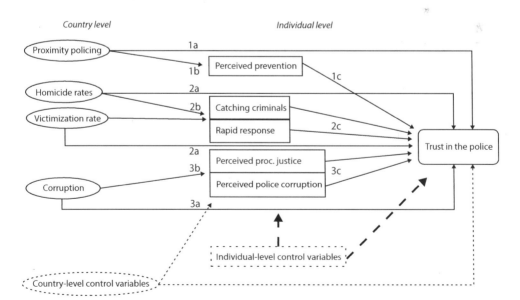

4.5   CONCLUDING REMARKS

In this chapter, I have outlined a quantitative approach toward describing differences and developments of trust in the police as well as explaining differences. I have
formulated theses and hypotheses aimed at answering my research questions.

    In Chapter 5, we shall delve into the diachronic aspects of the analyses, study-
ing developments in trust in the police over time. Moreover, that chapter will
examine the cross-national and longitudinal measurement equivalence of the included data. In Chapter 6, attention shifts to differences at a fixed moment in time:
2010. After briefly describing differences at that time, I shall attempt to explain
them through the full theoretical model shown in Figure 4.1.

Describing developments in trust in the police in Europe from 1981 until 2014

Data and measurements: The European Values Study and the European Social Survey

In this chapter, I will address two research questions. First, Research Question 1 asked to what extent measurements of citizens' trust in the police are empirically comparable across European countries. While this question concentrates on cross-country comparisons, we should also take care to ensure that time-series measurements within the same country are equally comparable over time. Second, Research Question 2 aims, in a descriptive way, to chart differences in levels of trust between countries and developments in trust over time. The first research question, of course, is a precondition for meaningfully answering the second.

When aiming for international and diachronic empirical assessments of public trust in the police, the data sources are essential: we require data that are both cross-nationally comparative and longitudinal in nature. The sources we will use are hence international time-series data. The first necessity for these data is that they are cross-nationally comparative in design. Second, they should consist of several waves; different points of measurement in different periods in time. Third, for the purposes of equivalence tests as described in Chapter 4, the data sources should include questions about trust in the police as well as trust in other state institutions. Two publicly available cross-national surveys meet these requirements: the European Values Study (EVS) and the European Social Survey (ESS).

5.1.1 The European Values Study (EVS)

The European Values Study is a relatively long-running survey, gathered in four waves at the time of writing: 1981, 1990, 1999, and 2008 (EVS, 2011). Over the years, the number of participating European countries has increased from 16 to 47. I include the 28 countries that have participated in three or more waves. In each of the countries and waves, multi-stage random sampling was applied on the population of citizens above the age of 18 who had sufficient command of the national language(s). Interviews, generally numbering 1000 per country, were nearly always conducted in person. In every year, questions were included about confidence in various institutions: the army, police, parliament, civil servants, and the justice system. In the English core questionnaire, the question asked, followed by the list of institutions, is phrased as follows: '*Please look at this card and tell me, for each item listed, how much confidence you have in them: is it a great deal, quite a lot, not very much or none at all?*' This question has been reversed to a 0 to 3 scale, where 0 means none at all, 1 means not very much, 2 equals quite a lot, and 3 a great deal.

Since the measurements are of ordinal nature, they have been parameterized to the assumed underlying continuous variable following the procedure recommended by Jöreskog (2005). With this transformation, they can be dealt with as continuous variables, enabling comparison of means within the same country over time. The long-running nature of the survey also renders it possible to track changes within countries over a relatively long period of time. A limitation of the data, unfortunately, is that cross-country comparisons of levels of trust at the same moment in time in this data source are often found to be nonequivalent (for the results of the cross-national equivalence tests on EVS data, see Appendix B). This implies that mean levels of confidence in the police in the EVS data are not validly comparable *between* countries. I will hence limit these analyses to a longitudinal exploration of developments of confidence *within* countries.

5.1.2   *The European Social Survey (ESS)*

The second data source is the European Social Survey, a biennial repeated survey operating since 2002. While this also means that it lacks a substantial chunk of history that is included in the EVS, the ESS has several considerable advantages. First, while still flawed in several ways (see Billiet et al., 2007), it is methodologically among the most rigorous of international social surveys; documentation of sampling, data collection, possible biases, and questionnaire development and translation are extensive (ESS, 2011). Second, the fact that the ESS is repeated every 2 years gives us the possibility of discerning trends with rather more precision than is possible with the 9-year intervals of the EVS. This also means that, as of the time of writing, there are already seven waves available, allowing us to discern between longer- and shorter-term developments.

A total of 36 European countries have been included in at least one wave, although some countries have participated only once or twice. For the purposes of the present analysis, 27 countries have four or more points of measurement, allowing us to see potentially interesting trends; these countries are included in the analyses of the present study. Germany was split into an eastern and a western part, and the measurement for the U.K. was split into England & Wales and Scotland. Respondents from Northern Ireland (too few in number to be included separately) were removed. This left us with 29 cases for the ensuing analyses.

The ESS follows stratified two- or three-stage probability sampling as its procedure for selecting respondents, who should be aged 15 or older. The vast majority of respondents are interviewed face to face and response rates are, in most cases, high—around 60% or upward (ESS, 2011). In all of these years, questions were asked on trust in five different institutions: the police, the legal system, parliament, politicians, and political parties (the 2002 wave was the exception, as it did not include the question on political parties).

All indicators, all questions assessing trust in institutions, were measured in the same fashion: '*Using this card, please tell me on a score of 0–10 how much you personally trust each of the institutions I read out. 0 means you do not trust an institution at all, and 10 means you have complete trust.*' The resulting 11-point, interval-level scale is well suited for further analyses.

5.2   THE MEASUREMENT EQUIVALENCE OF THE ESS AND EVS: MAIN FINDINGS

Before we continue by tracing developments in trust over time and comparing them between countries, I will briefly report on the measurement equivalence tests conducted to ascertain cross-country comparative validity. Note that the details of these analyses can be found in Appendices A, B, C, and D, while the general logic of the analyses and their main findings will be presented in the main body of the text.

Three different analyses will follow throughout this section: for the benefit of our long-term diachronic descriptive assessment, the four waves of EVS data from 1981 to 2008 will be subjected to longitudinal equivalence tests. Then, the validity of our medium-term diachronic data, the ESS 2002–2014, will be similarly scrutinized. Finally, for the purposes of the explanatory analyses, cross-country equivalence tests of the ESS wave 2010 (the wave including the information we shall need to test our hypotheses) will be reported on. In all these cases, respondents with missing values on one or more types of institutional trust were removed from the analyses.

5.2.1   *Multi-group structural equation modeling*[1]

A solid way of testing for measurement equivalence is to apply structural equation modeling (SEM) in a multi-group setting. SEM is a powerful tool for testing a wide range of theoretical models (Hox & Bechger, 1998), including factor analyses of several manifest indicators measuring one or more latent constructs (Kline, 2011). Both our EVS and our ESS data are structured in this way.

SEM is a method based on the covariance matrix of all included indicators, providing (maximum likelihood) estimates for each parameter in this covariance matrix and computing a χ-square-based model fit. It is a flexible method for testing and improving theoretical models, such as the factor model of trust in various

---

1.   A different version of this section was previously included in Schaap & Scheepers (2014).

institutions that we aim to analyze. Not only can SEM test such models, but it can also compare them across different groups—be they countries, years, or other points of measurement. Through SEM, we can analyze whether a model of some theoretical construct fits in each separate country or year and what parts of the model do not fit and are hence nonequivalent. For this purpose, various global and specific fit indices have been designed. The part of the model in which we are primarily interested is the indicator 'trust in the police': if citizens' trust in the police is found to be nonequivalent by one or more of these fit indices, this has serious implications for its comparability.

Appendix A contains the technical and methodological details of the analyses and the stepwise diagnostics procedure that I applied to ascertain equivalence. Let it suffice to state here that I have combined the procedures and recommendations of multiple previous, similar studies.

5.2.2   Longitudinal measurement equivalence of the EVS, 1981–2008

While the detailed results can be found in Appendix B, the main findings of the diachronic equivalence tests of the EVS deserve some examination here as well. While configural invariance, the basic level of equivalence indicating shared frames of reference, was achieved in all years, the same cannot be said of the two other levels of equivalence: metric and scalar invariance. Metric invariance, the question of whether people attach similar weight to individual institutions in the composition of institutional trust at different moments in time, failed to materialize in **Finland** (the 1990 wave) and **Malta** (the 1981 wave). In addition, scalar invariance, the question of whether the base level of trust in each institution as compared to the others is equal at different moments in time, was not always achieved. This held for the two previously mentioned cases, as without metric invariance, scalar invariance can never be attained. Moreover, scalar invariance was rejected in the cases of **Bulgaria** (1990), **Estonia** (both 1990 and 2008), **East Germany**[2] (all three waves in which it was included), and **Poland** (1990).

Results of invariance tests are often hard to interpret, and these cases follow that rule. The hypothesis that some formerly communist countries have gone through so much societal change that it has affected the longitudinal equivalence of measures of trust and confidence appears to be relatively credible. This would be particularly salient in the rapidly changing contexts of Estonia, East Germany, and Poland. In these cases, and quite possibly in the Bulgarian one too, their noninvariance probably reflects genuine developments within society more than measurement artifacts. Such relatively straightforward explanations, however, cannot

---

2.   The EVS maintains an explicit distinction between former East and West Germany, even after the German reunification. Similarly, Great Britain is included as a case separate of Northern Ireland. This categorization might be considered somewhat anachronistic, yet in this case I will go along with the constraints of the data.

be provided for the other two countries showing evidence of longitudinal noninvariance: Finland and Malta. Regardless of why these particular contexts proved to pose equivalence issues, however, caution is advised when comparing absolute levels of trust in the police in these countries over time. In analyses based on EVS data, I will hence make clear when the validity of certain data points is hampered by equivalence issues.

5.2.3   *Longitudinal measurement equivalence of the ESS, 2002–2014*

Much like with the EVS, the detailed results of the diachronic equivalence tests for the ESS are presented in Appendix C. The first level of equivalence, configural invariance, was reached, albeit with some notes of caution. In the cases of Cyprus, Israel, Lithuania, Russia, Scotland, and Ukraine, one fit indicator (the RMSEA) had values slightly above what is commonly deemed to indicate good model fit. However, closer examination through the stepwise diagnostics procedure did not give any cause for concern: other fit measures yielded excellent results and there were no indications of misspecifications in the model.

A more serious issue was signaled in the metric invariance tests, indicating that the case of Ukraine was problematic in the measurement year of 2004. The misspecification in the structural equation model concerned the measurement of trust in the police. If full metric invariance cannot be achieved, by definition scalar invariance is out of the question as well. Hence, whatever the cause, in Ukraine, measurements of trust in the police in 2004 cannot validly be compared to those in other years within the same country. Developments in trust in the police in Ukraine hence need to be interpreted with care. For all other cases under study, metric invariance was reached without issue; while some countries (Cyprus, Israel, Russia, and Scotland) again featured a somewhat weak RMSEA value, no misspecifications could be found through the stepwise diagnostics procedure.

The scalar invariance tests again passed without major issues for most countries. Three exceptions were Spain (in 2006), Slovenia, and Ukraine (2004). In Slovenia, nearly all years were noninvariant as compared to the reference year 2014 (in 2004, 2006, 2008, and 2012). This means that in **Slovenia**, hardly any diachronic comparison can be made without running afoul of equivalence issues. Other diachronic analyses on ESS data's measurement of trust in the police can probably be safely conducted, with the exception of **Ukraine** (2004) and **Spain** (2006), where noninvariance did involve trust in the police.

5.2.4   *Cross-national measurement equivalence of the ESS, 2010*[3]

The previous two analyses presented were of a longitudinal, diachronic nature. These helped us decide which years of measurement to include in the descriptive, longitudinal analyses to follow. The present section, however, will shift focus to the cross-national comparison: tracing developments within the same country is one thing; comparing mean levels of trust across countries is quite another. If we wish to explain differences, however, we first need to ascertain that cross-national comparisons are valid. The consequence of this logic is that another series of equivalence tests is required: cross-national equivalence tests based on the ESS wave 5, the data for which were collected in 2010.

Unlike the previous sections, where multiple tests were conducted for each level of invariance (a separate procedure for every country), the present analyses take the form of a single model tested in its entirety for each level of invariance. The details are displayed in Appendix D, but despite the cross-national rather than longitudinal nature of the examination, the procedure is largely the same as in the previous tests. First, configural invariance was reached without issues, with satisfactory values on each fit indicator. The next stage, metric invariance, proved more problematic: in **Bulgaria**, **Cyprus**, **Finland**, **Russia**, and **Ukraine**, trust in the police had a deviant position in the composition of trust in legal institutions, with factor loadings that were either lower (Finland) or higher (the rest) than expected. This made these countries nonequivalent in a cross-national examination of trust in the police.

The scalar invariance test, conducted for all but the above-mentioned countries, yielded signs of noninvariant intercepts of trust in the police in **Israel** and **Spain**. Additionally, but inconsequentially for our specific purposes since it did not concern trust in the police, trust in parliament in the Netherlands showed evidence of being noninvariant. After correcting for these misspecifications, the model had achieved satisfactory fit; while some fit indices remained mediocre, particularly the RMSEA,[4] there were no misspecifications left and hence the stepwise diagnostics procedure yielded no more evidence for noninvariance.

The results of our cross-national equivalence tests of the 2010 ESS data mean excluding seven countries out of the 29 that were analyzed. This would have left us with 22 countries for the comparative explanatory analyses, but unfortunately

---

3.   The results of the analyses presented here are largely equal to those included in Schaap & Scheepers (2014)—the difference being that I have split the U.K. data into England & Wales and Scotland as two separate countries, and that I have removed the (handful of) Northern Irish respondents.

4.   It is worth noting, however, that simulation studies indicated the main weakness of the RMSEA to be model complexity: for simple models with few measured indicators—such as the one examined in the present study—the index yields higher values, thus pointing to a worse model fit than is justified (Fan & Sivo, 2007; Kenny & McCoach, 2003).

Austria was not included in the 2010 wave and could hence not be included in the explanatory analyses either. In Chapter 6, this results in 21 countries.

5.3   DESCRIBING DEVELOPMENTS IN TRUST IN DIFFERENT COUNTRIES

In this section, I will first address long-term developments in mean levels of trust over the long term, using EVS data for 1981–2008. We will pay special attention to three of the four theses discussed in Section 4.3: the desacralization thesis, the safety utopia thesis, and the post-authoritarian paradox. These will form the lens through which we will observe the long-term developments in the 28 countries included (counting Germany as two, with its eastern and western parts separated in the analysis). After that, we shall continue with medium- and short-term developments by examining the ESS data for 2002–2014. This should give us the opportunity to study all four theses, but particularly the final one: the socioeconomic crisis problem.

For both parts, it should be noted that evidence of nonequivalence will be stressed. While nonequivalent years or countries will not be rejected out of hand, they will be clearly indicated as being nonequivalent and hence possibly invalid. However, for the sake of reference it could be interesting to include these nonequivalent points of measurement. In the explanatory sections of Chapter 6, however, nonequivalent countries will be removed entirely, as they might skew the results of the explanatory analyses.

5.3.1   Long-term developments: The EVS

In the long run, based on the desacralization thesis, the safety utopia thesis, and the post-authoritarian paradox thesis we would expect levels of trust to decline; in the U.K. because of desacralization, across the rest of Western Europe due to the safety utopia, and in formerly communist Central and Eastern European countries as the result of the post-authoritarian paradox.

Figure 5.1 displays developments in confidence in the police across various European countries in the years for which we have information; although it should be noted that some measures show evidence of nonequivalence and hence should be considered with great caution. The data indicate that trends in confidence in the police are rather mixed.

In Great Britain, Figure 5.1 indicates that trust declined substantially between 1981 and 1999—as predicted by the desacralization thesis. However, it appeared to have slightly recovered afterwards. If processes of desacralization drove the trend in trust in the police before, between 1999 and 2008 they appear to have either stopped or been cancelled out by other processes. This result for Great Brittain is in line with the works of Reiner (2010) and Loader and Mulcahy (2003). The slight improvement in confidence since 1999 appears to chime with what Reiner refers to as *'fragile re-legitimation'* (2010: 99).

Looking at the rest of Western Europe, negative trajectories of trust have been predicted by the safety utopia thesis. Some of the included countries do feature such a trend to some extent: this holds for Ireland, the Netherlands, Northern Ireland, and possibly Norway and Sweden—although here, this trend is weak if existent at all. Other Western European countries either do not show a clear trend (Austria, Belgium, Denmark, West Germany, and Spain), or feature positive trajectories (Finland, France, Iceland, Italy, Malta, and Portugal). Clearly, the picture is rather diverse. Negative trends dominate in the British Isles[5], but Southern Europe in particular mostly shows positive long-term developments in trust. The overall trends are even more positive if we merely take into account the slightly more recent developments—between 1990 and 2008, discounting 1981.

Taking this into consideration, it is particularly the fall in trust in the British Isles that seems to be the exception to the overall neutral or even positive trends across most of Western Europe. The timing of the decline in confidence in the British Isles, however, diverges: in the U.K., the fall was steepest between 1981 and 1990, whereas it was most pronounced in Northern Ireland between 1990 and 1999, and in the Republic of Ireland between 1999 and 2008.

The safety utopia thesis may not even be the most appropriate explanatory mechanism in those countries that have witnessed a fall in trust. The development in Northern Ireland, for instance, likely has to do with its decades-long history of conflict and, in a Western European context, its unique position as a divided society.[6]

---

5.   Meaning, in the present study, the U.K. and the Republic of Ireland.
6.   Ellison and Smyth (2000: xviii) reported that the police in Northern Ireland had trouble justifying their methods and getting adjusted to the new situation after the 1994 ceasefire proclaimed by the IRA and the 1998 Good Friday Agreement. This reflects the broader notion that police tend to enjoy stronger support in situations of conflict and war than during times of peace and relative calm, when their actions come under more critical scrutiny by the society that they protect (Jonathan, 2010). For the Northern Irish police, a decline in trust is therefore perhaps a negative side effect of the peace process.

Figure 5.1   Developments in confidence in the police 1981–2008, EVS

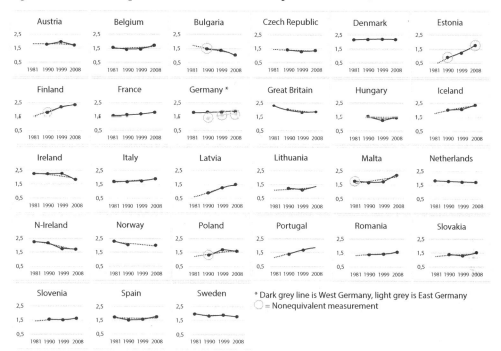

Moving to the post-authoritarian paradox thesis, we shift our attention from Western to Central and Eastern Europe. This thesis posits that levels of trust in countries recently emerging from authoritarian regimes will decline—although it does not tell us much about how strong or enduring this decline will be. Evidence for this thesis in the data, however, is scant. Contrary to what one would expect, there is a moderate to strong increase in trust across many of the Eastern European countries included in the present analysis, with Bulgaria as the only really negative exception. Although some of the countries and years included suffer from measurement equivalence issues, the overall trends appear to be positive. Latvia, Lithuania, Romania, Slovakia, and Slovenia all show positive long-term developments. This may hold for Estonia, East Germany, and Poland as well (but their trajectories are marred with equivalence issues). The Czech Republic and Hungary appear not to have witnessed much development, although both featured a decline between 1990 and 1999 and an improvement between 1999 and 2008.

The post-authoritarian paradox does not appear to accurately describe the main trends in the formerly communist part of the continent: on average, levels of trust increased between 1990 and 2008. There might be something to the thesis in a sense that the increase in confidence tended to be stronger after 1999—after the initial shock of the system change had passed. Between 1990 and 1999, more countries did feature a reported decline in trust, or at least weaker growth. To varying extent, this can be discerned from the graphs of the Czech Republic, Hungary, Lithuania, Romania, Slovakia, and Slovenia. On the whole, however, the post-authoritarian paradox thesis does not convincingly explain trends in confidence in the police across Central and Eastern Europe; as in Western Europe, reality seems to be more positive than expectation.

The results of this descriptive, longitudinal analysis yield a lot of food for thought. Most importantly, let us note that the majority of countries show a distinct improvement in terms of citizens' attitudes toward the police in 2008 as compared to the situation in 1990. We have already discussed the fall in public confidence in the police in the British Isles. If we discount these nations, only one country on the continent shows a clear decrease in confidence in the time frame between 1990 and 2008: Bulgaria. Even this is somewhat uncertain, since the measurement in 1990 proved nonequivalent.

The overall increase in confidence, however, is not uniform across Europe. Nor does it appear to be exclusively concentrated in specific areas. Whether it's the former communist Eastern Europe, Scandinavia, or continental Western Europe, some countries show a (strong) improvement in confidence, whereas others remain more or less the same or show a slight decline. Only the Mediterranean countries have witnessed a more or less uniform increase. This is, of course, good news for most police forces across Europe.

As posed by the desacralization and the safety utopia theses, there is a decrease of citizens' confidence in the police in the British Isles. Contrary to what one could expect, however, this decline remains mostly limited to that area. There are indications, especially between 1981 and 1990, that there was a fall in trust in Belgium, the Netherlands, Norway, and Sweden, but most of these negative trends have mostly been cancelled out by later, positive, developments. Hence, overall, there does not seem to be strong support for a universal or even common trend toward decreasing levels of trust in Western Europe, although there are pockets of growing distrust—particularly in the British Isles. In this rather limited sphere, both the desacralization and the safety utopia theses may find some support.

5.3.2   *Medium-term developments: The ESS*

Although we previously found only meager evidence for the desacralization and safety utopia theses, as well as for the post-communist paradox, the EVS data are not the most up to date; the most recent wave was released in 2008—already several years ago at the time of writing. Additionally, and as a result, we have not yet examined the possible impact of the socioeconomic crisis. Moreover, the long intervals between the EVS measurements make detailed explanations practically impossible. These inherent limitations to the EVS data are problematic, since they render us unable to study short-term changes and the theoretically very interesting time frame of 2008 onward.[7] Fortunately, as previously discussed, we have the ESS 2002–2014 data to mitigate this weakness.

The countries in this analysis unfortunately do not match perfectly with the ones included in the EVS, but such are the problems of cross-cultural research—the overlap is still substantial and the countries included will certainly give us some impression of the trends across Europe. I have split the UK into England & Wales and Scotland—not only do they have independent police forces, but they also have different histories and paths of socioeconomic development. Germany was again split into an eastern and a western part, to reflect its divided postwar history.

Figure 5.2 portrays the developments in public trust in the police across Europe from 2002 until 2014. In order to clearly portray trends, I have designed the graphs to cover a two-point area in terms of absolute levels of trust on the 0–10 scale. However, note that while the graphs are drawn with the same intervals, they are not necessarily on the same level. In some countries, this means that the trend, whatever direction it shows, takes place in a low-trust context. Other countries, while possibly showing a similar trend, may nevertheless have much higher levels of trust.

The relevance of repeating measurements every 2 years is illustrated by the fact that hardly any trend seems to be linear but, rather, shows ups and downs. On the surface, it appears hard to distinguish clear trends based on the graphs in Figure 5.2: trust oscillates. In a few countries, it clearly develops in a single direction, showing similar positive or negative changes every year. In most countries, however, positive developments and negative ones alternate, or are mixed with periods in which trust seems stable. Nevertheless, upon closer inspection, some general tendencies are distinguishable. First and foremost of these is that there are more countries showing an increase in citizens' trust in the police than a decrease in the time frame included here: 17 out of 29 countries show an overall positive trend, seven a negative one (Cyprus, Denmark, Greece, Ireland, Israel, Slovakia, and Ukraine), and in five countries there is no clear direction in developments in trust (Austria, Bulgaria, Finland, Russia, and Scotland).

---

7.   Or, for that matter, the effects of the theoretically equally relevant crisis during the 1980s.

Figure 5.2   Developments in trust in the police 2002–2014, EVS

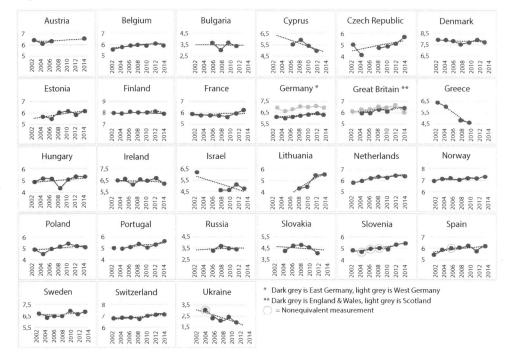

Albeit concerning a different time frame, the rather positive overall image is similar to the patterns discerned in the EVS analyses between 1990 and 2008. Where the increases in trust take place, however, differs somewhat from the previous analysis. While the EVS analyses indicated that trust in the police fell sharply in the British Isles, we see an increase in trust in England & Wales in the ESS. This trend also holds for Scotland, with the exception of the final year of measurement, when it suddenly shows a considerable drop in trust. In these countries, apparently, the long-term decline reported in the EVS analyses was countered in recent years (which, on a basic level, was already suggested by the final period of the EVS data, between 1999 and 2008). Whatever the value of the desacralization thesis in predicting long-term trends in trust in the police in England & Wales, it still does not appear to hold much sway.

Shifting our attention to the rest of Europe, we once again find little support for the increasing disillusionment with the police predicted by the safety utopia thesis. Similarly, the post-authoritarian paradox thesis, which argues for falling or continuously low levels of trust in post-communist societies, does not match the trajectories observed here very well. While there are places where trust appears to have diminished, the overall conclusion is that, across the continent, most developments are positive. Countries where trust has increased can be found in the continental Western European, Nordic, Mediterranean, and Central and Eastern European spheres, meaning that these gains are not limited to a specific area. On the basis of these results, popular ideas about generally diminishing trust simply have to be rejected; none of the three main theses examined so far holds up well against the observed trends in trust.

What about the fourth supposed mechanism behind changing trust rates? The socioeconomic crisis problem posited that there would be some effect of the crisis on trust in the police. This can be relatively easily assessed using the biannual data of the ESS. For this analysis, we will focus on eight countries specifically: Bulgaria, Cyprus, Greece, Hungary, Ireland, Portugal, Slovenia, and Spain. These eight nations, all EU Member States, required financial assistance from European funds, the World Bank, or the IMF, or were very close to requiring such at varying moments during the crisis.[8] The impact of the crisis on each of these countries arguably differed, and in some of them it is unclear what, apart from frantic official meetings and alarmist headlines, the impact of the crisis was on the average citizen. But if the socioeconomic crisis affected trust in the police, these are the countries that should prove most instructive in learning what that effect might have been.

Based on Figure 5.2, we can already see that in some countries, such as Bulgaria, Cyprus, Greece, and Hungary, there are strong indications that trust in the police has decreased substantially during the years of the socioeconomic crisis; the losses amount to between 0.60 and 1.20 points on the 0–10 scale. In Bulgaria, (presumably) Greece, and Hungary, this decline occurred early, in 2008, whereas it happened in Cyprus in 2010 and 2012. This is no surprise, since the latter country was hit by the effects of the crisis later than the other three. The positive news here is that Bulgaria and Hungary seemed to have witnessed a quick recovery in terms of trust in the police after the initial shock. In the other four countries that were in severe financial turmoil—Ireland, Portugal, Slovenia, and Spain—on the face of it, evidence of a fall in trust in the police appears weak or even entirely absent. Even so, to say anything decisive, we need a more thorough examination. This can be approached from a slightly different angle. Instead of looking merely at trajectories of trust in the police, we shall now combine this information with developments in trust in other institutions. For the eight severely crisis-struck countries, this is displayed in Table 5.1, which features levels of trust (as measured on a 0–10 scale) in four institutions between 2004 and 2014. The final column contains sparklines or mini-graphs tracing the developments in each institution.

---

8.   Similar countries that could not be included due to a lack of data are Italy, Latvia, and Romania.

Table 5.1   Developments in trust in four institutions in eight crisis-hit countries, 2004–2014

Country	Institution	2004	2006	2008	2010	2012	2014	Trend
Bulgaria	Police		3.65	3.04	3.67	3.41		
	Legal system		2.44	2.18	2.47	2.23		
	Parliament		2.13	1.86	2.38	2.07		
	Politicians		1.75	1.59	1.99	1.74		
Cyprus	Police		5.60	5.90	5.41	4.98		
	Legal system		6.07	6.24	5.54	4.74		
	Parliament		5.69	5.41	4.53	3.40		
	Politicians		4.29	4.37	3.59	2.53		
Greece	Police	6.06		4.85	4.62			
	Legal system	5.44		4.74	3.80			
	Parliament	4.71		3.57	2.04			
	Politicians	3.65		2.44	1.36			
Hungary	Police	5.15	5.13	4.32	5.09	5.31	5.31	
	Legal system	4.42	4.36	3.77	4.63	4.64	4.63	
	Parliament	3.62	3.39	2.59	4.23	3.91	3.85	
	Politicians	2.73	2.56	1.92	3.12	3.29	2.96	
Ireland	Police	6.64	6.15	6.52	6.44	6.64	6.25	
	Legal system	5.19	4.94	4.98	5.02	5.21	5.24	
	Parliament	4.75	4.78	3.79	3.62	3.55	3.77	
	Politicians	3.99	3.84	3.18	3.08	3.04	3.32	
Portugal	Police	5.01	5.08	5.33	5.07	5.33	5.64	
	Legal system	3.92	4.02	3.80	3.42	3.48	3.70	
	Parliament	3.69	3.86	3.52	2.93	2.57	3.17	
	Politicians	2.07	2.59	2.44	2.05	1.82	2.02	
Slovenia	Police	*4.66*	*4.95*	*4.98*	4.96	*5.35*	5.47	
	Legal system	*3.85*	*4.16*	*4.25*	3.09	*3.25*	3.12	
	Parliament	4.15	4.23	4.43	3.00	2.97	2.76	
	Politicians	3.10	3.22	3.42	2.27	2.30	1.92	
Spain	Police	5.97	*6.16*	6.19	6.32	5.96	6.35	
	Legal system	4.88	*5.16*	4.52	4.49	3.69	4.14	
	Parliament	5.12	5.08	5.17	4.36	3.50	3.88	
	Politicians	3.76	3.56	3.46	2.70	1.93	2.31	

The first thing to note in this table is that in all included countries (as, incidentally, in the other 21 countries in the ESS analyses), trust in the police is higher than in other institutions. Also, all the crisis-struck countries listed in Table 5.1 have experienced some fall in several types of public trust. However, differences and different trajectories can be observed.

What we can see is that Bulgaria, Cyprus, Greece, and Hungary appear to have more or less similar trends for trust in the police as for trust in other institutions; the crisis appears to have hit trust in all four institutions more or less in the same way, albeit in varying intensity. In Cyprus and Greece, trust in the police has been hit less severely than trust in other institutions, while in Bulgaria, the impact of the crisis on trust was very weak in general—although, it being the country with the lowest levels of institutional trust to begin with, this was little cause for celebration. In Bulgaria and Hungary, the effect of the crisis appeared to have been temporary, with trust returning to its old levels in the next measurement.

The other four countries show very different trajectories. First, we should emphasize the nonequivalence of trust in legal institutions (police and legal system) in Spain in 2006 and in Slovenia in most years; this should make us proceed cautiously in interpreting those measurements. That being said, over the period of measurement, Portugal, Slovenia, and Spain featured increasing net levels of trust in the police (albeit with several ups and downs over the years), while trust in other institutions diminished substantially. These divergent trajectories between trust in the police and trust in other institutions are most clearly present in Slovenia.[9] In Ireland, finally, we see a distinction between trust in political institutions (parliament and politicians), which took a hit during the crisis and from which it had not yet recovered in 2014, and trust in legal institutions (police and legal system), which features ups and downs without a clear trend.

In several countries struck severely by the economic crisis, we can discern a fall in trust in the police. But how should we interpret and frame such a decline? In five countries (Cyprus, Greece, Portugal, Slovenia, and Spain), trust in the police has fared (much) better than trust in other institutions. Public trust in parliament and politicians, in particular, has declined during the crisis—with Greece and Cyprus as extreme cases. Overall, it appears as though the police in these eight countries have survived the socioeconomic crisis relatively unscathed as compared to other institutions. In none of these crisis-hit countries has trust in the police fared worse than trust in other institutions during the crisis.

The socioeconomic crisis problem, which states that trust in the police will have been affected in some way by the crisis but does not specify in which way exactly, has found a provisional answer. We have seen that the police are generally not immune to the negative effects of the crisis on public trust, but nor are they among its primary victims. Only two countries, Ireland and Spain, saw their trust in the police increase (mildly) while trust in political institutions fell. In one case, Slovenia, trust in the police remained at the same level—although equivalence issues make this uncertain. The other five countries featured declining trust in the police as trust in other institutions crashed. For the socioeconomic crisis problem, this

9.   Given the nonequivalence of most Slovenian measurements, we may wonder whether these results entail measurement artifacts or, rather, reflect societal changes that are so rapid and intense that they cause multi-group tests for measurement equivalence to raise a false alarm. I cannot answer this question straightforwardly in the present study. Still, while caution is advised, I would hesitate to reject these results outright, as the reported trend appears to be so strong.

implies that the crisis did affect trust in the police, and usually did so negatively, but was less harmful overall to trust in the police than to trust in other institutions.

5.3.3   *Intermezzo: Trends in trust in the police compared to other institutions*

The previous analysis, concentrating on the impact of the socioeconomic crisis on trust in institutions in eight countries, gives rise to a final, somewhat indeterminate question. This is the question of how trust in the police has actually fared generally as compared with trust in other institutions throughout Europe over recent decades. I would like to insert a brief intermezzo to address this question. We have seen trends in trust in the police show mostly positive trends since 1990 (with several notable exceptions and, as evidenced by the 2-year intervals of the ESS, occasional hiccups and bumps along the way). How does the overall trend of trust in the police compare with overall trends of trust in other institutions over the same period of time?

The results of this comparison are displayed in Appendix E. This appendix first includes longer-term developments (between 1990 and 2008) in confidence in the armed forces, the police, parliament, the civil service, and the justice system. Then, it displays data on medium- to short-term developments (contrasting 2002 with 2014) in trust in the police, parliament, politicians, and the legal system across Europe. While not the main focus of the present chapter, it is worth reflecting on the most important findings of this comparison.

In the EVS data, we have seen confidence in the police increase overall since 1990. A similar trend holds for confidence in the armed forces, although trends here appear to be more extreme: a large group of countries has shown large increases in confidence in the armed forces, while a smaller group has seen (usually more limited) decreases. Unlike confidence in other institutions, confidence in the armed forces has changed substantially in each country included. Confidence in parliament has featured less positive general trends, with countries showing negative developments clearly outnumbering those with positive trends. In many countries, however, confidence in parliament has not changed substantially. Confidence in the civil service, meanwhile, has looked more positive. Although the developments have been weak overall, the largest group of countries has shown small gains. The long-term trends for confidence in the justice system have been the most negative, with only a few countries showing (weak) improvement, and a substantial number of countries featuring negative or very negative trends in confidence.

The results for the ESS 2002–2014 data in some ways mirrored those of the EVS, but were quite different in others. Trust in the police, as in the EVS, and as discussed before, leaned toward positive developments. On average, however, trust in parliament as well as trust in politicians showed negative or very negative trends: while some countries featured substantial gains in trust in parliament and/or politicians, the largest categories consisted of countries with strong losses of trust in these two institutions. The negative long-term trend in confidence in parliament shown by the EVS is hence continued by the ESS data 2002–2014. Trust in the legal system, finally, showed mixed results, with countries spread out over the different categories: a roughly equal number of countries had positive developments as compared with those displaying negative trends. When contrasted with the EVS results, the ESS trends regarding the legal system looked more positive. The (very) negative trend of confidence in the justice system hence did not appear to continue as strongly in the more recent developments across Europe, although there is still a substantial number of countries where trust in the legal system continues to fall.

5.4   Conclusions

The EVS and ESS data combined provide us with something of an impression regarding trends in trust in the police across Europe over recent decades. Following the logic of some of the most popular ideas regarding developments in trust, one would be forgiven if one expected a bleak, negative picture of falling trust levels across the continent. Surprisingly, the empirically observed trajectories of trust in the police are, on average, considerably more positive than the desacralization thesis, the safety utopia thesis, and the post-authoritarian paradox thesis suggested. While they may have described the situation in some countries at some periods in time, the long and short of it is that trust in the police has, across most of Europe, tended to increase rather than decrease over recent decades. This trend is neither universal nor absolute—some countries have seen falling trust and most countries have witnessed years or periods when trust decreased—but nonetheless it is quite dominant. The main exceptions to these overall positive trajectories appear to be the time frame between 1981 and 1990, when developments in the (Western European) countries included were somewhat more negative; the situation in the British Isles, where trust in the police, as a whole, seems to have declined over the long term; and some of the countries most severely hit by the socioeconomic downturn that commenced with the 2008 economic crisis. Still, remarkably, trust in the police has shown more positive trends—both in the long and in the shorter run—than trust in other institutions. The only exception has been confidence in the armed forces, which could be argued to have featured even more positive long-term developments.

This implies that of the dominant theses and problems that I formulated in the previous chapter, only the desacralization thesis has found more than marginal support (at least until about 2000)—since it was chiefly directed toward the limited sphere of England & Wales. If there is anything to the safety utopia thesis, it must have concerned the period before roughly 1990. Two countries on the eastern fringe of the continent, Ukraine and Bulgaria, show negative tendencies from an already low starting level, which may indeed reflect the post-communist paradox as formulated by Krastev (2005). But, overall, the post-authoritarian paradox thesis found little support in the data—limited to specific countries in specific periods in time. The socioeconomic crisis problem, finally, proved to be a factor of some relevance in several countries, although trust in the police was harmed considerably less than trust in other institutions over the period of the crisis.

To summarize, the theses formulated previously appear to be of only limited value when examining developments in trust in the police, specifically where more recent trends are concerned. Either way, we can conclude that the crisis-like discourse regarding citizens' attitudes toward the police appears, in the light of these data, largely exaggerated. This is not to say that police forces should stop worrying about public confidence; rather, it is meant to infuse realism into the debate. The police remain among the most trusted public institutions. This gives rise to two obvious questions. First, why did the most popular theses regarding developments in trust in the police in most cases turn out to be wrong? And, second, if not through the previously posed theses, how can we make sense of the observed trajectories of trust?

Several possible explanations for the failure of the popular theses regarding developments in trust in the police to accurately predict trends can be discerned. First, the desacralization and safety utopia theses may mostly be focused on a period before the time frame included in this analysis. This implies that the actual decrease in confidence occurred before the start of measurements. A similar process may be at play for the post-authoritarian paradox; several Southern European countries emerged from various authoritarian regimes in the period just before the start of the measurements in 1981. This could mean that any harm to trust in the police based on the assertions of this book may have been done before our period of measurement.

Second, we may have a somewhat nostalgic, overly romantic view of the past. We may be harking back to a mystical 'golden age' of policing and of security that was actually not as perfect as we now tend to think it was. Nostalgia tends to color collective memories. On the other hand, incidents that are fresh in one's mind carry greater weight than those further into the past. The importance of recent negative events might hence be overstated; our assessment of their relevance may not correspond with their actual societal impact. This way, we may simultaneously have too rosy an image of the past and too negative an image of the present.

A third explanation is more specific to the southern and eastern parts of the continent. Democratization and reform in these mostly post-authoritarian societies (in two waves; during the 1970s and the early 1990s) has had a positive effect on the public's view of the police. The fact that the police are not purely a political tool for stabilizing the regime anymore, but are generally aiming to serve the public interest, may have greatly improved police–public relationships—despite the problems that might endure. However flawed, the current situation is still perceived as preferable to the authoritarian past. The post-authoritarian paradox theses, hence, could just be plain wrong.

A fourth explanation is more complex and may have somewhat different implications. Over time, the correct interpretation of the popular theses discussed previously may not be that they caused trust to decrease; rather, they may have altered the nature and meaning of trust. Already in 2002, O'Neill, aware of many of the processes related to the safety utopia thesis, had rejected a uniform, one-dimensional decrease in public trust in institutions. She argued that, no matter how fiercely we tend to criticize various institutions for failing to live up to our expectations, our very actions indicate that we still trust them. She emphasized the discrepancy between what people say and what people do. Increasingly critical attitudes toward institutions are one thing; how people act on them are quite another. Similarly, increasing criticism of the police may not automatically be reflected in growing mistrust; it could just reflect growing involvement and scrutiny. In this sense, it is interesting to note that citizens' willingness to report violent crime to the police, an indicator of 'trust in practice,' appears to have increased over recent decades (Baumer & Lauritsen, 2010; Tarling & Morris, 2010). This suggests that it may not be wholly accurate to discuss trust merely in terms of a degree or amount; rather, we could conceive of trust as one aspect of the multifaceted relationship between the police and citizens, which is subject to potential change.

With the fifth explanation, which concerns police practice, we turn to alternative ways to understand changes in trust. The popular theses stressing declining trust tend to assume that the police themselves have not changed much. However, successful trust-building strategies may have emerged. The rise of community policing, an increased emphasis on combating corruption, more attention to effectiveness and efficiency, a decreasing likelihood of using excessive force, and the curbing of what may be seen as wasteful spending may possibly have contributed to an increase in public confidence in the police across Europe over recent decades. While the empirical evidence is insufficient to make this case across Europe, there are indications that, at least in some countries, trust-building efforts have yielded some fruit (Myhill & Quinton, 2010; Skogan, 2006b).

Let us turn to the recent, positive, developments observed in England & Wales (and Scotland, discounting the 2014 measurement, to which we shall return later) as an illustration. These positive results do not run as counter to previous studies as one might think. Although several qualitative (Loader & Mulcahy, 2003; Reiner, 2010) and quantitative (Bradford, 2011a; Hough, 2003; Jansson, 2008) studies found that trust in, and the legitimacy of, the police in the British Isles was steadily decreasing, contributions employing more recent data have actually reported an increase after about 2003 (Innes, 2011; Myhill & Quinton, 2010). This is compatible with the present analyses. This positive trend moved in unison with the development of reassurance policing in the U.K. (Innes, 2004, 2005; Myhill & Quinton, 2010), a clear trust-building strategy. We will return to this particular case in Chapter 8, when discussing the development of trust-building strategies in England & Wales, but this does serve to illustrate that the police themselves can affect trust on a national scale. What we can see, at least, is that in some cases, trust in the police moves in unison with changes in policing and the police organization.

This could also have negative consequences. The regular repetition of the ESS survey rounds provides us with enough information to draw together a new thesis. My assertion is that besides the socioeconomic crisis, the short-term effects of certain other events also become visible in changing levels of trust. These events may well be directly related to the police. The results for Denmark, for example, showing a decrease in trust around 2008 and a relatively quick recovery afterwards, were also found in another diachronic study on the subject (Balvig et al., 2011; Holmberg & Balvig, 2013). The authors attributed this development to the troubled police reform that was introduced in Denmark in 2008. Interestingly, we see similar dips in trust after police reforms in other countries too, such as the measurement of trust in the police in Scotland in 2014 (see Fyfe, 2014; Fyfe & Scott, 2013; SIPR, What Works Scotland & ScotCen, 2017) and in Finland in the same year (see Haraholma & Houtsonen, 2013; Vuorensyrjä, 2014). This gives rise to a challenging notion: that police reforms (possibly specifically of the centralizing kind as collected by Fyfe et al., 2013), especially in the short run, can hurt trust in the police. This is remarkable, as they are often designed to improve trust in, and the legitimacy of, the police; as we will see in Part III of this book, this tends to be one of the central drivers behind police reforms.

A final note concerns trends in trust and confidence in institutions in general. It was remarkable to see developments in trust in the police being much more positive overall than trust in most other institutions. Only confidence in the armed forces fared similarly well. Trust in political institutions (parliament and politicians) and in the legal system has shown much less positive trends and indeed may give cause for concern. I will return to this notion in the concluding Chapter 12.

ExPLAINING DIFFERENCES IN TRUST IN THE

POLICE BETWEEN EUROPEAN COUNTRIES

6.1   INTRODUCTION

In the previous chapter, I traced developments in trust across Europe over time.
These analyses were descriptive in nature—although tentative suggestions as to
why certain trends occurred were provided. In the present chapter, however, the
endeavor will be to explain differences between countries. Section 6.2 will introduce the actual differences between countries in terms of levels of trust, as measured in 2010. While slightly dated, this year of measurement saw the ESS ask a full
set of questions regarding public attitudes toward the police—essential if we wish
to explain differences in trust between countries. Section 6.3 then proceeds with a
closer look into the data and the operationalizations of relevant variables under
study.

After these two preparatory sections, our attention will turn to explaining differences in trust in the police on the national and individual levels. In these explanatory analyses, we will be guided by the hypotheses formulated in Chapter 4. Section 6.4 sketches the main contours of an explanatory model of trust in the police,
assessing first the national-level and then also the individual-level determinants of
trust. Section 6.5 is devoted to analyzing the three intermediary mechanisms
hypothesized previously, providing more detail in the relationship between proximity policing, instrumentalism, and procedural justice on the one hand and trust
in the police on the other. After this, we will be able to reflect on the viability of the
hypotheses in Section 6.6. Section 6.7 will examine the oft-ignored possibility of
divergent effects of individual-level determinants across countries. Finally, in Section 6.8, we will be able to close this chapter with some concluding remarks that
reflect on our main findings.

6.2   DIFFERENCES IN LEVELS OF TRUST BETWEEN COUNTRIES IN 2010

In the previous chapter, we established cross-national measurement equivalence
for the ESS data in 2010 for 21 out of 28 included countries. With this equivalence,
we can now endeavor to compare mean levels of trust between European coun-

tries. Figure 6.1 displays mean levels of trust in the police across the continent. Nonequivalently measured countries are included separately.

We can observe high levels of trust in the included Nordic countries (Denmark, Norway, and Sweden, with the high trust measured in Finland being nonequivalent) and in several Western European countries. Switzerland and the former West Germany in particular do well in terms of trust, followed by the British Isles, the former East Germany, the Netherlands, and Belgium. Estonia is a notable former communist exception in this company of nearly exclusively northwestern European comparatively high-trust societies. At a substantial gap, these countries are followed by a mix of Mediterranean and Central European countries, with France and Poland doing relatively well. Hungary, Portugal, Slovenia, and the Czech Republic have rather mediocre levels of trust, while Greece, Slovakia, and Croatia feature relatively low trust.

The nonequivalent countries appear to have some of the lowest trust rates, with Bulgaria, Russia, and Ukraine in particular performing extremely poorly. Despite their nonequivalence, it seems unlikely that these low levels of trust in the police can only be attributed to measurement artifacts. Similarly, I would be hesitant to reject the extraordinarily high level of trust in the police measured in Finland outright—while equivalence issues prevent us seeing how well-trusted they are exactly, it seems clear that citizens in Finland tend to trust the police.

Figure 6.1   **Differences in levels of trust in the police across Europe in 2010**

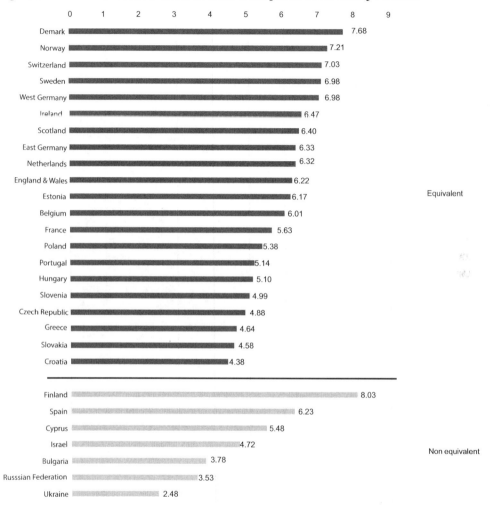

Note: I conducted all analyses on data file version ESS05e02, in which Lithuania unfortunately was not yet included. Hence Lithuania is not analyzed in this chapter.

As these descriptive data indicate, there are clear differences between countries in terms of trust. This is confirmed when observing the country-level variance in trust in the 21 countries where it was equivalently measured: 14% of the variance in the data, the differences between individuals in how much trust they have in the police, was explained by the country level. While the majority of differences between citizens in their assessments of the police depend on individual differences, the country in which they live affects their trust to a considerable extent. In the previous chapter, we have already witnessed sometimes strong developments in trust over time. These substantial differences and developments serve to illustrate the importance of explanatory analyses: recognizing all the differences within Europe, how can we explain that some countries have so much more trust in the police than others?

6.3   OPERATIONALIZATION

The general methodology behind the European Social Survey (ESS) has already been introduced in Chapter 5, while the methodological choices made in selecting the variables of interest have been explicated in Chapter 4. In this section, we shall delve deeper into the operationalization of the measurement model of trust in the police and its determinants.

First, we have included a range of variables on the national level, attaching a value for each of these variables to every country. The construction of most of these determinants, particularly those that are important to the hypotheses, has received extensive attention in Section 4.4. However, it is worth revisiting these variables to understand their operationalization for the present analyses.

Proximity policing is measured through the **proximity policing index**, the methodology behind which is addressed in Appendix E. The resulting index, where higher levels imply more adherence to proximity policing principles, ranges from 0 to 3. In reality, however, most countries adhere to these principles to at least some extent and none of them do so perfectly. This means that the observed values are between 0.40 and 2.55.

Instrumentalism has two macro-level indicators: homicide rates and victimization rates of burglaries and assault. **Homicide** rates were derived from the World Health Organization's European Mortality Database (WHO, 2017). The homicide rates are those from 2009; it appears reasonable to expect that if the public judge the police by their performance in reducing homicide, there should be a slight lag in the effect of homicide rates on trust in the police. From the database, the number of deaths by homicide and assault per 100,000 citizens were extracted to form the country's homicide rate. The other indicator of instrumentalism on the national level, **victimization (aggregated)**, was computed by aggregating the share of respondents in that country, as measured by the ESS, who indicated that they had been the victims of a burglary or (threatened) assault over the past 2 years. This resulted in an index theoretically between 0 (no one became victim) and 1 (everyone was victimized), but in reality ranging from 0.04 to 0.25.

Procedural justice on the national level was operationalized in terms of **corruption**. Transparency International (2010a,b) annually compiles the Corruption Perceptions Index, based on a range of expert and business surveys of every country. The resulting values arguably comprise an integrity index rather than a corruption index, as a higher value on the 1–10 scale means less corruption. For the purposes of the analyses, the values have been reversed so that a higher value also implies higher corruption. The lowest value in our analyses, the 1.7 of Denmark, is hence equal to the original 9.3. The highest corruption value, the 7.5 for Greece, was originally a 3.5 on the 1–10 scale.

Two more country-level determinants are taken into account in the analyses to serve as control variables. Income inequality is included as measured for the year 2010 by UNU-WIDER (2011a,b). This source collected income inequality information for every country and reported it as a **Gini coefficient**. Previous research has also relied on this data source (Jang et al., 2010), making it worthwhile to compare results.

Democracy has been measured by the Economist Intelligence Unit (2010, 2017). Democracy is ranked on a scale from 1 to 10, where higher values represent more democratic countries. The final score is a composite of a range of indicators, summarized in five categories: electoral process and pluralism, functioning of government, political participation, political culture, and civil liberties.

The individual-level variables included are all contained in the ESS survey wave 2010. The police-related variables, part of our hypotheses, are part of the special rotating module 'trust in police and justice' and were hence not included in other waves. These concerned the proximity policing-inspired perceived police successfulness in **preventing violent crime**; two instrumental determinants consisting of how often citizens perceive the police to **catch burglars** and perceived **rapid response** of police to calls after a crime is committed; and the procedural justice variables consisting of the perceived police inclination to accept **bribes** and the **procedural justice** scale. The development of all of these questions has been described by Jackson et al. (2010, 2011). Some of these variables had substantial percentages of missing values. Missing values on each of these questions were imputed through regression imputation with random error correction. All other variables included in these models were used as determinants for the regression imputation. Merely for the purposes of regression imputation, three extra determinants were added that generally have strong correlations with attitudes toward the police: satisfaction with life, political orientation on a left-right scale, and generalized social trust.[1] Two further choices surrounding these determinants are worthy of note. First, the rapid response variable has an answering category 'violent crimes never happen near to where I live.' Respondents indicating this were coded as 'missing.' Second, a sub-question of the procedural justice scale, asking how often the police explain their decisions and actions when asked, had an option to answer 'no one

---

1.   The reason why these three determinants are not included in the analytical model of trust in the police is that their causal relationship with the police variables is unclear; trust in the police might affect social trust, or the other way around, or an underlying determinant might explain both, making the relationship spurious. Without solid theoretical and preferably empirical underpinnings, we can only observe correlations between such attitudinal variables, but not include them as determinants in an explanatory model. Fortunately, when imputing missing data using regression analysis, we merely wish to accurately estimate substitute data for the missing values—in this procedure, causality is of no consequence.

ever asks the police to explain.' I recoded respondents choosing this response to the most negative 'never' category.

Other individual-level variables serve as controls and concern either demographic characteristics or personal experiences. Unless otherwise specified, respondents with missing values on one or more of these variables were removed from the analyses. **Gender** and **age** were straightforwardly included in the questionnaire. **Education** was measured according to the ISCED 1997 categorization: divided into seven categories, which range from only pre-primary education to the second stage of tertiary education. The ensuing 7-point scale is treated as being of interval level. Household **income** was originally indicated by a score on a 10-point scale, based on the national distribution of household incomes divided into deciles. Income distributions across these deciles greatly differed according to country. To compensate for this possible bias, income values were recoded as fractional rank percent values, meaning that income became more relative to mean and median incomes across the country—with values ranging from 0 to 100. In a country where only a small proportion of respondents is in the lowest income category, respondents in this category will receive a lower fractional rank percent value: this represents the fact that their position on the income scale is more extreme than in countries where many respondents are in the lowest income category. Missing values were substituted with the country's mean, except in Portugal, where no information about household income was available. To avoid removing an entire country from the analyses, income values in Portugal were substituted through regression imputation with random error correction.

The ESS also includes self-reported information on **minority membership**. In each country, respondents were asked whether they considered themselves part of an ethnic minority. Although proportions differed per country, about 5% of our respondents indicated minority membership. The small proportion of respondents not answering the question was considered part of the majority population. A respondent's **marital status**, a categorical variable, had multiple possible answers. I merged the married respondents and those with a registered civil union into a single 'married' category. Additionally, separated and divorced respondents were merged into one 'divorced' category. Next to these two, I discern the 'widowed' and 'single' categories. **Main occupation**, measured as a respondent's main activity during the preceding 7 days, was similarly measured into multiple nominal categories. The categories are employed, student, unemployed, retired, active in the household, and other. For reasons of parsimony, currently fulfilling military or community service counted as employed, whereas respondents indicating that they were sick or disabled were placed under the 'unemployed' header.

The **urbanization** of the household where the respondent lives was measured in five steps, ranging from a big city, to the suburbs or outskirts of a big city, to a town or small city, to a country village, to a farm or home in the countryside. I treat this as a continuous (interval-level) variable. **Religious attendance** was measured by asking respondents how often they attend religious services, apart from special occasions. The resulting scale has seven categories, ranging from every day, to more than once a week, to once a week, to at least once a month, to only on special holy days, to less often, to never. Again, this determinant is treated as a continuous variable, with coding being reversed so that a higher score means more frequent religious attendance. Previous **victimization** of burglary or assault was a straight-forward yes/no question and is hence included as such. **Police contact** consisted of two questions: first, whether the respondent had been approached, stopped, or contacted by the police over the last 2 years; and, second, to what extent the respondent had been satisfied with the contact if it had occurred. This evaluation was measured on a five-point scale ranging from very dissatisfied to very satisfied. I simplified this to three categories: those who were satisfied, those who were neutral, and those who were dissatisfied. Those stating that they couldn't remember whether the police had contacted them were considered not to have been contacted. This led to four separate categories in the analyses: those not contacted, those contacted and satisfied, those contacted and neutral, and those contacted and dissatisfied with the interaction.

A total of 36,617 respondents were originally included in the 21 countries under study. After removal of respondents with missing values on one or more of the included variables that were not replaced by any form of missing data imputation, 34,622 respondents remained. All variables were standardized except dichotomous ones, meaning that the continuous variables included all received a mean of zero and a standard deviation of one. This transformation enables easy comparisons between different effect sizes of various determinants. The descriptive characteristics of all included variables, before standardization, are displayed in Table 6.1.

Table 6.1   Descriptive values of the variables included in the explanatory analyses

N = 34,622		Range	Mean	SD
Country-level variables	Proximity police index	.40–2.55	1.63	.43
	Homicide	.30–5.61	1.12	1.07
	Victimization (aggregated)	.04–.25	.16	.06
	Corruption	1.7–7.5	4.33	1.82
	Gini coefficient	24.2–38.5	31.04	4.25
	Democracy	6.81–9.80	8.22	.78
Individual-level hypothesized variables	**Trust in the police** (dependent variable)	**0-10**	**5.89**	**2.50**
	Prevent violent crime	0–10	5.21	1.97
	Catch burglars	0–10	4.73	2.12
	Rapid response	0–10	5.80	2.25
	Police bribes	0–10	3.86	2.52
	Procedural justice	0–3	1.74	.55
Individual-level control variables	Gender			
	Female	0/1	.54	–
	Male	0/1	.46	–
	Age	14–101	48.32	18.59
	Education	0–6	2.65	1.81
	Income	0–100	55.55	25.12
	Minority membership			
	No minority	0/1	.95	–
	Minority	0/1	.05	–
	Marital status			
	Married	0/1	.51	–
	Divorced	0/1	.10	–
	Widowed	0/1	.09	–
	Single	0/1	.30	–
	Main occupation			
	Employed	0/1	.47	–
	Student	0/1	.09	–
	Unemployed	0/1	.09	–
	Retired	0/1	.26	–
	Household	0/1	.08	–
	Other occupation	0/1	.01	–
	Urbanization	0–4	2.07	1.21
	Religious attendance	0–6	4.40	1.56
	Victimization			
	No victim	0/1	.84	–
	Victim	0/1	.16	–

N = 34,622	Range	Mean	SD
Police contact			
No contact	0/1	.64	–
Satisfied with contact	0/1	.24	–
Neutral contact	0/1	.05	–
Unsatisfied with contact	0/1	.07	–

6.4   EXPLAINING TRUST IN THE POLICE IN 2010

6.4.1   *National-level determinants*

As the model we aim to test is a multilevel one—consisting of individuals nested within countries and containing country-level as well as individual-level determinants—the analyses need to take account of this hierarchical structure. Multilevel linear regression analysis is an approach that deals well with the model under study and, through the MIXED procedure in the SPSS statistical package, will hence be applied to test our hypotheses.

First, to test the appropriateness of such a multilevel approach, a baseline empty model (or null model) was analyzed. This yielded the variance within assessments of trust in the police on the individual and country levels. The null model level 1 variance—the variance on the individual level in this empty model—was 5.34. The null model level 2 variance—that on the country-level—was 0.88. As mentioned before, this is a substantial and highly significant proportion of the total variance, meaning that multilevel regression analysis is appropriate: enough of the differences in trust in the police are found on the national level and can hence be explained by national factors.

After this baseline model, we can commence with the actual analyses. First, in the Models A-a through A-f, we test the effects of the country-level determinants on trust in the police, without any controls. These bivariate analyses will be a useful starting point before we continue with the more advanced ones. The national-level indicators are then included together in a single model, Model A-g, to observe whether their bivariate relationships also hold when controlled for other country characteristics. Through this approach, we can test Hypotheses 1a, 2a, and 3a.

Table 6.2   Effects of national-level determinants on trust in the police

N = 34,622	Model A-a		Model A-b		Model A-c		Model A-d		Model A-e		Model A-f		Model A-g	
	B	s.e.	B	s.e.	B	s.e.	B	s.e.	B	s.e.	B	s.e.	B	s.e.
Proximity police index	.35*	.17											-.05	.07
Homicide			-.05	.21									.13*	.08
Victimization (aggregated)					.46**	.18							.01	.09
Corruption							-.91***	.07					-.80***	.13
Gini coefficient									-.21	.20			-.04	.07
Democracy											.76***	.11	.17	.13
Country-level variance	.74		.88		.66		.10		.84		.27		.08	

Two-tailed tests: * *P* = .05 |** *P* = .01 |*** *P* = .001

Table 6.2 shows significant bivariate relationships between several country-level determinants and trust in the police in Models A-a through A-f. Proximity policing and aggregated victimization levels appear to affect trust weakly. While the effect of the proximity policing index is as expected, the effect of victimization rates is rather surprising: the more citizens report being victims of crime in a country, the higher are the levels of trust. Stronger are the effects of democracy and, especially, corruption. While democracy serves as control variable, the powerful, negative effect of corruption on trust is quite noteworthy. Homicide and a country's Gini coefficient appear to be unrelated to trust.

In Model A-g, all country-level determinants have been included in a multiple regression analysis. Notably, most effects of these variables diminish or disappear when they are included together. Only corruption remains a powerful determinant of trust. And while the instrumentalist determinant of victimization rates is no longer a surprisingly positive determinant of trust when the other variables are taken into account, it is now the homicide rate that appears to be positively related to trust. Again, this is the opposite of what was expected. In Model A-g, moreover, we can observe that these macro-level determinants together leave only 0.08 of the original country-level variance of 0.88 unexplained, meaning that about 91% of the differences between countries are determined by the country-level variables included in the model.

Purely based on the country-level determinants, there does not seem to be much support for proximity policing: while there is a significant bivariate relationship between the proximity policing index and trust in the police, this effect disappears once other variables are taken into account. Instrumentalism fares even worse: its two indicators, homicide and victimization rates, are either nonsignificant or are significantly related to trust in the reverse direction to what was expected: higher victimization rates (bivariately) and homicide rates (when other macro-level variables are included) are positively related with trust in the police. This leaves only procedural justice, in the form of its negative country-level indicator corruption, as a powerful determinant of trust in the way it was expected to. Its powerful negative relationship with trust is hardly decreased at all when other variables are included in the analysis.

6.4.2   Individual-level determinants

With the country-level analysis as a basis, we can continue to add individual-level determinants to our model of trust in the police. Table 6.3 displays the results of three multilevel regression analyses; first, to contrast the other models, Model A-g is featured again. Then, in Model A-h, variables are added based on demography and experience. Finally, Model A-i is the full model of trust: it also features the individual-level determinants derived from the three theoretical perspectives. This gives us the opportunity to test Hypotheses 1c, 2c, and 3c.

Table 6.3   Effects of national-level and individual-level determinants on trust in the
              police

N = 34,622	Model A-g		Model A-h		Model A-i	
	B	s.e.	B	s.e.	B	s.e.
Proximity police index	-.05	.07	-.07	.07	-.11*	.05
Homicide	.13*	.08	.13	.08	.12*	.05
Victimization (aggregated)	.01	.09	.05	.09	.09	.06
Corruption	-.80***	.13	-.86***	.13	-.45***	.08
Gini coefficient	-.04	.07	-.06	.07	.02	.05
Democracy	.17	.13	.14	.13	.18*	.09
Female	ref.		ref.		ref.	
Male			-.08**	.03	-.10***	.02
Age			.09***	.02	.01	.02
Education			.08***	.01	.07***	.01
Income			.11***	.01	.07***	.01
No minority	ref.		ref.		ref.	
Minority			-.10*	.06	-.17***	.05
Married	ref.		ref.		ref.	
Divorced			-.22***	.04	-.10**	.04
Widowed			.11*	.05	.02	.04
Single			-.10**	.04	-.05	.03
Employed	ref.		ref.		ref.	
Student			.40***	.05	.21***	.04
Unemployed			-.40***	.05	-.23***	.04
Retired			.06	.04	.03	.04
Household			.00	.05	-.06	.04
Other occupation			.03	.11	.07	.09
Urbanization			.01	.01	.00	.01
Religious attendance			.18***	.01	.05***	.01
No victim	ref.		ref.		ref.	
Victim			-.31***	.03	-.07**	.03
No contact	ref.		ref.		ref.	
Satisfied with contact			.32***	.03	.11***	.03
Neutral contact			-.73***	.06	-.19***	.05
Unsatisfied with contact			-1.40***	.05	-.57***	.04
Prevent violent crime					.44***	.01
Catch burglars					.22***	.01
Rapid response					.29***	.01
Police bribes					-.34***	.01
Procedural justice					.54***	.01

N = 34,622	Model A-g		Model A-h		Model A-i	
	B	s.e.	B	s.e.	B	s.e.
Individual-level variance		5.34		5.01		3.62
Country-level variance		.08		.08		.03

Two-tailed tests: * P = .05 |** P = .01 |*** P = .001

Let us first observe the changes in the effects of the macro-level determinants throughout these three models. The initial bivariate positive relationship between the proximity policing index and trust disappears once other factors are taken into account and, surprisingly, eventually grows weakly negative in Model A-i. This means that, after accounting for spuriousness, there is eventually no support for Hypothesis 1a regarding the effect of proximity policing. Homicide rates remain (also weakly) positively related to trust in the police, which again contradicts the hypothesis—in this case, Hypothesis 2a. The other half of this instrumentalist hypothesis concerned a supposed negative effect of victimization rates on trust in the police, which again is not found in the data. This means a rejection of Hypothesis 2a and directly contradicts the central assertion of instrumentalism. The negative effect of corruption on trust in the police, although it weakens somewhat in the final Model A-i, remains the most powerful country-level determinant. This is in alignment with Hypothesis 3a. Finally, of the two macro-level control variables, the Gini coefficient appears unrelated to trust in the police, whereas the level of democracy is eventually shown to be weakly positively related to trust.

On the individual level, Model A-h shows that various demographic variables are significantly related to trust. Women, the elderly, those with higher education and with higher income, ethnic majority members, and those who attend religious services more often have more trust in the police. The same holds for students (as compared to those who are employed) and those who are widowed (as compared to married people), while the unemployed have considerably less trust in the police than the employed. Additionally, single and divorced people have less trust than those who are married. More interesting theoretically, however, is the effect of victimization and particularly the impact of encounters with the police. Victims of crime have less trust in the police. And while those satisfied with their police contact have significantly more trust than those who had no contact with the police at all, it is particularly interesting to look at the two other categories: people who evaluated their contact neutrally or even negatively found their contact to have more than twice and more than four times as much of a negative impact on trust, respectively. This implies that a positive encounter can improve trust, but even one that is experienced neutrally has a stronger negative effect on trust—let alone contacts that are evaluated negatively.

When we include the police strategy-related attitudinal variables in Model A-i, the effects of most other individual-level variables understandably decrease, although the strongest ones easily remain significant. All of the attitudinal determinants are related to trust according to expectations, although the strength of their effect differs somewhat. The strongest effects are procedural justice, followed by prevention of crime and perceived police susceptibility to bribes. Weaker effects are found for police rapid response and their perceived effectiveness in catching burglars. These findings align with all three theoretical paradigms and mean that Hypotheses 1c, 2c, and 3c all find a measure of support, but the strongest support holds for procedural justice and the weakest for instrumentalism. To some extent, this mirrors the findings on the country level.

The full model, Model A-i, shows substantially decreased individual-level variance (the fall from 5.34 to 3.62 means a reduction of 32%) and almost negligible residual country-level variance (a reduction of about 97%). The reduction in total variance is 41%. This means that factors included in the model explain 32% of differences in trust in the police between individuals and 97% of the differences between countries. The explanatory strength on the country level is considerable, especially if we take into account that this is predominantly because of the effect of a single variable: corruption. While we are limited in our ability to explain differences between individuals, differences between European countries in terms of trust in the police are overwhelmingly determined by the prevalence of corruption.

On the individual level, we see that much of the explanatory power of the model is determined by the police-related variables. People who evaluate various aspects of policing more positively also have considerably more trust in the police. In itself, this is not particularly surprising. The strength of the effects tells us something, but we need more stringent tests for any definite conclusions about the viability of the three theoretical schools in determining trust.

6.5   Intermediary variables

In the following analysis, we will take each of the five intermediary variables, the individual-level determinants closely connected to one of the theoretical schools, as dependent variables. To what extent can we explain those five different types of public assessments of the police? These analyses address Hypotheses 1b, 2b, and 3b.

First, we will examine citizens' assessments of police successfulness in preventing violent crime, seen to be an indicator of proximity policing. Hence we will pay particular attention to the relationship between the national-level proximity policing index and individuals' perceived police preventive success, as posed by Hypothesis 1b.

The second and third intermediary variables are indicators of instrumentalism: they concern the extent to which the police are perceived to be successful in catching burglars, and perceptions of how quickly they arrive at the scene of a crime. Both variables are expected to be shaped by homicide rates and victimization rates of burglaries and assault in the country, as defined by Hypothesis 2b.

The fourth and fifth intermediary variables concern individual-level indicators of procedural justice. Following procedural justice theory, both police susceptibility to bribe-taking and police following procedural justice principles, as perceived by citizens, will be determined in part by national-level corruption. This is predicted by Hypothesis 3b.

6.5.1   *Proximity policing: Prevention of crime*

The first intermediary variable is the extent to which citizens think the police capable of preventing crime. This is an indicator of proximity policing, albeit, as argued before, rather an imperfect one. As expected through Hypothesis 1b, proximity policing on the national level is expected to determine citizens' assessments of police preventive success. As perceived police successes in preventing crime has been found to affect trust in the police, this suggests an indirect effect of proximity policing on trust.

The first thing to note is that, contrary to trust in the police, differences between countries in terms of their average assessment of police successfulness in preventing crimes are actually quite small. This is indicated by the null-model country-level variance, which is only 0.07—as compared to the individual-level variance of 3.79. This means that differences between individuals in how they assess police preventive success are far greater than between countries. This small country-level variance (about 2% of the total variance), however, is still statistically significant, making a multilevel regression structure appropriate.

Three regression models are featured in Table 6.4: Model B-a features the bivariate relationship between the proximity policing index and perceived police successfulness in preventing violent crimes. Model B-b then adds the other country-level determinants to test the extent to which any initial bivariate relationship holds up when controlled for other factors. Finally, Model B-c contains the country-level and individual-level determinants.

Despite the small country-level variance, we can see from Model B-a that there is still a significant positive relationship between proximity policing on the country level and citizens' assessments of police preventive success. This is the outcome expected by Hypothesis 1b. However, the significance of the effect of the proximity policing index disappears once other country-level variables are accounted for in Model B-b: only corruption is a significant determinant.

Table 6.4   Effects of national-level and individual-level determinants on perceived police success in preventing violent crime

Prevent violent crime	Model B-a		Model B-b		Model B-c	
N = 34,622	B	s.e.	B	s.e.	B	s.e.
Proximity police index	.13**	.05	.06	.04	.05	.05
Homicide			-.05	.05	-.04	.05
Victimization (aggregated)			-.01	.06	.05	.06
Corruption			-.22**	.08	-.28**	.09
Gini coefficient			-.02	.05	-.07	.05
Democracy			-.07	.08	-.12	.09
Female	*ref.*		*ref.*		*ref.*	
Male					-.00	.02
Age					.06***	.02
Education					-.07***	.01
Income					.01	.01
No minority	*ref.*		*ref.*		*ref.*	
Minority					.18***	.05
Married	*ref.*		*ref.*		*ref.*	
Divorced					-.16***	.04
Widowed					.09*	.04
Single					-.05*	.03
Employed	*ref.*		*ref.*		*ref.*	
Student					.28***	.04
Unemployed					-.14***	.04
Retired					.06	.04
Household					.06	.04
Other occupation					-.02	.09
Urbanization					-.01	.01
Religious attendance					.19***	.01
No victim	*ref.*		*ref.*		*ref.*	
Victim					-.37***	.03
No contact	*ref.*		*ref.*		*ref.*	
Satisfied with contact					.17***	.03
Neutral contact					-.66***	.05
Unsatisfied with contact					-.96***	.04
Individual-level variance	3.79		3.79		3.60	
Country-level variance	.05		.03		.04	

Two-tailed tests: * $P = .05$ |** $P = .01$ |*** $P = .001$

Adding individual-level determinants in Model B-c does little to change the effects on the national level: corruption remains the only significant country-level predictor of perceived police success in preventing crime. Individually, we can see that there is a particularly strong negative relationship between victimization and perceptions of police prevention. Unsurprisingly, victims of crimes perceive the police to be less successful in preventing crimes from happening. Additionally, both neutral and especially negative contact with the police diminishes public perceptions of police preventive success. There is a much weaker, positive effect of positive contact. A final individual-level effect of note is that of ethnicity: while ethnic minority membership was previously found to go hand in hand with lower trust in the police, we find here that ethnic minorities have more positive assessments of police successfulness in preventing crime.

These results appear to show that there is only a weak indirect positive relationship between proximity policing and trust in the police through perceived police preventive successes. The initial relationship disappears once corruption is taken into account, pointing toward a procedural justice-like mechanism rather than one determined by proximity policing. This means that Hypothesis 1b finds only very partial support. Overall, however, only a relatively minor part of differences in public assessments of police preventive success can be explained by our model. Differences are also much larger between individuals than between countries, indicating that public opinions of police successfulness in preventing crime are probably hard to substantially influence by police organizations themselves.

6.5.2   *Instrumentalism: Catching burglars and rapid response*

The next intermediary variables test the instrumentalist Hypothesis 2b. We are looking at the influence of homicide rates and victimization rates of burglary and assault on citizens' assessments of police successfulness in catching house burglars and their rapid response to calls for help. The expectation is that higher homicide rates and victimization rates lead citizens to evaluate the police more negatively in these respects—meaning that there is a connection between actual crime rates and public perceptions of police effectiveness.

As with the previous analysis, there proves to be relatively little variance to explain on the country level. The null model of perceived police success in catching burglars shows an individual-level variance of 4.38 and a country-level variance of 0.12. Similarly, the null model of public assessments of police rapid response to calls has an individual-level variance of 4.90 with a country-level variance of 0.14. For both cases, this means that differences between individuals account for about 97% of the total variance, and differences between countries for about 3%. Public assessments of the police in these respects hence depend much more on individual characteristics than on characteristics of the country.

Table 6.5 displays the results of the analyses regarding determinants of public perceptions regarding police effectiveness in catching burglars and their rapid response to calls. Models C-a and D-a feature the estimates of national-level crime rates as measured by homicide and self-reported victimization of burglary and assault rates on the two individual-level indicators of instrumentalism. In Models C-b and D-b, other country-level variables are added to serve as controls. Finally, Models C-c and D-c see the individual-level determinants added, to give a full picture.

Model C-a shows that there is indeed a small, negative effect of victimization rates in the country on perceived police effectiveness in catching burglars. However, this effect disappears once other country-level variables are included in Model C-b and remains insignificant when individual-level factors are accounted for as well. Public assessments of how likely the police are to capture house burglars do hence appear to be only marginally related to actual crime in the country. On average, more burglaries in a country do not seem to substantially alter opinions of police successfulness in actually catching burglars. Homicide rates are entirely unrelated to perceived police effectiveness in catching burglars; there is not even a significant connection in Model C-a, let alone in the more extensive models C-b and C-c.

On the individual level, like previous models, Model C-c shows a particularly strong effect of how citizens evaluate their contacts with the police. Contacts that are experienced negatively substantially decrease perceived police effectiveness in catching burglars. This is hardly any better for neutrally experienced contacts, while there is a relatively small positive effect for positively evaluated interactions between police and citizens. It is also noteworthy that victims of burglaries or assault are much less positive about police successfulness in catching burglars than people who have not been victimized. On the other hand, students, ethnic minorities, and people who attend religious services more often have more positive assessments of police effectiveness in catching burglars.

Table 6.5   Effects of national-level and individual-level determinants on public perceptions of police effectiveness in catching burglars and of police rapid response to calls

	Catch burglars						Rapid response					
	Model C-a		Model C-b		Model C-c		Model D-a		Model D-b		Model D-c	
N = 34,622	B	s.e.	B	s.e.	B	s.e.	B	s.e.	B	s.e.	B	s.e.
Proximity police index			-.06	.07	-.07	.08			-.05	.07	-.07	.08
Homicide	-.03	.07	-.04	.08	-.03	.09	.01	.08	.06	.08	.05	.08
Victimization (aggregated)	-.15*	.07	-.12	.09	-.05	.10	-.13	.08	-.17*	.09	-.16	.09
Corruption			-.13	.13	-.20	.15			-.33**	.13	-.41**	.14
Gini coefficient			-.01	.08	-.08	.09			-.12	.07	-.13	.08
Democracy			-.13	.14	-.18	.15			-.19	.13	-.22	.14
Female	ref.		ref.		ref.		ref.		ref.		ref.	
Male					-.05**	.02					-.08***	.02
Age					-.01	.02					.07***	.02
Education					-.13***	.01					.07***	.01
Income					-.01	.01					.03*	.01
No minority	ref.		ref.		ref.		ref.		ref.		ref.	
Minority					.21***	.05					.06	.06
Married	ref.		ref.		ref.		ref.		ref.		ref.	
Divorced					-.11**	.04					-.07*	.04
Widowed					.06	.04					.11**	.05
Single					-.00	.03					-.05	.03
Employed	ref.		ref.		ref.		ref.		ref.		ref.	
Student					.41***	.05					.33***	.05
Unemployed					-.09*	.04					-.18***	.04

	Catch burglars						Rapid response					
	Model C-a		Model C-b		Model C-c		Model D-a		Model D-b		Model D-c	
N = 34,622	B	s.e.	B	s.e.	B	s.e.	B	s.e.	B	s.e.	B	s.e.
Retired					.13***	.04					.09*	.04
Household					.13**	.05					-.2**	.05
Other occupation					-.03	.10					.03	.11
Urbanization					-.02*	.01					.23***	.01
Religious attendance					.19***	.01					.11***	.01
No victim	*ref.*		*ref.*		*ref.*		*ref.*		*ref.*		*ref.*	
Victim					-.54***	.03					-.29***	.03
No contact	*ref.*		*ref.*		*ref.*		*ref.*		*ref.*		*ref.*	
Satisfied with contact					.11***	.03					.26***	.03
Neutral contact					-.66***	.05					-.60***	.06
Unsatisfied with contact					-.95***	.04					-.86***	.05
Individual-level variance	*4.38*		*4.38*		*4.15*		*4.90*		*4.90*		*4.71*	
Country-level variance	*.09*		*.08*		*.11*		*.12*		*.08*		*.09*	

Two-tailed tests: * *P* = .05 |** *P* = .01 |*** *P* = .001

Small differences exist with public evaluations of police rapid response. Interestingly, there is no significant relationship between either homicide rates or victimization rates and perceptions of rapid response in Model D-a. Model D-b, however, displays a weakly significant negative effect of victimization rates. Surprisingly, there is a more robust negative effect of corruption. The effect of victimization loses its significance when individual-level factors are included in Model D-c, but corruption remains a significant determinant of assessments of police rapid response. Hence, public assessments of police quickness to respond to calls are more determined by corruption than by national-level measures of crime. This does not offer much support for Hypothesis 2b. On the individual level, the most eye-catching difference between Model C-c and Model D-c is the strong positive relationship between urbanization and perceptions of police rapid response. Perhaps unsurprisingly, citizens in rural areas have more negative perceptions of the speed with which the police will arrive at the scene of a crime.

These results suggest very little support for the instrumentalist hypothesis. Homicide appears to be entirely unrelated to considerations of police effectiveness, and even victimization rates of burglary and assault in a country are weakly, if at all, connected to individual perceptions of police effectiveness—although victims themselves are considerably more negative, particularly about police capacity to catch burglars. The connection between country-level corruption and citizens' assessments of police rapid response is remarkable, and suggests that aspects traditionally more related to the procedural justice school of thought might affect considerations of police effectiveness—more so than actual police effectiveness in terms of reducing crime.

6.5.3   *Procedural justice: Accepting bribes and the procedural justice scale*

The final two intermediary variables concern aspects of procedural justice or process-based policing, displayed in Table 6.6. Models E-a, E-b, and E-c study the factors that affect perceived police inclination to accept bribes, whereas Models F-a, F-b, and F-c inquire about the determinants of procedural justice—a scale based on three strongly related items: police fairness, police explaining their decisions, and their respectful treatment of citizens. Unlike the intermediary variables discussed before, we actually see considerable differences between countries in how they assess the police in terms of process-based policing. The null-model individual-level variance of perceived police bribe-taking is 4.88, whereas the country-level variance is 1.45. Although this means that differences between individuals remain larger than between countries, the country-level variance is considerable at 23% of the total variance. Perceptions of police bribe-taking are hence relatively strongly dependent on the country under study. To a lesser extent, this holds for perceived procedural justice too. Measured on a different scale (0–3 rather than 0–10), the variance on the individual level is 0.28 and that on the country level 0.03. While the total variance to be explained by the model is less than of the other intermediary variables, even when accounting for the different scale, a relevant part of the variance can be found on the level of countries: about 11% of the differences in perceived procedural justice depends on the national level.

The expected relationship between corruption on the national level and individual opinions of police bribe-taking and procedural justice (Hypothesis 3b) is present in all models. The strong effect of societal corruption on perceived police bribe-taking barely decreases in size when other national- or individual-level determinants are controlled for in Models E-b and E-c. The strength of this effect is confirmed by looking at the country-level variance: this decreases from the null-model 1.45 to 0.11 in the model that only includes corruption. This implies that 92% of the differences between countries in respondents' assessments of police susceptibility to accepting bribes is explained by the countries' score on the corruption index. Hence a country's societal corruption and citizens' estimates of police corruption are extremely powerfully related. But this effect of corruption is not limited to perceived police bribe-taking: it also holds, albeit to a lesser degree, for perceived police procedural justice. In countries with a high degree of societal corruption, the public are considerably less likely to perceive the police to act according to principles of procedural justice—corruption negatively affects perceptions of police fairness, respectful treatment, and their explaining their decisions. This effect remains robust even when other national-level (Model F-b) and individual-level variables (Model F-c) are included.

Table 6.6   Effects of national-level and individual-level determinants on public perceptions of police susceptibility to bribe-taking and police procedural justice

N = 34,622	Bribes						Procedural justice					
	Model E-a		Model E-b		Model E-c		Model F-a		Model F-b		Model F-c	
	B	s.e.	B	s.e.	B	s.e.	B	s.e.	B	s.e	B	s.e.
Proximity police index			-.09	.07	-.08	.07			.04*	.02	.03*	.02
Homicide			-.06	.08	-.05	.07			.01	.02	.01	.02
Victimization (aggregated)			.03	.09	.00	.08			-.03	.02	-.02	.02
Corruption	1.20***	.08	1.04***	.13	1.07***	.12	-.15***	.02	-.12***	.03	-.13***	.03
Gini coefficient			.11	.08	.12	.07			-.02	.02	-.02	.02
Democracy			-.13	.14	-.10	.12			.02	.03	.02	.03
Female	*ref.*		*ref.*		*ref.*		*ref.*		*ref.*		*ref.*	
Male					-.35***	.03					-.00	.01
Age					-.20***	.02					.03***	.01
Education					-.10***	.01					.02***	.00
Income					-.07***	.01					.02**	.00
No minority	*ref.*		*ref.*		*ref.*		*ref.*		*ref.*		*ref.*	
Minority					-.23***	.06					-.03**	.01
Married	*ref.*		*ref.*		*ref.*		*ref.*		*ref.*		*ref.*	
Divorced					.18***	.04					-.05***	.01
Widowed					-.09*	.05					.03**	.01
Single					.08**	.03					-.03***	.01
Employed	*ref.*		*ref.*		*-ref.*		*ref.*		*ref.*		*ref.*	
Student					-.17***	.05					.02*	.01
Unemployed					.25***	.04					-.07***	.01

	Bribes						Procedural justice					
	Model E-a		Model E-b		Model E-c		Model F-a		Model F-b		Model F-c	
N = **34,622**	B	s.e.	B	s.e.	B	s.e.	B	s.e.	B	s.e.	B	s.e.
Retired					.07*	.04					-.00	.01
Household					-.04	.05					.02	.01
Other occupation					.08	.11					-.03	.02
Urbanization					.02	.01					-.02***	.00
Religious attendance					-.14***	.01					.04***	.00
No victim	*ref.*		*ref.*		*ref.*		*ref.*		*ref.*		*ref.*	
Victim					.13***	.03					-.05***	.01
No contact	*ref.*		*ref.*		*ref.*		*ref.*		*ref.*		*ref.*	
Satisfied with contact					-.16***	.03					.10***	.01
Neutral contact					.47***	.06					-.19***	.01
Unsatisfied with contact					.72***	.05					-.32***	.01
Individual-level variance	4.88		4.88		4.71		.28		.28		.26	
Country-level variance	.11		.08		.07		.01		.00		.00	

Two-tailed tests: * P = .05 | ** P = .01 | *** P = .001

On the individual level, we find few surprising results. As before, citizens' evaluations of the contact they had with the police are particularly strong determinants of their judgment of the police; this time in terms of procedural justice-related dependent variables. One interesting difference is that men consider the police far less likely to take bribes than do women. Such a gender difference does not recur in the questions about police procedural justice. It is also intriguing that ethnic minority members consider the police to be less likely to accept bribes, but also less likely to act in a procedurally just manner: while they appear to trust in police integrity, they do not have much faith in being treated fairly.

A remarkable and unexpected finding on the national level is the weak, but enduringly significant, positive relationship between proximity policing and perceived procedural justice. This effect holds even when individual-level variables are accounted for: in countries that adhere to a larger extent to proximity policing principles, citizens have more positive perceptions of police procedural justice. This points to possibly intertwining processes between the proximity policing and process-based policing schools. If we recall that corruption on the national level also affects individual-level indicators of effectiveness and proximity, we can conclude that the three theoretical models, while conceptually and theoretically distinct, have some empirical overlap and are possibly at least partially mutually reinforcing.

6.6   MAIN RESULTS: REFLECTING ON THE HYPOTHESES

Now that the key analyses have been conducted, we can proceed to reflecting on what they mean for our hypotheses, and with them the theoretical perspectives that we have derived them from. While the main results concerning the hypotheses are summarized in Table 6.7, it is worth reflecting on some of these results. First, however, let us briefly recall what was examined in this chapter.

Our main interest was to find the factors on the national and individual level that determine public trust in the police and hence explain differences in levels of trust between countries. To do so, we were guided by three theoretical perspectives and the trust-building strategies that they proposed: proximity policing, instrumentalism, and procedural justice. To measure proximity policing, the proximity policing index was constructed as a country-level indicator, while perceived police successfulness in preventing crime was its individual-level determinant. We expected both a direct effect of proximity policing on trust and an indirect one through perceived police prevention. Instrumentalism was represented by two country-level indicators: homicide rates and victimization rates of burglaries and assault. The individual-level indicators were perceived police successfulness in catching burglars and the perceived quickness of police response to calls—both referring to perceptions of police effectiveness. Again, both a direct effect on trust in the police was expected and an indirect one, through individual perceptions of police effectiveness. Procedural justice, finally, had one country-level indicator, corruption, and two individual-level ones: perceived police susceptibility to bribes and perceptions of police adherence to procedural justice principles. As with the other two theoretical schools, procedural justice also implies both a direct effect of corruption and an indirect one, through its individual assessments.

The previous sections have tested both these expected direct effects (Section 6.4.1) and the indirect ones (Sections 6.4.2 and 6.5). There were vast differences in the degree to which the hypotheses found support in the empirical findings. Some expected effects, in the data, appeared to be absent or even reversed. Additionally, some unexpected cross-relations were found where country-level determinants expected to be related to one theoretical school affected individual-level indicators from another.

Table 6.7 features the main results regarding the hypotheses. In my assessment of how well each hypothesis passed the empirical tests, I have distinguished five rough judgments: hypotheses could be strongly supported, mostly supported, neither supported nor rejected, mostly rejected, or strongly rejected. These various degrees in between acceptance and rejection of hypotheses are necessary to reflect the sometimes nuanced results from the analyses; sometimes a hypothesis is partially supported as, for instance, the expected relationship is present bivariately or with only country-level controls, but disappears once other factors are accounted for. It is worth bearing in mind, regardless, that even when hypotheses find strong empirical support in the data, this by no means implies that we have found a universal rule or mechanism. It merely shows that in the particular data we have at our disposal, the expected trend is strongly present.

What does this list of results teach us? First, and most notably, the procedural justice-inspired hypotheses all find strong support in the data: there is a strong, negative direct connection between societal corruption and trust in the police; a strong effect of corruption on perceived police bribe-taking (positive) and their adherence to procedural justice principles (negative); and strong effects of perceived police bribe-taking (negative) and police adherence to procedural justice principles (positive) on trust. All of this is exactly as was expected in the hypotheses. Based on these results, we hence cannot reject procedural justice as a useful mechanism to understand public trust in the police. What is more, societal corruption significantly impacts individual-level indicators derived from the other two schools as well: more corruption goes hand in hand with more negative assessments of police capacity to prevent crimes and their rapid response to calls.

Table 6.7   Conclusions regarding the hypotheses

	Hypothesis	Conclusion	Findings
	Proximity policing		
1a	In countries that adhere to a higher extent to proximity policing principles, citizens have more trust in the police	• **Mostly rejected**	• *Significant positive bivariate relationship, but becomes significantly negative when all other factors are controlled for*
1b	In countries that adhere to a higher extent to proximity policing principles, citizens perceive the police to be more successful in preventing crime	• **Neither supported nor rejected**	• *Significant positive bivariate relationship, but becomes nonsignificant when other factors are controlled for*
1c	Citizens who perceive the police to be more successful in preventing crime have more trust in the police	• **Strongly supported**	• *Significant and powerful positive relationship*
	Instrumentalism		
2a	In countries with lower homicide rates and lower victimization rates of burglaries and assault, citizens have more trust in the police	• **Strongly rejected**	• *Victimization rates are bivariately positively related to trust; effect disappears once other factors are controlled for; homicide rates are positively related to trust after other factors are controlled for*
2b	In countries with lower homicide rates and lower victimization rates of burglaries and assault, citizens perceive the police to be more successful in catching criminals and respond more rapidly to reports of crime	• **Strongly rejected** and • **Weakly supported**	• *No significant relationship found between homicide rates and citizens' perceptions of police effectiveness* • *Significant negative relationships between victimization and citizens' perceptions of police effectiveness when only country level is taken into account, but become nonsignificant when individual-level factors are controlled for*
2c	Citizens who perceive the police to be more successful in catching criminals and respond more rapidly to reports of crime have more trust in the police	• **Mostly supported**	• *Significant positive relationships, but relatively weak effects*

	Hypothesis	Conclusion	Findings
	Procedural justice		
3a	In countries with less corruption, citizens have more trust in the police	• **Strongly supported**	• *Significant and powerful negative relationship*
3b	In countries with less corruption, citizens perceive the police to act in a more procedurally just fashion and be less likely to take bribes	• **Strongly supported**	• *Significant and powerful negative relationship*
3c	Citizens who perceive the police to act in a more procedurally just fashion and be less likely to take bribes have more trust in the police	• **Strongly supported**	• *Significant and powerful negative relationships, albeit stronger for procedural justice than for bribe-taking*

For the two other theoretical schools, evidence is mixed. There is only a weak, if any, positive direct effect of proximity policing in a country on trust in the police— it even appears to be negative once other variables are controlled for. There is also only a weak positive connection between proximity policing and individual assessments of police successfulness in preventing crimes. Nevertheless, there is a powerful positive effect of perceived police successfulness in preventing crimes on trust in the police. Additionally, and unexpectedly, there is also a positive relationship between country-level proximity policing and individual assessments of police adherence to procedural justice principles; this suggests that proximity policing improves public perceptions of police procedural justice.

If anything, instrumentalism fares worse than proximity policing and much worse than procedural justice. There are indications that homicide rates, as well as victimization rates of burglary and assault, are actually positively related to trust: higher homicide and victimization rates are associated with more trust in the police. Homicide is unrelated to public assessments of police effectiveness in catching burglars or rapid response. Even victimization rates of burglary and assault are only weakly, if at all, connected with public perceptions of police effectiveness. Remarkably, the connection between victimization of burglaries and perceptions of police successfulness in catching burglars is so weak as to be nearly absent.

6.7   COUNTRY-SPECIFIC EFFECTS

While the hypotheses have been sufficiently addressed for now, there is still something lacking. If we wish to discuss police trust-building strategies, one aspect that is often forgotten is the diversity that we see across Europe. Our previous analyses dealt with the 21 included countries as a whole, providing varying measures of support for the three different theoretical schools and their implications for trust-building. This is perfectly logical when looking at the effects of national-level determinants. However, for the examination of individual-level determinants, such a global analysis is too crude: it assumes that effects of individual characteristics on trust will be equal across countries. This is an assumption that, in the past, has been proven wrong.

In the previous analyses, we have found several interesting results regarding the effects on individual-level control variables on trust in the police. Some of these results contradicted at least some previous research from some countries: ethnic minority members were found to have less trust in the police than the country's ethnic majority—unlike what was found by Kautt (2011); those professing that they had experienced positive interactions with the police had significantly more trust than those without any contact—contradicting, for instance, Lammers (2004) and Skogan (2006a); and urbanization was found to have no effect on trust—whereas Cao and Zhao (2005) found a negative relationship between urbanization and trust in the police. The question, also addressed in Chapter 4, is to what extent these results are influenced by the specific countries included. In other words: to what extent are the effects of several individual-level determinants of trust universal or, rather, unique to separate societies or countries? Fortunately, although uncommon in large-scale international comparisons, it is possible to simply split our analyses by country and observe the effects of individual-level indicators by country.[2] Does the positive effect of positively evaluated interactions hold up in each country? Are ethnic minorities disinclined to trust the police everywhere? This analysis—or, rather, this series of analyses—can shed some light on those policy-wise rather important questions.

If we split our analyses by country, it is necessary to take into account the fact that the statistical power of the regression analyses decreases substantially. This implies that weaker effects tend to become nonsignificant. In order to adjust for this, we will alter our thresholds for significance. This is justifiable when we take into consideration that we are not looking for rock-solid certainty in what effect is present in which country. Rather, what is of interest here is how effects do or do not differ across countries. Does a certain variable affect trust negatively in one

---

2.   One might argue that another way to control for different effects of individual-level variables in multilevel regression structures is to add the possibility of random effects of the determinants under scrutiny, thus creating a random slope model. However, while this procedure can successfully estimate the random effects component of a variable—providing a solid indication of the extent to which effect sizes or even directions differ across countries—it does not specify the countries concerned. To summarize, it does not tell us in which countries the effects of the variable of interest would be strongest or weakest, or in which countries the effects are positive or negative. Hence the results will be statistically accurate but theoretically and practically of limited value. The more straightforward approach to split the analysis by country (and hence ignore the nested structure of the data) is statistically less precise but does give us the required impression, and is capable of informing us exactly which countries show different results.

country, and positively in another? Does a positive net effect of a determinant in the main Model A-h, where all countries were included, perhaps obscure the possibility of some countries having a negative relationship instead? Table 6.8 contains Model G, the collected multiple regression analyses for the individual-level control variables previously included in the multilevel analyses.

What new information do these country-specific effects in Table 6.8 offer? Once we split the regression analyses by country, three different rough patterns can be discerned. The most obvious are the determinants that have a rather uniform effect: significantly positive, or negative, in all or nearly all countries. This is clearly the case for neutral or negative evaluations of contacts with the police—both of which have a negative effect in nearly all countries under study. Similarly, religious attendance has a positive effect on trust in most countries. It is also noteworthy that positively evaluated contacts, while often positively related to trust, do not improve trust in every country—in a substantial minority of eight countries, there is no evidence of such a positive effect.

Then, there are some determinants that have no significant effect in most countries, but do seem to affect trust significantly in some—leading to a weak or absent net effect in the cross-country analyses. These include being widowed or retired. With some variables, however, a minority of countries actually shapes a powerful net effect, while there is no evidence of a relationship for the majority of nations under study. Income and being divorced are examples; based merely on the cross-national Model A-h, we could be inclined to conclude that having a higher income is always positively related to trust in the police. However, in the majority of individual countries there is no evidence of such a relationship. In part, this could be attributed to the diminished statistical power when we split countries, but it probably also reflects substantive differences in effect size between contexts. In short, where trust in the police is concerned, income may play an important role in some countries, while it could be wholly irrelevant in others.

Table 6.8   Country-specific multiple regression analyses of trust in the police

Model G	Male	Age	Education	Income	Minority	Divorced	Widowed	Single	Student	Unemployed	Retired	Home	Urbanization	Religious attendance	Victim	Negative contact	Neutral contact	Positive contact
Reference cat.	Female				No min.	Married			Employed							No contact		
Belgium	0	0	+++	+++	–	0	0	0	+++	0	0	0	0	+++	–	–	–	+
Croatia	0	++	0	0	0	0	0	0	0	0	0	+	0	+++	0	–	0	+++
Czech Republic	–	+	0	+	0	–	0	0	+	0	+	0	+++	+++	–	–	–	+++
Denmark	0	0	+++	0	0	–	0	0	0	–	0	0	0	++	–	–	–	0
England & Wales	0	++	+	++	–	–	++	–	+++	–	0	+	0	+	–	–	–	+++
Estonia	––	++	0	+++	––	–	+	+	+++	–	0	0	0	++	0	–	–	++
France	–	0	+++	+++	–	0	+	0	0	–	0	+	0	++	0	–	–	+
East Germany	0	0	0	+++	0	0	0	0	++	–	0	+	+	+++	–	–	–	0
West Germany	0	0	+++	+++	+	0	+	0	0	–	0	0	0	+++	–	–	–	+++
Greece	–	++	––	0	++	0	0	–	+	–	+	–	–	+++	–	–	–	++
Hungary	–	+	+	0	0	0	+	0	0	0	0	0	0	+++	0	–	–	+++
Ireland	0	+++	+++	++	+	–	+	–	+++	–	0	–	–	0	0	–	–	0
Netherlands	0	0	+++	0	0	–	+	0	+	–	0	0	0	++	–	–	–	+
Norway	0	0	+	+++	–	–	+	–	++	–	0	0	0	++	–	–	–	0
Poland	0	+	++	//////	+	0	0	0	0	0	+	0	+	0	–	–	–	0
Portugal	0	+	0	0	+	0	0	0	0	–	0	0	0	0	0	–	–	0
Scotland	–––	+	0	0	0	0	0	+	0	–	0	0	+	0	0	–	0	0
Slovakia	0	0	+++	0	0	0	0	+	+++	–	0	0	0	++	–	–	–	+++
Slovenia	0	0	0	0	–	–	0	0	+++	0	0	0	+++	0	–	–	–	++
Sweden	0	0	+++	0	0	0	0	0	0	–	0	0	+	0	0	–	0	0
Switzerland	0	–	++	0	0	0	0	–	0	–	0	–	0	+++	–	–	–	0
Total																		
Positive	1	8	13	8	3	0	7	3	10	0	2	3	4	16	0	0	0	13
No effect	15	11	7	12	11	14	14	13	11	8	19	14	15	5	5	0	3	8
Negative	5	2	1	0	7	7	0	5	0	13	0	4	2	0	16	21	18	0
Effects model A-h	–	+++	+++	+++	–––	–––	+	––	+++	–––	0	0	0	+++	–––	–––	–––	+++

Significance levels .1 (+ or -), .025 (++ or --), and 0.01 (+++ or ---). All tests are one-tailed (previous findings serve as implicit hypothesis).

NB: we have no information on income in Portugal.

The largest and most interesting type of determinant to the present inquiry, however, consists of variables that have a positive effect in some, no effect in other, and
a negative effect in yet other countries. This becomes particularly important when
the positives and negatives appear to cancel each other out, leading to a very weak
or nonsignificant net effect. This is the case for those whose main occupation is taking care of the household, but also—and more relevant in policy terms—for urbanization and minority membership. In many countries, urbanization does not
appear to affect trust in the police. However, in the Czech Republic, Greece, and
Slovenia, there is a powerful positive relationship: citizens living in urban areas
have more trust in the police than rural respondents. On the other hand, in Ireland
and to a lesser extent Hungary, the opposite holds. Similarly, in seven countries
under study, self-defined ethnic minorities have less trust in the police than the
majority—leading to a weak overall negative effect—but in Greece, Ireland, and
Portugal ethnic minorities have more trust in the police than the ethnic majority. In
11 other countries, ethnicity does not appear to matter as far as trust is concerned.

Even variables that, on the surface, appear to have strong, unidirectional relationships with trust, such as education, prove to be subject to such diverse effects
upon closer examination: while, overall, higher levels of education are reliably positively related to trust, Greece is the exception to the rule, with a strong negative
relationship. This effect would be easily overlooked if only a cross-national analysis were conducted. Similar, albeit less striking, examples can be found in the
effects of age, gender, and being single: in the overall analysis, Model A-h, they
have robust effects in a clear direction, yet this effect actually runs in reverse in
some of the included countries.

6.8   Concluding remarks

In this chapter, after describing differences in levels of trust at a fixed moment in
time (2010), we have endeavored to explain public trust in the police through
hypotheses derived from three main theoretical schools: proximity policing, instrumentalism, and procedural justice.

While procedural justice found strong support in the data, proximity policing
yielded mixed results, and hypotheses regarding instrumentalism fared poorly.
Based on the preceding analyses, it is police integrity and fair treatment of citizens
that are particularly central in determining public trust in the police. Evidence for
these notions, derived from the procedural justice school of thought, is strong on
the national as well as the individual level. Societal corruption not only negatively
affects public perceptions of police procedural justice and of police inclination to
accept bribes, as expected, but also negatively impacts perceived police rapid
response to calls and their perceived ability to prevent crime. All of these individual assessments of the police are subsequently strongly related to public trust in
the police. Procedural justice, and particularly corruption, hence seem to provide

us with several leads for understanding and improving public trust in the police through trust-building strategies.

Proximity policing's mixed results mean that the national-level proximity policing index only weakly, if at all, influences trust in the police and perceived police preventive successes. A country's score on the proximity policing index does, however, affect perceptions of police procedural justice in that country. Police preventive successes also determine trust in the police. While this provides only partial support for proximity policing as a school of thought and hence as a police practice paradigm, the empirical support that is present means that I would be reluctant to reject proximity policing strategies outright. The implications for the proximity policing paradigm, I would suggest, are nuanced. One note we could make, for instance, is that it will most likely be best to pay special attention to procedural justice when implementing proximity policing reforms, and vice versa.

Most surprising, meanwhile, are the results regarding instrumentalism. Higher crime rates, if anything, are associated with more trust in the police. Additionally, there is barely any connection between actual crime rates and popular perceptions of police effectiveness. This runs counter to popular notions within the police organization and policy circles, and poses a fundamental challenge to the core principles of instrumentalist thinking—carrying implications to which we shall return in Chapter 12.

To what extent can we combine insights from the previous Chapter 5, the descriptive, longitudinal analyses, with those derived from the analyses of Chapter 6? The link is less direct than could, on the face of it, have been expected. For instance, the strong connection between corruption and levels of trust in a country would suggest a simple mechanism: successfully combating corruption will increase public trust in the police over time. We should, however, caution against such simplified reasoning. It is true that several countries under study show long-term increases in trust as well as a decrease in corruption.[3] This holds for instance for Estonia, Poland, and France. But whether these relationships are as straightforward as this would suggest remains to be seen. If we look at the developments between 2012 and 2014, for example, France shows an increase in corruption, but also an increase in trust. In this same period, Poland showed falling corruption, and yet also falling trust. And while Estonia's corruption scores have been on a steady downward slope in recent years, its levels of trust in the police have tended to oscillate—even though the general trend has been positive. Other countries, such as the Netherlands, Slovenia, and Spain, have, although on different levels, featured constant or gradually rising levels of corruption, and yet have also seen

---

3.   Transparency International emphasizes that its Corruption Perceptions Index, the values of which we use in the present study, have historically not been designed for longitudinal analyses. Only from 2012 onward has the procedure for composing the index been standardized in such a way as to allow historical comparisons. Before that year, however, very clear changes in the index over time probably do give some indication of the general trend.

an overall increase of trust in the police. Apparently, while the factor definitely plays an important role, mere trends in corruption in themselves are insufficient to understand trajectories of trust.

These examples serve to illustrate that explaining differences between countries at a fixed moment in time is something different altogether from understanding trends. While it appears credible that, on average, a decrease in corruption will lead to trust in the police increasing, this is not a straightforward, fail-safe mechanism. Corruption, like trust, is a multifaceted concept that is hard to measure. Moreover, it is likely that other determining factors are at stake as well.

The additional analysis has yielded several relevant results. It has shed some light on the consistently contradictory findings regarding the effects of certain variables on trust in the police, such as ethnic minority membership, urbanization, or contacts with the police. It has shown that while universal or near-universal effects of some variables do exist, it is far more common across the European continent to observe differing or even contradictory effects. What this means for cross-national investigations of trust in the police will be addressed in Chapter 12.

We have seen, over the preceding chapters, that trust in the police in Europe varies greatly from country to country. Additionally, trust can fluctuate: over relatively brief time frames of 2 years, substantial developments can and do take place. Finally, we have seen that at least at a fixed moment in time, it is possible, to a substantial degree, to explain differences between countries and between individuals in terms of trust in the police. To tie all these findings together, however, requires yet more understanding. The things we still do not know, and that are essential to understanding the dynamics of trust in the police, are mainly related to governmental and police actors. It is, as of yet, unclear how police organizations and governments respond to, for example, sudden decreases in trust. In what terms or concepts do they understand such a problem and what is their diagnosis of the issue? Do they correspond to any or more of the three theoretical perspectives addressed in the preceding part of the study—proximity policing, instrumentalism, and procedural justice? Then, based on this problem definition, how do they respond to the problem? What approaches, or—more accurately phrased—what strategies, have been formulated to deal with the problem of trust? This emphasizes the 'dialogic character' (Bottoms & Tankebe, 2012) of trust and legitimacy. Again, we may ask to what extent such trust-building strategies are inspired by or drawn from the three theoretical perspectives discussed previously. Of course, these questions are not always related to sudden decreases in trust; they may also depend on other moments or circumstances in which trust is in some way defined as something that needs attention and improvement. But these circumstances and responses to such events or processes are likely to differ across contexts—both in terms of time and of space. Finally, then, we may wonder how the answers to such questions differ across countries and how we can understand such differences.

These are the challenges that will be addressed in Part III of this study, starting from Chapter 7 and proceeding with three case studies: England & Wales, Denmark, and the Netherlands. Combined with the insights yielded in Part II, we should be able, in the concluding Part IV, to answer our research questions and achieve a more complete understanding of trust in the police from the perspective of the police, the public, and other actors involved in the relationship and the resulting tensions.

PART III

POLICE TRUST-BUILDING STRATEGIES

7.1   INTRODUCTION AND RESEARCH QUESTIONS

In the previous part of this book, the focus was on citizens' trust in the police from the perspective of the public. Through a range of quantitative survey data, I first addressed the question of the extent to which we can validly compare questionnaire data across European countries. Finding that trust in the police could be compared across most, if not all, European countries, I proceeded to tracing developments in levels of trust in the police in different European countries. In this process, we were guided by various popular theses predicting more or less specific developments in trust in different countries. Then, the analyses went on to compare levels of trust at a set moment of time, 2010, finding substantial differences in levels of trust across the continent. I finally aimed to explain those differences by applying three theoretical lenses, each of which yielded distinct expectations and hypotheses on the factors that determine the relationship between the public and the police.

All these efforts, although quite varied in nature, had in common that they focused on the perspective of citizens, rather than the police. As I argued in Chapter 1, in order to gain a richer, more complete understanding of the dynamics of trust in the police and illuminate the 'dialogic character' (Bottoms & Tankebe, 2012) of trust, we need to learn more about the police perspective. We have learned of developments in trust, differences between countries, and factors determining how much trust people have in the police. The question arises, consequently, of how this interacts with the police and police work; trust and legitimacy are not only relevant among the public. Legitimacy can be divided into audience legitimacy—public trust in and views of the police—and power-holder legitimacy—police self-perception of their legitimacy, authority, and trustworthiness and their ensuing strategies to improve on these (Bottoms & Tankebe, 2012). We have very little information on how the police actually define the problem of trust, how they construct it, and how they attempt to deal with it. And when we move to the internationally comparative domain, that 'very little' starts to resemble 'none at all.' In the following chapters, I will hence take an exploratory approach focusing on theory-building and the generation of a framework for understanding trust-building strategies. The logic, hence, is different from theory-testing research.

The following chapters will focus on attempts by the police to gain, regain, or maintain citizens' trust. I will place all these attempts—to borrow a concept from Six (2004), later applied to the police by Goldsmith (2005) and Goldsmith and Harris (2012)—under the header 'trust-building strategies.' This means that there is a goal-oriented effort on the part of the police to gain public trust and confidence. The analysis of Six (2004), however, concerned the intra-organizational level—mainly concentrating on the question of how to increase interpersonal trust within organizations. The context of the present study is that of an organization seeking public trust; a markedly different situation (Goldsmith & Harris, 2012). However, it is not unreasonable to expect that police organizations in different countries all have their own ways of attempting to improve public trust—even though they might not use the word trust but, for example, prefer confidence, legitimacy, or even satisfaction. I will describe all these efforts using the term trust-building. Such trust-building strategies can be designed and acted out on the national stage as well as by individual street-level officers. However, we are primarily interested in trust-building on the institutional level. Police trust-building strategies concern, as discussed in Chapter 1, '*how institutional arrangements and practices associated with policing can be reshaped so as to make them more deserving of public trust*' (Goldsmith, 2005: 457).

Of course, trying to build public trust is easier said than done. The literature on police culture often emphasizes that police officers, as part of the nature of their job, tend to be suspicious toward outsiders and feel isolated in society (Reiner, 2010). Westley (1970; but based on much older research) already wrote of the difficulties police organizations face when dealing with the public. Although his portrayal of a violent, deeply racist Midwestern American police force during the late 1940s is in many ways unlikely to be typical for any contemporary Western European police organization, the stance of the police versus the public has ever remained ambivalent. Even when the police do not transgress the boundaries of the law or other norms, they are by the nature of their job involved with activities that are bound to antagonize at least part of the public through the use of force or other negative outcomes (Bittner, 1980; Reiner, 2010).

On the one hand, as was demonstrated in previous parts of this book, the police simply need the public in order to properly do their job (FitzGerald, 2010; Goudriaan et al., 2006; Jackson & Bradford, 2010; Sunshine & Tyler, 2003; Tyler, 2004). On the other, police officers are often deeply distrustful toward citizens. The combination of encountering quite a few criminal citizens in their daily work, fostered by a specific, somewhat isolationist subculture being ingrained into police officers from the moment they (often at a young age) join the service, can easily lead police officers to maintain a skeptical attitude toward the public. Police organizations in all Western countries therefore face the challenge of overcoming both their own suspicion as well as a reluctance on the part of the public to engage with them.[1] This tension, and how the police attempt to address it, is well worthy of study.

One potential remedy has been analyzed by Mawby (2002) in his in-depth study of police image work in the UK. He considers image work to be strongly related to *'the legitimation process, entwined with the seeking and retaining of legitimacy'* (Mawby, 2002: 2). I would agree. Yet image work is only one part of this seeking and retaining of legitimacy. And, as we will see over the course of these chapters, image work by itself, while potentially important and certainly something to take into account, has within the police organization generally been considered insufficient to forge ties of legitimacy between the police and the public—as evidenced by recurrent waves of police reorganizations and reform aiming to change not only communication or image, but also police practice.

It is my expectation that the police in different countries and at different points in time use different tools and strategies to foster public trust and their legitimacy in the eyes of the public. First of all, for these tools and strategies, we have to look at the problem definition. How a problem of trust or legitimacy is framed and understood is likely to shape the eventual strategy of dealing with it—although we should never assume that either the problem definition or the police response to the problem will remain the same over time. Second, the nature of trust-building strategies can be expected to depend on cultural, historical, structural, and political specifics of the local context and ratio. Third, such strategies are likely to be influenced by other, international or even global, factors including examples or perceived best practices from abroad. For instance, there are times when specific trust-building strategies are fashionable or popular. Perceived successes of a certain model in one country or context can lead another country to copy its central tenets through processes of policy transfer or diffusion (Crawford, 2009; Jones & Newburn, 2007). These considerations are addressed through the three research questions previously formulated in Chapter 1:

> Research Question 4: *When and how was citizens' trust in the police defined as a problem in different European countries, and how did it evolve?*

> Research Question 5: *What strategies and 'solutions' have since then been adopted by whom to address the problem of trust in these countries, and to improve police–public relationships in general?*

> Research Question 6: *How can we understand the differences we find between and within countries in terms of problem definition and trust-building strategies?*

---

1.   Police in non-Western contexts in many cases face even more daunting challenges, but this is beyond the scope of the current contribution.

In the following section, these research questions will be clad in a theoretical framework providing some necessary guidance for us to understand trust-building strategies in their context and build on existing insights and knowledge.

7.2   THEORY: UNDERSTANDING TRUST-BUILDING STRATEGIES

In this section, I will attempt to construct a framework for understanding thinking about trust and trust-building strategies. This entails the lines along which to study the concepts of interest, the common lens or focus required to give direction to the comparison (Nelken, 2010).

7.2.1   *Problem definition, policy generation, and political events*

To answer the research questions, I will pragmatically draw from concepts of Kingdon's (1995) work on understanding policy processes. While in some ways not fully applicable to the current project, Kingdon's book offers a compelling and well-structured framework for a systematic understanding of political agenda-setting—and, as was also noted by Terpstra and Fyfe (2014), we will see that political agenda-setting has many things in common with police agenda-setting. This, in turn, often provides the essential foundation for trust-building.

Kingdon aimed to formulate a systematic approach toward the question '*[w]hat makes people in and around government attend, at any given time, to some subjects and not to others?*' (Kingdon, 1995: 1). In his work, a key consideration for finding out why and how certain problems make it to the top of the political agenda is the distinction of three central processes. These processes, *problem recognition, generation of policy proposals*, and *political events*, need to come together in the right constellation at the right time. When this confluence occurs, a so-called policy window opens, providing '*opportunities for pushing pet proposals or conceptions of problems*' (Kingdon, 1995: 20). A certain problem definition, or a specific solution to a previously defined problem, can then reach the top of the agenda. Presumably, this will then lead to adoption and implementation—although this is not the focus of Kingdon's analysis. I consider the three processes that he discerns to be valuable concepts to use as guidelines for a study of police trust-building strategies.

One compelling contribution that illustrates these stages as related to criminal justice policies is the book 'Inventing fear of crime,' by Murray Lee (2007). It describes and analyzes the invention and emergence of fear of crime as a central policy topic throughout the U.S. and the U.K. From Lee's analyses, we can distill the central concepts and actors involved in Kingdon's work. Here, fear of crime is the *problem*, with the *policies* and *political events* differing according to place and time. For the U.S., Lee (2007) describes how the McClellan Subcommittee on Criminal Laws and Procedures proposed increased powers for the police and diminished rights of individuals dealing with them, resulting in the Omnibus Crime

Control and Safe Streets Act 1968. After the invention of the *problem* of fear of crime, therefore, *policies* were formulated to address them—in this case, the 1968 Act. These policies were then pushed by certain actors in *politics* who wielded power and influence at the right time, chief amongst them being a conservative Democrat Senator from Arkansas, John McClellan (Lee, 2007). Similarly, it might be possible to discern parallel concepts and processes in the present study.

An interesting and, for this study possibly fundamental, difference between the approach of Lee (2007) and the theoretical model of Kingdon (1995) is on the origin of problems. Kingdon remains unconvinced of the need to trace the roots of a problem or an idea back to its origin. His assessment is that '*it is [...] true that within a given case, when we try to track down the origins of an idea or proposal, we become involved in an infinite regress*' (Kingdon, 1995: 72-73). In this view, there is no predefined place in time to call the birth of an idea, because all ideas build on older notions. The risk is that this analysis treats the genesis of an idea as something of a black box, while the study of origins and developments of ideas can yield particularly important insights—these origins determine to a large extent how a problem is defined and understood. While the exact inception of an idea or strategy may be impossible—and often irrelevant—to pinpoint in time or place, it can prove insightful to discern when it entered public discourse.

This is why Lee (2007), in a Foucauldian history of the present, speaks explicitly of the *invention* of a concept—fear of crime. He can do this despite the challenging fact that '*there are continuities and discontinuities in the history of the concept*' (Lee, 2007: 10), because it is exactly those very continuities and discontinuities that he studies. This means that it is possible to discern several defining moments and phases in the social construction of the concept of fear of crime, but also, even if it takes place in stages, its invention. Similarly, we will see throughout the following chapters that an attempt to determine when trust in the police was first constructed as a relevant problem will yield some doubt about the exact timing of the occurrence. It is, however, certainly possible to narrow down the defining phases in the invention of trust to two or three periods in time, depending on the criteria one applies. Additionally, we will observe that the circumstances around the invention of trust in the police as a policy problem strongly influence the framing of the problem, and therefore the proposed policies and solutions.

How can we apply this theoretical approach to a study of developments in criminal justice, and trust-building specifically? An important thing to note is that the present study, unlike the work of Kingdon, does not delve deeply into the political realm—although we will certainly see instances where politics get involved with policing. Specifically, policies, as in policy measures, do have a central role, as was also the case in the study of Lee (2007). Furthermore, a political context, in the broader sense of the word, is of course present in all institutions. If we therefore bear in mind that the domain is different, we shall find that most concepts and ideas from Kingdon (1995) tend to recur in some form in criminal justice territory in general and policing in particular.

7.2.2   *Problem recognition: The invention of trust*

Applying these ideas to the present study, we first need to make sure that we start at the beginning; or at least, *a* beginning—the moment when realization starts to dawn that citizens' attitudes toward the police actually matter. When did police-citizen relationships first become an object of scrutiny, and how was this constructed and understood? What is the context of such an invention; what are the conditions for trust to be invented as a relevant concept? This is the moment when trust loses its taken-for-grantedness and becomes an object of reflection. It is imaginable that a sudden crisis situation may give rise to such a problem definition, but it is quite possible that other conditions are equally or more salient. And then: in what terms was the problem phrased; what was the diagnosis?

The initial scrutiny, for completeness' sake, need not be scientific—it is even unlikely to be so, as one matter of interest is who defined the problem of trust. We are looking for the social invention of trust as a vital concept by certain actors to understand and frame the relationship between the police and the public. Additionally, we can trace the development of trust as a problem up to the present day. How was the problem of trust defined by police and government and other relevant actors over different periods in time? Can we see distinct phases in the construction of trust, is there a gradual evolution, or has it remained static?

7.2.3   *Policy generation: The design of trust-building strategies*

This is closely connected to the next research question. Based on a certain understanding of trust and of police-citizen relationships, what policies and approaches have the police since adopted in order to work with the concept? How have they attempted to shape their relationship with the public, or what trust-building strategies have they applied? Who are the most important actors driving these strategies and why were these dominant as opposed to others? How did certain solutions to address the problem of trust emerge on top of the policy agenda, while others withered? How did ancillary notions, such as ideas about the relationship between citizens and the state, or about safety and security, affect the design of policies to build trust?

As a point of departure for trust-building strategies, it makes sense to start with the three perspectives employed in the previous part of this book: (neo)-instrumentalism, proximity policing, and procedural justice. The expectation is that each of these three perspectives suggests and promotes a certain trust-building strategy in archetypal form. Therefore, when we talk about police trust-building strategies, there are theoretically at least three different ways to go about Kingdon's (1995) process of policy generation.

Whenever a society is confronted with a perceived problem of lack of trust in the police, relevant actors can prefer to formulate a strategy based on instrumentalist notions and assumptions, for one founded in proximity policing, or for a procedurally just approach. These models, however, are, like all models, archetypes. It could be logical to expect that societies, at different points in time, borrow from more than one of these perspectives to design their trust-building strategies. Various blends and combinations can be imagined. Another complication is that the fact that these three models dominate the existing literature need not automatically imply that they are the only ways to think about how to improve trust in the police: it is entirely possible that police organizations will opt for trust-building strategies rooted in completely different logic. Here, we may have to acknowledge the importance of chance, and of the unique.

Kingdon (1995) describes the role of policy entrepreneurs: actors, usually individuals, who come up with certain ideas or strategies and promote them to the policy-making establishment. Often, individuals and their ideas will just remain in the 'primeval policy soup,' but sometimes, due to structural factors or sheer coincidence, a single actor or very small group of actors can emerge and seemingly single-handedly determine the course of an entire country. As we will see in the following chapters, the role of the individual can occasionally be decisive in shaping strategies and thinking about trust for years or even decades to come.

Alternatively, however, the police establishment might prefer not to generate any special policies at all but, rather, expect problems to blow over eventually. It is also possible that strategies have multiple functions and uses, of which trust-building is only one part. In this sense, we need to take account of the potential difference between the rhetoric of the strategy—for example, as posed in policy documents and other ways of presenting the strategy to the public—and its actual intentions and substance (Mawby, 2002; Reiner, 2010).

We will find out, in the following chapters, to what extent the three theoretical perspectives used in the previous part of this book form, in empirical reality, a basis for trust-building strategies and policies in different countries. We shall need to keep our eyes open for the possibilities of complicating factors such as those described above.

7.2.4   *Political events and changing contexts*

The third process in Kingdon's model is that of political events. When discussing politics, we should make a distinction between political in the narrow sense, as related to elections, politicians, or the ideological preference and agency of governments, and in the broader sense, concerning the presence of 'the political' in all organizations. Kingdon defines the political stream as '*such things as public mood, pressure group campaigns, election results, partisan or ideological distributions in Congress, and changes of administration'* (Kingdon, 1995: 145), referring to the narrower interpretation. This narrower interpretation is also applicable to the police; for various reasons, *'the police are in politics, whether they recognize it or not'* (Bayley, 1985: 189). But in the present study, while the narrower political will certainly play an important role, there is also the importance of the broader interpretation. Next to 'political events,' we should in this case probably also include changes in the context of policing in a wider sense, to adjust this theoretical framework to the context of the present study. This context of policing would include, but not be limited to, the factors mentioned by Kingdon (1995). Meanwhile, when I use the term 'political,' I will do so in the narrower sense.

When studying the adoption of certain proposals and strategies to improve public trust, it is essential to take into account the specific circumstances: the acceptance and implementation of a new strategy do not occur in a vacuum, but are affected by various events and actors, often of a political nature, but not exclusively: they include various shifts in social and power relations. They can include, among other examples, elections bringing new politicians and parties to power, riots and breakdowns of public order, scandals, or the rise of a new generation of police chiefs. The roles of such events can be either supportive for a new strategy, or impede or obstruct it. Any reconstruction of trust-building strategies needs to take these factors into account and view them through a comparative lens: to what extent do these shed light on cross-national differences or similarities?

Something has to change in order for a police trust-building strategy to be adopted and implemented. The definition of a problem is one part; the formulation of an agenda to deal with the problem is another. However, the acceptance and internalization of the problem definition and the policy proposals often requires a change in the policing context (rapid or gradual). Either the existing establishment, political or otherwise, alters its way of thinking, or the composition of this establishment must be changed substantially in order to open a policy window for implementation of the policy proposals. In order to be followed through, trust-building strategies require adoption by substantial parts of the police leadership and government.[2] Next to events, individual policy entrepreneurs can play vital roles here—for instance, by enthusing the establishment or leading by example. Especially if these entrepreneurs are widely known and respected—for example, if they are leading police chiefs—we shall see that they occasionally strongly influence the strategies applied. Certain policy documents can also prove to be particularly relevant.

---

2.   It is worthy of note that adopting a police trust-building strategy also requires a measure of support from rank-and-file officers. This is an important difference with Kingdon's theoretical model, and one we will return to in subsequent chapters.

7.2.5   A comparative analysis of trust-building

To conclude, the present study on citizens' trust in the police and police trust-building strategies will use the categorization of problem definition, policy genera-tion, and political events as first posed by Kingdon (1995) in a pragmatic, adjusted form. The present study will take into account the invention of trust in the police; the moment at which it was first constructed as a salient issue or problem. Addi-tionally, I will aim to trace developments in the social construction of this problem through time. Moreover, I will study the approaches adopted to deal with this problem: police trust-building strategies. Finally, where possible, we will say something on the actors pushing for these policies or problem definitions.

Like the previous part of this book, the research questions that I pose are both (cross-case) internationally comparative and (within-case) longitudinal. But unlike the previous chapters, the answers to these questions are of a qualitative nature, rather than quantitative. I aim to trace citizens' trust in the police, and the institu-tional ideas and strategies on this subject, diachronically from its inception as a policy issue, through the following years and decades, up to the present. If we wish to improve our understanding of these processes, by definition we require a diachronic perspective. One may, then, wonder why it is necessary to compare these policy processes across multiple countries. After all, surely trust in the police is important in every country. But here is the thing: problem definitions, as well as appropriate solutions, are often quite specific for a certain time and place (Nelken, 2010). Terms and language differ across countries and can have unique meanings (Crawford, 2009). And even if the same words and catchphrases are used, as is often the case with cross-national models of policing such as community policing, they tend to be interpreted and applied in different ways. A similar thing holds for policies, ideas, and laws that travel from one society to another: they are subject to significant change along the way (Twining, 2004). Such processes of criminal jus-tice policy transfer and policy convergence are increasingly common—among Western societies (Jones & Newburn, 2007; Savage, 2007), or from Western to non-Western contexts (see Blaustein, 2015; Brogden, 2005; Cain, 2000; Steinberg, 2011). Policy transfer, policy convergence, and diffusion are likely to be relevant concepts when studying police trust-building strategies, but the existing literature on crimi-nal justice policy transfer has taught us that these are no simple matters of cutting and pasting from one context to another—rather, there will be different interpreta-tions and applications of what initially appeared to be a single idea.

It is essential to attempt to capture some of these different interpretations and applications in a European context. They illustrate the richness of thinking about these subjects and therefore open our minds to what is possible (Nelken, 2010). They provide us with a more nuanced, complex understanding of reality than would otherwise be the case. Additionally, an emergent theoretical frame around trust-building strategies will be stronger when multiple cases are included. Moreover, paying sufficient attention to these differences will help us to prevent ethnocentric thinking regarding trust and police–public relationships.

I will compare three northwestern European police systems: those of England & Wales, Denmark, and the Netherlands. I shall clarify my choice for these three northwestern European societies in the following section.

7.3   METHODOLOGY

7.3.1   *Case selection*

In any international comparative study, a key question is the selection of the countries that we compare. The answer depends on a mix of options and constraints provided by the research question, the methodology, theoretical considerations, preexisting knowledge, and practical concerns. In the previous part of this book, I limited my research to European countries. It would make sense, if only for reasons of consistency, to take this as a starting point for the case selection in this part of the study too.

First, we should take care not to include too many units of analysis; more cases in the analysis will render the comparison more superficial (Nelken, 2010). Since this study aims to delve into rationalities and the social construction of a problem, and traces developments, we require a comparatively in-depth analysis. Hence, a small number of cases is recommended.

There are some principles to take into account when selecting this small number of cases. Previously, I described differences between countries in the comparability of trust in the police, and noted that comparability became difficult especially toward the edges of Europe. Then, I saw that there was also considerable variation within Europe in terms of absolute levels of trust, its developments, and its determinants. This variation could not merely be attributed to particular clusters of countries—although these did play a role—but were present even between societies that were, in most respects, otherwise quite similar. This implies that the main challenge for case selection in a qualitative study of trust-building strategies will most likely not only be to find a theoretically interesting degree of variation, but also, paradoxically, to maintain some constraints on the variation so that a comparison will still make sense (Nelken, 2010; Terpstra, Van Stokkom, & Spreeuwers, 2013). This suggests that a case selection strategy should reason from a 'most similar case' perspective, to prevent any comparison of 'apples' and 'oranges.'

The consequence of the requirement to both gain sufficient variation, as well as to ensure there is not too much of it, is that I will follow a two-stage approach toward reaching focused diversity. First, this means limiting the possible cases to be studied. It is preferable to select countries that are relatively similar, having a certain degree of commonality and proximity in culture and history. As a guideline for narrowing down the pool of potential countries, it will be most informative to select cases where we expect trust-building strategies and thinking about citizens' trust in the police to have a long tradition. This implies selecting countries with a comparatively long democratic history. Countries in northwestern Europe are in that sense preferable: Southern European countries have a legacy of military dictatorships, whereas Eastern Europe has existed under totalitarian communist regimes until relatively recently. Hence, the selection of three cases from the northwestern parts of Europe should reduce comparability issues to a greater extent than if we were to pick countries from all over the continent, and these countries are also likely to yield the rich information required for a meaningful analysis.

The second stage takes place after applying these criteria of comparability and democratic history. We now need to define which countries to choose from our narrowed-down northwestern European sample. In order for this research to have potential implications and broader value for more than just the cases under study, implying a degree of analytic generalizability, we are looking for variation on theoretically relevant dimensions (Eisenhardt, 1989). One option to achieve this would be to select our cases at random from the population of northwestern European countries, in order to gain a random distribution on the dependent variable and prevent selection bias. In small-N case study research, however, this is a risky approach, due to its likelihood of yielding a skewed selection (Seawright & Gerring, 2008). A random selection is also undesirable in other ways. This being a theory-building case study rather than a theory-testing one, it is useful—that is to say, more informative—to select one's cases based on theoretically interesting values of the dependent variable (Geddes, 1990). This leads us toward a 'diverse cases' criterion as a guideline for case selection.

A challenge when attempting to select diverse cases in the present study is that little systematic knowledge exists about the dependent variable—police trust-building strategies. Therefore, we have to apply other criteria for our case selection. My selection strategy is based on what I theoretically expect, on the basis of potentially important factors or independent variables for trust-building strategies, to be diverse cases. Within previously defined boundaries—countries with a long democratic history—we are hence looking for diversity in such factors.

A solid way of ensuring such focused diversity is to select cases from different groups of countries; clusters that differ on some key characteristics. I discern three such key characteristics: (a) the type of state or society, (b) structural characteristics of the police system, and (c) levels of and developments in public trust in the police.[3] All these factors can reasonably be expected to *potentially* make a difference in police thinking about trust and in trust-building strategies that the police then opt for—to potentially help determine them. Based on these criteria, I select three

---

3.   Levels of and developments in trust can logically be expected to be the cause as well as the result of trust-building strategies and police thinking about trust; they may interact. However, as they serve at least partially as independent variables, and potentially very important ones at that, it is worth including them as criteria for case selection.

cases: England & Wales, Denmark, and the Netherlands. Throughout the rest of this section, I will elaborate on how these cases make for a diverse selection based on the three key characteristics mentioned above.

Considering societal differences, we can expect the relationship between the state, the police, and citizens in a country to be an important factor in the development of possible trust-building strategies. In this sense, it is valuable to have representatives from different clusters of countries. England & Wales represents an Anglo-Saxon state, Denmark a Nordic one, and the Netherlands a continental Western European country. But this is more than a geographic categorization. In the distinction of Esping-Andersen (1990), they each represent one of the three 'worlds of welfare capitalism,' a categorization reflecting different constellations of relationships between the state and its population. There is a liberal welfare state (England & Wales), a corporatist-statist one (the Netherlands, although it presently resembles more of a mixed model), and a social democratic welfare state (Denmark). How the type of welfare state affects and shapes police trust-building strategies is, a priori, still unclear. Given that these types of welfare states represent different types of relationships between the state and the public, however, it is more than likely that this distinction matters in some way. For instance, we can observe that the presentation and contents of recent police reforms in England & Wales (Loveday, 2013), Sweden (Wennström, 2013), and Finland (Haraholma & Houtsonen, 2013) were at least partially shaped by considerations rooted in their countries' respective welfare systems.

The structure of a police organization is a multifaceted issue, but one relevant and well-studied aspect is the degree of centralization of the police organization. While many countries have recently experienced waves of centralization (Fyfe et al., 2013; Van Sluis et al., 2013), they tend to strongly differ as to their past. An informative comparison would do well to include countries with different (historical) degrees of centralization. Centralization, too, is a multidimensional concept, and most European police systems have centralist as well as decentralist characteristics (Bayley, 1985). There are, however, certainly differences between countries— with some being more centralized than others. Historically, the police system is relatively centralized in Denmark and rather decentralized in the other two (Van Sluis et al., 2013). The Netherlands, though, has gone through strong administratively centralizing reforms since the early 1990s, turning into arguably the most centralized organization of the three at the time of writing. It is thus a case that has more or less moved from one extreme to the other, at least in terms of the administration of the police organization.

Another essential structural feature of police organizations is their accountability or control (Bayley, 1985). Who determines policing, to whom are the police accountable, and is supervision coming mainly from inside or outside? While practice turns out to be more complex than suggested by archetypes, the three countries feature profoundly different fundamental assumptions about this issue. In

England & Wales, the police are ideally accountable to local communities. There is a comparatively high degree of external supervision. In Denmark, national parliament is, as a matter of principle, the actor controlling the police (with the Minister of Justice as its representative). This more distant relationship means that there is more reliance on internal supervision. In the Netherlands, control of the police is historically relegated to the local mayors (and the prosecution service). In this respect, the Netherlands is hence more decentralized than in terms of the police administration.

In terms of structure and position of the police in society, the following things can be said about each of the three cases: England & Wales features a regional police system, with 42 different police organizations that were designed to have a relatively high degree of autonomy and independence from central steering. The notion of constabulary independence is essential here, meaning that the police are ideally independent from the state. Rather, following number seven of the so-called Peelian principles, named after the Home Secretary who famously founded the London Metropolitan Police, *'the police are the public and the public are the police.'* In the influential Peelian model, the police are supposed to serve and represent 'the community': citizens, rather than the state.

Denmark, by contrast, has had a national police organization since before World War II. The central state has a relatively strong hold on policing, as on many other fields, with the result that the police, in the eyes of the public, represent the authority of the state on the streets. Here—as, for instance, in Sweden (Terpstra & Fyfe, 2013; Wennström, 2013)—the police are part of the social-democratic welfare complex.

If England & Wales and Denmark occupy two different ends on the state-citizen continuum, and can therefore in some respects be considered polar types (Eisenhardt & Graebner, 2007), the Netherlands is considerably harder to classify—but is probably best positioned somewhere in the middle. The Dutch police system has historically been an amalgamation of German, French, and English influences and features state-centered as well as local authority-oriented elements. This provides us with considerable, if focused, variation in police systems and models within our three-country selection.

The final criterion for selecting the cases is that of different trajectories and developments of trust in the police. An advantage of selecting only northwestern European cases is that we have long-ranging data on the subject of trust in the police, so that we can discern trends. Again, we are interested in diverging trends to keep our cases diverse. Let us see how these three cases have developed in terms of trust over recent decades.

England & Wales

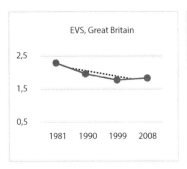 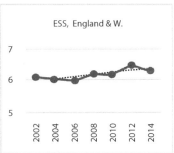

Our first country is England & Wales. Although measured in the EVS as Great Britain, and so including Scotland as well,[4] it featured a strong decrease in trust over the 1981–1999 time frame. It appears to have been a high-trust society around the first point of measurement, but it rapidly moved into what is for European standards more average territory. The EVS data suggest a small recovery between 1999 and 2008. This is confirmed by the ESS measurements, although this source indicates that the decline was reversed only after 2006, while data from the well-reputed British Crime Survey feature the 2002/2003 wave as the turning point (Myhill & Quinton, 2010). Considering the substantial fall in public confidence in the police until at least 1999, we may wonder how the English police, once considered by the English public to be the best in the world (Loader & Mulcahy, 2003), have responded to this diminishing trust, or, again in the words of Loader and Mulcahy (2003), in a broader sense their desacralization. What have been their strategies to (re)gain public trust? How have they experienced the apparent gains in confidence from the early to mid-2000s up to 2012?

Denmark

---

4.   Policing in Scotland was steered from Westminster until devolution in 1999, making a distinction between policing in Scotland and in England & Wales less conceptually useful before this time, but rather essential after this moment.

Our second case is Denmark, a country with remarkably high rates of trust in the police. Longitudinal data show neither a clear increase nor a decrease in trust over time. This is the case for the long time frame of the EVS, where we see only minute differences between measurement points, but also for the ESS; which indicates that there was a dip of trust around 2008–2010, after which trust recovered (and decreased again). This is roughly in line with the results of more in-depth Danish research (Holmberg & Balvig, 2013). This raises several interesting questions regarding Denmark, as follows. Given its consistently high levels of trust, to what extent is trust in the police a salient issue in this country? Do the police feel that they have to work with the subject, or is trust, and a good relationship between police and citizens, taken for granted? Second, considering that there was in fact a considerable drop in trust for a short period of time, how can we understand police thinking around this period? Were they aware of diminishing public confidence, did they act on that notion, and if so, how did they do it?

Netherlands
Denmark's trust in the police has remained remarkably constant at a very high level over time, while trust in the police in England & Wales has strongly declined from high to medium rates—although it has bounced back considerably in recent years. The Dutch case, however, is perhaps the most complex to understand.

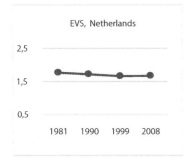
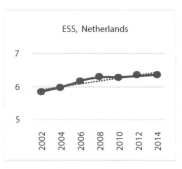

Starting as a more or less medium-level country in terms of trust in 1981, we can see a gentle downward trajectory between 1981 and 2008 in the EVS data. Looking at the more recent ESS data, however, we see, on the contrary, a robust increase in trust between 2002 and 2014, with most of the gains taking place between 2002 and 2008. Based on the near-equal levels of trust in 1999 as compared to 2008 in the EVS, one would therefore expect a powerful decrease between roughly 1999 and 2002, a time frame about which my two international data sources have no information. Dutch national survey data confirm this assessment (Centraal Bureau voor de Statistiek, 2006). This data source points at 2001–2002 as the period in which trust in the police in the Netherlands took a serious hit, after which it rapidly recovered and the previous downward slope slowly bent upwards until at least 2012 (Centraal Bureau voor de Statistiek, 2013; Schaap, 2014).

Not unlike in Denmark, therefore, this means a considerable but brief drop in trust amid otherwise rather gradual trends. Like England & Wales, though, there was an overall negative trend during the last decades of the 20th century, combined with a strong improvement in levels of trust over recent years. Therefore, developments in the Netherlands seem to share some characteristics with both Denmark and England & Wales. It is unique, however, in that trust has not been particularly high in any point of time of the measurements. What does this mean for thinking about trust and trust-building strategies?

A final remark about my case selection concerns the within-case analysis. After all, we can hardly expect the policing of a large metropolitan area to be the same as policing the countryside. This difference may also hold for trust-building strategies and thinking about police–public relationships overall. This is why I apply not merely a multiple case design—studying more than one country—but, rather, an embedded multiple case design (Yin, 2009), including multiple sites within each country. This approach has the benefit of being more sensitive to within-case variation, hopefully preventing the drawing of overly deterministic conclusions regarding trust-building strategies and also providing insight into the degree to which these strategies can differ across the country. This is important because much trust-building can be expected to be specific to local or regional contexts.

In no way do I expect to have covered all of the meaningful differences within the country with regard to trust-building activities; nor do I assume that any one of the locations I study is fully representative of the country as a whole. But what I can say is that I found certain strategies and ways of thinking about police–public relationships in a specific country, and not just in a country, but also in different contexts within that country. I will explain my within-case selection rationale further in the next section.

To summarize, my case selection has been based on two main arguments: first, to enhance comparability, narrowing down the possible pool of countries included in the study to those sharing certain characteristics; and, second, to observe different trust-building approaches in different regions and cities or towns within a country.

7.3.2   *Data collection*

In this section, I will describe my approach in each of the three countries under study. My main method for answering the previously formulated research questions is through analysis of face-to-face semi-structured interviews, in which I asked key persons questions on a wide range of trust-related issues in their country and in their work. In addition, I studied a range of policy documents in each country, consisting of vision documents, white papers and proposals, evaluations, and enquiries. When studying trust-building strategies, such written sources can be as informative as personal accounts by key persons. The documents were selected based on their relevance for answering research questions, or were mentioned as being relevant by informants.

A considerable part of the interviews was conducted on the national level, attempting to gain insight into the situation—and, in particular, the policing-related history—of the country as a whole. Within each of the three countries, however, I also followed the approach of selecting two locations to study trust-building in specific local contexts, making this an embedded multiple case study (Yin, 2009). These locations are not exactly equal in each country; differences in country characteristics, police organization, and my own ability to gain entry all shaped the within-country case selection. The purpose of including two different locations within each country was to remain sensitive about meaningful variation within the country in terms of police–public relationships in general and police trust-building strategies specifically. One particularly salient division was that between city and countryside or, more roughly, urban versus suburban and rural areas. In all three countries, I aimed to gather sufficient information on police thinking about trust and trust-building strategies in urban as well as in rural areas.

As a result, the locations I selected in each country vary strongly in terms of population density, area size, and the nature of the challenges to policing. Additionally, while I was sometimes able to study an entire police district by speaking with people in many different locations, and with very different functions and ranks, in other cases I was forced to concentrate on one part of the district, such as a certain urban area, while only getting cursory information or anecdotal evidence about the rest of the organizational unit.

In England & Wales,[5] I selected a large metropolitan police force, Case E1, and a medium-sized county force, Case E2. E1 was a heavily urbanized area with typical big-city challenges and a highly diverse population in terms of employment, income, crime rates, and ethnic background. E2 was a county force in the South of England that combined a few urban hubs with a large rural periphery. Most of my research was conducted in one of the urban centers, a medium-sized, densely populated city with relatively high unemployment, comparatively high violent crime rates, and a predominantly white, traditionally working-class population. The police unit responsible for this urban center, however, also worked in several suburban and rural areas beyond the outskirts of the city.

In Denmark, most of my research was conducted in two police districts (*politikredse*) that shared several characteristics but proved to be quite different when studied up close. Both districts featured large rural areas (like nearly all Danish police districts) and one sizeable city. Case D1 was an island force with compara-

---

5.   Note that when I speak of England & Wales, I refer to it as the police system. My empirical research was conducted in England; it is possible that findings apply to Wales only to a limited extent.

tively small distances from the urbanized center to the rural periphery. It had a high proportion of ethnic minorities concentrated in one relatively deprived neighborhood of its main city, which was the primary challenge for policing in the otherwise reasonably affluent district. Case D2 was a Jutland (mainland) force with long distances between the one urban center and the many outlying towns and villages. The composition of its main city was a bit more balanced than in D1, with various less affluent neighborhoods and ethnic minorities more equally distributed over the region's capital. Poverty, substance abuse, and unemployment were perceived to be more important problems across the district as a whole, but the main challenge in D2 was the large geographic and cultural distance between the urban and the rural areas.

The Dutch case studies included one metropolitan area, Case N1, and one partly urbanized area with a medium-sized city at its heart, Case N2. N1 took place in one of the major cities in the west of the country (in the metropolitan cluster called the *Randstad*) and included densely inhabited, heavily urbanized areas as well as suburban parts. This meant that the police faced a diverse range of challenges, juggling among other things serious organized crime tasks and youth problems, but also many requests regarding minor incivilities. N2, on the other hand, was a police district well outside of the *Randstad*. Not unlike the English case E2, it included a former working-class industrial city with low diversity and high unemployment that was in the process of attempting a shift toward a more knowledge-based economy. N2, overall a less challenging area for policing than N1, also included surrounding suburban and rural areas. The case selection is summarized in Table 7.1.

Table 7.1   Within-country cases

Country	Code	Fieldwork	Context
England	E1	October 2014	Metropolitan
England	E2	October 2014	Part urban, part rural
Denmark	D1	February 2015	Part urban, part rural
Denmark	D2	February 2015	Small part urban, large part rural
Netherlands	N1	August–October 2015	Metropolitan, part suburban
Netherlands	N2	August–September 2015	Part urban, part suburban/rural

One could argue that locations in Denmark tended to be more rural as compared to the other two countries—thus potentially challenging the comparison. However, we should bear in mind that Denmark is, with the exception of its capital Copenhagen, overall a much less urbanized society than either England or the Netherlands.[6]

6.   The population density is about 400 inhabitants per square kilometer in England and in the Netherlands, but only slightly over 130 in Denmark.

Therefore, the different research contexts accurately reflect differences between societies.

In addition to these six locations, I interviewed police chiefs and officers from various other police districts and regions—particularly in Denmark, which for me was the most unfamiliar country, but also in the other two. This was to gain insight into the broader context and further ascertain to what extent specific ideas and strategies had spread beyond the context in which I first encountered them. Where appropriate, I will refer to these other locations by another number. In Denmark, for instance, that means I will sometimes refer to interviews in location D3 or D4.

The informants were not selected at random. Rather, I enlisted the advice and help of contacts in each of the countries under study—often previous informants who could recommend others based on the criteria that were key to my research design. There were two main criteria for the selection of informants: (a) their seniority (both in age as well as in position) and (b) their type of work and sector. Also, in matters where opinions strongly differed, I attempted to select informants from multiple sides of the debate.

In the vast majority of cases, interviewees were either (retired) police officers, government officials, or scholars. Selecting on variety in seniority meant, for police officers and government officials, that I included police chiefs as well as street-level officers, and municipal street workers as well as top civil servants. This variety in seniority as well as type of work was for different reasons: first, to familiarize myself with policing in different countries; second, to gain insight into trust-building on different levels, from national policy-making and policies to how these affected the operational level;[7] and, third, to achieve maximum ecological validity —in a broad sense—ensuring that the informants represented the real variety amongst actors involved in and concerned with all aspects of trust-building activities.

All of the scholars and a substantial number of the (retired) police officers and government officials had the role of expert in their field, being key informants for understanding a specific historical event or process. Many of them had personally been involved in trust-building or in designing strategies and policies. These expert interviews made for a slightly different style and nature of interviewing, more geared toward reconstructing a process such as the invention of trust or the development of a particular trust-building strategy (Tansey, 2007).

I conducted interviews with 76 people, usually individually but occasionally in duos when explicitly preferred by my informants. Interviews ranged in duration from just under 30 minutes (an exception) to about 2 hours, but had an average length of 1–1.5 hours. Twenty-three people were interviewed in England during October 2014, 31 in Denmark during January and February 2015, and 22 in the

---

7.   While semi-structured interviews are inadequate to study the acts and practices of police officers as related to trust-building in their daily work, they can provide insights in their attitudes, knowledge, and ways of thinking on the topic—which is the aim of the present study.

Netherlands between July 2014 and October 2015, with the vast majority of the interviews taking place between June and September 2015.

The semi-structured interviews were conducted with the aid of a topic list, which consisted of three parts: a core set of topics, a country-specific module, and respondent-specific questions. Most of these topics aimed to answer the research questions; some were designed to help me understand the local or national context. There were occasional deviations from all three parts and the sequence in which the topics were addressed varied. The core topics and country-specific modules are included in Appendix E. Interviews were recorded on tape, with a few exceptions, and transcribed verbatim.[8] Written notes taken during the course of the interview exist for every interview, along with field notes of remarkable observations. Next to the interviews and the policy documents that I analyzed, additional information was gathered through regular e-mail exchanges to request clarification, often while I was in the process of analyzing the initial data.

7.3.3 *Analytical approach*

With the exception of the policy documents, all written sources were thematically analyzed through the software package Atlas.ti. Codes were categorized along different aspects of the research questions and along trust-building strategies.

First, the initial research findings were summarized in three detailed, country-specific case reports, which contained extensive description as well as a round of analysis. This was done so elaborately to allow distinct, unique patterns to emerge (Eisenhardt, 1989). Only after each of the case reports was written were chapters then distilled aiming to answer the research questions for each country. This was essential to discern and pin down the context-specific aspects of trust-building strategies, and to illuminate how different circumstances can matter in all stages under study: from problem recognition and definition to the very implementation of trust-building strategies. Throughout the following chapters, I will make use of various quotes and statements of my informants. I have selected these statements based on their relevance for answering the research questions. Subsequently, the resulting draft chapters were read and commented on by native specialists in policing and police science to check for factual errors, misinterpretations, and omissions —while I obviously take full responsibility for any remaining mistakes.

Only when we have established a solid understanding of the basics of the dynamics and processes at play, in each of the different contexts under study, can we proceed to the third stage of the analysis: a systematic comparison of the three cases to answer the research questions, in Chapter 11. I aim to discern the most important differences and similarities, and to construct a provisional framework

---

8.   Two entire interviews and several segments of others were lost due to technical failure or, in one unfortunate case, ineptitude on my part; one other interview was not recorded as it took place over the telephone. In these cases, the transcripts are not accurate word for word.

for understanding police trust-building strategies in a contemporary Western European context.

8 | ENGLAND & WALES

8.1 THE FOUNDATIONS OF POLICE WORK[1]

The first of my case studies is England & Wales. Much has been written about policing in England & Wales, and many readers will be familiar with some of the processes described in this chapter. Regardless of this fact, my specific approach will hopefully shed new light on this police system.

The origin of English police work is well known, and oft romanticized. Still, it is worth revisiting the birth of modern policing in this country for a bit before we move on to more recent history, if only because of the central role this origin still plays in the memories and identity of the English police. The importance of what Reiner (2010) calls the 'orthodox story' of police history is illustrated by one senior police officer reflecting on the origin of British policing as follows:

> Chief superintendent, E1: 'Sir Robert Peel made a number of statements when he set the Met police up. The police are the community, and the community are the police. It was the absence of crime that he saw as a good indicator of whether police service has been successful. He saw policing by consent as indicator that we are all public servants. With those principles, it's bound to be seen as a good model. [...] It is a model that the public they serve would like.'

The Metropolitan Police Act of 1829 laid the foundations of modern British police work. The late 18th and early 19th centuries had seen an ebb and flow of societal unrest, especially in London. Riots were frequent and the existing decentralized system of parish constables and watchmen proved ever less capable of keeping the peace. One possibility was to model a British police force on the existing, centralized French system. This was rejected, as local authorities feared an infringement on their autonomy, and opposition factions in parliament suspected that the ruling Tories wished to employ a state police to entrench their power (Lyman, 1964). Furthermore, framing the police reform in terms of public order was expected to infu-

---

1. The text throughout this chapter is spelled in American English, consistent with the rest of the dissertation. Quotes, however, are in British English, since most informants are British. The same holds for British phrases like 'neighbourhood policing.'

riate the public (Smith, 1985). Therefore, Home Secretary Robert Peel concentrated on arguing for a unitary London police organization as a solution for rising crime rates.

The aims of the Metropolitan Police Act became to establish a professional police service that could stem crime by means of preventive patrol, as well as to deal with riots in a less violent way than by sending in the army (Smith, 1985).[2] In order to win acceptance by the public, who—not entirely without reason—were likely to view the new police primarily as an instrument to protect the rich and powerful, the new Metropolitan Police had to be careful not to provoke the working classes. To win public trust and confidence, great emphasis was placed on police conduct and on the importance of prevention (Lyman, 1964). Additionally, a uniform was introduced to emphasize that policemen were no spies, and they were unarmed to indicate that they were no soldiers either (Emsley, 2003).

An important additional step in the formative process of the police in Britain was the 1839 and 1840 county police legislation, which aimed to spread the Metropolitan Police model across the country, but with substantial space for local interpretation (Emsley, 2003). In subsequent decades, this gave rise to a police system with high local autonomy. With the fact that the police were unarmed and therefore were perceived to require popular support to be effective, the idea gained dominance that the British police had to be locally and democratically accountable (Reiner, 2010). This, in addition to delivering public services that the public demanded, solidified the rhetorical dominance of the notion of policing by consent (Brogden, 1982).

The factors mentioned above—an emphasis on the importance of prevention, unarmed police, and a high degree of local autonomy and accountability—remained present during the subsequent century and are important for understanding thinking about trust and legitimacy in present-day England & Wales. They play a vital role in police trust-building strategies and aspirations.

8.2   POLICE WORK IN THE POSTWAR DECADES

The notion of trust has been present in British policing for a long time. Ideas around confidence, or at least public acceptance, were part of the debate surrounding the 1829 Metropolitan Police Act. More than a century later, Banton wrote that *'the public in Britain are able to trust the police because the actions of individual officers follow a common pattern so that the subject knows what to expect'* (Banton, 1964: 167). His contribution emphasizes an overall harmonious relationship between the police and the public in Great Britain—as opposed to signs of police brutality and ethnic tensions in the US. In the 1960s, there was hence no awareness of serious

---

2.   Historians do not fully agree on the relative weight of each of these two goals, but they do agree that both appeared to have played a role (Reiner, 2010).

problems with trust in the police—quite the contrary; the British police prided itself on being trusted. The assertion of Banton (1964) was that the police in the Great Britain of the 1950s and 1960s were often working in homogenous communities with shared values. The policeman, being part of this stable social order, only had to *'oil the machinery'* (McLaughlin, 2007: 34). This was also how a retired chief constable experienced his first years in the police:

> DS. *'Can you recall when the concept of trust or confidence was first used? Was it used already when you joined [the police]?'*
>
> Retired chief constable 1: *'No. When I joined in 1958 there was complete, almost blind acceptance, of the police. Which was a paradox, because the standards in some forces... in some forces, trust was clearly being abused. Yet the generality of views was that the police was one of the rocks on which society was built.'*

A curious side effect of this status meant that the police were being seen as embodiments of a near-sacred institution, not as individual people with lives and families (Banton, 1964; Cain, 1973). For the most part, the role of the police in the apparent harmony in society was celebrated. However, *'nuances and ambivalence'* (Brogden, 1982: 198) in the relationship between the police and the public were historically present, albeit hard to measure. During the 1950s and certainly the 1960s, underlying tensions and societal developments started to nibble away at the edges of the public image of the police. Previously present class-related fault lines (Brogden, 1982) were strengthened and supplemented by rising crime rates, waves of moral panic, increasing ethnic diversity, corruption scandals, and the presence of youth countercultures since the 1960s. All of these were factors that would, over time, prove increasingly serious issues for policing (Loader & Mulcahy, 2003; McLaughlin, 2007; Reiner, 2010). An additional complicating factor, although initially largely disconnected from police work in England & Wales, was the start of the Troubles in Northern Ireland during the late 1960s, with the Royal Ulster Constabulary taking a militarized, repressive role (Weitzer, 1985). At the time, the police did not yet experience these processes as a fundamental challenge to their function and societal role.

> Retired chief constable 1: *'[T]he question 'why' arose at the end of the 1960s. 'I know my rights, why are you saying this? I don't agree with you.' It made life actually quite difficult. So you had to justify your actions. Even while you're backed up by law, you didn't want to throw legal quotations at them. You'd have to win them over to a large extent by personality and attitude. You had to win their respect. [...] [Y]ou'd have to demonstrate the sense of what you were doing. [...] If you accept, as I do, that society is constantly changing, and if you accept the British police model that the police must be in tune with society, then you have to change as well.'*

8.3   THE 1980S: THE BRIXTON RIOTS, THE SCARMAN REPORT, AND THE
           INVENTION OF TRUST

Despite increasing challenges during the 1960s, the police had no reason to doubt
their legitimacy in the eyes of the public. However, a first step in the transition
from the 'sacred' to the 'profane' had been taken (Loader & Mulcahy, 2003). Further developments took place during the 1970s, including increasing occurrences of
deaths in custody, a series of corruption scandals, and strengthening ties between
the Police Federation and the Conservative Party (Reiner, 2010). These factors set
the stage for arguably the most tumultuous years for police-citizen relationships
since the 19th century: the 1980s.

    In April 1981, a multiple-day confrontation took place between the police and
mostly black youth in Brixton, London. Large numbers of buildings and cars were
torched, many members of the public and the police were hurt, and dozens of rioters arrested. The impact of the Brixton riots was not as much material, however,
but largely psychological. A wave of inner-city riots followed across England over
the course of the year, signifying a problem that was wider than just the area of
Brixton. It was not the first period of unrest, nor would it be the last, but what
made it unique is the inquiry that followed, by the respected Lord Scarman. In the
Scarman report, published in November of the same year, the Brixton riots were
explained by multiple factors, including unemployment and poverty in the local
communities involved. However, the most immediate source of the riots was oper-
ation Swamp 81, a heavy-handed stop-and-search project by the Metropolitan
Police to deal with street crimes (Scarman, 1982). Police actions sparked serious
indignation by the mostly ethnic minority inhabitants of the area, who felt that
they were being unjustly targeted. But, according to Scarman, there was more at
stake than simply a police tactic. In fact, he argued that he had

> '*no doubt that a significant cause of the hostility of young blacks towards the police was loss of confidence
> by significant sections, though it should not be assumed by all, of the Lambeth[3] public in the police. It is
> clear that the two Members of Parliament whose constituencies cover the area of the disorders were fully
> aware of the crisis of confidence.*' (Scarman, 1982: 79)

It is remarkable that Lord Scarman not only wrote of a *loss of confidence* in the
police amongst the public, but even summarized the situation as a full-blown *crisis
of confidence*. This sort of phrasing in the Scarman report probably helped create an
awareness within the police that they had, in fact, an unprecedented problem with
trust and confidence of a significant minority of the population. Consent proved to
be fragile (Brogden, 1982). The impact of the Brixton riots and the Scarman report
on the police in England & Wales should hence not be underestimated. Several of

---

3.   The London borough that includes Brixton.

my more senior informants, for instance, referred to this moment as a watershed in their thinking. One example:

> DS: 'In your career, was confidence an issue at the very beginning?'
>
> Retired chief constable 2: 'Most definitely. Within my first year, we had the Brixton riots and then the Scarman report, which was about those things. I'm not sure Scarman used quite those terms, but he used a set of terms that amounted to that.'

If we attempt to define the invention of trust and confidence in the police as a concept, it is therefore probably the Scarman report that has the most valid claims to its inception.

In a related development, it was shortly afterwards that Home Secretary Leon Brittan introduced the concept of confidence to the Home Office (Faulkner, 2014: 90). A later European Commissioner and life peer, Brittan lasted only for a little over two years as a Home Secretary in the second Thatcher administration, but was in office during a pivotal period in time: from June 1983 until September 1985. His tenure was to have a lasting impact. In the experience of a former civil servant:

> Retired senior civil servant, Home Office: 'It was the first time that I became conscious of it as a subject that was going to be talked about for itself. [...] To take public confidence as a subject you look at first, and then talk about how you can improve public confidence [...]. That was the first time. It was linked with fear of crime as being another subject which had to be addressed in its own right, separately from improvements in policing and security. Public reassurance became an issue.'

But why did Home Secretary Brittan introduce this concept? Based on the previous considerations, we may expect he was driven by notions from the Scarman report. However, in the words of this former Home Office civil servant, there were also more personal reasons.

> Retired senior civil servant, Home Office: 'Leon Brittan's position was complicated because he was following Willie Whitelaw, who was the most powerful person after the Prime Minister. [...] [Whitelaw] didn't have to cultivate political support, and the Prime Minister left him alone. He didn't have anyone to fear. Leon Brittan was a much less established character. He'd been Chief Secretary to the Treasury, but he hadn't been a departmental cabinet minister. He didn't have a very strong position in the Conservative Party. He was Jewish and was encountering some anti-Semitic feelings.'
>
> DS: 'Within the party?'
>
> Retired senior civil servant, Home Office: 'Yes. So his position was more precarious and he had to work hard politically to maintain his credibility and position in the party. That was the context, I think, in which he thought public confidence, which in some ways meant confidence in him, was a subject he wanted to build up.'

Next to nationwide developments and realizations that there was tension between the police and at least certain segments of society, there appears to have been a distinct political dimension to the invention of trust and confidence. Given the somewhat lukewarm initial reception of the Scarman report by the first Thatcher administration (Benyon, 1984), it may be that the policy window for putting trust on the political agenda only opened with the appointment of Brittan as Home Secretary. It could have created the sort of open situation that is required for new ideas to make it to the agenda (Kingdon, 1995).

To what extent trust and confidence actually became a top policy priority during this period remains unclear, but there was certainly a break with the past. The consequences of the invention of trust were almost immediate. One example is that the second wave of the British Crime Survey, from 1984, included a question on public attitudes toward the police for the first time (the first wave was conducted in 1982 and nearly exclusively featured questions about victimization). It would soon be followed by other projects on the topic, such as the left realist approach of the Islington Crime Surveys. Trust and confidence had become issues with which police, scientists, and politicians were involved.

8.4   THE 1980S: INITIAL TRUST-BUILDING STRATEGIES AND THE MINERS' STRIKE

The Scarman report simultaneously defined a problem and proposed a range of solutions. Recommendations by Lord Scarman to improve the relationship between police and citizens included an independent complaints procedure and citizen consultative boards to enhance police accountability, and implementation of community policing strategies to improve proximity to the public (Scarman, 1982).

The first two of Lord Scarman's recommendations were partially followed through with the Police and Criminal Evidence Act 1984, or PACE (Savage, 2007). It paved the way for the Independent Police Complaints Commission (IPCC), thought to be a fair way of investigating supposed police wrongdoings. PACE also meant the beginning of police–public consultation platforms, which were intended to improve citizen oversight of policing, but also to ensure local support for locally specified and designed policing strategies:

> *Retired chief constable 1: '[Collaboration with citizens] was formalized following the Brixton riots and the Scarman report. He advocated citizen cooperation through consultative committees. In fact he copied what the West Midlands Police were doing [...]. Scarman liked it and it was rolled out nationally. That was a formalized way of sharing information and problem-solving. The model has got to be a good one. There has to be a link between the street and the people who make the policies.'*

In addition to the formal changes, the police themselves were also expected to initiate experiments with proximity policing ideas, following the Scarman report. In response to the perception that the police had drifted too far away from the communities that they served, there were efforts to restore this connection. Brogden (1982: 206) labeled these efforts as part of the construction and reconstruction of public consent. This was echoed by a former civil servant from the Home Office, who framed community policing experiments as part of a broader attempt to regain public trust and help solve social problems, acknowledging a crucial role for the Scarman report:

> *Retired senior civil servant, Home Office: 'The pressure on the police [during the 1980s] was towards improving public confidence and not to see their job in the narrow role of mopping up villains. So they were concerned with preventing crime as much as with detecting and prosecuting. And once they got into crime prevention and the sort of discussions we were having about the design of housing estates, the maintenance of property, the security arrangements, they started to move more into social questions. And that was being led from the Home Office as a deliberate attempt to civilise policing, I suppose. [...]*
> *The crime prevention division was set up within the Home Office. There was some discussion about where it should be. And it was placed in the police department as a demonstration that this was something that the police should be interested in doing and do something about.*
> *[...] The police themselves were quite happy to develop these ideas of neighbourhood or community policing and so they became more of a social service—as probation moved the other way.[4] [...] There was, I think, a generation of both senior and junior officers who wanted to do that. And when they became involved in things like race riots in Brixton and so on, they realized there was something going on in places like that. The Scarman report was crucial in part of that story.'*

One retired chief constable reflected on this period, during which he was participating in designing new schemes and projects:

> *Retired chief constable 2: 'In terms of public confidence, the [scheme we were working with] most definitely was framed around delivering a better service to the public. It was a fundamentally community policing-based approach, about dealing with problems and tactical issues of concern to the public, more than about crime figures. So that was 1981, 1982. There were a number of other forces in the U.K. attempting something similar.'*

We can conclude, therefore, that there appeared to be a cautious advent of initiatives designed to improve public trust during the first half of the 1980s. Most of these initiatives paid at least lip service to community policing, a concept that had recently emerged in the U.S. and was rewritten for the British context by early adopters such as the chief constable of Devon and Cornwall, John Alderson (Alderson, 1979).

---

4.   Probation in England & Wales developed from a social service into an enforcement or correctional agency, a gradual process that had commenced during the late 1960s but gathered considerable traction during the Thatcher administrations (Lacey, 2014).

This period of experimentation with trust-building, however, encountered growing challenges in the form of growing societal unrest, leading to protests, riots, and strikes. Becoming increasingly Janus-faced in their approach, the police simultaneously experimented with community policing and professionalized their riot control methods to the point of being more militaristic than at any point in recent history (Waddington, 1992). This strongly contrasted with the attempts to 'civilize policing' as described by the retired civil servant quoted above.

The most serious, almost lethal setback to trust-building attempts came in the form of the 1984-1985 miners' strike. The second Thatcher administration wished to scale down the unprofitable national coal industry, proposing the closure of a large number of coal pits. A large-scale strike ensued, with participants picketing to prevent anyone from working in the mines. Prime Minister Thatcher opted to use criminal law measures to deal with the picketers. As a consequence, large numbers of police officers, often from forces outside the mining areas, were deployed to harshly crack down on the strikers. This placed the police directly at odds with entire communities:

> *Retired senior civil servant, Home Office: 'The Prime Minister took this very hard-line position of seeing the miners as traitors to the state. And that produced confrontations with the police. [...] the police were divided in some ways in how they dealt with [the strike]. It was a situation they weren't used to. Police officers were moved to the mining areas from other parts of the country, where they didn't know anything about the social dynamics of a mining community. They were, I think, much more ready to deal with the situation via arrest or prosecution and firm action than the local police who knew the mining communities. Some of them came from it. They were much more willing to talk and contain and deal with things quietly than the police who came in.'*

The fact that many of the police officers having to deal with the picketers came from outside the region meant that the potential for conflict was much greater. Subsequently, these conflicts clearly showed the police as the opponent of local communities, and created the image that the police were tools of the government who could not be trusted—neither by the mining communities themselves (Green, 1990) nor by the public at large (Loader & Mulcahy, 2003). In public image terms, the police *'lost whilst appearing to win'* (Mawby, 2002: 23): they suppressed the strike, but only with serious consequences for their image and hence, presumably, public trust in the police. To make matters worse, the massive police deployment also meant that forces outside the mining areas were depleted. This went at the expense of community policing experiments designed to improve relationships between the police and the public, as illustrated by one retired chief constable:

> *Retired chief constable 2: '[The community policing reforms] hadn't lasted. [The miners' strike meant] a complete diversion of many a reform process. It was 18 months of chaos. Most police officers were work-*

ing 12 hours a day just to keep officers on the streets, because we had sent off so many north to Notting-
hamshire and such.'

While the strikes ended in 1985 and the police did initiate new experiments with trust-building, notably community policing, the second half of the 1980s was again plagued with scandal, this time related to miscarriages of justice: the Guildford Four, the Maguire Seven, and the Birmingham Six all referred to suspects of different pub bombings presumably committed by the IRA, while the Tottenham Three concerned suspects of the murder of constable Keith Blakelock during the Broadwater Farm riots of 1985. In all of these cases, initial verdicts were eventually overturned because of flaws in or manipulations of the original investigations. To what extent these events actually hurt trust in the police is unclear, but media attention placed the police in an increasingly unfavorable light (Mawby, 2002; Reiner, 2010). It showed that trust could no longer be taken for granted (Johnston, 1992).

8.5   THE 1990S: FIGHTING CRIME AND PERFORMANCE TARGETS

The challenges were about to become greater. During the 1980s, the police had remained remarkably untouched by Thatcher's drive toward a more businesslike public sector, arguably because the government required police loyalty during the civil and industrial unrest of that decade. With crime rates continuing to rise, however, this changed in the early 1990s—with great consequences for trust-building. Police performance became an issue on the political agenda of the Major government (Loveday, 2000). The central notion here was that police should redirect their effort to their 'main job' of catching criminals, rather than being preoccupied with other functions (Home Office, 1993).

The 1994 Police and Magistrates' Court Act can be seen as the concretization of the effort to systematically decrease crime rates by making the police more businesslike, more efficient, and more accountable, introducing 'value for money' as a central guideline. The most important step in this process was forcing local police services to set objectives and targets that were based both on local concerns and Home Office instructions (Loveday, 1997). With this act, a new trust-building strategy was effectively signed into law: what I call instrumentalism. The assumption here was that citizens in fact wanted the police to fight crime, rather than anything else (Home Office, 1993).

After the 1997 elections, the New Labour government under Blair built on this assertion and greatly expanded the target framework. This framework included targets for arrest rates (should increase) and for crime levels in different categories (should decrease), among other things. Another element of this system was a high degree of central control, something very uncharacteristic of the formerly decentralized English policing model. Not reaching Home Office targets could have consequences for one's position or job (Loveday, 2006). The rationale behind this was clear. In the words of one former chief constable:

> *Retired chief constable 2: 'We already had objectives, and under Labour they became increasingly sophis-*
> *ticated. [...] Labour's approach in that era was that more transparency of what police performance was,*
> *and better ways of demonstrating police performance, would lead to increased public confidence.'*

The performance framework was hence part of a trust-building strategy. In the following years, the performance culture rapidly spread throughout the organization. Although initially praised for supposedly causing a decline in crime rates, it proved to be at best a rather double-edged sword.

First, increasing pressure to reach targets in certain categories of crime was bound to lead to ever more creative ways of recording (or, in many cases, rather nonrecording) of crime. Crime rates would, as an unintended consequence of performance culture, be manipulated in order to achieve the target (Eterno & Silverman, 2012; HMIC, 2014). Except for simply opting not to record a crime—for example, by choosing not to believe a victim's story—other ways for police officers to deal with performance pressure include arresting 'usual suspects' or 'low-hanging fruit,' or to move around with labels so that the crime falls into a less serious category:

> *Director, independent policing think tank: 'Improving arrest rates consisted of arresting kids and people*
> *for possessing cannabis. The police would do all sort of things to skew police targets.'*

> *HMIC inspector 2: 'Vulnerable victims, rape in particular—there are lots of issues with recording rape.*
> *There are issues about performance culture, where the police service is more concerned about showing*
> *good figures, low crime, and high detections. If that means that you don't record a crime and you don't*
> *believe the victim, it won't get into the system.'*

A second problem with performance indicators is that they give a powerful message to the police that these things are all that matter. Tasks that are not included in the performance regime are likely to be neglected. Several of my informants summarized this problem with the line 'what gets measured, gets done'—implying that everything else does not, including those things that simply cannot be measured:

> *Chief superintendent, E1: 'I have a lot of pressure on me from the center on delivering performance. The*
> *confidence and trust question would not be so accountable as the others. The senior people put less*
> *emphasis on it. If I'm going to get questioned in front of senior officers, my focus is to answer their main*
> *questions, which are not about confidence and engagement.'*

Inspector, E2: 'The problem when you focus on targets is that you focus on numbers and manipulating the numbers, and not on the individual, the member of the public, and the crime.'

8.6   ANOTHER VIEW OF THE 1990S: 'INSTITUTIONAL RACISM'

While important, the increasing emphasis on fighting crime and performance management is only one part of the story of trust-building during the 1990s. Continuing the trend of the 1980s, tensions between the police and sections of the population remained high. The Stephen Lawrence murder became a symbol for everything that was wrong in the relationship between the police and ethnic minorities. In April 1993, Stephen Lawrence, a black teenager, was stabbed to death by five white men on the streets of London while he was waiting for a bus. Despite strong indications that the murder was racially motivated and completely unprovoked, detectives from the Metropolitan Police let racial stereotypes and prejudice determine their investigation. The investigation was a spectacular failure and the suspects were to walk free for decades to come.

Years after the murder, a combination of pressure from the victim's family and the media led the new Labour administration to establish an inquiry. The Macpherson inquiry and subsequent 1999 report, which famously labeled the Metropolitan Police as 'institutionally racist,' served as a painful suggestion that nothing much seemed to have changed in the relationship between the police and ethnic minorities since the Brixton riots. Macpherson concluded that

> *'there is a striking and inescapable need to demonstrate fairness, not just by Police Services, but across the criminal justice system as a whole, in order to generate trust and confidence within minority ethnic communities, who undoubtedly perceive themselves to be discriminated against by 'the system.' Just as justice needs to be 'seen to be done' so fairness must be 'seen to be demonstrated' in order to generate trust.' (Macpherson, 1999: 46.30)*

The Macpherson report bore striking similarities to the Scarman report, but had a stronger emphasis on notions of fairness and other terms out of the procedural justice book, while Scarman featured stronger proximity policing-oriented notions.

It is hard to estimate the impact of the Macpherson report. Clearly, it placed the notion of confidence prominently on the agenda once again, although it concentrated primarily on the Metropolitan Police. Additionally, a range of race-related measures was passed to promote equality and counter discrimination by the police —and other government agencies. Cultural diversity awareness training, revision of recruitment, and consultation with ethnic minority groups were examples of measures passed to improve treatment of ethnic minorities (McLaughlin, 2007; Sharp & Atherton, 2007). Most of these measures can be interpreted as attempts to improve procedural justice.

Not surprisingly, being labeled 'institutionally racist' was not exactly to the delight of the police, even though Macpherson (1999) was careful to emphasize that he considered it to be a problem at the organizational level and that many officers were in fact not racist at all. This grave label could have caused a backlash within the organization, or at least a resistance against new policies. While some sources indicate that the report has lead to many changes in the way in which the police deal with ethnic minorities (House of Commons Home Affairs Committee, 2009), some of my informants noted that in their opinion many of the post-Macpherson changes were cosmetic or mechanical in nature, rather than reflecting a true difference in practice and attitude. Hence, there are indications that the Macpherson inquiry was more successful in (re)defining the problem of police–ethnic minority relationships than in providing solutions. Beyond this, it is hard to say what the effects of the MacPherson report have been in terms of procedural justice and trust-building.

8.7   The 2000s: PCSOs, reassurance policing, and neighbourhood policing

At the turn of the millennium, the Labour government began to realize that a focus on crime meant that the police were steadily drifting away from other functions. This meant an estrangement not only from ethnic minority groups, but from the majority of the population. Responses to counteract this undesirable effect rapidly gathered steam. Inspiration was drawn from the Netherlands, where forms of auxiliary police staff were experimented with during the 1990s. Such auxiliary police could possibly also increase police visibility and public feelings of safety in England & Wales (Savage, 2007: 68-69). The first step toward implementation was made with the White Paper *Policing a new century: A blueprint for reform* (Home Office, 2001). To compensate for the pull toward measurable crime tasks, the paper introduced a new type of police staff: the Police Community Support Officer (PCSO). 'Middle England' had been deprived of a visible police service and had the feeling that nothing was being done about community concerns (McLaughlin, 2007). Quoting one of my informants, this had led to '*if not a diminished trust, certainly an increased disappointment*' (interview with retired chief constable 1). The introduction of PCSOs, non-warrant-carrying police personnel who specialize in low-level disorder and visibility, meant an attempt to deal with these concerns and restore lost confidence. PCSOs were perceived to be particularly useful in restoring ties with ethnic minority communities, a policy goal that had been high on the agenda since the Macpherson report. Members of these communities were reluctant to join the police as constables, but might be tempted to join as PCSOs instead, thus making the police more representative of the context in which they worked (Johnston, 2005; McLaughlin, 2007). Therefore, the introduction of the PCSO was a (partial) remedy for two major problems of the police as related to confidence and trust: performance management removing police from visibility in the community, and strong mistrust of ethnic minorities. In summary,

> 'PCSOs are tasked to undertake visible street patrol and to contribute to the reduction of low level crime and disorder, thus enhancing levels of public reassurance. In London, the PCSO initiative was also seen as an opportunity to diversify the recruitment profile of theMPS [Metropolitan Police Service], thereby making it more representative of the communities it polices.' (Johnston, 2005: 243)

During my interviews, it became apparent that there were divergent views on PCSOs and their introduction as a trust-building strategy. Some informants were highly enthusiastic: PCSOs improve police visibility and proximity to the public. Additionally, they can gain access and win public trust in situations where regular police officers are more likely to elicit antagonistic responses, due to their enforcement powers:

> Inspector, E1: 'The nice thing about [having PCSOs] is that they are an unobstructed police resource. They can't arrest, they can't be deployed in public order somewhere, they can't be tied up investigating crime. So they spend a huge proportion for their time being visible on the street. And when they ask me what to do, I often tell them that: be visible.'

> PCSO 1, E2: 'With my role, we have the luxury of time. We can sit in the play park and talk to the kids, and the parents may come out and say to the children not to talk to us. We then tell the parents we're just checking, making sure they're okay, talking about school and what they did today. And some parents will realize that you're okay, that you're not a threat to them. And you get the trust of a couple of them, and the others will see the relationship building, and they will want to see what's going on.'

Other informants, however, viewed PCSOs in a less positive light, emphasizing that they only exist because the police had neglected visibility in the first place, or that they are not up to par with regular police constables:

> Chief superintendent, E1: 'In my personal opinion, they should not have introduced the PCSOs at the time. They should have made the police do the job they were paid to do and stick to that: visibility.'

> Retired assistant chief constable, E2: 'The public know the difference between police and PCSO. They know they're not getting the same service. The person they're talking to doesn't have the same training, capability and capacity to deliver the same thing as police. In my view, PCSOs were a mistake.'

PCSOs can be considered as one way of returning to a more community or proximity-oriented approach. A broader, more cohesive ideological return to proximity policing principles was soon to follow.

This development commenced in the early 2000s, when the term 'reassurance gap' became popular to characterize the relationship between the police and the public. This referred to the discrepancy between decreasing crime rates on the one hand and stagnant or even worsening levels of fear of crime and confidence in the police on the other (Fielding & Innes, 2006). This discrepancy was puzzling, and perceived to be increasingly problematic. The very existence of the reassurance gap meant that the assertion that demonstrating police effectiveness to the public would increase trust and confidence had to be rejected: instrumental approaches had not had the desired effect.

In 2003, the National Restoring Reassurance Programme was introduced: a large-scale experiment that aimed *'to address the gap between broadly improving indi-cators of risk of criminal victimization and declining indicators of public confidence'* (Fielding & Innes, 2006: 130). Reassurance policing was essentially drawn from older conceptions of community policing, with the addition of the Signal Crimes perspective developed by Innes (2004)—which, in turn, was a highly sophisticated adaptation of the *broken windows* hypothesis as first posed by Wilson and Kelling (1982). This fusion of ideas made reassurance policing a trust-building strategy that placed much emphasis on proximity and visibility, but also on dealing with those specific incidents and problems that have the largest impact on people's sense of safety. Ideally, this was done in cooperation with citizens and with other members of the 'extended police family.' This extended family included, but was not limited to, the recently introduced PCSOs and community wardens—the latter having sim-ilar tasks to PCSOs, but in the employment of local councils rather than the police.

The Restoring Reassurance Programme was well received overall and, accord-ing to participants, showed potential for improving confidence in the police (Millie & Herrington, 2004). Before long, the term 'reassurance policing' was replaced with 'neighbourhood policing' (Home Office, 2004; Innes, 2005). With the help of considerable funding, neighbourhood policing was rolled out across the country:

Chief superintendent, E1: 'The big change in 2004 is that every ward got this [neighbourhood policing] service, even the ones that had no crime. And they loved that, because in wards where they had no crime they wanted to see the police too. But from a busy borough command perspective, it seems like a waste of resources. It's good, but I need to use these people where it's really bad. The boss at the time kept us to this model and that was very good.'

Superintendent, E2: 'what I think has made a huge difference is neighbourhood policing. It really was nothing new, but it needed reinventing because we swung away from that, being reactive. The whole idea is ring fencing local officers, who aren't changed around all the time, who will stick to a very small area, and stay there for a while to build up confidence and trust, and engage with their community and really understand the community. [...] What I think we've done well in [E2] is problem-solving. Rather than reacting to crime, we try to work out what the priorities are and address the root causes for a proactive solution. I think the neighbourhood teams in [E2] are good, very active. [...] People love to see them.'
DS: 'They love to see them?'
Superintendent, E2: [laughs] 'Give or take. The majority does.'

Until today, neighbourhood policing is considered to be a successful trust-building strategy, even if it occasionally went, as Chief superintendent, E1 suggests, at the expense of police effectiveness. Neighbourhood policing was credited with the first increase in public confidence in England & Wales since the start of measurements:

> HMIC inspector 1: 'There's quite strong evidence that the increase [in confidence] in the 2000s was due to the introduction of neighbourhood policing. So we assume that increased visibility, public reassurance, and problem-solving helped contribute.'

> Retired chief constable 2: 'We saw a significant rise in confidence since the introduction of neighbourhood policing. Given the research we had already done, it was reasonable to expect that causation.'

It is important to note, however, that the implementation of neighbourhood policing initially did not mean the end of performance targets. Quite the contrary: the performance framework was extended with several indicators on public satisfaction and confidence. In the final years of the Labour administration, from 2008 until 2010, a radical overhaul of the target framework was conducted, leaving the police with only a single target: public confidence. Despite the clear change in government strategy, the effect of this reform appeared not to be immediate. My informants were very clear as to why this was the case:

> Retired chief constable 1: 'Police managers had become so used to performance targets that they left them in place, having added some targets of their own. It's a simple dynamic, isn't it? If you are promoted because you are very good at hitting targets, very quickly, like a Pavlovian dog, you react and you don't want to operate where targets don't exist [...]. The point I make is quite an important one: in the end, so ingrained had the culture become, that some people in the organization can't operate without them.'

To conclude, even though central government had abolished all targets, local police organizations largely left them in place or even extended the framework. No longer did performance management function as a supposed trust-building strategy—the idea that it improved trust had long since been discredited. It had merely become a standard way for police forces to operate; one that tended to impede the neighbourhood policing reforms.

8.8   FROM 2010 ONWARD: CONSERVATIVE-LED GOVERNMENTS

Thinking about trust would take a strong turn after the election of the coalition government of Conservatives and Liberal Democrats under Cameron in 2010. In only a few years, the coalition government *'transformed policing beyond recognition'* (interview with police researcher 2); but how and why it transformed is harder to pin down.

The foundation of the coalition government's trust-building strategies (and arguably even more under the second, Conservative Cameron administration) seemed to be that the police can actually not be trusted as they are and need to change in order to deserve trust. This was a radical departure from previous governments, both Conservative and Labour ones. But in what sense the police should change is much less clear. We shall see that different strands were being followed at the same time by different actors.

One of the key agencies in this respect is the policing inspectorate, HMIC. Its function was described as follows:

> *'Her Majesty's Inspectorate of Constabulary (HMIC) will become a stronger advocate in the public interest, independent from the Government and the police service. We will ensure that HMIC has the powers to be able to undertake this critical role and strengthen the public's trust and confidence by providing them with objective and robust information on forces.' (Home Office, 2010: 17)*

While the Home Office emphasizes that HMIC should work to strengthen public trust and confidence in the police, its near-constant flow of highly critical reviews and reports is more likely to be intended to achieve the opposite. This is no coincidence: despite its formal independence, HMIC is funded by the Home Office—and has received considerable additional funding over recent years. This was also noted by several of my informants, who saw the approach of HMIC as part of the wider government policies regarding the police. One HMIC inspector acknowledged that the police faced unprecedented pressures:

> *HMIC inspector 2: 'There are some interesting dynamics in policing at the moment. You may be aware of the News International case, the phone hacking. Because the police have been arresting journalists and prosecuting journalists, the media have turned against the police. This government is trying to reform the police service, so their agenda seems to be quite tough on policing. The IPCC [Independent Police Complaints Commission] is desperately trying to prove they're independent and worthwhile, so they're quite tough on the police as well. So there's lots of things going on.'*

This led one journalist to sum up the relationship between the Cameron government and police as *'five years of barely concealed running warfare'* (Dodd, 2015). Although perhaps a slight exaggeration, this journalist's assessment does chime with broader sentiments:

> *Retired chief constable 2: 'Government has tried to make the problem the police, rather than the public. They've put the focus on the police and spent basically the last four years slagging the police off and telling them they're useless, and there's certainly been enough stuff tumbling out the news to make that a realistic position.'*

What was the cause of this animosity, most prominently by Home Secretary Theresa May, toward the police? Most of my informants pointed out that the police had perhaps become a little spoiled during the New Labour era, receiving unprecedented levels of funding. Most likely, the causes for the worsened relationship between government and police are a combination of Conservative antipathy toward the Labour inheritance, a perceived need to substantially cut expenses, and a desire to restore some form of oversight of the police—since they were perceived to have become too arrogant and independent. The tension between police and government is therefore a result of different political ideas and processes. There was also a more positive, ideological wish to democratize policing and give the public more of a say, a drive that was even stronger amongst Liberal Democrats (Reiner, 2013).

This intense scrutiny and drive for reform made for a rather harsh climate for the police, or what some of my informants labeled a 'siege mentality' within the police organization. Thinking about trust in the post-2010 era probably cannot be disconnected from this difficult relationship between the police and government. Approaches that could be considered trust-building strategies also serve political goals, such as weakening police autonomy. It is hard to determine which of these purposes is, in fact, most important.

One example that illustrates this ambivalence is the changed role of HMIC; yet another is the recent institution of police and crime commissioners (PCCs), first elected in 2012 but based on one of the ideas formulated (and ultimately rejected) in a 2003 vision document (Loveday & Reid, 2003). These democratically elected officials distribute the police budget, hold the chief constable of their region to account, and determine police priorities. One of the goals of having Police and Crime Commissioners is explicitly to increase public confidence in the police. PCCs are therefore by design a trust-building strategy by means of democratizing policing (or strengthening the traditional ideal of policing by consent). In the words of the coalition government:

> 'We will empower the public: introducing directly elected Police and Crime Commissioners who will give the public a voice and strengthen the bond between the public and the police through greater accountability and transparency so that people have more confidence in the police to fight crime and ASB [antisocial behavior].' (Home Office, 2010: 8)

The institution of Police and Crime Commissioners was to give the public more influence on policing, and this increased influence was expected to generate confidence. An additional reason why having elected officials in control of the police would improve trust was summarized by a police researcher with the statement 'Politicians understand confidence and public opinion better than the police' (interview with police researcher 2).

Politicians are, following this logic, expected to be better at gaining public trust. After all, they are forced to care about public confidence in order to be reelected. But PCCs are not only a trust-building strategy, since a clear effect of their introduction was that chief constables lost a degree of power (Davies & Johnson, 2016). Democratizing policing also meant that police autonomy was diminished, thus achieving several goals at once. Paradoxically, the influence of PCCs is considerable and strictly limited at the same time—depending on the way one looks at it. Severe budget cuts imposed by the government on the police limit the space for PCCs to pursue their own policies considerably. One PCC said of these pressures:

> *Police and crime commissioner, E2: 'I think it's not so much up to the local, especially now, since local spending has diminished so much over the last 20 years, and local control, despite the localism agenda of this government, is neutered by central government influences and demands.'*
> *[...]*
> *DS: 'You are part of that localism agenda.'*
> *Police and Crime Commissioner, E2: 'Absolutely, in theory. But I'm finding it in practice not quite as free as it would say on the tin, if you like.'*

Hence, PCCs, while presented as part of a democratizing trust-building strategy, are perhaps better understood as new actors in a political struggle between government and police, where the highest priority is to decrease police autonomy. Additionally, turnout for the first PCC elections was so low that their connection with the public remains rather doubtful.

A final noteworthy development during the coalition years is the recurrence of procedural justice ideas to the policy agenda. In what appears to be another episode in the story of tense relationship between police and ethnic minorities, the 2011 London riots once again placed treatment of minorities in the spotlight. Soon after, the Home Secretary, Theresa May, started challenging the police on their overuse of the stop-and-search measure concerning minorities, which was seen as one of the causes of the unrest (Lewis et al., 2011; Newburn et al., 2016). Certainly it contributes to mistrust of the police, albeit mostly among the part of the population that is most subject to it (HMIC, 2013):

> *Retired senior civil servant, Home Office: 'There's a long story here of police culture, of canteen culture, and of race. This goes back over 30 years. It's still a story; the Home Secretary has picked up on this in a courageous way: to try and confront the police on stop and search, and reduce its use and misuse, during last week's party conference. Although it wasn't in the news much, it's a very significant change on such a political event. It's very rare for a minister to take on the police in such a way. In fact, I can't remember a minister ever doing it, but it's all part of a very tense relationship between government and the police at the moment.'*

The use of stop and search, despite resistance from chief officers, has been considerably reduced between 2011 and 2015 (Home Office, 2015). This development is best understood as an attempt to decrease the number of interactions that harm trust, and hence it falls into the trust-building category. However, the debate is also connected to the power struggle between government and the police.

Other developments similarly related to procedural justice concerns include experiments with police body-worn cameras, aimed at improving the quality of police public interactions; the formulation of a Police Code of Ethics; and experiments with direct entry of outsiders into senior policing functions to counter adverse elements of police culture.

8.9   CONCLUSIONS

Over the past chapter, while necessarily limited in scope, I have aimed to trace the development of trust in the police as policy issue and the formulation of trust-building strategies in England & Wales. We have seen that trust, as a policy problem, was most likely invented in the first half of the 1980s. While various efforts were made to improve trust and confidence at the time—sometimes phrased instead in historical terms of consent, such as by Brogden (1982)—the issue rapidly disappeared into the background during the rest of the decade. A failed attempt to restore trust by instituting a strict regime of performance indicators with the addition of strained police–ethnic minority relationships led to a reinvention of the concept during the late 1990s, when realization dawned that demonstrating dropping crime rates was in itself insufficient for gaining public confidence. The problem of trust has remained prominent on the agenda ever since.

Policies for dealing with the problem of trust have seen many changes and developments. We can roughly discern four categories of strategies, three of which have already been prominent in the rest of this book: proximity policing as an umbrella term for various community-oriented strategies, procedural justice, and instrumentalism. In addition to these three, we also find the trust-building strategy of democratic accountability, albeit mixed with the policy goal of diminishing police independence.

Peelian notions of policing by consent have characterized and shaped most of these strategies. They match well, for example, with strategies such as community policing (Alderson, 1979; Brogden, 1982) or neighbourhood policing—strategies that visibly position the police within local communities and attempt to let them act on local priorities. Procedural justice principles have also been present since the establishment of the Metropolitan Police; for example, in its emphasis on correct police conduct. Similarly, democratic accountability, present in some form throughout recent decades, is certainly strongly related to the Peelian principles. Its latest and most visible incarnation being the Police and Crime Commissioners, the idea of democratic accountability in policing is more prominent than ever. This is despite the fact that considerations other than those related to public trust have played a role in their institution.

The only apparent exception in this group of trust-building strategies is instrumentalism, with its notions of demonstrating police effectiveness. While reduction of crime has always been a vital goal of most Western police organizations, it has only relatively recently, since the rise of the NPM model, been coupled with notions of confidence and legitimacy.

Looking at the moment in time at which certain policies are adopted, an important determining factor appears to be a moment of political change. This is a moment that can temporarily open a policy window (Kingdon, 1995). What we have seen in England & Wales is that this often means a complete shift of governing parties, for example with New Labour reverting to proximity principles that the Conservatives had largely abandoned, or with the coalition government opting for democratic accountability rather than proximity. In other cases, however, a change in one or two key functions can suffice. Examples are the replacement of William Whitelaw by Leon Brittan in 1983, which first allowed public trust to reach the top of the policy agenda, or John Major taking over the prime-ministerial function from Margaret Thatcher, which paved the way for the advent of instrumentalism in policing. However, we should bear in mind that not all trust-building strategies are closely connected to a political shift. They can also be developed during one political era, an example being the fine-tuning of neighbourhood policing during the New Labour period. It appears evident, however, that every time frame has its own rationality around trust and confidence, and therefore its own specific trust-building strategies.

9.1 THE FOUNDATIONS OF DANISH POLICE WORK

In Denmark, trust has long been a less prominent issue than in the other two cases under study. This is not to say it is irrelevant—quite the contrary. The problem of trust took a long time to unfold as a policy issue, but had been in the making for decades. For various reasons, until quite recently Danish society did not frame police–public relationships in terms of trust, or did so to a lesser extent than many other European societies. Throughout this chapter, we shall trace police attempts to improve their relationship with citizens over time, and how this would eventually come to be defined as a relationship based on trust.

A vital difference between police in Denmark and those in England & Wales is that the Danish police are considered, and consider themselves to be, civil servants —employees acting on behalf of the state. Again unlike in England & Wales, such a strong connection between police and state is, in general, considered to be an advantage. This is because the state itself is in general viewed as a benign actor (Jespersen, 2011), rather than as a 'meddler' (Loader & Walker, 2007) against which citizens should be protected. This has massive implications for trust-building and police-citizen relationships.

The notion of the state as an actor that works to the benefit of its citizens goes a long way back. Jespersen (2011) explains it through the 1660 institution of the absolute monarchy. This de facto coup was the result of a power struggle between the king and the nobility, in which the commoners supported the king. It was only because of public support that the king could institute the absolute monarchy and subjugate the nobility. This made the connection between the Danish monarchy and the public particularly strong. The monarchy, while absolute in terms of its legal powers, considered itself to be an expression of the will of the people, and therefore always had to take public opinion into account. This lent the state a high degree of public legitimacy. It has also resulted in a Danish state apparatus that is traditionally, on the one hand, quite large and powerful—something it shares with the French model—but, on the other, also strongly decentralized and reliant on local communities, a characteristic that is more like Anglo-Saxon countries. The combination of these two aspects reflects the historical alliance between the state and the public.

A related characteristic is that Danish laws tend to be drawn up on the principle of legal opportunism, giving relatively large discretionary autonomy to law enforcement agencies (Björk, 2005). Danish police officers appreciate this—from an international angle very substantial—autonomy, since it allows them to treat citizens in the way they think is fair under the circumstances (interviews with police assistant and police inspector 1, both D2; see also Holmberg, 2000). The powers of the Danish police are legally far-reaching, but tend to be applied with considerations of public acceptance and legitimacy. In a wider sense, this legal opportunism allows much space for informal, nonstate legal constellations and solutions (Jespersen, 2011). Next to a strong state, this fosters a strong civil society. The consequence of all this is a *'fundamental attitude of modern Danes that the state is a friend and ally, not an adversary, a protector and not an enemy'* (Jespersen, 2011: 53).

It is in this element of protection that the police have an essential function. We cannot disconnect Danish police work from the broader state's responsibility to care for its citizens. This protective function of the police is conceptualized in a somewhat unusual way in Denmark as compared to many other contexts. It is consistently described using the Danish adjective *tryg* or the noun *tryghed*—as an ideal, a desirable state of being. Danish social order in general is even thought to be ultimately concerned with creating or maintaining a *tryg* society (Levisen, 2012). Here, the police play a central role. The responsibility of the police to contribute to building a *tryg* society is stipulated in Section 1 of the Danish police law:

> *'The police shall work for* tryghed, *security, peace and order in society. The police shall promote this end by means of prevention, assistance and law enforcement.'* (Bekendtgørelse af lov om politiets virksomhed, 2004, §1; my translation)

Since it appears to be such an essential term, to understand its implications for policing it is important to understand what the concept of *tryghed* actually means. What is a *tryg* society? While *tryghed* will in dictionaries likely correspond to either 'safety' or 'security,' such translations are rather narrow and actually may prove to be misleading.[1] In an insightful analysis, Levisen (2012) sheds light on the world of meaning surrounding the word:

> *'Tryghed conceptualizes an ideal for social life based on the values of, roughly, 'trust', 'familiarity' and 'predictability'. A* tryg *universe idealizes well-structured, well-organized, and nurturing social environments.'* (Levisen, 2012: 115)

---

1.   Occasional alternative translations include 'comfort' and 'confidence.'

A state of *tryghed*, in Levisen's (2012) analysis, reflects the world of the child; not just in its safety and protection, but in the very absence or denial of any threatening factors within or without. The provision of *tryghed*, clearly stated as one of the primary aims of the Danish police, is part of the role of a parent or teacher.[2] Certainly this does not mean that the police in Denmark are unwilling or unable to use force or fight crime—they do use force. The limited evidence available even indicates that the police in Denmark tend to be more robust in their use of coercion than those in other Nordic countries (Holmberg, 2002, 2015; Olsen, 2008). However, since the vast majority of police work (as in other Western European countries) does not entail the use of force, these facts need not be contradictory. The use of force can, after all, be required for the restoration or maintenance of a *tryg* society. Hence, the police consider as their function not just to keep society safe, but to help create an environment characterized by *'aspects of 'warmth', 'trust', 'everyday well-being', 'safety' and 'freedom' at the same time'* (Levisen, 2012: 119). This is a broad responsibility that is not, as such, enshrined in legal rules and may not always be obvious in everyday police practice, but is latent in the organization and in the dispositions of individual police officers.

9.2   POLICE UNTIL THE 1970S

In the dominance of *tryghed*, trust has an ancillary, implicit function. A relationship between police and public that is characterized by trust is a requirement for a *tryg* environment. Building or gaining public trust is something that should intuitively fit well with the Danish perspective on police work and its function. For a long time in history, this trust was not in question. The taken-for-granted nature of trust in the police, as we saw it in England & Wales until at least the 1960s, endured for a rather longer time in Denmark. This is not to say that trust has not been an issue on occasion. We shall explore the main developments in the construction of trust in the police and of trust-related concepts, and we shall see that these developments culminated in the eventual advent of trust as a policy issue in recent years.

The origins of the Danish police were not unique in a European context. The Danish police as an institution goes back all the way to 1682, when they were established under the absolute monarchy. Around the (peaceful) transition from an absolute to a constitutional monarchy in 1848, the old, high-policing based mode of working proved to be increasingly outdated. It took the new system of government until 1863 to finally reform the police on a British-inspired model of municipal-based low policing. This developed into a highly decentralized system in which the preexisting network of *landbetjenten* (countryside police officers) and *sognefogeder* (parish bailiffs) was also integrated, functions which remained in place until 1973,

---

2.   The concept of *tryghed* is known and used in other Scandinavian languages as well, so Denmark is not unique in this sense. In Sweden as well as in Norway, *'trygghet'* is a central concept in public safety discourse.

when the number of *landbetjenten* was decreased and the *sognefogeder* only remained on minor islands. Finally, the *landbetjenten* were also all but abolished with the police reform of 2007 (H. Stevnsborg, personal communication, March 10, 2015).

It was with this reform that the police took up their role as a civil police operating close to the public. There was, however, a certain tension with this decentralized system: it was mainly a model for times of peace and tranquility. Once a considerable multi-ethnic European power, Denmark had, by the second half of the 19th century, been diminished to a tiny, mostly agricultural state with nearly exclusively Danish inhabitants. The military and territorial losses of the previous centuries had, and to some extent still have, a distinct psychological impact on the self-perception of the Danes (Jespersen, 2011). By the late 19th century, there was a strong internal cohesion, which did favor a decentralized system of government and policing, but also a great fear of outside powers—especially the newly founded Germany.

Fear of the outside grew particularly urgent with the tensions of the 1930s. Threats of communist and fascist movements were running high, posing a serious challenge to the capacity of the municipal police forces. Fears of Nazi infiltration in minority-German parts of southern Jutland from 1933 onward compounded the risks. To face this threat and better mobilize the police if trouble arose, the local forces were integrated into the national police, the *rigspolitiet*, in 1938. For the Social Democrat government, this had the ideological benefit of yielding uniform labor conditions for all police employees (Stevnsborg, 2010).

During the German occupation, the police, like other state institutions, initially continued to function. They were made to participate in the arrests of communists from 1941 onward, but unlike in several other European countries, they did not contribute to the internment and deportation of Jewish citizens—since most of them were evacuated to neutral Sweden by the resistance movement. During the last year of the war, the Germans, who had seen the Parisian police rise up against the occupying force once the Allies approached the city, disbanded the Danish police. The former officers were either transported to concentration camps or went into hiding. This absence of a clear authority on the streets led to a period of chaos and anarchy. Because of this, years of organizational chaos ensued as Denmark attempted to rebuild its police after the war.

The police, in the eyes of the public, had mostly acted in an acceptable fashion during the war (unlike, as we will see, in the Netherlands), but several scandals did tarnish their name. Most prominent of these was the so-called Spider Case, a corruption scandal involving the Copenhagen investigation department (Stevnsborg, 2010). Corruption being a rare phenomenon in Danish society, this had a distinct impact on how policing was to be conducted in the following decades:

Retired police commissioner: 'At that time we had a serious case which involved lawyers within the police, police officers, and of course people outside the police. And two or three police officers were fired. I remember that, because when I started in the Copenhagen police in 1965, that case from 1948 was still remembered. The way the criminal [investigation] police worked was very much influenced by what had happened at that time. They didn't dare to go to restaurants and mingle with criminals and so on.'

In spite of this scandal and the organizational chaos after the war, trust in the Danish police was not in question. There was no direct need for large scale reform, so the police system itself had remained mostly the same as before the war. A national police commissioner (*rigspolitichef*) was responsible for dividing the budget across the local police districts and for police recruitment and training, while in each of the districts, the district police commissioner (*politimester*) dealt with all operational affairs of the police and public prosecution.[3] This led to a continuing power struggle in which district police commissioners could act almost completely independently in their geographic areas. The national commissioner could use budget allocation as leverage to achieve his goals. This constellation lasted until 2007.

9.3   THE 1970S AND 1980S: CAREFUL REFORM

In 1973, a reorganization reduced the number of police districts from over 70 to 54. This matched the reduction in number of municipalities at the same time, reflecting the shift from a fundamentally agricultural society to a more urban one (H. Stevnsborg, personal communication, March 10, 2015).

The police reform was intended to increase the strength of the local police forces, which were often perceived to be too small to adequately serve their area and deal with increasing crime rates. Each of these new, larger districts was provided with a main station that was to be opened 24/7. It did mean, however, the first police pullout from local villages and communities. While municipalities without a main police station kept a single-officer *landpoliti* office (H. Stevnsborg, personal communication, March 10, 2015), police visibility was perceived to have decreased (Stevnsborg, 2010). The benefits of having a permanently opened main station were also somewhat questionable, as illustrated by one police inspector's memory of the 1970s:

Inspector 3, D2: 'When I started in the police, it was accepted that if you had night duty, and the clock hit one, you would get your night coffee and sit back in your chair, sleeping until there was a phone call.'

---

3.   Unlike in most other Western countries, the Danish police and prosecution are one and the same organization on the district level.

As society changed, however, rising crime rates began to lead to feelings of *'utryghed'* (the antonym of *tryghed*) among the population. The call was for the police to be more visible to counter these feelings. It was also in this period that fear of crime, a concept more concrete and specific than *utryghed*, started to gain salience (Balvig, 1990).

In 1983, action was finally undertaken. With the motto *'mere synlighed, større tryghed'* ('more visibility, greater *tryghed'*), experiments with proximity policing (*nærpoliti*) commenced. These *nærpoliti* were designed to be a supplement to regular policing. One important task they soon received was that they represented the police side of the newly instituted SSP networks; a cooperative venture between schools, social services, and police on the local level all across Denmark. These networks were primarily designed to prevent youth crime, which at the time was perceived to be increasingly problematic, from getting worse (Stevnsborg, 2010).

While these attempts to increase visibility and cooperation were popular with local authorities and the public, they had little impact on either crime or *tryghed* (Stevnsborg, 2010). Current police officers also tend to look back on this period as a rather primitive experiment:

> Police commissioner, D1: 'I remember they did community policing in 1972 or 1973 or so. They gave some police officers a district. But it ended up only being paperwork with that district, and he went out only to find a man who didn't pay his fine or didn't show up in court. [...] You used old policemen for that, who couldn't do patrolling anymore.'

This means that a sense of urgency may have been lacking in the attempts to increase visibility through proximity policing. There was probably also little cause for this urgency at the time. There was a certain concern with crime levels, as well as regular and sometimes violent conflicts between the police and far-left movements and squatters, but public trust in the police in general was not in question (O. Scharf, personal communication, November 11, 2015). At most, there was an undercurrent of worry that Danish citizens might not feel as *tryg* as they did before and that the general climate might be changing.

9.4   The 1990s: Trust invented?

Despite the concerns and challenges addressed in the previous section, postwar policing, up until the 1990s, remains in public memory as a relatively tranquil period in terms of police reputation and police–public relationships. It was remarkable in itself how few of my informants could even recall a single issue or scandal within policing that affected the public in any way. Except for the Spider Case, one exception was the surveillance of far-left movements program by PET, the Danish intelligence service, that has broadly been criticized for being too all-encompassing (Stevnsborg, 2010).

This general lack of scandal was not, or not only, because the Danish police were exceptionally well behaved or because there were no fault lines within society. Postwar but pre-EU Denmark was still not entirely free from the impact of the long period of existential threat from the outside, strengthening internal ties and loyalties. A compounding factor was that most local police chiefs had worked in the Ministry of Justice or the prosecution service earlier in their careers—and vice versa—making for a close-knit criminal justice community and inhibiting internal conflict. The consequence, according to one police researcher, was as follows:

> Police researcher 3: 'Scandals seldom are constructed as real scandals, because apparently people [within the criminal justice chain] then stick together. The only thing that had a really big impact was the Nørre-bro shootings, after the Maastricht treaty referendum. That was as if a bomb had dropped, and it led to changes in public-order policing. But usually, these things are played down with relative ease.'

This is a serious difference with the English and the Dutch contexts, which with high regularity, albeit in varying degrees, featured highly mediatized scandals and conflicts between the police and the public.

The one large exception mentioned by the police researcher took place on May 18, 1993. It was the day of the referendum on the Maastricht treaty—whether or not to join the EU (under condition of four opt-outs). When it became apparent that the yes vote had the majority, protesters took to the streets in the traditionally problematic neighborhood of Nørrebro, Copenhagen:

> Police researcher 1: 'They set the neighborhood on fire. Police of course tried to restore order, but they hadn't planned for it. They almost lost it; it was very close. So they shot at the rioters, and that was a scandal [...]. 113 shots were fired, and afterwards a number of investigative committees and so on tried to find out what really happened. Even these days, nobody knows for sure. [...] In spite of the fact that two times the local commissioner in Copenhagen tried to find out what happened, then the state prosecutor had two investigations, then the ombudsman had an investigation, and finally a parliament committee took four or five years and came with a report in 2000. The years then passed and nobody cared anymore. What really happened [...] remains unclear. Police have been trained to solve these situations without force.'

In previous decades, Danish citizens had gotten used to protesters and police struggling on a regular basis. The use of force, however, had remained limited to batons and teargas. Additionally, the protesters had been a left-wing minority and were thus not broadly supported by the public at large. In the case of the 1993 Nørrebro riots, however, these two factors were different. First, the repeated use of firearms, injuring several protesters, was unlike anything seen before. Second, since nearly half of the Danes had voted against the Maastricht treaty, the protesters had a considerable degree of, if not sympathy, then at least understanding.

These elements contributed to a serious challenge to the legitimacy of the police (H. Stevnsborg, personal communication, November 9, 2015).

The main result of the crisis around the Nørrebro riots, except for a series of inquiries, was a reform of Danish public-order policing—mostly improving communication, organization, and technology. Next to these responses, there did not seem to be a particular policy to restore trust and legitimacy. The perception of the riots was probably predominantly that they were the result of primitive public-order strategies, not of a wider problem with policing in general. Once the issue of public-order strategies was sufficiently addressed, the problem was perceived to be solved.

9.5   THE PROXIMITY POLICING EXPERIMENTS OF THE LATE 1990S

It is not clear to what extent, if at all, the gradual resurgence of proximity policing was related to the events in Nørrebro. Proximity policing had certainly been receiving more attention from the early 1990s onward, but was still suffering from issues ranging from low status, to being a place for officers nearing their retirement, to a preoccupation with administrative duties (Holmberg, 2002). These problems gave rise to a need to revise the system. Around 1996 or 1997, the concept therefore got a distinct new impetus with a series of experiments, ranging in scope from insignificant to rather extensive. Then national police commissioner Ivar Boye argued that the police should focus more on prevention, problem-solving, on public feelings of safety, and even on quality of life (Holmberg, 2005).

The most likely incentives for the comeback of proximity policing were probably the ineffectiveness of the old system of *nærpoliti* and influences from abroad, rather than the Nørrebro riots or a public call for reform (Holmberg, 2002). Inspiration for the proximity policing experiments came from the U.S., but also from nearby Sweden—which had already implemented its similar '*närpolisreformen*' in 1994 (Peterson, 2010). Danish police let the Swedish experience influence the way in which they organized proximity policing. Regarding the U.S., one former police chief who was involved in the experiments makes the link explicit:

> Retired police commissioner: 'I read a book called What works in policing, *from the U.S. [DS: by David Bayley]. It's quite old now, from the 90s. They had done a series of evaluations of quite a lot of police practices. What happens if you send more police officers on the street? What will happen if you are more visible? That sort of thing. And there was only one thing that maybe had a positive result, and that was community policing. Everything else didn't work. No result. But community policing could maybe be the way.'*

There were several reasons to start the experiments with proximity policing in the late 1990s, and different goals and ideas played a role. But it is important to note that the reason was not a perceived *problem* with trust. Although the primary purpose of the experiments is probably best summarized as an effort to modernize and improve the police in general, as suggested by the retired police commissioner quoted above, they were also intended to increase trust—so that it would become even higher—and work on police–public relationships. Upon being asked when the concept of trust was first used in public discourse, one informant confirmed that this was a central idea:

> Police researcher 2: 'I think at least [trust] was taken to the forefront with the community policing experiments and the drive towards community policing. From 1995, 1996 onwards, there was a strong drive within the national police towards community policing. The then national police commissioner said that it would be the police's task to enhance people's quality of life, which I think is a very, very big agenda to put on the police, right? I think what it came from was the notion of quality of life crimes, from the U.S. That was sort of mistranslated or exaggerated to the idea that the police should now enhance quality of life.'

While this police researcher could certainly be correct that there was mistranslation involved, illustrating, en passant, the problems with policy transfer, there may also be more to it than that. After all, a focus on general quality of life, albeit a big agenda to place on the police, does match well with the police goal of *tryghed* that had long been central, and would be enshrined in the newly drawn-up Police Act.[4]

This does not necessarily mean that the police see all things related to the complex and multidimensional concept of *tryghed* as part of their duties. But it does imply that in Denmark, more than in many other countries, these different things are intertwined: police work contributes to *tryghed*, as does the work of many other agencies and institutions. Police work is part of a greater whole. This idea is reinforced by the considerably wider array of tasks and responsibilities that the Danish police have as compared to the English or Dutch police. These include duties related to fines and court summons, conducting driver's tests, and checking whether farmers abide by EU regulation concerning fertilizers. The weakness of the private security sector[5] and the near absence of other uniformed actors in the public safety domain further explain the broad role of the police.

It is in these factors that we can possibly find part of the appeal of proximity policing to the Danish police. After all, one of the most central tenets of proximity or community policing is for the police not to define their role too narrowly in terms of crime reduction. One can question whether these often administrative tasks are in any way related to proximity (in many cases, they are not), but what

---

4.   The 2004 Police Act was the first of its kind. Previously, aspects of policing had been arranged through various other laws.
5.   According to the Confederation of European Security Services, Denmark was among Europe's lowest-ranking countries in terms of private security sector size in 2011. The only EU country with—barely—a comparatively smaller sector was Italy (CoESS, 2011). Additionally, Van Steden and Sarre (2007) noted a general reluctance on the part of the Danish police and government to cooperate with private actors in security matters.

they do is make sure that the police are less purely focused on crime than they are in many other countries. This makes for relatively fertile ground for proximity policing ideas. Why, then, did this wave of proximity policing experiments that commenced in the late 1990s and lasted until the early 2000s subside again?

The proximity policing reforms were evaluated thoroughly (Balvig & Holmberg, 2004; but several interim reports were published from 1999 onward). The results of this evaluation were mixed. Feelings of *tryghed* and police-citizen relationships did not improve, police visibility and availability to citizens actually decreased, and police job satisfaction did not increase. On the other hand, there were indications that crime had fallen and police cooperation with other local actors had improved (Holmberg, 2002). The fact that the experiment was evaluated so thoroughly—a rare occurrence in Denmark, and arguably elsewhere—was also considered to be a positive thing in itself.

The fairly critical evaluation is probably one thing that stemmed the enthusiasm for proximity policing in Denmark. An additional reason is that community policing is to a large extent a trust-building strategy. However, we may wonder what the use of a trust-building strategy is when there is no shared perception of a problem with trust. The attention paid to the experiment (for instance, in the local media) may actually have emphasized police deficiencies to the public—certainly in the first stages of the project, when the police organization was still struggling with the new concept. This was even more so because the most comprehensive experiment was conducted in a rather affluent area; not traditionally the sort of context with the highest need—or potential gain—for proximity policing. Enthusiastic police chiefs may also have oversold the concept, promising more than they could deliver, inevitably leading to disappointment (Balvig & Holmberg, 2004).

All this leads to the conclusion that despite the most serious scandal in Danish postwar policing, and regardless of attempts to introduce proximity policing as a trust-building strategy, trust in the police was still a poorly understood subject during the 1990s. There was no structural challenge to trust, which we found in England & Wales to be the foundation of any trust-building strategy.

9.6   THE 2000S: TOWARD A NEW MODEL OF POLICING

Proximity policing was never formally abandoned, but in practice it was mostly put on hold. In fact, it was shelved until later, when it would be integrated into a new police system. Debate around a new police system had been ongoing for a while, and gathered pace when a commission was formed by the Social Democrat government in 1998. The Police Commission (Politikommissionen), consisting of academics, senior police officers, and civil servants, had two purposes. The first was to propose a Police Law, to collect all regulations regarding police work into a single piece of legislation. As mentioned before, the Police Law was eventually passed in 2004. The second goal was destined to have a rather more complicated history: it was to rethink and revise the system of 54 different police districts (Stevnsborg, 2010). The Police Commission proposed to reduce the number of districts to 25, so that the capacity of each district would be greater—a perceived necessity to deal with changing patterns of crime, and also perceived to yield a more efficient distribution of limited resources. Of particular interest is that the Commission, in its 2002 report, spoke of the need for these new, larger districts to provide what it called 'reel tryghed': real or actual tryghed (Politikommissionen, 2002). This is the Danish near equivalent of objective safety—that is to say, crime numbers—as opposed to subjective safety (Stevnsborg, 2010). This marks a decisive shift in thinking from the 1970s, when the slogan was still 'more visibility, greater tryghed,' in a reference to a more holistic interpretation of tryghed. While it is hard to say for sure, it seems likely that this development was to some degree influenced by English discourse at the time—the Police Commission's distinction between 'regular' tryghed and 'reel tryghed' coincided with the English debate on the 'reassurance gap,' the discrepancy between fear of crime and actual risk of victimization. This reflected a similar, albeit certainly not equal, distinction between subjective and objective notions of safety-related concepts.

It is worthy of note that the Police Commission did not abandon the notions of visibility and proximity. The Commission stated that 'proximity, tryghed and visibility are quite central concepts in relation to police work' (Politikommissionen, 2002: 50; my translation), as well as that 'larger districts do not in themselves mean that closeness to the individual citizen is lost, but larger districts rather on several points provide better possibilities for reel tryghed and proximity in police work.' (Politikommissionen, 2002: 66; my translation, emphasis added). In rhetoric, this reflects a continuing prominent position of the proximity policing ideal, while we can also see encroaching instrumentalism. In the views of the Police Commission, the two were intertwined and did not need to be mutually exclusive.

The reform proposed by the Police Commission never happened. The year 2001 saw a change in government, when the right-wing Venstre party took power. The then Minister of the Interior and later Prime Minister Lars Løkke Rasmussen soon composed a new commission, the Vision Committee, to revise the proposals of the initial Police Commission and added to its mandate the question of hierarchy: the division of tasks between the national commissioner and the district commissioners, which had remained untouched since World War II. The Vision Committee consisted of the Danish national police commissioner Torsten Hesselbjerg, a representative from the Police Union, one from the Chief Police Officers' Association, several people from private businesses, a few mayors, representatives from different ministries, representatives from the courts and public prosecution, and several scholars. The chairman, Erik Bonnerup, was a former bank and insurance CEO, while a former national commissioner of the Swedish police was also included, since Sweden had undergone a police reform in 1998 (Visionsudvalget, 2005). The committee was therefore quite a mixed bag, with notably few police representatives and a strong influence from business and government.

While right-wing parties were traditionally in favor of decentralization and localized policing, the Vision Committee made a curious turn in that it proposed even larger districts than the original Police Commission: 12 instead of 25. Additionally, it advocated a 'normalized management structure' (interview with former senior civil servant, Ministry of Justice), where the district commissioners were to be subordinate to the national commissioner, who would in turn answer to the Minister of Justice.

In exchange, however, the local commissioners would be granted influence over their budget allocation (Holmberg & Balvig, 2013). The new police districts were also expected to tackle all serious crimes themselves, rather than leave these cases to the national police as had been the case before. These latter notions lead Kruize and Jochoms (2009) to consider the reform a decentralization, which is also how it was presented by the Venstre government. The argument was that localized, decentralized policing could only be successful if these local units were 'sustainable' enough to function independently on their own—a similar argument to that proposed by the original, Social Democrat-initiated, Police Commission. Currently, most informants agree that the reform primarily entailed a centralization, but, in the words of Holmberg and Balvig (2013), rather a 'centralization in disguise.'

This move was not limited to the police: Rasmussen also arranged the amalgamation of the municipalities into considerably larger units, with the same arguments. This seems to have been a primarily political process, unrelated to public concerns. Asked about the motivation for the police reform that would eventually come to pass in 2007, a former civil servant involved with drafting the new system said:

> *Former senior civil servant, Ministry of Justice: 'It didn't come from a wish or demand expressed by the man on the street, but in a way you knew at a political level and within the police and prosecution, that you'd have to deal with the new challenges regarding crime. If you didn't prepare the organization, then you would have a problem with politicians and citizens.'*

The proposals of the Vision Committee for a new police system were strongly influenced by NPM notions of value for money, efficiency and effectiveness—a movement that began its ascent a few years earlier with the first parliamentary multiple-year agreements for police funding (Holmberg, 2002). For instance, it included the imposition of strict and detailed performance contracts with the 12 local district commissioners.

With the Vision Committee, the language around *tryghed* and citizens' attitudes and demands was once again changing. Note the growing similarity to English-language discourse around safety: while the 2002 Police Commission had introduced *reel tryghed* as notion of objective safety (as opposed to 'regular' *tryghed*), the Vision Committee spoke of *tryghedsfølelse*, or 'feelings of *tryghed*.' Alternatively, the authors used '*subjektiv tryghed*': subjective *tryghed*. In other words, while the Police Commission used *tryghed* as the regular concept and only referred to *reel tryghed* when objective safety was specifically intended, the Vision Committee saw *reel tryghed* as the standard, while *tryghedsfølelse* was just the emotional experience of *tryghed*, an approximation of fear of crime. What this seemingly superficial rhetorical change meant for the Vision Committee's view on the police is made clear by two quotes from its 2005 report:

> '*In the Vision Committee's opinion, the tendency in the media and political debate to focus on assumptions about citizens' subjective sense of* tryghed *is problematic for an appropriate prioritization and use of police resources.*' (Visionsudvalget, 2005: 33; my translation)

> '*Entirely in line with the various studies on the population's low anxiety and high* tryghedsfølelse *[feelings of* tryghed*], the Vision Committee has also been able to ascertain that the average Dane does not even ask for a police effort directed at a stronger subjective* tryghed, *more visible police, etc.*' (Visionsudvalget, 2005: 34; my translation)

The implications were clear: political and media attention to subjective perceptions of safety distorted police efforts to fulfill their actual proper tasks. There was no problem with citizens' perceptions of safety, so the focus must be on fighting real crime. Visibility was also deemed to be irrelevant; according to the Vision Committee, citizens needed to actually be safe, rather than feel safe (Holmberg, 2014). Danish citizens, the Vision Committee concluded, therefore wanted an effective and efficient crime-fighting police. An important part of the focus should be on organized and transnational crime. This may not lead to increased trust, but the assumption was that this was best for the public. It is important to note that the Vision Committee based its design of a future Danish police organization on very specific assumptions about the developments in crime and other challenges for the police: crime was expected to shift from property crimes to crimes against the person, crime was supposed to become more international, organized, and technologically advanced. Investigations were therefore to become more complex and would require more specialized skills. Additionally, the Vision Committee expected societal tensions to grow: respect for authorities was expected to decline, challenges with male ethnic minority members were thought to be growing, recreational drug (ab)use was perceived to be on the rise, and psychological problems among the population were thought to be leading to ever more serious crimes (Visionsudvalget, 2005). The demands on the police were expected to be much more related to crime-fighting, specialized investigation, and public-order issues, perceived by the Vision Committee as 'objective,' than with lower-level issues, seen as 'subjective.'

The 2007 police reform, with its strong NPM influence and focus on measurable crime indicators, reflected these expectations.

Despite this dominant instrumentalism, the proximity policing movement that had been so influential before had not entirely disappeared; it was integrated into the new police system through a separate pillar of police officers: that of the *'lokal-politi,'* or local police. These local police would be an adaptation of the *nærpoliti* from the 1990s and would also absorb the remaining countryside police officers, the *landpoliti*. This part of the reform was not as much intended to improve citizens' trust but, rather, to alleviate undesirable negative effects of the police reform on localized policing and therefore on police–public relationships:

> *Former senior civil servant, Ministry of Justice: 'It was in fact a quite important part of the reform, that the politicians, despite the larger districts, wanted a police who knows about the local areas, who work with the community and schools and social services. [...] Of course, it was also to stress that... looking at the map of Denmark, going from 54 to 12 districts, it looks like we're centralizing. It looks like it'll be hard to keep your local police officer if you're living in a small community. How should you deal for instance with young people in your community going into crime, in that new system? This was to stress: we know that, we are aware of that. That's why we have a dedicated part of the police working with these issues as well, and working with smaller types of crime; the things that hurt citizens in their everyday lives should also be an important part of police work.'*

The word 'trust' (*tillid*) is mentioned three times in the Vision Committee's report (Visionsudvalget, 2005): twice to refer to citizens' trust that the police know best where to place their own priorities, and once to state that trust in the police is high. None of this indicates that the Vision Committee had an explicit trust-building strategy in mind. Rather, it suggested that trust, like 'subjective *tryghed*,' was taken mostly for granted. The institution of a separate local police pillar meant an effort to maintain trust at its previous levels.

9.7   AFTER THE 2007 POLICE REFORM

Developments since the 2007 police reform have been myriad, often occurring in rapid succession and occasionally in seeming contradiction. I will argue, however, that the concept of trust has been central in post-reform Danish policing in several of these developments.

9.7.1   *Short-term impact*

The short-term impact of the 2007 police reform has been extensively documented elsewhere (Balvig et al., 2011; Holmberg & Balvig, 2013; Kruize & Jochoms, 2009). To summarize, there were several years of organizational chaos, public discontent with police response, and police loss of local affiliation. New, centralized police call centers did not work and lacked well-prepared employees; police did not respond to calls; clearance rates dropped; and a national newspaper, *Berlingske*, even launched a campaign highlighting police shortcomings.

Citizens' trust in the police took a distinct and, in a historical context, possibly unique dive from its previous high levels. Eventually, national police commissioner Hesselbjerg was fired due to this crisis. This series of issues put the police in a very public, highly unfavorable light, a position they were certainly not used to:

> *Police commissioner, D3: 'We had [these issues] here as well. Some of them were real, because we were in a situation where everything was changing, some weren't specifically… some had nothing to do with the police reform. But we were in a situation that there were quite a number of critics. People were criticizing the reform, so more people than usual would be inspired to call the local media and tell them they also had a story about when they called the police and they didn't come. Every time a citizen said how the police didn't react as he'd wished, it hit the headlines.'*

Hesselbjerg's successor, Jens Højbjerg, succeeded in stemming the worst organizational chaos within the police. The negative effects of the police reform on citizens' trust in the police, their dissatisfaction with police work, and their fear of crime had largely disappeared by 2010-2011 (Holmberg & Balvig, 2013). Clearance rates also improved. The experience of several years of crisis, however, had not been forgotten. For the Danish police, not used to crisis, the immediate aftermath of the reform had been unparalleled in its criticism. It was probably the closest thing to a crisis of trust in recent Danish history, bringing public attitudes toward the police to the top of the agenda, where they have remained over the following years. Over the following pages, I will first describe the problem definitions, and then proceed to the perceived solution to address these problems.

9.7.2   Local policing and satisfaction

Even though trust in the police had recovered several years after the reform, citizens' assessment of local police work remained worse than before: police were perceived to have less knowledge of local affairs, to patrol local neighborhoods with lower frequency, and citizens were less satisfied with local policing. Partners complained that they had lost their personal contact with the police, that the police did not know their way around local affairs anymore, and that the police were investing less effort in preventive activities (Holmberg & Balvig, 2013). This implied that the institution of local police as a separate pillar had not yielded the expected result of compensating for increasing centralization. That finding matched the experience of several of my informants:

> Board member, Police Union: 'It is of crucial importance that local police have knowledge of local affairs. That's very nice on paper, but that's not what we see in the small cities and what we hear. [...] It had high priority in the police reform, but how did it work out in practice?'

There are several factors that contributed to the problems with successfully establishing the local police pillar, at least during the years immediately following the reform.

First, the initial chaos in the police organization led to a serious situation in which the police did not respond to calls, or did so very slowly. This was the most publicized failure of the police reform, and therefore the part that needed addressing most urgently. The way of dealing with this was by pulling out officers from local police work to move them into response positions.

Second, the police reform was also combined with budget cuts, the assumption being that the reform would yield a more efficient way of working—therefore requiring fewer officers. Unfortunately, since the anticipated efficiency gain did not materialize, the logical choice was to once again pull out local officers to compensate for the diminished manpower on response tasks. Additionally, to achieve the desired savings, local police stations were either closed down or became very limited in their opening hours. This also spelled an end to the network of local *landpoliti* officers, who were deemed too expensive to maintain. One police officer in a small-town police station shared the common sentiment that I encountered regarding the effects of these budget cuts:

> Police assistant 4, D2: 'You lose contact with people. People here know we are just open one hour a day, and in the end, everyone will think: I don't bother. I'll just go on the internet and call, and if I can't reach anyone, that's it. You lose the contact.'

A third issue was that the police reform also meant that a framework of performance management and benchmarking was introduced. This system has evolved a lot in the years following the reform, but the initial structure was a rather rigid framework, where targets purely focused on crime numbers and response times. Local police work and crime prevention were not measured at all in this performance framework (Holmberg & Balvig, 2013). As we saw in England & Wales, 'what gets measured, gets done.' Things that were not measured were hence not prioritized. For local district commissioners, there was no incentive to focus on local police work, so it dropped to the very bottom of the agenda.

Within the local districts, this led to an awareness that the police reform may have built a larger scale and therefore potentially more clout for the local districts, but that this came with a serious downside. The rigid performance structure, the focus on organized crime, and hierarchy between the national commissioner and local commissioners led to a discrepancy between public expectations and what the police actually delivered:

Police commissioner, D1: 'We have gang crime, cyber crime, and all police officers are thinking that to be professional they need to increase their investigation skills, their tough-on-crime skills. The problem is: we see all kinds of crime, but the population in general don't. The biggest problem, if you ask them, is bikes. Bikes riding where they're not allowed to. Mopeds, same thing. And dogs shitting on the pavement. You can ask them. And here we are being skilled to tackle gang crime and so on.'

Deputy commissioner, D4: '[Citizens] don't care about organized crime. They care about petty theft, about mopeds driving in their local area, disturbing the peace. [...] We have to deal with it, we have to deliver what they think is important. If we don't do that, we won't be successful.'

These statements by senior district officers are remarkable: the belief, prominent on the national level and within the Vision Committee, that police work should focus on serious crime was not shared at the local level. Nuisance, antisocial behavior, petty theft—all these things are, in the eyes of the local district commissioners, important for citizens. These local commissioners hence challenge the foundation of the Vision Committee's strategy, including the assertion that the public do not desire police visibility. One local commissioner hesitated to call the result of this discrepancy a loss of trust, preferring to refer to it as a lack of satisfaction:

Police commissioner, D1: 'They trust us because we are not corrupt, we are fair, it is all based on legality. But they're not satisfied. They often say: where is the police when we need them? [...] In my neighborhood, I just assume people trust the police. Citizens say that they trust the police. But I'm getting more and more aware that they are not satisfied.'

This chimes with the assessment of Holmberg and Balvig (2013) that trust recovered from its fall just after the police reform, but that satisfaction with local police work remained poor. And while the term used is satisfaction rather than trust, it certainly has implications for trust: it means that citizens do not trust the police to act on their concerns. As illustrated above, this became a challenge for the local police districts that could not be ignored.

9.7.3   Ethnic tensions and trust

At about the same time that the police began to recover from the initial shock of the 2007 police reform and the criticism that accompanied it, a new problem made it to the top of the policy agenda. In 2010, the Ministry of Social Affairs, under the right-wing government of Lars Løkke Rasmussen, defined 29 'particularly vulnerable neighborhoods.' The Danish phrase reads *'Særligt Udsatte Boligområder,'* abbreviated to *'sub-områder,'* or sub-neighborhoods. Predictably, given this abbreviation, these neighborhoods are often referred to as ghettoes.

There is strong variation among these neighborhoods, the largest and most problematic ones being found in Copenhagen (Nørrebro/Tingbjerg), Odense

(Vollsmose), and Aarhus (Gellerup). The new national policy reflected the fact that troubled neighborhoods were increasingly seen as a problem that needed to be addressed.

The presence of high crime rates, gang problems, and riots in some of these neighborhoods also forced the police to take action. Additionally, the risk of radicalization of members of Muslim groups focused their attention on these areas. It was around this time that realization dawned within several local police districts that police work in these areas was inadequate at best and counterproductive at worst. The police were not being trusted and in fact did little to be trusted. While only pockets of mistrust as seen from a national perspective, such challenged neighborhoods are important to the police; many of them are overrepresented in crime statistics and often find themselves in the media spotlight. At the same time, the police had very little knowledge on what actually occurred in these neighborhoods:

> *Police commissioner, D3: '[We changed our approach in that problematic neighborhood] because we wanted to build respect and trust between the inhabitants and the police. We have had, before that, several occasions when there had been riots out there and patrol cars came out from the main station, and they didn't manage it in a very smart way. They had to use their batons and whatever, and it didn't de-escalate but it escalated the situation. Sometimes, over a week or two, we had to be present daily with a lot of police officers in order to try to de-escalate the situation.'*

Problems in these neighborhoods grew worse over the years, until it was clear that something had to be done. In a challenged area in D1, it came to a violent explosion in the summer of 2012, when a group of rioters directed its aggression toward a hospital. This deprived neighborhood, with high proportions of ethnic minorities, high unemployment, low social cohesion, and serious gang crime, was decidedly *utryg*. Citizens did not feel safe and did not perceive the state, including the police, to be there to protect them (interview with consultant, D1). The type of challenges that the police face in these neighborhoods is therefore completely different from those in the rest of the country.

The Danish police have no tradition of policing situations of high crime and low trust. They are used to working in a high-trust society where people feel *tryg*. They do so in remarkably low numbers (the police officer density in Denmark is substantially lower than in England & Wales or the Netherlands). However, the Danish police were, for a long time, inexperienced in dealing with ethnic minorities and in having to gain trust, rather than maintaining existing high levels. Ethnic minority officers are also severely underrepresented in the Danish police service. So how did the police, at least until recently, act in these difficult circumstances?

> *Police assistant, D1: 'The people considered us to be weak in hot-spot areas. We pulled back too often, refusing to conflict with gang members and hard-core criminals. That was seen as a weakness. People told*

us: when you face defeat, you have to come back a few hours later and actually do something. But what we
then did was stop and frisk the wrong people. [Citizens] felt that they were being let down twice. First,
the gangs took the area from them, [...] and when they defeated us because we had too few people, we got
the order to pull back too often. When we finally, too late, went inside the area to demonstrate our power,
all those hard-core criminals pulled back and we were targeting small criminals or well-functioning citi-
zens. This is how we through the years lost the legitimacy in the area, and how criminals could brand us
as not being just.'

There was a distinct unease among police officers about the way they had been dealing with problematic neighborhoods before; a discomfort I found in different areas of the country. After a series of incidents in several of these areas, and at different moments in time, various local police commissioners changed their strategies.

9.7.4   Proximity policing returns

The main problem with the police reform had been that the police had become too distant from citizens, too focused on serious crime and on internal processes, hurting trust, visibility, and local affiliation. The solution, then, was perceived to be a return to localized policing.

The particularly challenged neighborhoods did not improve under heavy-handed, reactive policing. There was a distinct crisis of trust in these areas. Besides this, proactive police strategies were perceived to be the way to deal with increasingly salient issues of radicalization. The alternative police strategy, then, was an intensive, proactive approach, again with a strong local presence, to build trust and connect with citizens: proximity policing.

Thus, very similar responses were seen as the solution to two quite different problems. The possibilities for this response, crucially, had been increased with the institutional rearrangement of the 2007 police reform. The local districts were theoretically now large enough to set strategic priorities, and had received the right to distribute their budget. As realization dawned on the national level that the previously rigid performance framework had counterproductive effects, in practice, the Ministry of Justice and the national police commissioner slowly granted the local districts the autonomy they already had on paper. Hence, the reform seemed to have simultaneously created a problem and the conditions for its—perceived—solution:

Police commissioner, D3: 'We changed things when we implemented the reform in 2007. Before that, we
had first four, then eight police officers in the local police station in [our most problematic neighborhood].
We increased the size of the police station, and today we have 26 police officers in that station, covering
the area. [...] we believe it is important to have this local police in the community being able to build
trust, work closely with the community, the youth clubs, the sports clubs, the management of the area,

representatives from the inhabitants, immigrant groups and so on. […] That was a result, or was inspired by the changes that came through with the police reform.'

The local districts (at least, the four I have visited) and the national police both recognized that more localized policing was required, particularly in challenged neighborhoods. On the national level, the National Center for Crime Prevention has expanded considerably between 2012 and 2015, while the local districts have developed their own initiatives around revitalizing *nærpoliti*. These processes have been encouraged by a national rhetoric that emphasizes 'co-creation' with citizens and other local actors. As of 2015, prevention as a topic has regained a place at the top of the agenda as well—and not only in police PR material:

Senior manager for prevention, D2 municipality: 'I think it's a different way of thinking around prevention now. I think there's more prestige in there than five years ago. […] I have discussed this often with police, and they said at first: oh, it's only for policemen who couldn't get the real jobs. But they don't say that now. I think there's a change of thinking about prevention and collaboration with us, now. Five years ago they said: oh, government, they only drink coffee. They'll only talk. But I don't feel that anymore. There's a very good respect between us now. I hope they see it the same way. [laughs]'

The change of strategies initially led to surprised responses, also within the police organization. Bear in mind the historically low status of proximity policing, as one proximity police officer recalls what happened after he was asked to join the local police immediately after graduation:

Police assistant 6, D2: 'When I first went out here, people thought I did something wrong in Copenhagen. They thought I was going through internal affairs or something: why would I come to the local police otherwise? People didn't believe me. They didn't believe I was actually headhunted. Why do you do that? Don't you like being a policeman anymore?'

But the strategy seems to have yielded some fruit in that it has gathered a considerable degree of enthusiasm and support throughout the organization. *Nærpoliti* officers previously had a reputation for being too old to chase criminals. This has changed—officers need to be able to build trust, especially with young people:

Deputy commissioner, D2: 'To tackle these problems [in our problematic neighborhoods], we need young officers with a special profile. They need to be able to talk with young people, and they need to be willing to engage with the neighborhood. Not everyone is fit for being a local police officer there.'

Simultaneous with the comeback of proximity policing as a strategy, the concept of *tryghed* returned. *Tryghed* no longer was interpreted in the way the Vision Committee had presented it—focusing on a narrow, crime-related definition—but was once again interpreted in a very broad fashion. When asked about the meaning of *tryghed*, one police analyst said:

> Analyst 1, D2: 'In [our project] Tryg [D2], we are working with [tryghed] in different ways. There's the
> project with nightlife, there's one about whether young people get the help they need in education, one
> about people in the street feeling unsafe, it includes so many different things in a way. It's really subjec-
> tive, a feeling, so it's hard to explain it. [...] It's the actual violence in the nightlife, but it's also the expe-
> rience of feeling unsafe in the nightlife. So the actual crime and the feeling is not the same thing. But our
> project is about both things.'

Note that this project to increase *tryghed* not only deals with objective and subjective safety, but also with education. Other elements of that same project, which
was a cooperative venture between the municipality and the police, concerned
helping young troublemakers find a job and countering loneliness among old people. This suggests that the concept of *tryghed* retained much of its original, holistic
meaning. The same resurgence occurred with visibility, a concept that had fallen
from grace during the time of the Vision Committee and the police reform:

> Board member, Police Union: 'We want police officers to be visible in the public, to be seen as being part
> of the public. [...] Not because a crime has been committed, but just to show the uniform and show people
> that we are there, give them some comfort. That way, they can feel they are secure in the smaller cities in
> Denmark as well as the larger ones. [...] That might be part of the reason that we have this high trust of
> the public, that we are there to help. We are there to answer questions.'

This gives the impression that the instrumentalist notions presented by the Vision
Committee, regarding organized crime, have lost at least part of their appeal over
the 8 years between the police reform and 2015. Besides, a renewed emphasis on
proximity policing initiatives means that there are conscious attempts to improve
public satisfaction with local police work, police visibility, and work on *tryghed* in
the broader sense of the word, and to gain trust and legitimacy in areas where this
is weak or absent. These concepts are all closely intertwined and sometimes hard
to tell apart: it is difficult to say where an attempt to increase *tryghed* aims to
improve concrete safety, visibility, satisfaction, trust, legitimacy, comfort, or a combination of all these.

9.8   SINCE 2012: THE INDEPENDENT POLICE COMPLAINTS COMMISSION

Previously, I have mentioned the relative scarcity of scandal surrounding the Danish police. Obviously, this does not mean that the police are free of problems in
their dealings with citizens. One key aspect in this matter is the complaints system.
As in England & Wales, the Danish police complaints system has undergone several changes over the past few decades. Before 1996, local commissioners decided

on complaints, advised by police complaints boards—consisting of representatives from the police and from local authorities. This was considered a seriously flawed system, since this meant that the police investigated themselves (Amnesty International, 1994). Between 1996 and 2012, police complaints were directed to district prosecutors. This system was still unable to guarantee independence from the police:

> *Senior manager, Independent police complaints commission: 'Young prosecutors from the police districts worked in the district's prosecutor's office for two to four years, after graduating. That raises the discussion, of course, that they are employed in an office that handles police complaints, while they really want to go back to the police after these two or three years in the prosecutor's office. Therefore, independence wasn't assured.'*

This problem lead to doubts about procedural fairness and a potential loss of trust in the police (Amnesty International, 1994, 2008). Critical assessments by Amnesty International, among others, meant an incentive to once again change the complaints system. As of 2012, Denmark featured an Independent Police Complaints Commission (*Den Uafhængige Politiklagemyndighed*), particularly influenced by the Norwegian and English models. This independent office has its own investigators and lawyers. While it does not have the right to prosecute, it has strong leverage and its reports enjoy constant media attention. As a result, there have been some high-profile debates between the Complaints Commission and the Police Union; for instance, about the circumstances in which the use of pepper spray is justified. On the other hand, there is also appreciation within the police for the work the Commission does and how it reflects on the police as a whole:

> *Police assistant 7, D2: 'Half a year ago, two police officers were caught in southern Denmark issuing fines to people, and they just had to pay in cash. It was mainly tourists from outside the country who had to pay the fines and the police officers then pocketed the money. This was investigated by the Independent Complaints Commission, absolutely to the bottom. The police officers who did it will without a doubt be imprisoned and kicked out of the police. I don't think that this makes us any more or less corrupt, but normal Danish people can see that if you make a mistake in the police, you will be investigated.'*

As in other countries where similar schemes have been introduced, the institution of the Danish Independent Police Complaints Commission can certainly be seen as a procedural justice-based trust-building strategy (Johansen, 2014).

9.9   Conclusions

In Denmark, the notion of public trust in the police has seldom been challenged. It was only with the police reform in 2007 that the police first experienced anything approaching a crisis of trust. Additionally, and possibly partially because of this, it proved hard to disentangle trust-building as a policy goal from related strategic goals such as improving visibility, preventing crime, and contributing to *tryghed*. This purpose of ultimately creating a *tryg* society makes any analysis of trust-building strategies confusing. It at once includes a presumption of trust and adds conceptual complexity regarding the function of the police in society and police–public relationships that is lacking in other countries. The concepts are strongly intertwined, but in different degrees depending on the moment in history. For instance, trust in the police was not salient during the 1970s and 1980s, when proximity police experiments aimed to improve *tryghed*. Trust as a concept was used during the proximity police reforms in the 1990s—but it was probably still best understood as part of the constellation of concepts that entail *tryghed*. Finally, it has really come to the fore in the most recent wave of *nærpoliti* initiatives, particularly in troubled neighborhoods.

The incrementally more prominent role of trust in police strategies geared toward the public may indicate that trust is, to a growing extent, no longer taken for granted. Trust, and therefore trust-building, is increasingly relevant, because it has been challenged more often and more seriously than before. Trust-building as a practice is strongly connected with proximity policing strategies, which is understandable given its roots as part of a wider complex of *tryghed*. A wide scope and rather holistic interpretation of police work is still an important aspect of Danish police work.

The history of the police in the Netherlands is, more than in any other country, an amalgamation of ideas and concepts. In nearly equal measure, although varying through time, the Dutch system was influenced and shaped by French, German, and British policing models (Fijnaut, 2007; Meershoek, 2007). It was a complex model with national-level as well as municipal police forces and many different actors who determined different aspects of policing. Governmental responsibility for policing was shared (or, in practice, competed over) by the Ministry of the Interior and the Ministry of Justice. In the context of the present study, until very recently the Dutch policing system featured considerably less police autonomy than formally enshrined in the English model, but was also less subject to central, national influence than the Danish system. Instead, it was traditionally characterized by a powerful role of local governments and especially of the (unelected) mayors.

If we wish to understand trust-building in the Dutch context, the best place to start is probably in the 1950s. As in other Western European countries, this was considered a relatively tranquil, stable period in Dutch society. The postwar reconstruction was in full swing, crime levels were low, and the political system had settled into a predictable pattern. Police authority was not challenged. The Netherlands had a conservative, somewhat boring reputation. It was a society divided into different religious and political groups, who in their daily routines lived separate, almost segregated lives in a system that was known as 'pillarization' (Lijphart, 1968a). Each pillar, meaning each of the social groups composing the Netherlands, had its own media outlets, associations, and even small businesses. Every pillar was dominated by a highly educated, influential elite—labeled the '*regenten*,' as the Dutch ruling class had been named since the 17th century. These elites together formed the roof over the state of the Netherlands, supported by their respective pillars. With considerable distance to the group they were representing, each of these elites negotiated on behalf of their own pillar's interests. Together, they attempted to reach a consensus. With this modus operandi, the *regenten* were in fact '*enlightened oligarchs*' (Kennedy, 1995: 152). As long as it worked, this system was characterized by strong internal social control and discipline within each pillar. This made the work of the police relatively straightforward. Internal tensions remained hidden below the surface.

These tensions, however, were present. They probably had a lot to do with the inheritance of World War II. While the war had contributed to a new social cohesion and expanded awareness of national identity, the Dutch authorities had also been implicated in some of the worst excesses of the conflict (Daalder, 1990). The police—and particularly the police of Amsterdam—had emerged from the war with a poor image, a bad reputation, and low social status (Meershoek, 2000). This had to do with the very proactive role of several police forces in the persecution of Dutch Jews and the resistance movement, during the years of German occupation. As a result, one might speak of *'remaining skepticism, if not mistrust'* (Daalder, 1990: 154; my translation) in postwar public attitudes toward state actors, and a mix of *'fear ánd allergy, in contacts with representatives of state power'* (Daalder, 1990: 154-155; my translation, emphasis in original). More specifically, *'especially if the behavior of the authority awoke associations with actions of dignitaries or police officers during the time of occupation, the memory of 'the war' could attribute a certain aura to new forms of resistance'* (Daalder, 1990: 231; my translation).

The careful phrasing above already suggests that the inheritance of World War II was a complex one in terms of relationships between the police and the public. The police were aware of this as well and the memory of wartime events remained a contentious issue within the organization for decades after (Van der Vijver, 2006). Within the police, the complex relationship between the police and the public was partially interpreted as the result of a lack of appreciation of police work and a 'natural' tendency of the Dutch people to disregard authority (Prick, 1959). It was unclear how or by whom this poor relationship between the police and the public should be addressed: *'The* Tijdschrift voor de Politie *[Journal for the Police], the only independent professional journal to return after the war [...], also noted public discomfort concerning the behavior of the police, but criticized the government as well, since it did nothing to repair public trust in the police.'* (Meershoek, 2007: 338; my translation)

The Dutch police did realize that trust was a critical issue; that it had been damaged during the war, and that something had to be done about it (Fijnaut et al., 2004). It is, however, unclear to what extent the postwar lack of trust in the police actually endured over the following decades and what consequences it had (Fijnaut et al., 2004). It is likely that it mostly remained an undercurrent of worry.

The proposed way of dealing with this concern was, for the police, primarily through further professionalization. The rebuilding of the relationship with citizens was to be done through building authority and prestige. Police officers needed to be fully educated, impeccable professionals with authority, acting on behalf of the state—as skilled and sophisticated as the judiciary (Rijksen, 1946). The main difference between the postwar years and the interbellum—especially the 1920s, which had been the peak of the professional movement—was that the German police were no longer the main role model but, rather, the English (Meershoek, 2007).

10.2   THE 1960S AND 1970S: A CRISIS OF AUTHORITY

After the 1950s had passed in a relatively well-ordered atmosphere, the police soon found the problems to be mounting. As in the rest of the Western world, youth movements were forming during the 1960s, challenging the status quo—the most prominent being Provo, a youth movement with the main goal of challenging all forms of governmental authority. But while other Western countries witnessed a similar rise of youth movements and social unrest, it was in the Netherlands that the chaos had arguably the greatest impact and led to the most profound changes.

The police had initially responded to all disturbances of peace and quiet in a heavy-handed fashion. This was facilitated by the strict, authoritarian strategies they had developed over the previous decades. This repressive approach did little to restore order but rather, to the bewilderment of the police, caused an aggressive backlash. Although it is debatable to what extent the acts of the police during the war still played a role in people's minds (Fijnaut et al., 2004), the protesters were quick to adopt insulting language, including references to fascism and Dutch war-time collaborators, when addressing the police. The year 1966 marked a low point: on several occasions, the police failed to anticipate riots; and then they proved incapable of controlling rioting crowds. One informant who had been in service during that time remembered the impact of the events on the police:

> DS: 'What happened for individual police officers? They came from a certain traditional system and sud-
> denly everything was reversed. How did they deal with that?'
> Retired chief constable 3: 'Incomprehension. I even remember that I had study leave from the Police Acad-
> emy during the day of the Telegraafrellen[1] and I went to Amsterdam with a few fellow students to have a
> look. We heard the crowd yell to police officers: 'fascists, SS men'. That was such a shock, that the author-
> ity was no longer accepted.'

While serious, this challenge to the police could have been surmountable, had they found active support in society. As it was, they did not.

Media scrutiny of police violence was unprecedented. This was illustrated by the release, by a group consisting of a professor in criminology and several journal-ists, of a booklet documenting various instances of aggressive police behavior (Charles, Hofland, & Vrijman, 1964). Included was a rare survey of public attitudes of police responses to various incidents in Amsterdam. While the largest group of respondents indicated support for the police, a substantial and very vocal minority

---

1.   The Telegraafrellen were large-scale riots against what was perceived as biased reporting by the
        main right-wing newspaper on June 13 and 14, 1966.

did not, and many others either did not know or refused to answer. The afterword of the booklet harshly concluded that the relationship between the police and citizens had been profoundly neglected, that police attitudes toward the public were best characterized as disdainful, and that mistrust of the police was only the logical consequence of police behavior (Lammers, 1964). These arguments clearly reflected the spirit of the time in that they attributed to the police the same characteristics of arrogance and lack of responsiveness that were blamed on the political elite. This assessment was, in hindsight, to a large extent shared by a younger generation within the police who recognized that rigorous enforcement of the rules was no longer a suitable way to work:

> Retired chief constable 1: 'The police had absolutely no connection, couldn't read the city, did not know what was going on, were preoccupied with internal matters. They were an instrument detached, estranged from society.'

The open criticism from the media had the police reeling. Possibly, this, combined with their distance from citizens, camouflaged indications that public support for the police at the time was still very high.[2] For this reason, Knibbeler (1966) refused to speak of a 'crisis of authority,' a popular phrase at the time. It was, nevertheless, certainly perceived as such by the police and by the political authorities. Additionally, it is not entirely impossible that shifts in public opinion occurred as rapidly as in the political climate, so that a hypothetical repetition of this survey could have yielded very different results if conducted several years or even months later.

If societal and media hostility caused widespread confusion throughout the police organization, it was processes within politics that eventually proved to be the final step in determining the police's self-perception as being in a crisis. Elite attitudes toward the new youth movements were hesitant at first, alternating between permissiveness, on the basis of the right to free speech, and repression, rooted in public-order considerations (Daalder, 1990). Soon, however, the various political elites started to adjust. Even within the younger segments of conservative political parties, there was a sympathy toward protesters rejecting the status quo and the old-fashioned, authoritarian dominion of the *regenten* (Kennedy, 1995). Local mayors, who in the Netherlands have the formal authority over the police with regard to public order, prioritized averting violent clashes in their streets (Meershoek, 2007). The national government, meanwhile, had been taken completely by surprise by the events of the mid-1960s and, as a result, may have overestimated the gravity of the presumed crisis in Dutch society (Kennedy, 1995). After the elections of 1967, a more progressive government came to power, which was more inclined to give in to the protesters' demands.

---

2.   Knibbeler (1966: 123) referred to a national survey conducted in March 1966 where 92% of the Dutch population had trust in the police (with 60% indicating 'a lot' of trust).

Calls for democratization, social equality, and acceptance of alternative life-styles by youth movements were therefore, after an initial stage of shock, relatively smoothly accommodated. The elite's arguments to do so, as publicly stated, tended to be rather vague. Statements that 'the time' had simply come and that 'the writing was on the wall' (Kennedy, 1995) were rampant. It can probably best be understood as a reflection of the Dutch politics of accommodation—the system of negotiation and compromise characterizing pillarized Dutch society in order to prevent open conflict (Lijphart, 1968b). This remarkable about-face of the Dutch elites reflected a shift from an originally mostly repressive attitude toward the protesters to a much more permissive one.

Elite accommodation to the protest movement left the police in the cold, as the final vestige of traditional ideas about law and order in society. When asked how the 1960s were experienced by the police, one police scientist and former officer therefore summarized the state of police leadership as follows:

> *Police scientist 2: 'Powerlessness. The chief constable of Amsterdam was fired after the riots of 1966. During that whole period there were attempts of police chiefs to make peace with this, but it was a process of soul-searching. It mostly lead to restraint and avoidance of violence.'*

10.3   CHANGING POLICE

Unlike in the period directly following the war, the paralyzed police organization did not frame the crisis it was experiencing as one of trust,. Instead, the most popular term to understand it was authority; the self-perceived monopoly of the police in having the authority over public space was challenged. Soon, the concept of legitimacy was added to this vocabulary.

The first theoretical contribution on the subject of police legitimacy in Dutch scientific literature reflected the previously described developments. Van Reenen and Verton (1974), two police officers who had taken to sociology, considered the legitimacy deficit of the police to be a manifestation of a trust or legitimacy deficit of the state as a whole:

> *'Falling trust in the political government leads to a diminished acceptance of police actions. The lack of legitimacy of the political government is manifest where political decisions are translated into action.'*
> *(Van Reenen & Verton, 1974: 74; my translation)*

The problem, in the view of the authors, was perceived to be with the strong connection between the police and the unpopular state. The logical consequence of a crisis of legitimacy of the state was a lack of legitimacy of the police. The solution would be for the police to create and maintain their own power base, separate from the legitimacy of the state (Van Reenen & Verton, 1974).

For a new generation within the police, it was this translation from authority to legitimacy that was a distinct eye-opener. A small group of university-educated young inspectors had been set the assignment to draw up a proposal for more efficiently redistributing police resources in the Netherlands. In a bout of creative insubordination, they wrote a vision document concerning the future of the Dutch police in general instead (Heijink et al., 1977). This document, 'Changing police' (*'Politie in verandering'*), was intended as a blueprint for police work in post-1960s Dutch society. One author summarized the rationale behind their approach as follows:

> *Retired chief constable 3: 'The question was: if positions based on authority become less stable, because traditional power relationships disappear, how to compensate for that instability? Our message was societal integration: to know and be known. [...] People who know each other are less likely to use violence against one another. People who know each other know what they can expect from the other. That was our message: the police need to get back into the neighborhoods, need to care about the wishes people have in those neighborhoods.'*

The vision document proposed a radically different view of policing than the traditional, authoritarian approach: one based on communication with citizens. Clearly, the model proposed by 'Changing police' was one of proximity policing. More concretely, it advocated the division of the police into small neighborhood teams, at the expense of overhead and specialized policing functions. In the view of the authors, the crisis of legitimacy experienced by the police could only be solved when *'authority gets a more personal character in terms of 'to know and be known''* (Heijink et al., 1977: 54; my translation), and this was what neighborhood teams were supposed to do. Proximity policing was therefore first and foremost a tool to restore police authority. The essential way of doing so was supposed to be through gaining public trust. Additionally, the report contained features of (proto-)procedural justice in its emphasis on just treatment of citizens and the recommendation to decrease the use of violence. In a wider sense, it recommended movement from enforcing the law to contributing to the maintenance of social order.

'Changing police' also marked a rupture in the connection between the police and the state. The authors, police officers, noted that their problems were not with legality, but with the social legitimacy of their institution—in the eyes of the public. They were concerned with what the police themselves were to do. They explicitly disagreed with the notion that the police were merely a sword in the hands of the state, as was posed by the personification of the professional model, postwar police reformer Frans Perrick (Heijink et al., 1977: 21). This interpretation was argued to be too state-centric and top-down. Instead, the police should strive to build their own legitimacy regardless of the state.

This is not to say that the model proposed by 'Changing police' was swiftly accepted within the police—quite the contrary. There was strong resistance at the political and senior police levels. The authors were initially *'excommunicated'* (interview with retired chief constable 3). Slowly, meanwhile, the ideas of 'Changing police' took hold in the organization. One of the few empirical evaluations of the proximity-based model proposed by the vision document, as implemented in Haarlem, suggested that the introduction of neighborhood police teams had led to lasting positive effects on perceptions of safety among the population. Relationships between the police and the public improved substantially. Additionally, the occurrence of various types of crime in the included neighborhoods diminished, without problems moving to adjacent areas (Broer, Schreuder, & Van der Vijver, 1987).

Despite increasing attempts by the police to solve conflicts with problematic sections of the population through negotiation and compromise, the 1980s still featured various violent clashes, especially with the radical squatters' movement. However, the seeds had been sown. Proximity-oriented ideas soon began to influence a new generation at the police academy. The significance of trust and legitimacy was no longer challenged. Nor was the need for the police to work on this subject and improve themselves. This awareness has remained in the organization ever since:

> *Former member national police board: 'The police function needs to get its legitimacy from the public. That is what I grew up in, what I was raised with, and it has always determined my career in everything I've done. We were always working on getting the police organized in such a way there would be a good relationship with the population.'*

10.4   THE REORGANIZATION OF 1993 AND THE BLOSSOMING OF PROXIMITY POLICING

In 1993, the complex constellation of national and municipal police forces as had existed before was reformed into a regional police system with 25 police regions and one national force. This reform aimed to address various long-standing tensions within the system related to the perceived fragmentation of the system, a perceived lack of police effectiveness and efficiency, rising crime rates, an increasing need for specialized police units, and the changing demographics of the country (Broer & Van der Vijver, 1987; Cachet & Sey, 2009; Cachet et al., 1994; Gooren & De Zwaan, 1995; Straver, 2006). After disappointing results of smaller reforms during the 1980s (Van Reenen, 1993), a radical overhaul suddenly became possible in 1989 with the advent of a new government featuring two ministers (for Justice and of the Interior) who had had no previous involvement in the police organization (Gooren & De Zwaan, 1995). With this political shift, a policy window suddenly opened, paving the way for an unexpectedly large reorganization.

The new regional system could be understood as a compromise between different political actors, including the political parties in government, the competing ministries of Justice and of the Interior, the mayors, and the prosecution service (Cachet & Sey, 2009). Each police region was provided with a regional administrative 'triangle' of the police commissioner, the chief public prosecutor, and the mayor of the largest municipality of the region. The police commissioner had the responsibility for operational affairs in his or her region, while the mayor of the largest municipality (advised by the chief prosecutor) had the main responsibility for the administration of the regional force. Meanwhile, local mayors and prosecutors had formal authority over police work in their municipalities: prosecutors were granted authority over criminal justice-related police work, while the mayor of each municipality kept formal authority over the police in public-order affairs and service functions in their municipality—this included the mayor of the largest municipality, who therefore had a double function (Cachet et al., 1994). Long-term policy was decided on by the regional college of mayors, headed by the mayor of the largest municipality and also including the chief prosecutor and police commissioner. Their central positions in multiple aspects of police management and operations meant that the mayor of the largest municipality and the police commissioner were the most powerful actors in the new police system (Gunther Moor, Bakker, & Brummelkamp, 1998; Rosenthal et al., 1998; Schaap, Terpstra, & Van Stokkom, 2017).

To compensate for the loss of power and influence—municipalities lost administrative say on their local police—as perceived by local mayors, who were capable of instigating a powerful lobby through the Association of Dutch Municipalities and the Ministry of the Interior, several rhetorical and substantive concessions were made. The tradeoff entailed that in exchange for the mayors' loss of power over the administration of the police, the police would concentrate more on proximity policing initiatives (Cachet & Sey, 2009; Terpstra, Gunther Moor, & Van Stokkom, 2010). Additionally, a promise was made to maintain a decentralized approach in policing matters as a preferred modus operandi (Gooren, 1992).

In practice, the proximity policing strategy formulated by 'Changing police' was realized nowhere or almost nowhere in its entirety. Nevertheless, the 1993 police reform led to a period in which the principles of proximity policing were, at least at the level of rhetoric, very much accepted and internalized. The positive example set by the neighborhood team experiment in Haarlem (Broer et al., 1987) served as an inspiration for other police organizations to at least partially follow suit (Punch, Van der Vijver, & Zoomer, 2002). A decisive factor in this process was that the generation that either composed or accepted the principles of 'Changing police' gained positions in the leadership of many of the newly formed police regions at this moment in time, and started to experiment with neighborhood teams and more localized policing—since their relative autonomy in the new system allowed it:

DS: 'What influence has a policy document such as 'Changing police', if there are so many different police forces that all have their own approach?'

Police scientist 2: 'When you can convince young inspectors and chief inspectors that that is the way to go, they will start building once they become chief constables. They will start working with neighborhood teams. If you also have the good fortune that the education changes and training techniques to deal with conflicts in a non-violent way are developed [...], a common culture will grow. That is a process of 20, 25 years.'

Many police regions were unwilling or unable to fully implement neighborhood teams. There were several disadvantages to the concept: the formation of neighborhood teams led to a disappearance of specialized knowledge, to a lack of investigative capacity in larger cases, and to communication issues with other teams and the rest of the police organization. One rather popular adaptation of the neighborhood team was therefore the reintroduction of the individual neighborhood officer (Punch et al., 2002). While they had existed before, their reputation had been poor. It was only after 'Changing police' reinvigorated the interest in local police work that the institution of neighborhood officers was professionalized. Up until the present, the individual neighborhood officer is an essential part of proximity policing and trust-building in general in the Netherlands. Each of these individual officers has a large degree of discretionary autonomy and will have his or her own specific style of working (Terpstra, 2008) and therefore of gaining trust. This makes proximity policing in the Dutch context a flexible, but also hard to define, strategy.

   Proximity policing remains, certainly rhetorically but arguably also in practice, a central trust-building strategy in the Netherlands. During the period of the regional police system (1993-2013), the goal was first to extend proximity policing and later to professionalize it. Many ways of doing so entailed forms of information-sharing and standardization.[3] This reflects the increasing managerial influence on policing in the Netherlands in general during this period, including on local policing.

10.5   Fighting crime, New Public Management, and targets

The 1980s, and certainly the 1990s, were characterized by complex and sometimes contradictory developments in Dutch society and policing in particular. As in other Western countries, concern with crime gradually grew. A landmark was 1984, when the Committee on Petty Crime (otherwise known as the committee-Roethof, for its chairman), instituted by parliament, alerted Dutch society to rising crime rates. This concerned mostly common, large-volume crimes that, in the view of the committee, needed to be addressed. Although the committee recommended an

---

3.   One example being the 'Reference Framework Proximity Policing' (*Referentiekader Gebiedsgebonden Politiezorg*; Nap & Van Os, 2006).

'administrative preventive' approach to deal with the problem, matching with proximity policing ideas (Bruinsma, 1999), it also signaled a shift in political and societal discourse. Indirectly, it may have paved the way for the emergence of fighting crime as a central topic. This idea was reinforced by survey data suggesting that citizens wanted the police to focus more on large-volume crimes (Van der Vijver, 1993). Hence, Van Reenen (2006) hypothesized that effectiveness and legitimacy were, in the eyes of the police, becoming more and more closely connected.

Over the course of the 1990s, proximity policing was one powerful branch of police initiatives, but instrumentalist ideas steadily gained ground. The assertion was that the police had been preoccupied with too many tasks that were technically not their duty. Instead, they should focus on their 'core tasks' of response, maintaining public order, and safeguarding the rule of law (Van der Torre & Van Harmelen, 1999).

In a parallel, although not equal, development to this rise of instrumentalism, centralizing tendencies in the regional police system created the conditions for the introduction and development of NPM-influenced policies. These started to gain traction around this time with the new 'purple' coalition government of social democrats (red) and liberals (blue). One of these was the imposition of policy cycles and multiple-year strategic plans, but these differed greatly depending on the police region (Gunther Moor et al., 1998). In the wake of the evaluations of the regional police system (Gunther Moor et al., 1998; Rosenthal et al., 1998), a nationwide police policy plan for 1999-2002 was drawn up by the Dutch ministries of Justice and of the Interior. This plan introduced several broad policy themes to the Dutch police that started to reflect the concerns for the 'core tasks' (Ministerie van Justitie en Ministerie van Binnenlandse Zaken, 1998). From 2000 onward, this meant that the Ministry of the Interior determined national priorities for the police (Terpstra & Trommel, 2006). This resulted in a more demanding structure of policy goals and targets being contained in the previously existing policy cycle, mandatory for each police region—although initially, this cycle was followed by all actors in a ritualistic, form-over-substance way (In 't Veld et al., 2001; Terpstra, 2002).

In a parallel development, police effectiveness had grown to be an increasingly important criterion for judging police forces over the course of the 1990s (Van der Vijver, 2004). Up until this time, public trust had been a concept that was only indirectly associated with these reforms, but this was about to change.

Instrumentalist thought and NPM strategies became intertwined during the first three (right-wing) governments under prime minister Balkenende, in the period 2002-2006. The year 2002 had been exceptionally chaotic, even traumatic, for Dutch society and for politics specifically. It had first seen the meteoric rise of populist politician Pim Fortuyn, whose controversial views on immigration found strong resonance with the public—although he was at odds with the entire political establishment. On May 6 of that year, he was murdered by a solitary gunman. Fortuyn's only recently founded party won a strong representation in the ensuing parliamentary elections and was swiftly included in the new government. One of the central pillars of this first Balkenende government's agenda was security, perceived to be the main priority of a public that was profoundly shaken by the year's events. While there had been a latent concern in the decade before, trust now once again became a pivotal issue.

With the policy document *Towards a safer society* ('*Naar een veiliger samenleving*'), NPM-related concepts and ideas were even more systematically applied to the entire criminal justice chain (Ministerie van Justitie en Ministerie van Binnenlandse Zaken, 2002). Simultaneously, the previously latent concern with safety and security developed during the early 2000s into a full-blown obsession with increasing safety, fighting crime, and decreasing minor nuisances and incivilities (Van der Vijver, 2004, 2006). The policy document echoed this increasing emphasis on repression and maintenance of order (Cachet, 2002; Terpstra & Van der Vijver, 2005).

In 2003, a target framework in the form of performance contracts for each police region, controversially even including quantitative targets for (traffic) fines, was implemented as a tool for contributing to public safety and public trust by improving police effectiveness (Jochoms et al., 2006; Ministerie van Justitie & Ministerie van Binnenlandse Zaken, 2003; Van Sluis, Cachet, & Ringeling, 2005). Additionally, it aimed to reestablish police authority in public space and improve public satisfaction regarding police response and police–public interactions (De Kleuver, 2007). The expanding performance framework was used as a lead for benchmarking between police regions and for distributing funds—rewarding those regions that performed better in terms of output (De Kleuver, 2007). This performance framework, intended to improve trust, was based in NPM-related considerations of efficiency and effectiveness, yet also aimed to restore police authority.

As is often the case with NPM-related reforms, the introduction of NPM principles to the Dutch police hence entailed a wide range of measures to address an even wider range of perceived problems (Terpstra & Trommel, 2009). It included a perception of citizens as customers and borrowed many ideas and concepts from the UK in particular, following in the footsteps of the initial New Labour approach. The police were also quick to couple notions of efficiency and effectiveness with legitimacy:

> '*The police, as other governmental institutions, need to show that people get value for their money. The Dutch police are accountable to the relevant authorities and to society for their effectiveness and efficiency and consider this to be an essential precondition for the legitimacy of their actions.*' (Projectgroep visie op de politiefunctie, 2005: 40; my translation)

This looks like a brief summary of contemporary instrumentalist logic: proven effectiveness and efficiency (by means of target setting) was intended to improve police legitimacy in a marriage of NPM-based concerns and instrumentalist logic.

Nevertheless, in hindsight, few of my informants directly connected performance management to notions of trust or legitimacy. On the contrary, many of them referred to a potential loss of public trust due to the target culture (see also Van Sluis et al., 2006). Either informants had forgotten that increasing trust had been one of the policy goals connected with performance management, or they did not deem it relevant. Often, the supposed link was primarily with political demands, rather than public:

> DS: 'For instance the quota for fines and the control on output, derived from the new public management, did those have as their purpose to improve trust?'
>
> Member regional unit command 1, N3: 'No doubt, to some extent. [...] What was being said at the time, which is funny because it touches on trust, is that the police are a governmental institution subordinated to the authorities, and that we have to make arrangements with those authorities on what we are going to do. If we do that, we are a trustworthy police. That was not a trust-inducing police; they used the word 'trustworthy'. A different term.'

Interestingly, this quote illustrates another, less obvious shift in thinking about the police. It suggests that the autonomy that the police had bestowed upon themselves with 'Changing police,' their intentional disconnect from government and the state to build trust on their own terms, had been gradually muzzled (Jochoms et al., 2006; Van Sluis et al., 2006): the trustworthiness mentioned by the informant above is not trustworthiness in the eyes of the public, but in the eyes of governmental actors with authority over the police. This meant growing tensions between central demands and the local affiliation of the police (Jochoms et al., 2006; Terpstra, 2004).

It is hard to define what the effects of performance management have been in a broader perspective, in terms of effectiveness, efficiency, or trust and legitimacy (Terpstra & Trommel, 2006; Van Sluis et al., 2006). Over the following years, part of the target framework, including the quota for traffic fines, was abolished, but substantial parts of it remained until after the 2013 police reform.

10.6   THE NATIONAL POLICE

After years of relatively few new developments regarding police trust-building, events took a major turn in 2013. The regional police system was replaced by the Dutch national police, only 20 years after the last major reform. Instead of 25 independent police regions with the support of a national specialized organization—albeit one steadily growing in size—the police were reconstructed into a layered structure: one national senior management team setting out the national policies and priorities, 10 regional units,[4] divided into 43 districts,[5] divided into 168 so-called 'robust basic teams.' Although debates surrounding the Dutch police system go back well into the 19th century (Fijnaut, 2007; Meershoek, 2007), the rapid move to a national model was still surprising. As recently as 2004-2005, police leaders and other actors were clear in their rejection of a national police (Projectgroep visie op de politiefunctie, 2005; Terpstra, 2013). Political support for the reorganization, however, developed rapidly, and without dissent the proposal for a national police service was eventually passed through parliament in 2012 (Terpstra, 2013).

10.6.1   The political background

As with the Danish police reform of 2007, there were many different reasons for forming the national police in the Netherlands. First, it is important to note there was a widespread malcontent with the functioning of the regional system. In several key publications, it was portrayed as inefficient and ineffective; cooperation between police forces was seen as poor; and the online infrastructure faced serious challenges (Algemene Rekenkamer, 2011; De Koning, 2010; Inspectie Openbare Orde en Veiligheid, 2008, 2010). Nevertheless, such failings, while serious, masked underlying politics and interests. One important factor was that a national police can be seen as the ideological extension particularly of the first conservative Balkenende government in 2002 and its priorities of 'hands-on' crime-fighting and improving security. In 2010, creating a national police organization was a logical step for the newly elected right-wing minority government (propped up by the populist Freedom Party), which wanted to show that it was at least equally serious about dealing with crime. In order to successfully do so, the national government required a stronger hold over the administration of the police—until that time a matter for the mayors of the largest municipalities.

Reflecting these priorities was the merger of the Ministry of Justice with the policing part of the Ministry of the Interior into one 'super-ministry' of Security and Justice. This meant that the previously powerful link between the local mayors and policing matters through the Ministry of the Interior was severed. As a result, proponents of centralization (the former Ministry of Justice and the prosecution service, which itself had undergone centralization during the late 1990s) gained in power and influence, while those opposing it (the local mayors, in varying constellations, and the Ministry of the Interior) were diminished (Terpstra, 2013). In the decades-old struggle between the two ministries dealing with policing, the Ministry of Justice had prevailed.

The institution of the national police was primarily the result of a political process, but it would be incorrect to assume that it had no consequences for the public

---

4.   In size more or less corresponding to English police forces.
5.   In size more or less corresponding to Danish local police districts.

and for police–public relationships. Minister of Justice and Security, Ivo Opstelten, who was to implement the police reform, hailed from the liberal VVD party. The VVD had campaigned on a tough-on-crime platform during the general elections. Nationalizing the police was hence a matter of prestige as much as anything else. However, the minister required wide support in order to institute the national police. To satisfy different actors involved with policing matters, including political parties, various other notions and ideas were adopted and integrated into the design of the national police force (Terpstra, 2013). In the end, this meant that the reform was presented as the solution to a plethora of problems and challenges. One of the elements that featured prominently as a strategic goal in the eventual design of the national police was that a national police should enhance public trust and police legitimacy (Ministerie van Veiligheid en Justitie, 2012a). How and why a national police would contribute to trust and legitimacy remained vague in these initial plans: it was supposed to occur through 'better cooperation with local authorities,' having more 'authority in public space,' and better 'service to citizens,' including improved treatment of victims.

10.6.2   Trust in the national police

The aforementioned vagueness about how the national police would improve public trust was soon about to change. Terpstra and Trommel (2006) noted that in NPM-related reforms in Dutch police work, it was the logic regarding citizens as customers that had been the least specific in its consequences. With the establishment of the national police, this lack of clarity was addressed in a policy document describing the new 'service concept' (Biemolt et al., 2012). The service concept attempts to provide the national police with their own, specific vision on public trust, distinct from older models of trust-building. Although the previous strategies of proximity policing and instrumentalism both still find support within the police, it is this service model that has, at least for the time being, grown dominant. The basic logic regarding trust is summarized as follows:

'The police have a great interest in providing a good service, because this can safeguard their image. Additionally, citizen satisfaction is an important lever to [gaining] more trust. Citizens' personal experiences with the police have the largest influence on public trust in the police.' (Biemolt et al., 2012: 13; my translation)

The authors reason that good service leads to higher citizen satisfaction and a better image of the police. This then gives cause for more trust. Interestingly, they do not mention that there is an actual problem or deficit around trust. The policy document takes the foundation of procedural justice, namely the idea that the actions of all individual police officers together, all police–public interactions together, shape trust in the police. Curiously, however, these interactions are then almost exclusively defined in terms of the provision of service—decidedly not a central theme in the procedural justice literature, but one more common in NPM-related reasoning:

> *Member regional unit command 2, N4: 'The whole service concept … it is much easier to organize the same service across the Netherlands within the context of the national police [than in the regional system]. It would be strange that if you wanted to report a crime in Amsterdam, you would have to wait for an hour, while in Limburg you could do it by telephone and in North Netherlands you could do it on a 3d-location. […] That citizen has the right to one single level of service. The Rabobank wouldn't want to say that digital banking is only possible in the south of the Netherlands, either. So this is really geared towards the citizen. In the end, the whole matter of legitimacy is easier to realize on the scale of the national police than 26 times on the local level.'*

The trust-building strategy of the Dutch national police appears to be headed toward uniformity and standardization of the service that the police provide to citizens. The core idea here is that the police need to deal with citizens the same way as (large) companies are perceived to treat their customers. Standardized service is meant to reflect that the police are a reliable actor that citizens can trust. I will now introduce two measures of the service model that illustrate the logic behind it as well as its inherent flaws.

a   Reporting crime

Quite a central issue in the service concept of Biemolt et al. (2012) was citizens' reports of crime. The authors formulated a list of options for citizens to get in touch with the police, in preferential order—as preferred by the police, that is. Steering the public in their choice is an explicit goal. The sequence is (1) the internet, (2) the telephone, (3) in a police station, (4) via a 3d report,[6] (5) on location, and (6) through social media (Biemolt et al., 2012: 10-11). Citizens can choose—in fact, there is a great deal of choice—but in the service concept, the police are encouraged to direct them to the preferred choice. People are therefore given the *idea* of a choice. It is remarkable to see that the majority of the options keep the citizens at a distance: except for the police station and visiting a citizen at home, there is a strong reliance on technology and service from a distance. Considering the low priority given to face-to-face options, personal interaction and visibility are clearly not central notions in the service concept. That this comes with serious drawbacks is something many within the police are aware of, but they often consider it to be a fact of life, rather than something they can influence. Others state that they attempt to work around these drawbacks:

---

6.   A 3d report is a report recorded by camera on specific locations.

Chief basic team 1, N1: 'We have to get used to it. We have 3d reports [...]. People can also report things over the internet. But then I take a look at that old mother of mine, and she says: I just want to see police officers. And I understand that too.'

DS: 'How do you deal with that question?'

Chief basic team 1, N1: 'Well, we can't really deal with that, actually. Those are things we cannot influence.'

Chief basic team 4, N2: 'Where necessary, for instance with old people who cannot come here but there has been a burglary and we want them to report it, we can go there with our mobile stations and take their information. Well, in that way we try as well as we can to bridge the gap that actually sort of came into being.'

It is unclear to what extent the police actually do revert to alternative solutions such as visiting victims of a crime to take their report. It is certainly more labor-intensive. The fact that this option is low on the list of preferred ways of reporting crime also does not suggest that it is common.

b Mandatory feedback after reports of crime

After a citizen reports a crime to the police, the service concept makes it obligatory for the police to provide feedback by calling the citizen back after a fixed amount of time—within 2 weeks of the initial report. The reason to implement this measure was that citizens who do not receive any follow-up on their reports are likely to think that the police are not taking their cases seriously and will hence lose trust in the police (Kort & Terpstra, 2015).

While mandatory feedback was at first introduced only for so-called high-impact crimes (burglary, mugging, and assault, among other things), my informants were quick to stress that this model is supposed to be extended to all offenses. In addition to the reasons enclosed in formal documents, there are multiple other motivations for systematically returning on citizens' reports, as mentioned by my informants: it could make the citizen feel better to know that something is being done with his or her report; it can help the police to gather additional information; and it gives the police the opportunity to explain their work. Reflecting the core idea of the service model, one informant stressed the importance of being reliable in the eyes of the public:

Chief basic team 2, N1: 'I think we really need to do this. [...] You must let citizens know how things are going and in the case of a simple investigation, you should let the victim know what happened with their report.'

DS: 'Why is this so important?'

Chief basic team 2, N1: 'Because it increases trust in the police, of course. It shows we are a reliable agency and that people also can expect something of us.'

Very few informants disagreed with the desirability of informing victims of the status of an investigation, but there is a serious downside to this rule as formulated by the national police. Because the emphasis is more on reaching a perfect percentage of follow-ups, as a quantitative target, the actual content of the interaction takes a backseat. Feedback, intended to be personal, in practice takes place over the telephone, but also digitally or with a standardized letter. It is questionable to what extent this achieves the goal of making the public feel that they are being taken seriously. Police officers consider the rigid demand to respond within 2 weeks as a bureaucratic hassle and treat it as such (Kort & Terpstra, 2015):

> *Retired chief constable 2: 'It's not personal. What happens now with that feedback is that some sort of automatic letter is being sent: [...] for the time being we're not doing anything with your case, blah blah blah. Well, that absolutely doesn't increase trust.'*

> *Manager, national police quality control office: 'This is done in a managerial sense... how should I say it... it's being done in a lousy fashion, because the point of measurement is the question of whether or not there has been a call. The measurement is not the question whether citizens are satisfied with the way their report took place or with police actions on their case, which is much more outcome.'*

10.6.3   More distant police?

The Dutch national police were not primarily instituted to improve public trust—the reorganization had different purposes. As the political process developed, however, more goals and ideas were added to the design. The service model is intended as a strategy to build trust in a more centralized, distant institution, with the idea that distance is a relative concept and need not be problematic. These core assumptions have since been challenged (Boekhoorn & Tolsma, 2016; Terpstra et al., 2016).

One way to compensate for a potential loss of proximity to citizens was by enshrining in the law a previously formulated guideline to have at least one neighborhood officer per 5000 citizens (Koopman, 2013; Nap & Van Os, 2006). It was, however, reinterpreted in a rather less generous way: that every unit should have *on average* one neighborhood officer per 5000 people (Ministerie van Veiligheid en Justitie, 2012b: 49; Terpstra et al., 2016). One neighborhood officer in a rather troubled neighborhood was negatively affected by what was probably an unintended consequence of this development—one of his colleagues was moved away:

> *Neighborhood officer 1, N1: 'There had to be fewer neighborhood officers per area. [my neighborhood] has about 10,000 people. We had three neighborhood officers. So you have one neighborhood officer per 3000 people, while they are striving towards one in 5000. We say: that should depend on the problems. [...] The area is difficult, so that we used to have three was not strange.'*

While this standard for neighborhood police officers was intended to compensate for a possible loss in proximity and visibility, it was therefore interpreted in such a way that the opposite is sometimes achieved exactly in those areas where police presence could matter most.

Exacerbating the centralizing effects of the national police is the fact that police stations have been closed or are being replaced by 'support points,' much smaller stations that are not open to the public (Terpstra et al., 2016). This is primarily for budgetary reasons. The closure of stations, in the vision of the Ministry of Security and Justice, is a way to force the police to work in a more efficient manner (Boek-hoorn & Tolsma, 2016). An ancillary idea was that this more efficient manner of operating leads to better contact with customers—meaning citizens (interview with senior civil servant, Ministry of Security and Justice). This assessment is shared among some police chiefs:

> Member regional unit command 1, N3: 'We have a service concept in which we say: we want to be in contact with citizens in a multichannel fashion, so in many different ways and preferably the way the citizens want. In those preferences, a visit to a police station is actually only a minimal option, so why should we keep them open? If citizens do not need to, anyway… When did you last visit a bank? […] It's some sort of myth: you need to have stations in your village because of safety; you need to have a neighborhood officer on the streets because of safety. Well, I prefer that neighborhood officer to work with problems in his neighborhood, and he can let people know what he's doing through Twitter. That way, citizens don't need to see him walking around with his hands on his back, doing nothing.'

The reasoning behind closing the stations is, according to these informants, that citizens do not wish to keep them open anyway: it is efficient to close them. Similarly, police visibility on the streets seems to be rejected for being inefficient in terms of time management. The police should be 'cheaper' and more 'flexible,' and make better use of social media as well as modern tablet and smartphone technology (interview with chief of basic team 4, N2).

Several of my informants pointed at potential disadvantages of closing stations and relying more on modern technology to maintain contact with citizens: not everyone will be using social media to connect with the police; certainly not the elderly and low-income ethnic minorities. Whether it is a qualitative replacement for face-to-face interaction is also questionable—something that also holds for other parts of the service concept, such as the ways to report crime to the police. The closure of stations arguably raises the threshold for at least a significant part of the population to get in contact with the police. Additionally, some informants challenge the idea that physical proximity and visibility are no longer central to citizens and that private sector-like ideas about service are any sort of replacement for these notions. Hence, it remains to be seen to what extent trust-building elements within the national police reform will actually achieve their purposes.

A study among Dutch mayors has indicated that a substantial minority of informants felt that police local affiliation and knowledge of local affairs had decreased after the police reform (Terpstra, Foekens, & Van Stokkom, 2015). Additionally, the formation of the new basic teams since 2013 has led to considerable organizational issues and threatens to isolate neighborhood officers from the rest of the organization (Terpstra et al., 2016). The previously mentioned measures of standardizing the processes of reporting crime and of providing feedback, along with the closure of police stations and the loss of local affiliation of the police, led Terpstra et al. (2016) to refer to the Dutch national police as 'abstract police.' Expectations are that these processes will not prove beneficial to public trust in the police.

10.7   PROCEDURAL JUSTICE

A strategy that has received scant attention throughout this chapter is procedural justice. Many individual officers work with procedural justice principles, but seldom state so explicitly. Procedural justice has not played as central a role in Dutch trust-building throughout history as the others I have described. Related subjects have come to the fore for a while, only to disappear relatively quickly. One example was the debate surrounding police corruption in Amsterdam in particular, which started during the 1970s with the emergence of organized crime (Punch, 1985), and recurred as part of the agenda of 'Changing police' (interview with police scientist 1). However, in debates about the Dutch police, corruption has over recent decades seldom been a salient topic—certainly as compared to England & Wales.

Procedural justice-related debates tend to be less prominent than in the two other countries under study, although it is possible to trace several measures and developments over recent decades. One example consists of the changes implemented after the Salduz case, which had implications all over Europe. In the Netherlands, it resulted in suspects of a crime gaining the right to consult a lawyer before questioning by the police. Although still more limited than, for instance, the U.K.'s PACE regulations, this is a case of procedural justice principles forced on the police (and judiciary) from outside (Hodgson, 2014).

Another indication that procedural justice principles, at least in a formal sense, are not particularly prominent in the Dutch system is that there is no independent police complaints commission: complaints about the police are sent to the police, and the chief of the regional unit determines what action to take, or commences an investigation (in which case an independent panel will have an advisory function). If the claimant is dissatisfied, he or she can turn to the National Ombudsman.

This is not to say that there is no systematic thinking about procedurally just treatment of citizens. Recent decades have seen the rise of 'treatment profiles' (*bejegeningsprofielen*), codes of police behavior toward citizens under specific, often challenging, circumstances such as football matches or other public-order events (Muller et al., 2010). Such rules for just treatment are also being developed for interactions between the police and (young, male) ethnic minority members (interview with neighborhood officer 1, N1). In the Netherlands, as in England & Wales in particular, there is an ongoing discussion around ethnic profiling. The accusation is that the police let themselves be guided by ethnic stereotypes during stop and search of citizens, rather than by substantive criteria (Amnesty International, 2013). This entails a serious debate within the police around fair treatment and potential discrimination. One ethnic minority neighborhood officer, who emphasized that he himself had never experienced any such issues, describes what he considered to be an eye-opener:

> *Neighborhood officer 1, N1: '[I have] conducted a little bit of research myself amongst colleagues, talked to them, and spoken with colleagues who have a foreign background. I was shocked by their stories. If they take off their uniform, they are just regular foreign guys walking on the street. From them, I heard stories of how police officers treat them. It [DS: meaning ethnic discrimination] certainly exists.'*

In several interviews, I encountered a strong awareness of problems with police–ethnic minority relationships. Perceived solutions to these problems often remained a little vague—not formulated in terms of a strategy but, rather, as an ideal. Measures and policies to counter discrimination and increase the representativeness of the police organization have been taken, including diversity targets and cultural awareness training, but do not form a consistent or coherent whole and face resistance within the organization (Çankaya, 2015). Hence, they have a limited effect (Çankaya, 2011). Nevertheless, in this ideal and in these policies, notions of procedural justice are often central:

> *Member of regional unit command 2, N4: 'What is a good way to make sure colleagues keep thinking about the way they act? That is really connected with legitimacy. If you want to be trusted by the Moroccan community, you really need to have good policies in that domain.'*
> *DS: 'What are good policies, then?'*
> *Member of regional unit command 2, N4: 'In any case that as a policeman you show in your interactions with those people that you are not only checking them because they are Moroccan. That you are also willing to discuss this with them, and that you are willing to act in a different way because the environment asks for it. [...] In the end, it is very important to be the police for everyone, to take Article 1 of the Constitution[7] very seriously and to show that too. The moment you lose that and you don't consider that to be important anymore [...], then you lose trust, lose legitimacy, you're gone.'*

---

7.   Article 1 of the Dutch Constitution holds that all who are in the Netherlands are to be treated in the same way if they are under the same circumstances. It explicitly forbids all discrimination.

The Dutch police are struggling to formulate a coherent national strategy to deal with tensions around ethnic profiling and the potential for discrimination. Diversity within the police organization is a topic on the agenda (Ministerie van Veiligheid en Justitie, 2015), but how to affect police practice remains unclear. Policies and guidelines exist, but the extent to which they have an effect on trust-building practices is unclear. Rather, informants tend to evoke latent values that reflect procedural justice principles in abstraction: fairness, justice, equal treatment, and giving citizens a say. They also accept the importance of personal interactions. But although the problem is defined and accepted as one of trust, as of the time of writing, this has not resulted in a separate, procedural justice-inspired trust-building strategy.

10.8   Conclusions

Trust has been a central concept for the Dutch police for a long time—probably longer than in the other countries included in this study. While it has been defined in different ways and understood in varying terms throughout recent decades, it has only occasionally and very temporarily dropped off the policy agenda. We have seen that the initial postwar perception of lack of trust was addressed by professionalizing the police. The police were, however, unprepared for the challenges of the 1960s, when they dived head first into a crisis of authority. This was soon to be rephrased into a crisis of legitimacy. The policy document 'Changing police' formulated a proximity policing-based approach to address this crisis and has remained influential in thinking about trust and legitimacy up to the present day. The early to mid-1990s were the heyday of proximity policing, as many members of the generation adhering to the principles of 'Changing police' became the leadership of the new regional police system, as instituted per 1993. Increased proximity policing was intended to compensate for the centralizing tendencies of the regional model.

From the late 1980s onward, there was a growing concern with crime rates. Although the connection with trust and legitimacy was not as strong as during the crisis of authority of the preceding decades, there were indications that the increase in large-volume crimes could have consequences for trust in the police (Van der Vijver, 1993). Over the course of the 1990s, the emphasis gradually shifted to order maintenance and decreasing crime, summarized as the 'core tasks' of the police, as tools to restore police authority.

Also during the 1990s, the principles of the NPM model started to get applied to the police. Initially, this was related to the development of policy cycles and multiple-year strategic plans, which became increasingly harmonized toward the end of the decade. It was only with the societal turmoil of the early 2000s that NPM-related concepts were merged with instrumentalist assumptions about crime and security. Over the years, this evolved into a quantitative target framework for issues ranging from crimes and clearance rates to traffic fines, to measure police effectiveness and efficiency and to enhance public trust. With the advent of the national police, part of the performance management framework was abolished, but a substantial part remains.

The only development that is, at the time of writing, defined as a real problem of trust, the strained relationship with some sections within ethnic minority communities has not yet led to a cohesive trust-building strategy. This is despite the fact that it is understood mostly in procedural justice terms. Procedural justice, however, has no tradition of being an explicit strategy within Dutch policing.

In recent years, with the reform into a Dutch national police, the policy goals have still been to increase public trust, but we should keep in mind that this was not the main reason for the reform. A separate trust-building strategy did arrive with the national police: the service model. The application of this model is actually not the result of a perceived problem—if a reason is mentioned, it is to prevent a possible future problem with trust in a more centralized, potentially more distant police organization. I have indicated several potential pitfalls of this strategy, and studies conducted on the subject this far have shown that some of these pitfalls do prove problematic (Terpstra et al., 2015, 2016; Van der Torre et al., 2015).

COMPARING THE THREE CASE STUDIES

11.1   INTRODUCTION

Earlier on, I formulated three research questions regarding trust-building strategies that I aimed to answer by means of three case studies. Now that we have explored the three different contexts included in the research, it is time to return to these questions and attempt to formulate answers to them. In doing so, the aim is to construct an emerging theoretical framework for understanding police trust-building strategies in Western European countries. In the following sections, I will address each of these research questions:

> Research Question 4: *When and how was citizens' trust in the police defined as a problem in different European countries, and how did it evolve?*
> Research Question 5: *Since that time, what strategies and 'solutions' have been adopted by whom to address the problem of trust in these countries, and improve police–public relationships in general?*
> Research Question 6: *How can we understand the differences we find between and within countries in terms of problem definition and trust-building strategies?*

11.2   RESEARCH QUESTION 4: DEFINING THE PROBLEM OF TRUST

11.2.1   *Framing trust: Words and meanings*

Over the past chapters, we have seen that while the preferred term throughout this book may be trust, a wide variety of related terms are used when discussing police–public relationships. This variety occurs within countries as well, since all three cases under study feature a rich arsenal of concepts and vocabulary. Still, we can discern certain trends in each country. In England & Wales, the most popular terms are trust and confidence. Danish discourse rather stresses *tryghed*, while the Dutch have a tendency to describe the relationship between police and citizens in terms of authority and legitimacy—although trust is also being used more often in recent years.

To a certain extent, these differences could more or less amount to coincidence. The popularity of the term 'legitimacy' in the Netherlands, for example, is probably at least partially determined by its adoption by the authors of the influential vision document 'Changing police' (Heijink et al., 1977). But to a large extent, such variations in terminology are likely to reflect latent substantive cultural, historical, and structural differences. *Tryghed* reflects a typical Nordic understanding of an ideal community and suggests a governmental role as parent or teacher (Levisen, 2012). The Dutch tendency to phrase police–public relationships in terms of authority is possibly a reflection of the fact that governmental authority as a whole was challenged in a more direct and serious way than in the other two countries, during the late 1960s and 1970s. Trust and confidence are best used to reflect a less institutional, more interpersonal relationship and will be more prominent in contexts where such interpersonal relationships concerning the police are deemed more central. Their importance in British discourse and policy is hence '*closely linked to the position of the police in British social, cultural, and political life*' (Jackson & Bradford, 2010: 247). Legitimacy and authority, while used to varying extent in all three countries, may be particularly popular in countries where the police are known as a strong, state-connected institution; where state-centric, bureaucratic, and legalistic discourse and logic dominate. 'Satisfaction' is a term that has seen increasing popularity over the past two decades. It has more of a performance and consumer-oriented ring to it, and we have seen that it was more of a central concept in periods in time when notions from the NPM model were influential.

Language matters. Unfortunately, it is hard to say to what extent it matters and what difference it makes in practice. Two things are probably safe to conclude, based on these linguistic and conceptual differences. First, my tendency to speak of police initiatives as trust-building strategies is a simplification of a more complex and nuanced reality. These strategies may aim to address trust but, rather, often concentrate on a strongly related, but ultimately slightly different, notion. Second, conceptual differences between countries (and even within countries over time) will almost certainly lead to different problem definitions and are therefore likely to affect the nature of the strategies employed to address these problems.

11.2.2 *Problems and problem definitions*

The basis for any trust-building strategy is the acceptance of a problem that needs to be addressed. But what that problem is, how it came to be, and therefore how it is defined will differ substantially between countries. This is summarized by Nelken, who writes:

> '*It is misleading to assume that modern criminal justice systems all face the same 'problems' even if they deal with them in different ways. 'Problems'—and 'solutions'—are perceived and constructed differently within different cultures.*' (Nelken, 2010: 46)

This holds for each of the three cases under study. We have seen that England & Wales, Denmark, and the Netherlands have all had several defining moments in their more or less recent history that have made the problem of trust manifest as a policy problem. The Netherlands has struggled with the problem of trust since at least the end of World War II. In England & Wales, the emblematic status of the 'bobby on the beat' prevented any serious challenge to police–public relationships for a long time and obscured existing tensions, until inner-city strains and then the miners' strike shattered the image of harmony during the 1980s (Reiner, 2010). Arguably, Denmark did not experience a crisis of trust similar in scope and impact to those in the other two countries, but that does not mean that there were never problems with trust. It was only with the reorganizational problems after 2007 that a general problem was perceived in the relationship between the police and the public. Before that moment, issues tended to have a smaller scope and trust-building strategies, while present, lacked the urgency that was often present in the other two countries.

Trust-building activities are much more likely to come into being when relevant actors think there is an actual problem with trust. It should therefore be stressed that we are concerned with *perceived* problems. These are not necessarily objective ones by any fixed criteria, such as low public trust rates in surveys. The crisis of authority that the Netherlands went through in the late 1960s and 1970s was, as far as we can tell, not reflected in nationwide public opinion polls: public support of, and trust in the police was, by today's standards, even extremely high (Knibbeler, 1966)—although, lacking earlier measures, we do not know how this compares to levels of trust before the crisis of authority. Although it is hard to say so for sure, it at least appears likely that the level of Dutch public trust in the police, had it been measured cross-nationally, would not have been dissimilar to that of English and Danish citizens at the time. Despite this, however, the Dutch government and police experienced an unprecedented crisis of legitimacy and authority, while the English and Danish police organizations did not. They merely matter-of-factly noted that there were more youth movements to deal with and that they were asked to explain their decisions more often than before. There was more work to do, but despite increasing pressure, they did not experience a crisis or fundamental challenge. A problem of trust in the eyes of the police and the government does not, therefore, equal a problem of trust in the eyes of the public. This is an important finding. I have explained this specific case by including the attitudes of the media and local and national governments of the time, which in the Netherlands were much more conciliatory and lenient toward protesters, leaving the police isolated.

The wider societal context matters in the definition of a problem. This is not just a question of different concepts and meanings when comparing countries, but it is also related to the scope, extent, and area of the problem. Many problems with trust and police–public relationships in general were first clearly defined after a (violent) clash between the police and the public. However, the impact of such clashes can vastly differ depending on how they are assessed. For instance, compare the 1981 Brixton riots in London with the 1993 riots in Nørrebro, Copenhagen. On the face of it, there are strong similarities between these events. Both were deeply violent clashes that took place in the capital of the country, in one of the country's most problematic neighborhoods, and in both cases they led to extensive debates and inquiries on the political level as well as profound media scrutiny. However, while the Brixton riots were defined in terms of a broader crisis of trust between the police and large swathes of the public, the Nørrebro riots were not. They were seen as emblematic of outdated methods of riot policing, rather than signifying a deep societal problem that the police urgently needed to address. While the clashes in Nørrebro were, like those in Brixton, framed in terms of trust and legitimacy, it was the legitimacy of riot control techniques specifically that was perceived to be challenged, not that of the police as a whole. The problem of trust and legitimacy in England & Wales, following the events in Brixton, was therefore more serious and profound than the crisis in Denmark after Nørrebro. This had important consequences for the aftermath and ensuing policy measures.

A final matter in understanding problems and problem definitions is the question of who defines the problem. Sometimes, the problem is defined by only one actor, or by some actors, while some others do not participate in its definition, or even oppose it. One example can be found in the Stephen Lawrence case. The MacPherson report on the investigation of Mr. Lawrence's murder concluded that the police force was 'institutionally racist,' implying a major problem of trust (MacPherson, 1999). This was a diagnosis that many within the police vehemently opposed, even though it did chime with what certain segments of society were thinking.

This raises the serious question of the extent to which there can be productive trust-building strategies if one or more of the involved parties does not consider something to be an actual problem of trust—or does not define it in the same terms and relationships. Another example that reflects this tension is the Danish police reform of 2007: the Vision Committee that proposed the reform assumed there was a public call for the police to focus on crime-fighting as opposed to visibility, a demand the Committee suggested could lead to a problem of trust if unaddressed. There was very little evidence that the police and the public themselves perceived any such risk, and if so it was certainly not formulated in terms of trust. Given that the Committee assumed a problem in police–public relationships while other actors did not, it is perhaps not too surprising that the police reform led to more tensions than it resolved.

Regardless of these examples to the contrary, it is important to note that the presence of a problem is often understood collectively—that is, the government, the police, and the public all have some idea that a problem or crisis is going on. Naturally, these different actors often have different diagnoses of how the problem came to be and of exactly what it constitutes. In the Netherlands, from 1966 until all the way into the 1970s, the police experienced the problem that their authority was no longer accepted. However, an influential anarchist-leaning group of activists labeled 'Provo' (due to their provocative actions) considered it their primary goal to break state authority: a crisis of authority was perceived to be necessary—and hence not a problem, but a positive outcome for society (Daalder, 1990). In their eyes, the problem was rather the force that the police applied (Van Duyn, 1985).

In England & Wales during the 1990s, public trust in the police declined—and this was commonly accepted to constitute a problem. The prevailing idea within government was that this occurred because the police were not effective enough in dealing with crime: the underlying issue was a lack of effectiveness and efficiency. However, there was also an alternative diagnosis: declining trust could also be seen as one manifestation of the 'desacralization' (Loader & Mulcahy, 2003) of the police institution in the eyes of the public—the further the police moved away from what was perceived to be the traditional image of the 'bobby on the beat,' the more disillusioned the public grew. This had been the case since the 1980s with the Brixton riots and the miners' strike, and it only continued in the following years as the number of scandals mounted.

It is worthwhile to pay attention to the challenges in defining a problem of trust such as the examples I have illustrated above. Problem definitions and understandings determine the strategies applied to solve them, and different understandings of problems can give rise to counterproductive or contradictory strategies.

11.3   RESEARCH QUESTION 5: STRATEGIES AND SOLUTIONS

11.3.1   Different strategies

Over the past several chapters, we have seen the recurring presence of all three trust-building strategies derived from the theoretical perspectives defined throughout this book. Instrumentalism, proximity policing, and procedural justice have each appeared throughout all three cases. This does not imply that the existence of these three strategies is an imperative, a sort of naturally occurring universal rule. Still, it is noteworthy that we can recognize strategies derived from these theoretical perspectives under varying circumstances. That being said, their presence and dominance shift strongly over time, differ depending on the country and local context, and are neither mutually exclusive nor necessarily complementary in their occurrence. The strategies, although they sometimes compete for dominance, can exist more or less independently from each other.

Instrumentalism has been present in each of the three countries at times, albeit earliest (and strongest) in England & Wales and latest in Denmark. In all three cases, there was a connection between instrumentalist notions of effectiveness in decreasing crime on the one hand, and NPM ideas of an efficient, businesslike state on the other. Performance targets and systems of benchmarking have similarly risen across these different contexts, although different in execution and at varying points in time. In Denmark, the NPM model had only a weak link with instrumentalism. For instance, the 1990s saw a focus first in England & Wales, and in the Netherlands toward the end of the decade, on the so-called 'main job' (England & Wales) or 'core tasks' (Netherlands) of the police: catching criminals. In Denmark, police duties remained wide in scope and any related notion or desire to trim down the number of police tasks to focus more on crime (and measure those tasks with a performance regime) only came to the forefront around the police reorganization of 2007.

Proximity policing has, in different forms and with different labels, been arguably the most popular police trust-building strategy. Successive waves of proximity policing have tended to engulf police leadership in different phases since the 1970s. It is a school of thought that also has undergone increasing sophistication and professionalization, particularly in Denmark and in England & Wales. Much of the idealism underlying proximity policing in the early stages in the Netherlands (Heijink et al., 1977) and in England & Wales (Alderson, 1979) has faded in later years. Ambitions have been downgraded from rather general goals of fostering democracy and freedom, to better addressing local problems and improving police-citizen relationships. It is a strategy that has broad support across different layers of the police organization and has proven to be quite resilient, even though it has at times disappeared from the (top of the) policy agenda.

Procedural justice, then, is the theoretical perspective that has the weakest organizational representation in the cases under study. This is not to say that it has no relevance, but a broad awareness of the importance of procedural justice principles does not in every case lead to actual trust-building strategies founded on these ideas. This is especially remarkable in the Netherlands, where procedural justice-inspired rules and minor reforms are plenty, but seem to lack a common framework. It is somewhat stronger in Denmark, but in both countries any procedural justice-related considerations of fair and equal treatment, or giving citizens the opportunity to make their case, are also likely to find shelter under the broad umbrella of proximity policing initiatives. England & Wales is a bit different in this sense in that there has been a (much) stronger historical focus both on scandals within the police and on measures attempting to prevent future scandals. Relationships between the police and ethnic minorities have also been on the policy agenda for a longer time, giving easier prominence to issues of fair and equal treatment.

Aside from the three theoretical perspectives included in the rest of the study, I have also found indications of trust-building strategies rooted in different ideas and assumptions. These tended to be unique for the country under study, or at least be much stronger there than in other contexts. The most important of these is the central position of democratic accountability in the English police model. The historical notion that giving the public a say in policing matters is essential for trusted policing has shaped different schemes and constellations over time. Most recently, this idea has inspired the institution of police and crime commissioners— elected officials expected to be the link between the public and the police. In the Netherlands and Denmark, concerns about democratic accountability were weaker. In Denmark, the rather indirect exercise of democratic accountability through parliament was usually deemed to be sufficient. In the Netherlands, concern about weak influence of local councils on policing matters is regularly voiced, but seldom connected to trust.

In the Netherlands after the police reform of 2013, a new trust-building strategy has been formulated that is founded on certain heavily rationalized (in a Weberian sense) service principles. While as of yet limited in scope, and although the extent of its practical implementation is disputable, it has fundamentally different assumptions regarding public trust in the police. The core idea is that a distant, uniformly operating police can gain public trust by being predictable and systematic in their treatment of citizens. In this, it shares some properties with the old professional model of policing (popular until about the 1970s across the Western world), but borrows concepts and assumptions from the NPM model and the way in which large businesses operate. In England & Wales, inspired by the work of Ritzer (1983, 2008), Heslop (2011) has referred to the heavily standardized, controlled, calculable, and efficiency-focused style of policing that has been shaped by the combination of NPM influences and the professionalization movement as the McDonaldization of the police. With this, he means that attempts to rationalize the policing function and organization have led to various irrational outcomes. Examples are increasing bureaucracy and diminishing police discretion. In the case of the Netherlands, it is contact with citizens and trust-building specifically that seem to have aligned with Ritzer's (2008) aspects of calculability, efficiency, predictability, and control. Here too, the irrationality of rationalization looms: a police organization that is distant, far removed from citizens, and invisible might be efficient in its service in some ways, but also risks losing its ties to the very communities it relies upon for information and support.

In the preceding section, I have described the dominant trust-building strategies in the three countries under study. We saw that several strategies are or were present in all three, but that others appear to be unique. What this suggests is that thinking about trust and how to improve it is probably not limited to the models I have described here; in other contexts, other ways of thinking are certainly imaginable.

11.3.2   *Policy generation and how trust-building strategies come about*

Following the description of different strategies in the three cases involved, it is time to shift our attention to how these strategies come about; how policies with the goal of promoting trust are generated. We need to know more about the dynamics and internal logic of trust-building strategies.

First, as with the process of problem definition, policy generation is dependent on the actors involved. It is important to note, then, is that trust-building strategies need not necessarily be designed (exclusively) by the police. More often than not, they are composed by several actors working more or less in tandem. Even in these cases, however, it tends to be one dominant actor that initiates such a development, and this one actor is often from outside the police—most of the time, from a ministry or another branch of government.

This is not to say that the police are not capable of designing trust-building strategies. Many police officers across all ranks have a genuine interest in knowing what citizens want, and it is certainly no exaggeration to say that trust-building is a subject with which the police are deeply involved in each country presently under study. But at the same time, the police often leave the initiative for new strategies to government or others. For governmental actors, ideological motivations for designing trust-building strategies can play a role, such as the installment of police and crime commissioners, in England & Wales, but mundane electoral considerations can be involved as well. Politicians, by the nature of their job, require an affinity for public opinion.

Having said this, it is surprising to note that it is England & Wales where government has played a central role in every new phase of trust-building since the early 1980s. In Denmark and the Netherlands, the picture is much more mixed, with several strategies originating from within the police. This is a rather counter-intuitive finding: England & Wales features the proportionally smallest government and a strong historical connotation of constabulary independence, whereas in the Netherlands, and particularly Denmark, the role of the state in public affairs is traditionally stronger—the police are seen as part of the state. Therefore, one would expect government to play a more central role in the development of trust-building strategies in the latter two countries. Nevertheless, we can see that Denmark as well as the Netherlands went through multiple trust-building phases developed by the police, where governmental agencies or political parties only jumped on the bandwagon after several years of police initiatives. In Denmark, the second wave of proximity policing (from about 1995 onward) was strongly driven by the national police commissioner as well as several local ones, while the third wave (after about 2012) was initiated by local commissioners and their deputies. In the Netherlands, proximity policing initially built on the ideas of three lowly inspectors—while its increasing popularity during the mid-1990s can be understood as a political compromise between local and national actors. After the 1993 police reform, the increasing scale of police districts had caused local governments and mayors to fear that the police would become too distant an actor (Cachet et al., 1994). The stimulation of proximity policing was a way to keep the police closely connected with local communities and local actors, alleviating these concerns (Terpstra et al., 2010: 30).

Interestingly, in the U.K. after the Brixton riots, government and police chiefs both initiated their own separate trust-building strategies: the Home Office focused on developing the procedural justice-oriented Police and Criminal Evidence Act of 1984,[1] whereas police chiefs experimented with forms of proximity policing. In doing so, both were following some of the recommendations of Lord Scarman (1982), illustrating the influence of nonpolice actors on trust-building in the country. The invention of neighbourhood policing in England after about 2001 was also led by governmental efforts—albeit co-developed by police and scientists.

This gives rise to the question of why governmental actors tend to play such a central role in English trust-building strategies in particular, since it would be the country in which one would expect the contrary, and less in the other two nations. One possibility is that policing is a highly politicized subject in England & Wales. Note, for instance, that any change of government in the U.K. will almost certainly also result in serious changes in policing—or at least, this is what has happened since the first Thatcher government was elected in 1979. In an essentially bipolar political system, the main political parties in the U.K. differ strongly in their vision on policing (although it should be noted that these visions are in flux themselves). Both the Netherlands and Denmark, on the other hand, saw wide cross-party political support for the large-scale police reorganizations that they implemented in 2013 and 2007, respectively. But this is only one possible explanation for the marked difference between the countries in terms of the actors initiating trust-building strategies—and even so, it does not address the cause of the higher politicization of policing in England & Wales.

The actual contents of trust-building strategies greatly depend on the circumstances and on the actors themselves. Political ideology is one such factor, although we should be careful not to exaggerate its importance. Proximity policing initiatives, instrumental measures, and procedural justice-oriented policies all have been initiated by the political left as well as the right. But in times when social democratic ideas about the welfare state have been dominant, proximity policing initiatives have tended to be popular. Similarly, in a more punitive climate, actors are more likely to turn to instrumentalist strategies. Often, a new government is likely to turn to policies that are substantially different from those of their predecessors. Such an explanation of trust-building strategies is less connected with ideological than with electoral aspects of politics.

---

1.   Procedural justice was not a term regularly used at that time, but for instance former Home Office senior civil servant David Faulkner writes that the *Police and Criminal Evidence Act 1984 [...] had brought greater integrity to the process of law enforcement. Minorities and victims of crime came to be treated with more consideration and respect and their voices were more often heard'* (Faulkner, 2014: 153), thus ticking several boxes of the procedural justice paradigm.

More important, therefore, are probably influences of contemporary ideas and fashions that have spread across public-sector policies as a whole. When the NPM model affects many sections of government, it is likely that its principles will be applied to the police as well. Since the NPM model is supposed to address an enormously wide range of problems and issues with the public sector, it is only logical that it will eventually also be applied as trust-building strategy for the police. Similarly, a 'localism' agenda in British politics (first adopted by Labour) contributed to shaping new proximity strategies, as well as strategies focusing on (local) democratic accountability. The same could be said of the 'Big Society' agenda included in the 2010 Conservative manifesto.

A final factor that should be addressed here is the appeal of policy transfer of seemingly fertile ideas from abroad, something I encountered in all three countries under study, and on the national as well as the local level. For the different countries included in this study, there are varying police systems that function as an example. England & Wales does not appear to draw much on foreign strategies, except for those coming from the U.S. One exception, in the case of PCSOs, is the Netherlands (Savage, 2007). For the most part, though, they are probably best described as a net exporter of policing models and of trust-building strategies. This can be observed in Denmark and the Netherlands, where policy-makers use England & Wales as a role model for (part of) their trust-building efforts—although they also draw from each other. For Denmark, its traditionally strong ties with the U.S. mean that their proximity policing strategies are to a considerable extent inspired by those in certain American cities. Cooperation and sharing information on ideas and strategies is also common with Sweden and particularly Norway. For the Dutch, the entire policing model is an amalgamation of British, German, and French elements. In terms of trust-building, however, the influences are primarily Anglo-Saxon—the French are looked upon as a worst-practice case due to the perceived distance between the police and citizens there, while the legacy of World War II meant that for a long time the German police were anathema. In recent decades, interaction and cooperation have increased, but strong differences in police systems and cultures remain (Liedenbaum, 2011). I will address policy transfer more extensively in Section 11.4.2.

11.4   RESEARCH QUESTION 6: UNDERSTANDING DIFFERENCES

11.4.1   *The local and national context and agency*

Previous sections have dealt with problem recognition as related to trust, and with the design of trust-building strategies to address these problems. The sixth and final research question deals with our understanding of differences between countries in these aspects. Based on the three previous chapters, how can we frame the differences that we see in problem definitions and trust-building strategies between countries, but also between different moments in time within the same country?

My assertion, based on the previous case studies, is that an understanding of such differences relies entirely on appreciating the importance of context and agency. Factors shaping problem definitions and strategies can, in large part, be found on the national, local, or individual level. While the type of factor that plays these roles can be understood cross-nationally, the factor itself is often largely dependent on context and agency.

Table 11.1 displays how trust-building strategies are shaped. First, they consist of three phases that, in practice, can happen simultaneously or, at least, are permanently in flux. These are the process of problem recognition, the generation of policies (in this case, trust-building strategies), and the adoption of such strategies. The latter implies their formal adoption as can be seen in laws or policy documents, for instance, as well as the way in which they are adopted and internalized, and the intensity with which the trust-building strategy is actually followed through.

Each of these three stages is shaped by a few criteria. For instance, if and how a problem of trust is recognized depends on the conceptual understanding of trust—which terms are used to describe trust relationships in a country. However, it also relies on the diagnosis being made of the main problem at hand. What is the critical issue at hand? The second stage is the generation of strategies to address the problem of trust. The approach is formed mostly on the basis of the general type of strategy that is being preferred (proximity-related, instrumental, procedurally just, or otherwise) and by the main actors that are involved in the generation of strategies. These can, for instance, be various governmental or policing actors. Third, to what extent and in what way strategies are adopted depends on a wide range of potential stimulating and impeding factors.

Table 11.1   The trust-building complex

Policy process:	Defined by:	Context and agency:
Problem recognition	Conceptual understanding of trust Definition or diagnosis of problem	Language and history Acuteness of problem or crisis
Generating strategies	Preferred type of strategy Main actors involved	Influence of other countries Ideology and politics (Unexpected) events
Adopting strategies	Stimulating factors vs. Impeding factors	Preferences of key individuals Police support Cultural and structural factors

Table 11.2   A summary of trust-building strategies in England & Wales, Denmark, and the Netherlands

	When (±)	Concept used	Problem definition	Strategy designed
England & Wales	1981–1984	Confidence	Ethnic tensions & Brixton riots	Community policing / Procedural justice
	1994–1999	Confidence	Rising crime	Instrumentalism
	1999	Trust & fairness	Stephen Lawrence inquiry	Procedural justice
	2001–2004	Reassurance	Confidence gap / distant police	Neighbourhood policing
	2010	Trust & confidence	Police seen as spoiled & arrogant	Democratic accountability
Denmark	1983	*Tryghed*	Rising crime / police visibility	Proximity policing
	1993	Legitimacy	Nørrebro riots	Riot police reform
	1996–2000	Trust & quality of life	Local policing had slumped	Proximity policing
	2007	*Reel tryghed*	Public want more objective safety	Instrumentalism
	2009–2013	Satisfaction	Crisis in response & in visibility	Proximity policing
	2010–2014	Trust	Ethnic tensions	Proximity policing
The Netherlands	1945–1950s	Trust	Acts of police in WWII	Professionalization
	1966–1980	Authority & legitimacy	Crisis of authority in Dutch society	Proximity policing
	1993–1999	Societal integration	Police disconnected from local actors after reform	Proximity policing
	1999–2003	Satisfaction & authority	Rising crime / police seen as soft	Instrumentalism
	2012	Satisfaction & trust	Lack of service uniformity	Service model / instrumentalism

By whom	Stimulating factors	Impeding factors
Police chiefs / Government	Authority of Lord Scarman / concern of Home Sec. Brittan	Miners' strike / lack of government support
Government	Rise of NPM model across public sector	Organizational resistance in police
Government	Media campaign	Police cultural & organizational resistance
Government, police chiefs, & scientists	Public consensus / calls for visibility	Target culture / focus on fighting crime
Government	Media criticism & scandals	Public apathy / budget cuts
Government	Reforms popular with local councils	Little urgency perceived
Government	Some support for cause of rioters	Problem limited to one (large) incident
National and local police chiefs	Policy transfer / police wide range of tasks	Trust already high / concept over-sold to public
Government & national police chief	Rise of NPM model / power of Ministry of Finance	Resistance by local councils
National and local police chiefs	Media campaign and public demand	Performance framework initially not conducive
Local police chiefs	Reform strengthened local police capacity	Police cultural resistance
Police chiefs	British example / history of professional policing	Weak lustration / low-standard postwar recruits
Middle-ranking officers	Political interest / matched societal climate	Old police chiefs adhered to professional model
Police chiefs & mayors	New generation of police chiefs / political compromise	Push for funds for investigative and specialized departments
Government	Murder of Pim Fortuyn / security prime concern	Police preference for proximity policing
Government	Establishment of national police	Organizational chaos

This is where the crucial role of the local and national context comes in, as well as that of agency. Various aspects can shape all previously mentioned criteria. The conceptual understanding of trust (which eventually determines problem recognition) is itself determined by factors such as language and history, by cultural and structural factors, by ideology or politics, by unexpected events, by preferences and agency of key individuals, or by yet other factors. Similarly, the definition or diagnosis of the problem, the preferred type of strategy, and the main actors involved are all shaped by such aspects of the local and national context, as well as by the agency of individuals. Contextual factors and agency, then, can also directly serve as impediments or stimulants for the adoption of a new trust-building strategy. Contextual aspects and agency, such as advocacy by key individuals, can enable a trust-building strategy to make it to the top of the policy agenda. The other side of the coin, though, is that context can also inhibit the adoption of a strategy; circumstances can greatly narrow or obstruct a strategy's way to the top of the agenda, or key individuals can block its access. In this way, the national or local context and agency can impede the blossoming of a trust-building strategy. We can see that every strategy discussed over the past chapters has its context. Often, as we have seen before, some contextual factors will serve as impediments while others will function as stimulants—all at the same time. This also means that a multitude of factors will be at play simultaneously: interacting, competing, or mutually reinforcing. The outcomes of such processes are the way in which strategies will be adopted, the intensity with which this will happen, and how successful such a strategy will ultimately be considered to be.

Contextual factors, as an umbrella term, still appear somewhat vague. What is part of the national or local context, and what is not? And how could individual agency make a difference? In Table 11.2, I have summarized the most important phases of trust-building in all three of the countries I have studied in this part of this book. I have displayed the concrete outcomes of the trust-building complex outlined in Table 11.1. In terms of stimulating and impeding factors, I should note that I have vastly simplified them here, only displaying the most important factors of context and agency. However, what is clear from Table 11.2 is that even such a simplified portrayal of the main stimulating and impeding factors at play offers a rich array of often unique processes, actions, or events.

It is important to note that I do not mean context to be a static concept. An obstructive context can evolve into a greatly conducive one for a new strategy within years or even months. Context is shaped, determined, and changed by events. (Political) events are what Kingdon (1995) considered to be the third step in the policy process: events open policy windows during which alternative ideas and policies can gain dominance. In terms of police trust-building strategies, factors of interest are openings for new strategies and new ideas to improve public trust. After defining a problem and generating a policy to address the problem, often an event and hence a change in context is required for this policy proposal to become reality. For the purposes of the present study, events can be political in nature—as in the case of elections or changes in governments, for example. They can also rely on acts of key individuals. But, on the other hand, they often turn out to entail some sort of scandal or a conflict between the police and the public. Public-order breakdowns, large-scale riots, or widely publicized instances of police brutality can provide a window of opportunity to place trust-building at the top of the policy agenda and push certain strategies or reforms (Savage, 2007). Such events tend to reflect larger perceived underlying issues and problems that a strategy can address. Therefore, this sort of event not only plays an essential role in problem definitions, as described in Section 11.2.2, but also helps to define and adopt a solution.

Events are often influenced and determined by individual agency, but in turn also influence individuals. These dynamics are hard to pin down or explain through any general theorizing. How and why specific individuals reasoned or acted under specific circumstances is often difficult to reconstruct or even understand—although this can be quite important. It is even more daunting to predict for the future: individual agency or responses to events can be related to personal chemistry between two or more actors, or attributed to personal convictions, preferences, faith, or even sudden insights. Often, it is not abstract mechanisms or structures that allow for a trust-building strategy to develop, but individuals in certain positions who cultivate this for a variety of reasons of their own. Using the term of Kingdon (1995), such individuals can act as policy entrepreneurs pushing their own solutions and strategies. Whether they manage to achieve their ends depends to a large extent on their *'creativity, energy, and political skill'* (Mintrom & Norman, 2009: 650). This is the importance of agency. It also illustrates why cross-national comparisons need to take very careful account of local and national context as well as the agency of key individuals.

I shall discuss one case that illustrates these individual dynamics. In Denmark, I visited one police district where two key individuals from very different backgrounds met after a highly publicized incident in a troubled neighborhood. Together, they then designed and pushed a trust-building strategy for this neighborhood, working as policy entrepreneurs in this district:

> Police commissioner, D1: '[Consultant, D1] was a well-known person, had a lot of jobs involving integration, been a politician, publically known and read and said lots of things. We talked after [a television panel we had both been attending]. We were both annoyed that it was the same [sort of incident] every time. We had never talked before, and we wondered whether we couldn't find a way to stop this.'
> [...]
> Consultant, D1: 'I have lived in [that neighborhood] for several years. I remained active afterwards. I know the area and the local issues, because I have worked inside and outside the area as social advisor, with dysfunctional families specifically and social issues more generally. It's part of my profession: develop new methods, networking, how to use resources instead of only focusing on the problem. And

when [Police commissioner, D1] and I talked together, we were both frustrated that we had had the same problems for 20 years: the same troubles, the same persons, the same criminals, the same issues every single year. If we keep doing what we always have done, we will get the results that we always have gotten. So maybe we just have to sit down and try to get something different to reach a different result. We had a brainstorm, and I liked the way [Police commissioner, D1] was thinking.'

[...]

Police commissioner, D1: 'We had the idea we had to start a dialogue with the well-functioning people [in the neighborhood]. [Consultant, D1] knows how to do it: you can do it wrong and you can do it right. If you go to the wrong people, others will mistrust you even more. We had to find people who are trusted by a lot of well-functioning citizens. Find the right people, people they trust.'

In the particular case above, a local trust-building approach was based on proximity ideas and dialogue with local communities, as part of the recent revival of proximity policing strategies in Denmark. But it is questionable whether this strategy would have been adopted had these two policy entrepreneurs never worked together, had they not shared their respective ideas and resources, and had they not led by example (Mintrom & Norman, 2009).

Trust-building strategies can also be a near-accidental outcome of individuals' preferences in other fields. One can think of Leon Brittan, the British Home Secretary whose focus on improving public confidence was probably as much a response to a perceived problem of trust as it was a strategy to strengthen his own vulnerable position in the Conservative Party. Remaining in the field of Tory Home Secretaries, Nelken (2010) noted how Douglas Hurd and his successor Michael Howard had entirely different interpretations of public attitudes toward crime and punishment. While the former relied on his moderate senior civil servants for many of his policies, the latter was driven by his own, punitive convictions. The difference between these individuals could possibly account for a part of the shift toward instrumentalist thought regarding trust-building during the 1990s —parallel to what Loader (2006) described as the 'fall of the Platonic guardians.' This connection confirms that national, contextual developments are never disconnected from personal, individual agency.

Finally, it is important to note the role of the police: if they were not involved in designing the trust-building strategy, a measure of police support is eventually essential in order for the strategy to be adopted, accepted, and internalized. Such support can be cultivated in various ways. We have seen that financial incentives, education and training, or the promise of more professional autonomy are tools employed by governments to make trust-building strategies attractive to the police. Attempts can also be made to first experiment with newly designed strategies or to implement them in limited or watered-down versions. Proximity policing in particular has seen countless such experiments and trials in the three countries under study, but this also happens with procedural justice-inspired ideas such as the introduction of body-worn cameras in England & Wales. These small-scale experiments can take place if the strategy is a top-down initiative, but also if it grows from the grassroots level. Systematic evaluations of strategies, on the other hand, are still not commonplace. Often, small-scale experiments or implementations are intended not to test whether the core idea of a trust-building strategy holds but, rather, to smooth it around the edges and cultivate further support for and involvement in the new approach.

Over the previous pages, I have attempted to shed light on the complex shaping and influencing of trust building strategies in the three countries under study. These are factors that we need to take into account when attempting to explain how and why a certain trust-building strategy is applied by the police in a given place at a given moment in time. What appears clear in this analysis is that if we wish to understand trust-building strategies, we need to make a serious effort to understand national and local context and have an appreciation of the role of individual agency. Without this crucial awareness, any cross-national comparison of police trust-building strategies is almost guaranteed to fall flat. Such a comparison would miss the vital point of police trust-building activities: they are, more than anything else, nationally and locally determined.

11.4.2   Policy transfer and foreign imports

Now that we have established the importance of national and local context as well as individual agency in shaping trust-building strategies, let us turn our attention toward that other aspect that shapes trust-building: international influences. We have seen over the past several chapters, as illustrated in Table 11.2, that the three different countries have often opted for (on the surface) quite similar strategies to address the problem of trust. For example, proximity policing strategies have in several instances been applied to restore the connection with citizens in all three cases under study. Despite this observation, it is important to note that similarity does not mean that things are identical. This is where the national and local context interact with international influences. Imagine the difference between the rhetoric or official language often applied in policy documents and the various local interpretations of a strategy, and we can already see that this poses challenges. Given the paucity of cross-national or in-depth studies on different locations within the same country on the topic, it is easy to underestimate the relevance of these differences and the way in which context and agency shape strategies or ideas imported from abroad. The national or local characteristics of a receiving setting can insure that core concepts from an imported strategy can change totally in meaning.

Some discrepancies can be remarkable, but are in practice probably inconsequential. One such example was derived from the (former) London Metropolitan Police commissioner Hogan-Howe, who labeled his trust-building strategy across London 'total policing.' Such a slogan would certainly be frowned upon in most continental countries, since throughout history many of them have had experiences with regimes that, in practice, applied forms of total—implying totalitarian—policing. The actual contents of Mr. Hogan-Howe's trust-building activities connected to this slogan, however, are probably less controversial—referring to temporary intense ('total') attention to select types of offenses. According to one of my informers, *'it has the symbolic value of 'total commitment''* (interview with HMIC inspector 1).

A potentially more problematic issue can occur when the language and manifest logic used to argue for certain strategies in preference to others are in fact similar across countries. Words and terms associated with a certain strategy or paradigm can appeal to policy-makers and police chiefs from different backgrounds and in different countries (Crawford, 2009). Police organizations, governments, and other actors draw inspiration and ideas from other contexts—sometimes taking place as gradual diffusion, but often in a more systematic form of policy transfer. Obviously, learning from others can be profitable and has the potential to genuinely improve policing practice. The underlying assumptions and goals of a (trust-building) strategy, however, can still strongly differ despite the superficially universally compelling language. What is perceived as a great success by people in one context, can, if transferred to another context, fall flat or have seriously adverse effects—and even the very definition of success is strongly context-dependent (Nelken, 2010). Many issues and challenges around policy transfer to developing countries in particular are by now well known (for various examples from all over the globe, see Blaustein, 2015; Brogden, 2005; Cain, 2000; Dammert & Malone, 2006; Kyed, 2009; Peacock & Cordner, 2016; Steinberg, 2011). Similar albeit probably less hazardous issues are involved with Western countries drawing from each other. Ideas about the state and citizens are reproduced in policing and in trust-building strategies specifically. This implies, as illustrated in the previous section, that trust-building strategies reflect the national culture, history, and sensitivities. In the importation of ideas from abroad, this fundamental point is often ignored.

There is one significant advantage for Western societies subject to policy transfer as compared to their counterparts in the global South: there is a much more equal relationship between the donor country and the receiving context. This also makes it less likely that a strategy will be fully transplanted into the new context. Rather, the receiving side can be expected to sieve the foreign model through its own interpretation and will attempt to fit it in with its own policing traditions (Jones & Newburn, 2007; Punch, 2007). Rhetoric is often rapidly copied and adopted to be applied in the form of buzzwords, but underlying ideas, assumptions, and actual practice are likely to strongly deviate from the original model and be adjusted to the new context. As Punch (2007) noted in his analysis of the policy transfer of zero-tolerance policing from the U.S. to the Netherlands and England & Wales, regular visits by senior police officers to the donor country lead to quick adoption of foreign catchphrases and expressions. However, *'[b]ehind the cosmopolitan façade, there are hidden conventions and [...] a resilient parochialism'* (Punch, 2007:

33). Actors in the receiving context have the ability and autonomy to select which ideas to implement and in what fashion to do so. They will, among other things, be guided by historical, cultural, and structural characteristics: by national and local context.

In some situations, we can discern an interaction between internationally relatively standardized and more local terms—they may merge, with all sorts of possible effects on police practice and trust-building strategies. An important example is the shift in Danish safety related discourse, where the initial term was the holistic word *tryghed*. In the early 2000s, it received an adjective in some cases: *reel tryghed*, to indicate objective security as a segment of the holistic interpretation. Finally, the original *tryghed* was turned into *tryghedsfølelse*, turning it into a purely subjective experience or perception—suggesting, en passant, that it was not as important to take into account, since it 'only' concerned feelings rather than *reel*, 'real' or 'objective' safety. This transfer (and translation) of English-language discourse to the Danish context had consequences for the practices of the police after the 2007 police reorganization, and by neglecting the original, Nordic conception of *tryghed*, led to probably faulty assumptions about what citizens wanted from the police. It ignored an core aspect of the receiving context.

Policy transfer and the translation of foreign trust-building models explain to a certain extent why the countries under study resemble one another in some respects and at some moments. At the same time, how these processes play out in different contexts also illustrates differences between the countries. We can see that while similar terms are often used in different countries, the substance and practices beneath this rhetoric strongly depend on context: context absorbs ideas and strategies, but also has the strength to adjust foreign models until they are almost unrecognizable.

11.4.3   *Switching strategies*

Once commonly accepted and adopted, a trust-building strategy can become institutionalized as a dominant paradigm—so powerful, sometimes, that it becomes hard to remember that it was not always like this. All activities and the entire discourse seem to be geared toward a certain strategy, a certain way of thinking and reasoning not only about police–public relationships, but even about the function of the police in society. The strategy, in this sense, has solidified. But after a while, despite, or perhaps because of, the dominance of such a trust-building paradigm, dissenting voices tend to emerge. Evidence, either research-based or anecdotal, indicates that all is not well with the paradigm. As trust-building strategies are characterized by a desire to strengthen specific elements of policing, after a while, other aspects can be perceived to be withering away. Instrumentalism often implies a preoccupation with measurable results; proximity policing will concentrate on local policing; while procedural justice tends to emphasize interactions between police and citizens. Almost by definition, such a strong focus often means that other aspects of police work receive less attention. A backlash from proponents of these other aspects is therefore to be expected; they are likely to feel that their preference is being neglected and will stress the negative consequences of this, in their view, single-minded preoccupation with one aspect of policing. The longer a certain paradigm dominates, the stronger the opposition is likely to grow: the shortcomings of the dominant strategy tend to become more visible and problematic the longer they endure. Eventually, this process is one of the main drivers behind changes in trust-building strategies.

This process has been manifest throughout the recent history of all three countries under study. We can see that the instrumental thinking dominant in England & Wales during the late 1990s and early 2000s, designed to improve public trust, was eventually perceived to increase the distance between the police and the public and make the police unresponsive to local demands. This made the national and local contexts conducive to a different trust-building strategy. The countermove consisted of reassurance and neighbourhood policing initiatives, which became dominant strategies over the course of the 2000s. With the start of the coalition government in 2010, these strategies were found to be too expensive and, therefore, the government argued, wasteful in the eyes of the public. The Home Secretary argued that high funding under the previous government had made the police arrogant in their treatment of citizens. The context had changed and individual agency—in this case by the Home Secretary—led to a change in strategies. The new dominant trust-building strategies, responding to the perceived shortcomings, emphasized correct treatment through procedural justice and democratic accountability through the institution of police and crime commissioners.

The examples listed above illustrate that shortcomings with a trust-building strategy will also be perceived to affect police–public relationships in a negative way. This suggests that the problems of this strategy are not merely limited to side effects in fields that have little relevance to the public, but will in fact mean that the strategy as a whole is perceived to no longer contribute to improving public trust in the police. This shift in thought tends to occur gradually and often involves the rise of a new generation within the police or in policy circles. This is a requirement because police paradigms tend to have their own frames, consisting of specific language, causal reasoning, and archetypes (Terpstra, 2013). This makes it hard to change or even develop such a strategy—it would to a large extent require one to step outside this frame. Different strategies have entirely different logic, sensitizing concepts, and problem definitions. The paradigm shift necessary for a change in trust-building strategies is therefore likely to take time and requires people from outside the old paradigm. But as the decline of a dominant trust-building strategy takes place, actors within and outside of the police will start to formulate their own analysis of the problems involved with the dominant paradigm, and then draw up a solution to address these problems. Under the right conditions, one or even more of these alternatives can eventually replace the old strategy. It is not a given that such a process will actually take place; there is no a priori reason to state that trust-building strategies can never last. However, as more contextual changes take place and more time passes with one paradigm or strategy dominating, the likelihood of an eventual shift grows.

11.4.4   *Convergence of trust-building strategies?*

If we accept that processes of diffusion or policy transfer affect police trust-building strategies, and that dominant trust-building strategies in different countries tend to change, is it then unreasonable to expect that these strategies will eventually start to resemble one another more and more? Echoing Crawford's (2009) question on the direction of crime prevention strategies across Europe, to what extent can we see convergence of police trust-building strategies in the three countries under study? The fall of a formerly dominant paradigm can be a possible opportunity for a foreign model to take its place: often, such imported models show great promise and have enthusiastic advocates, on the face of it making such a convergence of trust-building strategies in different countries quite credible.

There are certainly reasons to expect a convergence of strategies across Europe. Processes of globalization, increasing exchanges of police staff, the establishment and flourishing of various supranational policing bodies—all of these factors could contribute to countries being inspired by strategies from abroad and copying their central tenets. With these trends, challenges to policing and trust could also start to grow more similar. At least one major recent collection of studies does suggest that converging tendencies in terms of police organization can be found throughout Northern and Western Europe. The collection of Fyfe et al. (2013) shows a (predominantly) centralizing trend across these parts of the continent. In their introductory chapter, Terpstra and Fyfe argue that the recent police reforms in this region indicate '*if not a transformation, at least a fundamental set of changes to the relationships between police organizations, governments, and citizens.*' (Terpstra & Fyfe, 2013: 1). Nevertheless, cross-national convergence in the constellation of police organizations, governments, and citizens does not automatically equal convergence in trust-building strategies per se.

Observing the more or less recent history of trust-building strategies in the Netherlands, Denmark, and England & Wales, several indications of convergence do come to mind initially. For example, there is the series of waves of proximity policing initiatives in all three countries from roughly the 1970s onward. Even stronger is the converging nature of NPM-influenced models. The rise of the NPM model across the continent has done a great deal to standardize large parts of the police organization—including dealings with citizens and reasoning about trust. This is quite visible in all three cases. Based on these trends, there is hence certainly cause to speak of convergence.

It would nonetheless be too simple to speak only of convergence of trust-building. Aside from the cross-national trends mentioned above, there is also evidence to the contrary. Recently, this has come to light with various strategies that have been followed since about 2010-2012. As Table 11.2 shows, the focus has been on entirely different strategies in each of the three cases: different strategies rooted in completely different assumptions on what people want from their police, executed on different governance levels with support (and opposition) from very different actors. England & Wales has seen a Conservative–Liberal Democrat government concentrate on democratizing policing and a Home Secretary in open conflict with the police organization in an attempt to change police behavior, but also to create a clear break with the earlier Labour governments. At the same time, Denmark has featured a resurgence of proximity policing to deal with issues around diminished police visibility and unrest in troubled neighborhoods. Only a short time after the other two countries designed these strategies, the Dutch police were reorganized on a national basis with, at least on a rhetorical level, a coherent trust-building strategy based on uniform service provision to citizens. Given that in doing so, all three countries discarded some notions derived from the NPM model (to varying extents, all of them shifted attention away from measurable performance frameworks, although the Dutch case still leans considerably on instrumentalist notions and maintain a tough-on-crime rhetoric), their trust-building strategies do not appear to be converging at all. Quite the contrary: this is a clear case of diverging strategies. In all three countries, a shift in context, in national circumstances, forced a change in trust-building strategies. As the national contexts differed, the trust-building strategies too drifted apart.

Interestingly, both the English and the Danes looked for inspiration for their most recent trust-building strategies to the U.S.: for their police and crime commissioners, the English were inspired by the election of local officials in the U.S. (see Loveday & Reid, 2003—although the policies that were eventually implemented rather differed from the initial recommendations); I found that Danish police officers and city council officials in both case D1 and case D2 modeled their proximity policing initiatives partly on the approach of cities such as Seattle and Minneapolis. A single country can therefore be the source of multiple, highly diverse ideas for trust-building strategies. What is more, this example indicates that even having a single donor country does not at all guarantee convergence of policies and strategies between receiving countries.

Additionally, it is noteworthy that policy transfer can also occur from a context in which the initial idea or strategy was quickly abandoned, to a new one in which it is adopted with relative success—albeit in an altered form. The Dutch model of introducing police patrollers as auxiliary police officers, for instance, was soon dropped in favor of more extensive authorities for and numbers of municipal wardens (Terpstra et al., 2013). In England & Wales, however, the Dutch concept of having special police patrollers (re)connect the police and the public was implemented in the form of PCSOs. Their success was indicated by their rapid increase to over 16,000 fte: 7% of the total police workforce in 2010 (Home Office, 2016).[2] This means that the idea of auxiliary police officers, hatched in the Netherlands, took root in England & Wales through a process of policy translation, even though it largely failed in its original context. This was a case of policy transfer that hence led to divergence, rather than convergence.

To conclude, we can observe both converging and diverging tendencies, depending on the moment in time. There does not appear to be a clear trend with countries becoming more similar in their trust-building strategies: they draw ideas from other locations, certainly, but pick the ideas they prefer and adjust them to fit in with their own local, 'homegrown' style of policing. National and local context as well as individual agency in the receiving context tend to obstruct converging tendencies. Periods when convergence can be observed alternate, due to changes in national contexts, with periods of divergence. And the tendency to switch strategies, discussed in the previous section, also holds for influences from abroad: sometimes the influence of one specific strategy or from one country is strong, and at other times another country or strategy is seen as the prime example. Additionally, there are also phases when foreign influences are weaker and local factors dominate.

It is important to take foreign influences into account when studying trust-building. This includes processes such as policy transfer, policy translation, and diffusion. But many developments—if not most—in trust-building strategies are in fact due to local or national factors, or are at the very least strongly shaped by them. In shaping police trust-building strategies, we see a dynamic interplay between international, national, local, and individual influences. If we wish to understand differences between police trust-building strategies in different countries and at different moments in time, we need to take all of these levels into account.

---

2.   Their numbers had dropped to under 11,000 in 2016 due to budget cuts, casting doubt on the future of PCSOs.

Part IV

Conclusions

12 | Conclusions and discussion

12.1   Summary: Main findings

Chapter 1. This study aimed to provide more insight into trust in the police. Trust is essential for the police, as it improves citizens' feelings of safety, their willingness to intervene in minor cases of disorder, and to cooperate with the police and report crime. It is hence a precondition for the police to do their work well. Our knowledge about public trust in the police, as well as about how the police understand and attempt to improve trust, however, remains limited in several ways: in terms of theory and geographic and temporal range, the existing body of work still features considerable lacunae. Most importantly, few if any previous studies have included perspectives on trust from both citizens and the police.

Emphasizing its 'dialogic character' (Bottoms & Tankebe, 2012), I studied public trust in the police cross-nationally and diachronically, and I analyzed police trust-building strategies and how they developed in three Western European countries: England & Wales, Denmark, and the Netherlands. I was guided by six research questions. The first three concerned public trust in the police, the second three dealt with police trust-building strategies:

> Research Question 1: *To what extent are measures of citizens' trust in the police empirically comparable across European countries?*
>
> Research Question 2: *What are the differences between European countries in terms of citizens' trust in the police, and how has trust in the police developed across Europe over the past few decades?*
>
> Research Question 3: *What factors on the national and on the individual level explain differences between countries in terms of citizens' trust in the police?*
>
> Research Question 4: *When and how was citizens' trust in the police defined as a problem in different European countries, and how did it evolve?*
>
> Research Question 5: *Since that time, what strategies and 'solutions' have been adopted by whom to address the problem of trust in these countries, and to improve police–public relationships in general?*

Research Question 6: *How can we understand the differences we find between and within countries in terms of problem definition and trust-building strategies?*

Chapter 2. Before we could begin to answer these research questions, the study's central concepts required clarification: trust, confidence, and legitimacy dominate the discourse surrounding public attitudes toward the police. Trust and confidence are, in English-language publications, often considered to be different concepts. Internationally, however, few if any other languages feature a distinction between the two, leading me to treat the two as de facto synonymous. Both concepts, accepting the properties of the police, are defined as *the belief and expectation that the police, either as individuals or as an institution, fulfill their function 'well.'*

Legitimacy is an issue that is no less complicated than trust or confidence and equally popular in use. Legitimacy is a characteristic of the institutional level—the police as an institution have a certain degree of legitimacy. I distinguish two different types: formal and informal legitimacy. The Weber-influenced formal legitimacy consists of system-level frameworks of legal and social rules and norms, hence including legality and wider norm conformation. Durkheimian informal legitimacy includes citizens' understanding and acceptance of police authority, their cooperation and compliance, as well as confidence and trust. All systems of power and authority strive for self-legitimation. In democratic societies, the constitution of informal legitimacy implies that the police also seek to be trusted. Next to these central concepts, concepts of secondary relevance to this study were satisfaction, authority, and consent.

Chapter 3. There are three theoretical paradigms of thinking about trust in the police and how to improve it that have been applied throughout this study to help understand trust, derive hypotheses, and frame trust-building strategies. These paradigmatic schools of thought have different core assumptions and suggest different strategies: there are supposed to be specific means for police officers and organizations to make the public trust them. The first of these schools of thought is that of proximity policing. This movement emerged in a response to perceived weaknesses of the old, technology-focused professional model of policing. Proximity policing emphasizes improving police–public relationships by decreasing the distance between the two. The police should be approachable and visible, focus on addressing a broad range of (social) neighborhood problems such as disorder and feelings of insecurity, collaborate with partners, and be proactive in the battle against crime and disorder by involving the public. Often, this implies a decentralized command structure and large discretionary autonomy for officers. From the 1980s onward, proximity policing has seen its popularity among police and policymakers grow and decline in waves.

The second paradigm I discerned was that of instrumentalism. This school of thought emphasizes the effectiveness-centered aspects of professional policing and NPM-influenced ideas about efficiency and measurable output in improving trust and police legitimacy. In order to gain trust, the police should be able to demonstrate effectiveness, particularly in their 'core business' of fighting crime. Since the 1990s, this model of thinking about police–public relationships has grown to be quite dominant in policies and views of relevant actors, particularly police management.

The third school of thought is that of procedural justice. This interpretation focuses on police–public interactions, emphasizing correct treatment of citizens. Procedural justice-based policing entails, in the words of Tyler (1988), various elements: opportunity of representation for the citizen to make his or her case, and consistency, impartiality, quality of decision, correctability, and ethicality on the part of the police officer. When the police show respect, let citizens explain their views on situations, and show their commitment to making informed decisions, citizens are expected to comply more often and have more confidence in the police. Police corruption and unnecessary use of force will have the opposite effect. Procedural justice is predominantly an academic school of thought, but has slowly garnered attention over recent decades in policy and police circles.

Chapter 4. In answering the first three research questions, we first needed to define the extent to which measures of citizens' trust in the police were comparable across Europe. This was done through the introduction of measurement equivalence tests on cross-national, multiple-wave survey data: the European Social Survey (ESS) 2002–2014 and the European Values Study (EVS) 1981–2008. Then, for the cases where we had established cross-national and longitudinal comparability, the second question could be addressed: assessing differences between and developments in levels of trust within European countries. I introduced several popular theses about supposed developments in trust in the police and, if they held any validity, how they should be reflected in survey data: the desacralization thesis, the safety utopia thesis, the post-authoritarian paradox thesis, and the socioeconomic crisis problem. Most of these had negative implications: the expectations, popular in scientific, public, and political discourse, are that trust in the police is, on average, on the decline.

Having assumed that differences between countries in levels of trust were found, we could proceed to explaining them using the cross-national survey data of the ESS 2010 wave. These data were supplemented with information on the country level. For this part of the study, the three theoretical paradigms were employed to inspire sets of competing hypotheses. The proximity policing school of thought provided the expectation that citizens have more trust in the police in countries adhering to proximity policing principles to a greater extent. The instrumentalist paradigm led us to expect negative relationships between crime rates in a country (homicide rates and victimization rates of burglary and assault) and citizens' trust in the police. The procedural justice school of thought yielded the hypothesis that in countries with higher levels of corruption, citizens have lower trust in the police. Additionally, each paradigm hypothesized relationships between specific individual-level perceptions of the police and citizens' trust in the police, as well as between the previously mentioned country-level factors and the specific individual-level perceptions of the police. Finally, I included a range of control variables on the individual and country level.

Chapter 5. Multi-group structural equation modeling was applied to test for measurement equivalence of measures of trust in the police cross-nationally and longitudinally. The results indicated that mean levels of trust could validly be compared across most points of measurement over time included in the EVS 1981–2008 and ESS 2002–2014, yet not across all. Additionally, we found that mean levels of trust in different countries could be validly compared in most, but not all, countries included in the ESS 2010 wave.

The tracing of developments in trust over time was split into two parts: long-term developments as measured by the EVS, and medium- to short-term developments as captured by the ESS. Over the long run, confidence in the police had increased over much of Europe. This particularly held for the time frame between 1990 and 2008. The overall increase in confidence, however, was not uniform across Europe, as some individual countries showed constant levels or slightly declining trust. Nor did it appear to be exclusively concentrated in specific areas. One notable exception was the overall long-term fall in confidence in the British Isles. The medium- and short-term analyses of the ESS yielded a mixed picture: trust goes up and down across Europe. A majority of countries, however, again showed overall increases in trust. While each of the four popular theses regarding trends in trust held some validity in some period of time in some regions of Europe, the overall image in terms of developments in trust in the long as well as the short run was far more positive than is generally assumed. An additional finding of relevance was that trust in most other institutions seemed to fare much more poorly than trust in the police; while trust in the army in the EVS data tended to increase like trust in the police, evidence was mixed for trust in the legal system and the civil service, and trust in political institutions had declined across Europe over recent decades.

Chapter 6. After tracing developments in trust over time, I showed differences between countries in 2010, and then proceeded to explain those differences. We saw that trust tends to be highest in the Nordic countries, with other Western European countries following suit. Southern and former communist Central and Eastern European countries tended to have lower levels of trust in the police. This made for sufficient cross-country variance to explain in multilevel regression analyses. On the national level, while several determinants featured significant bivariate relationships with trust, only the effect of corruption remained significant, as expected, after controls were added. After the inclusion of control variables, proximity policing appeared to be unrelated to trust, while crime rates (homicide and victimization of burglary and assault) were surprisingly, if weakly, positively related with trust. On the individual level, all specific perceptions of the police (as derived from the three theoretical schools) were significantly related to trust; the strongest relationships, however, were with procedural justice-derived determinants, followed by the variable reflecting proximity policing and finally the two determinants related to instrumentalism. To conclude, the results offered firm support for procedural justice-derived hypotheses, weak support for proximity policing-derived hypotheses, and no support for instrumentalism. Additional analyses indicated that the effects of various individual-level control variables, such as ethnicity, on trust in the police differed substantially across countries—being positively related to trust in some and negatively in others. Other determinants, such as religious attendance, income, and contact evaluations, had more or less uniform effects across countries.

Chapter 7. After studying trust in the police extensively and answering the first three research questions, we turned to the police themselves as the object of research; without understanding the main actor involved, a study of trust in the police remains lacking. In formulating a theoretical approach to frame Research Questions 4, 5, and 6, I drew on elements from Kingdon's (1995) work on problem definitions, policy generation, and political events. In applying a case study approach selecting several of the previously included countries, the goals were multiple. First, we set out to chart when trust in the police was first defined as a policy issue, as a problem. Second, we traced the process of policy generation and the invention of strategies to address the problem of trust. As in the previous part of the book, this gave prominent roles to the three paradigms of thinking about trust—proximity policing, instrumentalism, and procedural justice. Here, these paradigms were not used to derive hypotheses regarding explanations of trust but, rather, to frame police trust-building strategies and their underlying logic. Third, the purpose of the analysis was to shed light on the role of unique circumstances, events, individual actors, and institutional and cultural contexts in the processes of trust-building from the inception of the initial problem to evaluation of the strategies.

I selected three Western European countries, England & Wales, Denmark, and the Netherlands. This selection meant including different cultural and historical cases that still had enough in common for a comparison to make sense. Moreover, their relative proximity offered some likelihood of coming across examples of policy transfer and diffusion. Within each country, multiple sites were selected for in-depth study. Data collection consisted of semi-structured interviews with experts and practitioners within and without the police and of varying seniority.

Chapter 8. England & Wales has long been known as an exemplary country in terms of police work and trust in the police, due to a near-mystical connection between the police and citizens (Loader & Mulcahy, 2003), with a central role for the notion of democratic accountability. However, in recent decades this picture has become muddled. A decisive period in the formation of trust as a policy topic, as well as in the development of trust-building periods, took place in the 1980s.

Waves of urban disorder including the Brixton riots emphasized mounting tensions and mistrust between the police and poor minority groups. The responses entailed a first wave of community-oriented policing (on the part of the police) and an emphasis on fair treatment and increasing democratic accountability (on the part of the Home Office). Much of the impetus for building trust, however, disappeared with the miners' strike in the mid-1980s. The course of the 1990s saw increasing emphasis on fighting crime and on value-for-money logic, influenced by rising crime and the popularity of NPM rationalities. Trust in the police, it was reasoned by the New Labour government of the late 1990s, could only be improved if the police could demonstrate success by reaching their performance targets.

In the early 2000s, evidence surfaced of a 'reassurance gap,' a discrepancy between police successfulness in reaching their targets and falling public trust in the police. This led to the introduction of neighbourhood policing—a new wave of proximity policing. Neighborhood teams were formed and a new type of police official, the PCSO, was introduced especially to improve relationships with citizens and reassure the public. With the economic crisis, however, came a change of government and a period of austerity in which neighbourhood policing was much reduced. The new Conservative-led government was skeptical toward the police, emphasizing a perceived lack of efficiency and openly attributing blame for various scandals to the police. A two-pronged approach toward trust-building ensued. First, the much-strengthened police inspectorate (HMIC) was supposed to make police forces more trustworthy. Second, the role of elected police and crime commissioners was designed to strengthen democratic control over the police and hence improve trust.

Chapter 9. Denmark is a high-trust society that, arguably, has never faced a serious crisis of trust in the police. Characteristic of the relationship between the public and the police in Denmark is that it is part of the broader cultural complex, with the state as a benevolent actor providing safety or, rather, the unique, harmonious notion of *tryghed*. A largely rural society with a national, but de facto decentralized police organization embedded in local communities, trust in the police was, for a long time, taken for granted. Rising crime and changing demographics led to careful proximity-oriented police reform in the 1970s. The police were subject to some scrutiny in the early 1990s after the well-publicized, violent Nørrebro riots, but these were not perceived to be indicative of a deeper problem with trust.

During the late 1990s, and with mixed results, a new wave of proximity policing experiments commenced, mainly influenced by foreign examples, aimed at further improving already high levels of trust. With fading confidence in proximity policing reforms (two waves had yielded little result), attention turned to a different approach. In a *'centralization in disguise'* (Holmberg & Balvig, 2013), a large overhaul of the police organization was conducted, based on notions of increasing police effectiveness and efficiency. This 2007 police reform led to organizational chaos and placed the police at a greater distance from citizens. Under a sudden wave of criticism, the police experienced a problem with trust. The failures of the reform and rising tensions between ethnic minorities and the police caused local police districts to reintroduce aspects of proximity policing, this time with the explicit goal of restoring trust. That the police were no longer an institution that was off limits for criticism was illustrated by the foundation of an independent police complaints commission in 2012.

Chapter 10. The Netherlands has historically featured tensions between police and citizens. While trust in the police in general was high, police authority was challenged earlier than in the two other countries under study. The 1960s saw a range of large-scale street protests and clashes between police and protesters, with the stunned police perceiving an acute crisis of legitimacy. Over the following decades, this inspired the police to design proximity policing strategies to reconnect with citizens, in order never to be caught unawares again. The policy document 'Changing police,' authored by police officers, played a central role—proposing, among other things, the introduction of neighborhood teams (Heijink et al., 1977).

With the regionalization of the previously fragmented police system in 1993, proximity policing became the leading trust-building strategy of the Dutch police. Gradually, this strategy evolved: individual neighborhood officers took the place of neighborhood teams, and with increasing collaboration in local networks. In parallel, however, concern with crime and insecurity was growing and NPM notions of efficiency gained traction. An important turning point was 2002, when the murder of politician Pim Fortuyn meant a watershed in Dutch thinking about public safety. The government's focus became chiefly to fight crime effectively. Inspired by the English example, an expanding framework of performance targets was imposed on the police.

The year 2012 saw a revolution in the Dutch police: a new reform nationalized the entire organization. With it came a trust-building strategy centered around improving public satisfaction and trust through efficient service delivery. The limited evidence so far points toward several negative side effects of this strategy, caused by the larger distance between citizens and the police.

Chapter 11. After the three case studies, it became possible to answer the research questions. While trust in the police was a relevant policy topic in each country, there were wildly differing moments in time when trust was defined—or, rather, invented (Lee, 2007)—as a problem. Moreover, the problem was often understood in different terms and was subject to different problem definitions. These problem definitions tended to gradually evolve. Similarly, different strategies were applied by different actors to address the problem of trust in each country at various moments in time. In particular, forms of proximity policing and instrumentalism have seen long bouts of popularity in each country, but in each case were pushed by different actors or constellations of actors, all with different interests. As a result, nominally equivalent strategies, such as proximity policing, had quite different interpretations and implications in each country under study.

Both the invention or definition of trust as a policy problem and the development of trust-building strategies are strongly dependent on the national or even local context—historical, structural, or cultural. Processes of policy transfer and diffusion do play visible and sometimes less visible roles in both problem definition and policy generation, but local circumstances as well as individual agency and often unpredictable events remain crucial. This means that there is no clear trend toward the convergence of trust-building strategies in the three countries under study. It is important to take foreign influences into account when studying trust-building; this includes processes such as policy transfer, policy translation, and diffusion. But many developments—if not most—in trust-building strategies are in fact due to local and national factors, or are at the very least strongly shaped by them. International, national, and local influences compete and negotiate over how the problem of trust is defined, what strategies are formulated, and how they are being implemented.

12.2   THE PUBLIC

We have been able to answer Research Questions 1–3 by establishing cross-national and longitudinal measurement equivalence, tracing developments in trust over time and comparing levels between countries, and finally testing for determinants of trust. We found that trust in the police is empirically comparable across most European countries and points in time, if done carefully, that trust is determined at least in part by factors that the police can influence, and, finally, that trust can change substantially over time, implying that the alteration of these factors can potentially make a real difference for trust.

Trust in the police varies greatly, per individual but also across countries. Some European countries have so far failed to allow the public to enjoy even a minimal degree of trust in the police. In these cases, this is usually indicative of broader failures of the state to gain a basic level of trust in its core tenets. Countries with very low trust in the police are often countries that are deeply challenged on the whole —fundamentally troubled states. Improving trust in the police in these cases implies addressing core societal problems—for reflections on such challenges and attempts to address them, see, for instance, Kupatadze (2012) and Light (2014) on Georgia or Beck (2005) and Peacock & Cordner (2016) on Ukraine. In most of the countries under study, however, the public had neither high nor low trust in the police. These are countries where failures and successes in gaining public trust alternate, where a basic level of trust has been achieved but where flaws and challenges and skepticism abound. Governments and police organizations in these countries may have the potential to reform particular institutions or formulate specific strategies to improve legitimacy, but often face significant obstacles when trying to implement them. This holds for many Southern and Central and Eastern European countries. A third group of countries featured relatively high levels of trust. This held for many northwestern European cases, including the three in-depth case studies for trust-building strategies. These countries often have a long history of thinking about trust and formulating trust-building strategies. Yet despite all this experience, this is a task that never seems to be finished. Strategies run into trouble or are shown to have adverse or perverse (side) effects; moreover, new developments in policing and society keep posing challenges for the police with regard to maintaining or building trust. Hence, almost regardless of the level of trust in the police, all countries included have reasons to think about trust and how to work with it.

The tracing of developments in trust in the police has shown that it is not a static concept: it can increase, and it can fall. On average, the majority of countries under study have seen an increase in public trust in the police since about 1990. The main drivers of this development remain unclear, although this invites further discussion in Section 12.3, where I discuss some inherent features of the police in contemporary society. What appears clear either way is that the crisis-like rhetoric that is popular within the media, in politics, and occasionally amongst the police themselves, regarding decreasing police legitimacy, is mostly unfounded. On the contrary, the police are, on average, trusted more than they were before. This is unlikely to relieve them of any obligation to work on improving trust, but the per-ception of a crisis of trust appears, in most countries, to be unjustified. The public may have different expectations from the police and be increasingly vocal about those expectations, but this is not reflected in levels of trust as measured through large-scale surveys.

What makes people trust the police? First of all, we should note that it is unlikely that there is something of a universal formula to determine trust in the police. We have not only found differences between countries in levels and devel-opments in trust, but also in the determinants of trust: different things matter in different ways in different countries. Remarkable here was, for instance, the rela-tionship between ethnicity and trust in the police. In some countries, ethnic minor-ity members have more trust in the police than the majority, yet in other countries they have less trust. This reflects the mixed findings on the relationship between ethnicity and trust in the police found in various previous studies (Cao et al., 1996; Goudriaan et al., 2006; Kautt, 2011; Sato et al., 2016; Skogan, 1978; Wolfe et al., 2016). Such divergent effects were observed for many variables. This could (and possibly should) have consequences for the police and for trust-building strategies across Europe: no assumption should be made that relationships are uniform across Europe; that equal strategies will work in different countries. Nationally and locally conducted, high-quality studies are of the essence here—something to which I will return in Section 12.5.

That being said, I would like to add some general remarks regarding the rela-tionship between trust and notions derived from our three main theoretical per-spectives on trust. According to the previously presented results, fair treatment of citizens and police integrity could be key in building and preserving the trust of the public across Europe. This chimes with results from several previous studies (Alalehto & Larsson, 2016; Kääriäinen, 2007; Jackson et al., 2013). Possibly even more remarkably, what does not appear to affect trust in the police is a popular measure of police effectiveness: levels of crime in a country. For the police, as one would expect after reading the qualitative part of this study, this is a rather counterintuitive finding. While trust is higher when citizens believe the police to be more effective in fighting crime and to be responding more rapidly to reports of crime (see also Tankebe, 2008; Weitzer & Tuch, 2005), perceptions of police effectiveness and actual crime rates are unrelated. This is different from what is commonly assumed by policy-makers and the police themselves (Home Office, 1993; Loveday, 2000), including in the three countries where I examined thinking about trust and trust-building. This European finding also contradicts, for instance, the global results of Sung (2006). Nor does the actual occurrence of crime in the European countries included decrease trust; higher levels of crime may even improve levels of trust slightly. Again, this goes against popular beliefs and the results of several previous studies (see Jang et al., 2010; Sampson & Jeglum Bartusch, 1998; Sindall et al., 2012; and to a lesser extent Jackson & Bradford, 2009).

As there are very few indications that measures of police effectiveness affect trust in the police, it appears that the public do not assess the police in the same way as they would judge a company or a business. The police are seen, by citizens, in a rather different light. In the comparative analyses, police fair treatment of citizens, more than any other factor, determined trust in the police. For citizens in the wide range of different European countries included, the level of crime is simply not central in shaping their trust. This finding might be counterintuitive for police organizations—police officers often define their work in terms of fighting crime, and have over recent decades frequently been told by external advisors, media, and politicians that this is what the public want. This is not a call for the police to stop addressing crime. Obviously, dealing with crime is an important part of the police function. Yet it is no more than just that: an important part. Other aspects of police work—for instance, the way in which the police interact with citizens on a day-to-day basis—appear to matter more in terms of shaping public trust in the police. Public understanding and appreciation of the police is more complex than mere crime-fighting, and so are police activities. Police trust-building efforts should, I suggest, mirror this complexity and versatility. In Section 12.4, I shall provide several leads in order to do so.

The results appear relatively clear for procedural justice and for instrumentalism. However, for proximity policing they are mixed. This carries several implications, both methodological and theoretical, that I would like to delve into in Section 12.5. For now, let it suffice to say that proximity policing found neither strong support nor strong rejection in the data and warrants more examination.

12.3   THE POLICE

Switching focus from the public to the police, the results of this study offer much food for thought. For instance, what do we make of changing levels of trust in the police, as compared to changing trust in other institutions? It has been remarkable to see trust in the police (and in the armed forces) increase across Europe over recent decades, while trust in political institutions has fallen. A tantalizing question is what these divergent processes mean for contemporary European societies.

Trust has more than an instrumental value: it is not merely the automatic outcome of several antecedents; nor is it a tool to enhance public safety or societal stability. There is another way to look at trust in the police, while still placing it in a diachronic context. This is related to what trust in the police may symbolize or signal. Loader and Mulcahy (2003) drew attention to the symbolic meaning of the police institution in people's minds. Although their argument concerns the English situation specifically, the relevance of their general argument to other European societies may still hold: the police are a unique institution. The police, like the army and the judiciary, are a 'legal' or 'order' institution, theoretically and empirically distinct from a political one (Rothstein & Stolle, 2008; Schaap & Scheepers, 2014; Wallace & Latcheva, 2006). And even if we take into account that much police work and decision-making shares features with that of politicians, we should remember that their proximity to citizens is far greater (Muir, 1977). Their diabolical powers, their multitude of tasks and activities (Bittner, 1980; Brodeur, 2007; Muir, 1977), and their visibility on the streets, in popular culture and in media attention (Loader & Mulcahy, 2003; Reiner, 2010; Mawby, 2002), which are different from those of other order institutions, make them a pivotal actor in people's views not only of the state, but of society. We may, as a result, wonder what trust in such an institution signifies.

In countries increasingly characterized by fragmentation and more liquid social ties (Bauman, 2000; Giddens, 1990, 1991), the police, more than the political realm, represent something greater than the individual. Much like the army, they symbolize a sense of order and unity bridging the many fault lines that run across ever more complex societies. It is my hypothesis that this is the main driver behind the long-term trends that we see in terms of institutional trust, where trust in parliament, politicians, and the justice system is on average steadily falling, while trust in the police and the military is mostly on the increase. That this is not necessarily good news must be clear; neither the police nor the military should be trusted unconditionally, and political institutions require trust in order for citizens to participate in the democratic process.

A pessimistic reading of these trends could be that citizens across many European countries are growing more authoritarian in their beliefs and preferences, and less inclined toward supporting democratic systems of checks and balances and the rule of law. Some researchers have, over recent years, reported alarming results that are much in line with this interpretation[1] (Diamond, 2015; Foa & Mounk, 2016).

A more positively inclined researcher, however, would emphasize that our explanatory analyses found that citizens trust the police more when they adhere to values such as integrity, fair and equal treatment, and the granting of opportunities for citizens to make their case. These are arguably democratic characteristics—all to some degree included by Bayley (2006), Jones et al. (1996), and Sklansky (2008) —and indicators of the procedural justice paradigm. Increasing trust in the police would then suggest not a growing authoritarian attitude but, rather, a belief that the police are capable of delivering means of policing that align with the rule of law, even as political actors and institutions are perceived to be falling short of those standards. The police, then, are attributed with more of a role as arbiters in public spaces. This growing public confidence in the police as opposed to political state institutions, however, aligns with continuing scrutiny of the police: faith is combined with fear. The burden that this places on the police is considerable; no matter how ambitious some of their trust-building endeavors are, we can hardly expect the police to live up to a role as a unifying factor in our increasingly fragmented societies. The challenges that they face in this symbolic function are certainly larger than mere questions about finding effective trust-building strategies. As an organization, the police tend to be occupied with different, more day-to-day questions. Most police officers cannot do their work in such a way that it corresponds to the unrealistically high public expectations. However, regardless of their actual capacities in forming an ever more important part of the otherwise seemingly weakening fabric that holds European societies together, this view suggests that, more than ever before, the police are a source of hope.

At the same time, some processes within the police raise serious questions about their future ability to maintain their central role, not just in symbolizing societal unity, but even in the maintenance of order and public safety. In different Western countries, a variety of developments have been challenging the position and role of the police, such as the rise of plural policing—including municipal disorder policing services (Eikenaar, 2017; Terpstra et al., 2013) and private security organizations (Button, 2007; Van Steden & Sarre, 2007)—police centralizations (Fyfe et al., 2013) and, related to this but by no means synonymous, arguably a development toward a more abstract, distantly operating police in some countries (Terpstra et al., 2016). These processes are ongoing and probably interlinked to some extent, making it hard to predict their ultimate meaning. However, it is not impossible that such a changing role and position of police organizations will gradually diminish their function as symbol of order and peace.

---

1. See also the gloomy assessment of the state of U.S. public attitudes toward political institutions by Gallup CEO Jim Clifton (2016).

Related to this remark is the finding that police organizations, at least in Western Europe, appear to be in a permanent state of flux themselves. There is a state of continual change, of constant reform. Noted more than a decade ago by Brodeur (2005), this cycle of nonstop revolutions has only seemed to pick up speed ever since (Terpstra & Fyfe, 2013). This, too, is problematic for the police. Each reform brings substantial risks to the organization itself and its climate (Mendel, Fyfe & Den Heyer, 2017). This in turn risks making police officers less inclined to police their communities fairly and in a procedurally just fashion, and to adhere less to proximity policing principles (Trinkner, Tyler, & Goff, 2016). In a broader sense, an organization that is subject to change itself can hardly be expected to serve as a beacon of societal stability.

To what extent these processes are problematic or desirable is hard to say. Many would argue that several of these developments have changed the security landscape and police services for the better. What seems clear is that they will complicate, or impede, the possibilities for the police to formulate trust-building strategies to address the problem of trust.

Concerning trust-building strategies, the endless waves of reform and implementation of new policing strategies have not consistently led to increasing policy convergence between different European countries. To some extent, this was surprising. After all, countries have long looked to one another for inspiration on how to organize their police and how to gain public trust in that police (although with regard to 'trust,' it must be said that alternative terms were often used). Sometimes, that inspiration was negative, an example from the very distant past being the foundation of the London Metropolitan Police. It was organized on a completely different basis than the French police to prevent the suggestion that the new police organization was meant to suppress citizens (Emsley, 2003). But most of the time, throughout the latter half of the 19th and the entire 20th century, police organizations have tried to learn from positive examples of foreign police services. Before World War II, the German and to a lesser extent French police were seen as examples in the Netherlands due to their professionalization and their clever use of technology. Postwar, the British police fulfilled this function and had the particular appeal of showing excellent relationships between the police and the public (Prick, 1961). This exemplary leading role was always temporary, and few people would argue that this foreign inspiration ever led to serious copying or convergence of strategies over the course of the 20th century. Quite the opposite: foreign models and strategies have always been interpreted and changed, or 'mistranslated,' to suit local contexts and interests. One example is provided by Christensen (2017), who detailed how the Danish police system introduced in the late 1850s was formally copied from the Metropolitan Police, but actually served as a compromise between liberal and conservative elites during the shift from the Danish absolute monarchy to a constitutional monarchy.

There is something very illuminating about this. The transfer of models and ideas from abroad always seems to be accompanied by national interests and motivations for importing such models. This means that they are likely to be altered before or after they arrive in their new context. And as it was with other aspects of the police organization, so it is with trust-building strategies. The adoption of PCSOs in England & Wales was an idea imported from the Netherlands (Savage, 2007). However, in the Netherlands this trust-building strategy fell flat and was soon abandoned (Terpstra & Van Stokkom, 2014), whereas it became a main driver of gaining public trust in the police in England & Wales as part of proximity policing initiatives for a relatively long period of time. Value-for-money notions transplanted from England & Wales to Denmark after the 2007 police reform were tweaked and reinterpreted by some local police commissioners, who claimed that a proximity policing strategy would, in the end, yield more value for money than a short-term instrumental focus on measurable output, as was superimposed by the national police. The result of all this is that while certain models or strategies have been popular at particular times in all three countries, they have differed fundamentally in their application and interpretation (and popularity) in different contexts—both nationally and locally. This makes policy convergence a poor term to describe the actual processes at stake—which are nominal adherence to shared central concepts leading to essentially different strategies and practices regarding trust-building.

Not only was there little evidence of convergence of trust-building strategies in the countries under study, but I would argue that such convergence would also carry considerable risks. Because the three theoretical schools have such completely different central assumptions and logic, they can—inadvertently and without anyone immediately noticing—affect one another: implementing one strategy, for instance after it was imported from abroad, could cause severe adverse effects in spheres better understood by other paradigms. This became particularly salient when discussing trust-building in an international, or policy transfer-related, context.

To illustrate what I mean, we briefly need to return to the previous discussion on proximity policing. The ideological success of community-oriented policing in the U.S. and the U.K. during the 1990s and the zeal of experts in exporting this model has led many governments across the globe to adopt proximity policing principles when reforming their police forces (Baker, 2009; Blaustein, 2015; Brogden, 2005; Caparini & Marenin, 2005; Frühling, 2007; Haberfeld & Cerrah, 2007; Meško & Klemencic, 2007; Van der Spuy, 2000). This could be argued to entail a form of policy convergence. However, when implemented poorly, such reforms can lead to cases of severe procedural injustice. Often, these countries are in various stages of the complicated transition from former authoritarian regimes toward more or less Western-styled democracy and have a turbulent, conflict-ridden past. Although there is evidence that proximity policing can be adapted to suit local, non-Western contexts (Baker, 2008; Cain, 2000; Maguire et al., 2017), there are many examples of unsuccessful, highly problematic or downright disastrous attempts to implement proximity policing principles abroad—various degrees of such unsuccessful endeavors are reported by Blaustein (2015), Brogden (2005), Kyed (2009), and Steinberg (2011). One can imagine several causes for such *'hubristic failure'* (Loader & Walker, 2007: 114): local communities might not consent to being policed (Steinberg, 2012), the concept of community may not even exist to begin with (Herbert, 2006; Lau, 2004; Szikinger, 1993), or resources could be too thinly stretched for successful community-oriented policing (Baker, 2007; Blaustein, 2015). But the most risky issue with the implementation of proximity policing principles lies in the nature of the police.

In previously authoritarian countries such as formerly communist Eastern Europe or large parts of Africa, the police tend to still habitually act in a repressive, often violent fashion, without much regard for human rights (Gerber & Mendelson, 2008; Steinberg, 2011). If such a police force is granted more autonomy, as is common with most—although not all—forms of proximity policing, we may expect abuse of power, police violence, corruption and (continued or worsened) paramilitary styles of policing (Kyed, 2009). This holds especially when personnel purges or processes of lustration have been weak or absent (Goldsmith, 2005; Light, 2014). The attempted implementation of proximity policing models might then lead to exceptional degrees of procedural injustice, since these activities are the opposite of procedural justice. Briefly after the fall of the Iron Curtain one Hungarian author, foreseeing this problem, argued against the adoption of proximity policing principles, estimating that it would be *'more than dangerous to invest any proactive power in the existing police organization'* of his country (Szikinger, 1993: 148). In this way, the flawed implementation of principles from one theoretical paradigm—in this case, proximity policing—can have adverse effects on the characteristics of another one—in this example, procedural justice-based policing. This can result in serious harm to trust. What makes matters worse in such instances is that those schooled in one paradigm are often unable to properly assess this unforeseen negative impact, as it affects traits and characteristics that fall outside of the familiar theoretical model.

This is not the only example I could provide in this context; similar concerns, for instance, can and sometimes have arisen with instrumentalist reforms negatively affecting proximity. The rise of quantitative target setting in England & Wales, Denmark, and the Netherlands, inspired by an international wave of NPM-based reforms and crime-focused political discourse, implied instrumentalist reforms. According to many of my informants, this went at the expense of local affiliation and of police willingness to meet public demands and priorities—concepts aligned with proximity policing. This emphasizes the importance of taking multiple theoretical perspectives into account when trying to study trust in the police and police trust-building strategies; it goes beyond an academic drive for theoretical saturation, but implies having a broader scope not only in observing the expected phenomena but also possible drawbacks and perverse effects. Likewise, it illustrates the importance of taking national and local context into account when implementing trust-building strategies inspired by foreign examples. It is useful to be inspired by nonnative strategies about what could be possible to address the problem of trust. However, blindly copying and pasting such a strategy into a new context without sufficient attention to national and local contexts (and what, indeed, the problem of trust entails in these contexts) is a recipe for disaster.

12.4   The pursuit of trust

This brings us to the problem of trust itself, and to trust-building strategies. The problem of trust is recognized in each of the three countries under study. Possibly, it is recognized in most places across Europe. Quite possibly, it is incorrect to speak of *the* problem of trust, as it seems more appropriate to mention *problems* of trust: while many European countries may recognize a challenge or problem or issue with police–public relationships, they will phrase and understand this in rather different terms and/or concepts, and with different cultural and historical connotations. This, of course, can have profound consequences for trust-building. Moreover, there was clear evidence of path dependency: to a large extent, decisions taken in the past, as well as past events and reforms, shape how trust is being dealt with in the present. Trust-building strategies are developed in a context partially formed by genuine wishes to improve police–public relationships, either for pragmatic or more idealistic reasons, but also by all sorts of cultural, historical, and structural stimulants or impediments.

Inevitably, the debate about what trust-building strategies are being followed and why leads to the question of what trust-building strategies should be followed. This, of course, touches on the fundamental question of 'what is good policing'—a hard question to answer. We should do well to reject a blueprint where concepts or strategies such as community policing or crime-fighting pose universal answers. This is reductionist, counterproductive, and sometimes dangerous, as has been illustrated by a range of studies—some of which have previously been mentioned —on policy transplants of specific strategies to different countries and contexts (see Blaustein, 2015; Brogden, 2005; Cain, 2000; Dixon, 2000; Ellison & Pino, 2012; Kyed, 2009; Lau, 2004; Peterson, 2010; Steinberg, 2011; Szikinger, 1993; Van der Spuy, 2000). On the other hand, nor should we blindly accept the thesis that good policing is entirely culturally and locally dependent. General focus areas or general guidelines can be imagined that are likely to help contribute to good police–public relationships in most contexts, as long as they are fitted in with local systems of power relations and mutual expectations.

What could such focus areas look like? Trust-building and the problem of trust are often particularly interesting to observe in contexts where trust is low (Goldsmith, 2002, 2005; Goldsmith & Harris, 2012). Efforts to build trust in low-trust areas often reflect issues and problems that may be quite common in many other places as well, but do so in a magnified fashion. This is why one of the Danish police regions under study planned to implement its trust-building strategies, which had previously been applied in one problematic neighborhood, throughout the entire district: lessons drawn from proximity policing in one area also provided inspiration for trust-building in other, less challenging, environments. Similarly, in the Netherlands through the 1990s, various police chiefs adopted regional or city-wide proximity policing strategies in one form or another after an arguably successful experiment in one problematic neighborhood in Haarlem (Broer et al., 1987).

It pays, in this perspective, to consider where trust really needs to be built. Citizens who already have reasonably high levels of trust in the police need not necessarily be accorded the first priority in trust-building efforts: quite often, the police feel they need to concentrate on groups and areas and neighborhoods where trust is lacking. It is here that trust-building in European countries could show strong parallels with building trust in developing nations. Recall the Danish neighborhood police officer to whom we were briefly introduced in Chapter 1, a former soldier in Iraq who saw strong parallels between his work over there and at home. He was not naïve; he knew he was operating in a wholly different context policing Danish neighborhoods as compared to being stationed at a military base in Iraq. Yet he saw parallels where they mattered most, recognizing echoes of the Iraqi public's attitude in how citizens in his neighborhood perceived the police and hence what type of challenges (albeit with a different intensity) he faced. In either circumstance, to be able to do his work, he needed to convince citizens that he was trustworthy.

The key to having a trusted police organization in such contexts is then, on the face of it glaringly obviously, to construct a trustworthy police service (Goldsmith, 2005). This is not as easy or straightforward as it seems; many trust-building efforts rely on changes that do not, in fact, primarily aim to improve police trustworthiness: better public relations, improved communication, and/or changing the structure of the police organization. A trustworthy police service, in the view of Goldsmith and Harris (2012), on the other hand, is an organization that deals well with citizens' vulnerability. For us to be prepared to take the risk of relying on the police for aid or assistance, we need to deem the actor to which we expose ourselves in our vulnerability to be trustworthy. As a consequence, for police officers, handling vulnerability carefully is key: it determines police trustworthiness (Montgomery et al., 2008). This is particularly salient in contexts where citizens are especially vulnerable; for instance, in neighborhoods where citizens' financial and social resources are limited. The problem here is that '*even single acts that violate local expectations can do substantial damage to [...] trust-building agendas*' (Goldsmith & Harris, 2012:

234): handling citizens' vulnerability poorly signals that the police are unworthy of trust and invites protest (Newburn et al., 2016).

This reflects the finding that violations of procedural justice principles hurt trust. Moreover, it implies that such a negative interpretation of procedural justice (in terms of violations such as corruption, preferential treatment for some groups, and excessive violence) is probably the most appropriate way to understand and approach the problem of trust. Trust-building, ironically, is hence probably best understood negatively: trust is (slowly) built by not doing harm.

That being said, it is worth noting that the procedural justice paradigm has recently run into some unexpected problems. While survey-based studies have consistently found strong connections between perceptions of procedural justice and citizens' trust, willingness to comply, and the legitimacy they attribute to the police, a number of recent studies employing experimental designs have, in different ways, yielded rather less positive results. MacQueen and Bradford (2015), conducting a field experiment in Scotland, found a negative effect of a procedural justice training intervention for police officers. After traffic stops by officers who either had (experimental condition) or had not (control group) undergone procedural justice training, public trust in, and satisfaction with, police officers declined for the experimental group as compared to the control group. Ariel et al. (2016) recently reported that body-worn cameras, among other things intended to improve police procedural justice, do not reduce police use of force and actually increase assaults against officers.[2] Finally, Worden and McLean (2017) indicated that citizens' perceived procedural justice is only loosely related to actually observed procedural justice as followed by police officers in practice; in their view, perceived police procedural justice is part of a broader complex of attitudes, including trust, that citizens brought *to* the encounter rather than it being shaped *by* the encounter. The authors argued, furthermore, that attempts to implement procedural justice-based styles of policing are adopted to rather varying degrees by mid-level and rank-and-file officers, further impeding implementation: it is *'incompatible with police work as some officers experience it'* (Worden & McLean, 2017: 183). The researchers did find, however, that procedurally unjust behavior negatively affected public subjective experience and hence trust.

In fact, these challenges point, much like the work of Goldsmith (2002, 2005) and Goldsmith and Harris (2012), to a reframing or reinterpretation of a procedural justice paradigm to a procedural injustice paradigm. They illustrate that changing police behavior to avoid violations of procedural justice and prevent doing harm is complex and challenging, but do not dispute the importance of doing so. This aligns with the approach taken in the present study. Hence, based on my findings

---

2.   But see the later contribution of Ariel et al. (2017), which is based on the same data. The researchers found that body-worn cameras do reduce citizens' complaints. Whether this is because police behavior improves or because citizens are discouraged from complaining (for instance, because they feel that video evidence could be used against them selectively) remains unclear.

and these additional considerations, it could be valuable to formulate some general principles or focus areas for the police to build, or at least not harm, trust. I would suggest the following:

A.   The police should not mistreat citizens (and take swift and honest action when evidence of the opposite emerges)
B.   The police should not be corrupt (and take swift and honest action when evidence of the opposite emerges)
C.   The police should take full account of local context (but never so as to compromise the principles above)

My argument would be that these admittedly vague and simple statements are the general focus areas that the police should treat as guidelines—the closest thing to universal rules or principles possible with something as diverse, multifaceted, and complex as trust in the police. However, these principles, bare-boned as they may be, are still fraught with tension in practice: inherent characteristics of the police organization and of police work in Western Europe—but likely elsewhere as well —challenge all three of these general guidelines. This is not to say that the police are by definition violent or corrupt; there are, however, mechanisms at play that make violence and corruption more likely than in many other professions. These tensions, I expect, cannot be permanently resolved; although attempts can and should be made to reconcile them as much as possible.

First, as already emphasized by Tyler (1990), the police are by the nature of their job often forced to create negative outcomes for citizens: they arrest, fine, and otherwise try to restrict or regulate citizens' behavior. More generally, the police are central actors in social conflict, pressured to align with one side in such conflict (Fielding, 2005; Green, 1990). The mere experience of being on the receiving end of coercive or repressive police attention, for instance during protests, is likely to result in citizens perceiving unfair treatment and can easily reinforce preexisting negative opinions of the police. This is particularly likely to occur under circumstances where trust in the police is already low (and hence where trust is in most dire need of improvement).

Second, the police are among the institutions that are most vulnerable to corruption (Punch, 2009). Their frequent interaction with citizens, their relatively high degree of discretionary autonomy, and their socialization in an often closed internal culture (Reiner, 2010; Westley, 1970) provides them with ample opportunities to accept bribes or otherwise abuse their power. At the same time, these traits make fighting corruption exceptionally difficult. Unsurprisingly, then, the fight against police corruption knows very few outright success stories (Light, 2014).

Third, the police, in many European countries, are almost by definition inclined to be somewhat detached from local contexts and communities. They represent the authority of the state and uphold national laws, although the national or central orientation of police forces differs by country and by police organization (Brodeur, 2007). The contemporary centralizing tendencies in police organizations across Western Europe (Fyfe et al., 2013) are likely to exacerbate this challenge: top-down institutional pressures tend to discourage the police from taking account of the local context. And even if the police understand this local context, are well connected with local citizens, and are involved in the communities they police, it could be argued that the risk of favoritism and vulnerability to corruption grows.

None of these complications should discharge the police or policy-makers from a duty to pay attention to these general focus areas. Even when police officers show evidence of corruption or if they have mistreated citizens, the organizational response to such occasions is of the essence. Swift and honest action with consideration for citizens could limit the damage substantially. What such action entails exactly depends on the context and the issue at hand; most important is that the police show that they care—about treating citizens fairly and about issues of integrity.

To summarize, while a critical attitude toward the procedural justice paradigm remains warranted, a negative interpretation of this school of thought, in which police officers are encouraged not to commit gross procedural injustices and where swift action is being taken once these do occur, while taking the specifics of the local context into serious consideration, appears to offer much space for the police to gain public trust.

This is a good starting point for principled trust-building, but we need more. An important final note regarding the pursuit of trust has to be made. So far in this study, I have treated trust in the police as a neutral social scientific concept. When I attached normative value to trust, I did so by considering it a public good: something that generally ought to be increased to the benefit of society. In reality, I would argue that trust in the police is a more ambiguous concept. Rather, if we ask the question of the extent to which trust in the police is a good thing, something we should always strive for, the proper answer ought to be: it depends.

Large segments of the population in Western European countries trust the police a lot, sometimes even unconditionally. However, an organization with the type of diabolical powers that the police possess should, as a matter of principle, never be trusted unconditionally. In a fundamental, essential sense, contradicting the famous Peelian description of the police, the police are empathically *not* the public and the public are *not* the police. By virtue of their function, their demographic composition, their culture, and their powers, the police are sharply divided from the public. This means that a healthy skepticism and a critical attitude of the public versus the police keeps the police on their toes and the public on the lookout. This, in turn, implies that trust does not need to be gained among all of the populace. Where, then, do the police need to improve trust and where not? As I discussed before, it is often particularly informative to observe the problem of trust in low-trust contexts. And, I would argue, as many police officers know well, it is also here that trust-building strategies are most necessary. This assertion, however, means that I have to part ways with a presently dominant way of thinking about trust-building.

A popular logic in academic circles regarding trust in the police is that it can and should always be stimulated—due to its obvious beneficial effects such as increasing public willingness to report crime and take action themselves in cases of minor disorder. This logic aims to ever improve trust through the promotion of shared values, in a sort of newly formed trust-building strategy integrated in aspects of existing strategies: '*A trustworthy police force is seen by the public to be effective, to be fair, and to have shared values, interests, and a strong commitment to the local community*' (Jackson & Bradford, 2010: 245). Despite its appeal, there are several issues with this line of thought.

First, I would argue that this shared values (or normative alignment[3]) perspective is flawed in one essential respect: it is at risk of following circular logic. By definition, shared values conceptually imply a measure of trust. This explains the powerful statistical relationships that are often found in these studies (Hough, Jackson, & Bradford, 2013; Hough et al., 2010; Jackson et al., 2012, 2013; Tyler & Jackson, 2014). When one trusts the police to have the same values as oneself, one will by definition trust them to a large extent. However, trusting the police does not necessarily imply sharing their values.

Second, it is here that most trust-building occurs: amongst those very people with whom the police do not share values, and yet need to cooperate. A great trust-building achievement would be to gain trust among groups of citizens with completely different values than the police. This is what often happens in challenged neighborhoods with diverse populations. And this is the type of achievement that is arguably most necessary.

Third, in highly diverse Western European societies, as well as in Eastern and Southern European countries where tensions between the policing apparatus of the state and the public historically run higher, shared values are not even achievable without major societal changes that it is not up to the police to enforce. Achieving shared values between the public and the police suggests that either the public or the police need to adjust their values. Societies, however, are diverse—it is unrealistic to expect all citizens in a country to adhere to the same, uniform set of values. Changing something as fundamental as values in one's citizens is a near-impossible goal for any source of authority. Logically, we would then expect the police to change their values so that they are in line with those of the public. But how can a

---

3.   While authors often use term 'normative alignment' (Huq, Jackson, & Trinkner, 2017; Jackson et al., 2013), it is more accurate to refer to this construct as one regarding shared values. This is clearly reflected in the items being included in the construct. These are: '*The police usually act in ways that are consistent with my own ideas of right and wrong,*' '*The police can be trusted to make the right decisions,*' and '*The police generally have the same sense of right and wrong as I do.*' All of these directly concern values.

police organization be expected to share citizens' values when there is no such thing as universally accepted societal values? Whose values should they adopt?

We can conclude that the shared values perspective is rooted in circular logic, concentrates on the wrong social strata, and is deeply problematic in its practical application. I would propose an alternative to this reasoning, one based on norms rather than values, that aligns with the general focus areas described earlier in this section. In this view, the police and the public need to share norms. An adherence to norms (not the same as laws, nor fixed rules) that are fair—and hence neutral— in a consistent, predictable way builds trust. It is not necessary (nor even likely) for the police to share values with the citizens whom they police, and certainly not with the citizens whose trust needs to be gained the most.

A good police organization does not, as its main priority, have the promotion of trust among citizens with whom the police share similar values. These citizens will by definition have a basic level of trust in the police—a level that could possibly be subject to further improvement, but not as a top police priority. Rather, a good police organization manages to achieve a level of trust even among those parts of the population with whom police officers have little in common. The police, in this interpretation, are a neutral, fair organization, maintaining well-established and agreed-upon norms in the same way for everyone—without under-policing or over-policing any particular group (Goldsmith & Harris, 2012). This implies complete police integrity and equal treatment of citizens, and particularly avoidance of violations of these norms. Whenever such norms are not agreed upon, a good police organization seeks to establish them in alignment and compromise with the populace that is being policed. This is a contribution of proximity policing principles to trust-building, and this is what we see neighborhood police teams and neighborhood officers doing in difficult neighborhoods and areas in England & Wales, in Denmark, and in the Netherlands. Therefore, awareness of local contexts is of the essence for any worthwhile trust-building effort.

The influence of the procedural justice perspective and the contribution of proximity policing are reasonably clear in this perspective. But what of instrumentalism? Having notions of effectiveness and efficiency at its core, what does this perspective mean for building trust? I would argue, based on the statistical analyses and the qualitative study, that actual police effectiveness in fighting crime, one of the central notions of instrumentalism, does not contribute to public trust in the police. Rather, the opposite may be true. An increasing emphasis on fighting crime effectively and efficiently will often be achieved at the expense of fair, equal treatment, disconnects the police from the policed, and hence tends, through police unilateral action, to violate shared norms.

12.5   CHASING KNOWLEDGE

That the police are not merely spending their time in pursuit of criminals but also, as an institution, chase public trust has been amply demonstrated. Meanwhile, we, as scholars and academics, are involved in a different pursuit altogether: that of knowledge. Like the endeavors of the police, our attempts to further our knowledge are comprised of a wide array of possible options and approaches—each with their potential weaknesses and strengths. Here, I would like to reflect on the scientific contribution the present study has made, the lacunae it leaves unaddressed, and the leads for future research that it provides.

I looked at trust in the police from two very different, yet also interrelated, sides: the perspective of the public, and that of the police. Where did this combination take us? Let us briefly reflect on some of the benefits and potential pitfalls of this approach, before we widen the scope and consider future directions of research.

First and foremost, while there is a strong appeal to balancing a study so that both the trust of the public and the rationalities of the police are included, this also brings complications. Some of these are practical: combining different methodologies in a single study is challenging and requires a researcher to juggle different types of logic—it requires a balancing act. Other complications are of more consequence: different methodological approaches yield different kinds of answers. In our study of public trust in the police, we could point to quantities: levels of trust, intensity of developments, strengths of covariances, size of effects. Inquiries into police trust-building strategies, however, rely on dissecting rationalities, path dependency, and policy processes.

It could be argued that such different types of explanations are incompatible—they concern different planes of logic. My aim was to illustrate the ways in which this juxtaposition could in fact yield complementary insights, exploring the tensions surrounding the problem of trust in the police. Both approaches dealt with the problem of trust and the functions of police trust-building strategies from an internationally comparative as well as a diachronic, historical perspective. Levels of trust change, just like problem definitions of trust and trust-building strategies. As trust differs across countries, so do ways of conceiving the problem and ways to address it. Valid comparisons of superficially straightforwardly measured levels of trust in the police between countries are as fraught with complications and challenges as comparing nominally similar trust-building strategies across countries. Neither trust nor trust-building strategies should be examined without taking the unique national or local context into account, without remarking on the cultural, historical, or structural factors at play, or without notes of caution regarding the generalizability not only of the results, but also of the meaning of the results.

Had I limited this analysis merely to the quantitative half, we would have been left wondering why not all police organizations simply follow a procedural justice strategy to gain public trust. However, the qualitative part of this study shed light on how police organizations have different perceptions of the problem of trust and how to address it, how these are shaped as much by the actual problem as by history, structure, and culture, how other actors and key individuals influence the direction and design of trust-building efforts, how empirical findings sometimes clash with the institutional logics of the actors involved, how popular or influential ideas from abroad or other parts of the public sector can shape strategies, and how different priorities and demands can affect or obstruct trust-building strategies.

What this does not mean is that the two approaches are unconnected: trust-building strategies can be influenced by the public and their preferences or protests. Similarly, public trust in the police has, in the past, been shown to be determined to some extent by trust-building activities. The public and the police are hence inexorably bound together and constantly influence each other.

My particular approach of the public, the police, and the pursuit of trust did come with several weaknesses. Some of these are inherent to the research design, while others were methodological or depended on the available data. Future studies may take heed and address these aspects of this study—I suggest some leads for improvement.

The first issue that warrants attention here is connected to the three main theoretical schools included in this contribution. In the in-depth analyses of trust-building strategies, one vital result was the popularity of proximity policing-inspired strategies with police organizations. Police institutional logic is, at least within part of the police organization, intertwined with notions of proximity, cooperation, and integration in society. It is hard to reconcile this important finding with the fact that the quantitative studies conducted so far have had great trouble operationalizing proximity policing—often omitting it altogether. The vast majority of research on trust in the police, certainly cross-nationally, has not even mentioned proximity policing perspectives. I consider this to be a serious flaw in the existing body of knowledge.

Unfortunately, the present study has also had difficulties doing justice to proximity policing, opting for a flawed operationalization rather than not including it at all. The proximity policing index I constructed was, after controlling for other factors, not positively related to trust. I wish to be clear in stating that the proximity policing index I constructed should not be considered the definitive cross-national tool in comparing nations' adherence to proximity policing principles. Due to its reliance on individual experts in each country, and to the skewed distribution of existing knowledge on proximity policing in each country, the proximity policing index is an unsatisfactorily rough tool to approximately assess actual police adherence to proximity policing principles. This means that while the analyses did not find the expected positive relationship between proximity policing and trust in the police, I consider this result to be far from conclusive. On the individual level, information was even more scant, as the only variable that could be included in the proximity policing paradigm was that of perceived police successfulness in preventing violent crime. While this reflects proximity policing notions more than any other strategy, it is only a (very) partial indicator of the rich spectrum of proximity policing activities as a whole.

Future analyses should focus on better operationalization of proximity policing aspects, clearly and explicitly separating them from instrumentalism and from procedural justice aspects. While we might accept that proximity policing is the most complex of the three theoretical schools as far as concretely measuring the consequences is concerned, it should not be considered impossible to do so. Indeed, there were indications that even with our flawed operationalization, there may be a role for proximity policing initiatives in shaping public trust. Future contributions should also concentrate on measuring it on the levels where it is most applicable.

This reflects one important aspect inherent to proximity policing that has as of yet not been sufficiently addressed: proximity policing is hard to grasp on the levels on which quantitative analyses usually operate. Procedural justice is most salient on the level of individuals, as it focuses on interactions (even though these can be aggregated). Instrumentalism is primarily concerned with the macro level, that of countries or organizational units (even though these can be split into lower levels). Proximity policing, however, seems to be somewhere in the middle. This was made clear during the inquiry into police thinking about trust and trust-building strategies. When police organizations apply forms of policing inspired by proximity policing, as we found in the qualitative study on trust-building strategies, they are most often and most thoroughly applied in particular areas, specific neighborhoods, or communities that are the most challenging to the police. Hence proximity policing is a school of thought that primarily concerns the level of communities, not that of countries or individuals. Our quantitative analyses were geared toward these latter two levels, and were not designed to take into account the level of neighborhood or community. Conceptually, there is a bit of a mismatch behind most quantitative methods of analysis and the primary focus of proximity policing, making it difficult to assess its possible effects. However, the qualitative part of the study did include the examination of police strategies on the level of local areas and neighborhoods, and based on these analyses there is one more important comment I would like to add.

Proximity policing strategies are often most intensively applied in neighborhoods and areas where trust is lower and problems are most rampant. This focus means that not only is the effect of proximity policing on trust in the police hard to measure—due to the different level of inquiry—but also it suggests initially a negative, rather than positive, correlation between trust and the application of proximity policing. Proximity policing, more than anything else, is a set of strategies designed to improve trust where it was perceived to be problematically low by restoring a lost connection between police and citizens. In this perspective, it is interesting to see that the proximity policing index, the index indicating the extent to which the police in a country tend to adhere to proximity policing principles, was positively related to citizens' perceptions of police procedural justice.

This aligns with findings from the qualitative examination of trust-building strategies, where I found that proximity policing was a strategy to gain public trust step by step. This was done in areas where it was particularly challenging, by showing a different face of the police. Its effects on levels of trust as measured nationally may not be immediately visible, but it is likely to portray the local police as fairer and more respectful. Police officers working with proximity policing strategies in challenged neighborhoods often indicated, in my interviews, that they paid particular attention to treating citizens fairly and correctly, and listening to their points of view. In their minds, considerations of proximity policing and procedural justice were closely intertwined. What this also suggests is that the successfully application of proximity policing strategies needs to incorporate considerations for procedural justice.

As evidenced by the quantitative analyses, this connection is the same for citizens; the academically clear distinction between different theoretical schools with wholly different research traditions and intellectual adherents is to some extent artificial. In itself, this is not particularly surprising. First, the three theoretical schools studied in this contribution are archetypes, and hence are never observed in a 'pure' form. Second, these schools are also closely entwined with normative approaches toward the problem of trust: they recommend that certain types of police work or activities are strengthened and emphasized. They would not claim a monopoly on police activities. Even the fiercest proponents of one of these schools would rarely argue for the police to drop all activities not directly following from this school. In reality, then, we see that aspects and activities from multiple strategies tend to mix.

This close connection between factors or aspects derived from different theoretical schools is evidenced in other instances as well: we saw corruption, an indicator drawn from the procedural justice school, affect measures of perceived police effectiveness—reflecting instrumentalism—and of perceived police preventive success —derived from proximity policing. The individual-level assessments of specific aspects of policing (their effectiveness in catching criminals, their adherence to procedural justice principles, etc.) all were powerful determinants of trust in the police. Previous research, moreover, has also found that these individual-level determinants of trust are strongly correlated with each other (Brandl et al., 1994; Koster, 2017).

What such high correlations and large effect sizes might mean, other than suggesting powerful explanatory mechanisms, is something potentially problematic. This is the second main issue that I would like to address. Procedural justice-derived determinants had extremely powerful relationships with trust—so powerful, in fact, that we perhaps should question their meaning. We may wonder to

what extent there could be an inherent conceptual overlap between procedural justice principles and the concept of trust. Here, it may help to discern perceptions of
procedural justice from actual procedural justice. The previously mentioned recent
study by Worden and McLean (2017), combining survey data with observations of
police-citizen interactions, indicated that citizens' perceptions of police procedural
justice were shaped more by the opinions of the police that citizens already had
before the interaction than by the actual procedural justice with which they were
being treated during the interaction. This, it could be argued, challenges the usually assumed causality between these attitudinal variables: rather than being an
antecedent of trust, perceived police procedural justice might be an integral part of
trust. Like the work of Worden and McLean (2017), future contributions might do
well to discern actual procedural justice from perceived procedural justice.

A similar issue may arise with instrumentalism and perceived police effectiveness. Interestingly, here we saw that perceptions of police effectiveness were positively related to trust, yet objective crime rates, in the instrumental view considered evidence of police effectiveness, were not. Rather than mixed results, this
points, in my view, to a rejection of instrumentalism in the way it is often phrased.
Thus, instrumentalism warrants rephrasing or reconceptualization. I have studied
it here in a relatively narrow sense, focusing on indicators of crime and crime-
fighting (with the exception of perceptions of police rapid response to calls, which
reflects effectiveness in a somewhat broader sense). The results, as was clear from
the analyses, were rather negative: crime appears to be wholly unrelated to trust in
the police, and actual crime and perceptions of police effectiveness are only weakly
connected. Instrumentalism, in the crime-fighting sense, does not affect trust positively. What other kinds or measures of police effectiveness mean to the public
remains unclear: individual assessments of police effectiveness might conceptually
overlap with trust, as they could with perceptions of procedural justice. A new,
more fruitful interpretation of instrumentalism should hence be understood:
broader than just crime-fighting, but not merely based on public assessments
either. Instrumentalism, I suggest, could potentially contain something of value if
police performance were reformulated to entail all three aspects of police duties as
encapsulated in most police laws: dealing with crime, helping citizens, and maintaining public order. If we want to assess instrumentalism more informatively, we
should consider studying the relationship between police effectiveness in each of
these three separate aspects and trust in the police, rather than merely focusing on
crime-fighting.

Two more remarks need to be made regarding weaknesses of the present study
that could be addressed in the future through different research designs and questions. Both aim to encourage more in-depth, qualitative examinations. The first of
these concerns my selection of cases in the study of police trust-building strategies.
I selected three northwestern European countries, and within each of those countries I concentrated on two different locations to learn more about trust-building on

a local level. This nested structure certainly had some merit: it proved that there were differences within, as well as between, countries in terms of trust-building strategies and even problem definitions. At the same time, however, we learned nothing about trust-building outside of these three countries. The pursuit of trust may take entire different forms even in neighboring countries, let alone in completely different parts of Europe. Much more research is needed before we can say anything meaningful regarding trust-building strategies in Europe as a whole. Similarly, we have found that trust-building strategies can take on vastly different interpretations in different places within the same country. This held even for national or centralized police systems. Local examinations of trust-building strategies may hence teach us a lot about how the police deal with the problem of trust, but first of all they teach us that there is great diversity. In the three countries included in the present contribution, that means the reported results, particularly when they concern local situations, are to a large extent dependent on the specific contexts that were examined. We need to accept that the situation may (or rather, will) be different in other parts of the same country, and at different points in time. A systematic inquiry into differences in trust-building within the same country provides many possibilities for future research.

A final remark that needs to be made concerns the matter of comparability. Much attention has been paid in the present study to the question of whether or not we can validly compare concepts or constructs across countries. In my qualitative study of trust-building strategies, I found that thinking about trust and trust-building already greatly differed across the three, on the face of it reasonably comparable, societies included. Occasionally, even in these relatively similar northwestern European countries, differences in culture, language, or structure were so complex that they posed tough challenges to my ability to meaningfully compare some central concepts, logics, or strategies. But at least in in-depth, qualitative studies we can see what the problem is.

In the quantitative cross-national analyses, attention to cross-national comparability took the form of measurement equivalence tests. Such tests, while among the best statistical tools to ascertain valid comparability, are still conceptually deeply flawed. They might tell us, for instance, in which countries comparability issues arise, but they are unable to teach us much about why there are such issues. Thinking about trust in the police, a nonequivalent measurement in a country, tells us only that there is a comparability issue—it might depend on linguistic differences, differences in historical associations with the policing function, cultural peculiarities, something else entirely, or a mix of all of the above. This, of course, is deeply unsatisfactory for anyone who really wishes to gain a deeper understanding of trust in the police. Why was trust in the police in Spain nonequivalent as compared to other countries? How come measurements of trust were nonequivalent in Slovenia at certain moments in time but not at others? Such questions may never be fully answered, but a more complete and nuanced examination should be attempted than through equivalence tests. This is where qualitative, in-depth approaches are of the essence. We could talk to citizens, discovering what trust in the police means for them (and what it does not), what historical or cultural associations and implications it has for them, and what practical consequences. We can speak with the police, uncovering how they view their relationship with citizens and what it means to be trusted or mistrusted. What form, according to them, should trust take and why? It is this sort of inquiry that, in my view, could yield essential information about what it means to compare trust in the police between different contexts. Of this type of information I could, through a quantitative analysis, only observe echoes embedded in data patterns of covariance matrices. Measurement equivalence tests, by necessity, assess mere statistical simplifications of a complex reality that is well worth digging into by other means.

Aside from these lacunae and weaknesses left by the present contribution, there are some suggestions that I could offer for future studies' general directions. One direction is the following. Returning to the notion of its dynamic approach, I should note that the two directions taken in the present study—quantitative assessments of developments in trust and qualitative examinations of the shaping of trust-building strategies—could, in a future contribution, be bound together even more closely. The best way to do so would probably be on the local or regional level within a country. Here, the dynamics of, on the one hand, police perceptions of citizens and their implementation of trust-building strategies and, on the other, public expectations of and trust in the police, could be contrasted. In the present study, I found rather different police approaches toward trust in different places within the same country. Such differences could be observed between police forces serving millions of citizens, but also between police stations in neighboring villages. The benefit of such a study of trust in the police and of police trust-building on the local, rather than the national or cross-national level, is that we could see the interactions between the two. A localized study can, more easily than a national or international one, assess how a particular approach toward trust-building shapes citizens' trust. On the other hand, it can also pinpoint how citizens' attitudes, complaints, or protests could determine the way police work and how they design or adopt new trust-building activities. Such a dynamic approach makes the most of qualitative and quantitative research methods, and could provide us with vital information on trust and trust-building on the level where current research on these topics is scant: that of local communities, towns, and neighborhoods.

A quantitative direction that future studies could take might concentrate on developments in trust in different countries. Ideally, a quantitative longitudinal analysis could take the shape of an explanatory analysis of trust-building strategies, or at least it could attempt to explain changing trust through changing contextual factors. This is more informative than attempting to explain differences in levels of trust between countries at a fixed moment in time, which has by now often been done. As of yet, available data for such a longitudinal study are probably still insufficient—or a great deal of additional data should be collected by the researcher. In the future, however, as additional waves of ESS and EVS and other survey data are collected, I expect the application of, for instance, growth curve modeling (Singer & Willett, 2003) to be useful in explaining changes in levels of trust in the police across European countries.

In a more qualitative direction, our study of police trust-building strategies and of problem definitions of trust could be expanded to different contexts, outside northwestern Europe. One result of the in-depth examination of England & Wales, Denmark, and the Netherlands was that their police institutional logic, their problem definitions, and their proposed solutions are often completely different—even though parallels, mutual influences, and (often superficial) similarities exist. Even this endeavor was quite modest from a European perspective, as it concerned relatively similar countries with moderately high to high levels of trust. I would hence encourage researchers from different parts of Europe to conduct similar inquiries into their police organizations, most notably in the Mediterranean region and in former communist countries. These are regions where trust has often increased dramatically (or occasionally collapsed) over recent decades and where society has undergone drastic changes. This invites in-depth analyses into how the police perceive (and have perceived) the problem of trust, into their institutional responses and trust-building efforts, and the interplay of institutions and public trust generally.

A final question raised by conducting this research was a fundamental one. Throughout this study, we have seen levels of trust change and trust-building strategies evolve.[4] We have theorized the problem of trust, attempted to explain differences between countries, and assessed the empirical comparability of measures of trust. One of the more remarkable results, here, however, is that despite the regularly stated perceptions of the police regarding a public that will never be happy with the police whatever they do, we have, on average, seen trust in the police increase, whereas trust in other institutions has fallen. What does this finding mean? Wat does it imply for the police, what for the public, and what for democracy? As mentioned in Section 12.3, there is something disconcerting about these results and they definitely call for more, and more in-depth, attention to the subject. Such contributions could take many shapes and approaches, but do appear to suggest fruitful directions for furthering our understanding of contemporary society. More than anything else, this serves to illustrate the vast complexity of the problem of trust, and why even rising levels of trust in the police are not merely cause for celebration.

Trust in the police touches on questions of state legitimacy. These matters lie at the very foundation of democratic societies and should be of interest to all. The

---

4.   Although, to be fair, the alternation of different trust-building strategies often had the characteristics of a Kuhnian paradigm shift rather than that of an evolving body of commonly accepted practices to improve trust.

web of complex, sometimes contradictory, processes and phenomena involving legitimacy, authority, consent, satisfaction, and trust is worthy of our full attention and cannot be discussed in isolation. As evidenced in the opening pages of this contribution, I consider the work of individual police officers in their own local areas to lie at the very foundation of addressing and understanding this complex. This, I believe, is a truism that researchers, police chiefs, and policy-makers everywhere should take heed of.

I have attempted to expand our knowledge of trust and trust-building and, in the process, endeavored to shed some light on the complexity of cross-national and multi-method examinations. Much more work needs to be done, and in some ways the present contribution has only managed to raise more questions than it has answered. I can only call on police and on researchers to keep addressing these questions. Meanwhile, trust in the police will remain an issue of debate for citizens, politicians, and police officers themselves for decades to come. And that, I think, is to the benefit of all.

Samenvatting

Deze studie richtte zich op vertrouwen in de politie. In **Deel I** van deze studie stelde ik dat vertrouwen van groot belang is voor de politie, aangezien meer vertrouwen maakt dat burgers zich veiliger voelen, sneller zelf ingrijpen in geval van kleine ordeverstoringen, en meer bereid zijn om samen te werken met de politie en aangifte te doen van misdrijven. Vertrouwen is dus een voorwaarde voor de politie om haar werk goed te doen. Onze kennis over vertrouwen in de politie en over hoe de politie zelf vertrouwen begrijpt en probeert vorm te geven laat in een aantal opzichten te wensen over: er zijn theoretische, geografische en temporele lacunes in het huidige onderzoeksveld. Het belangrijkste is echter dat er nauwelijks bestaande studies naar vertrouwen zijn die ingaan op zowel het perspectief van burgers als van de politie. In navolging van Bottoms en Tankebe (2012) beschouw ik vertrouwen dan ook als een dialoog tussen deze twee partijen.

Ik bestudeerde vertrouwen in de politie vanuit een landenvergelijkend en diachronisch perspectief. Daarnaast richtte ik mij op politiële vertrouwensstrategieën en hoe deze zich hebben ontwikkeld in drie West-Europese landen: Engeland & Wales, Denemarken, en Nederland. Ik liet mij daarbij leiden door zes onderzoeksvragen; het eerste drietal gaat over vertrouwen van burgers in de politie, het tweede drietal richt zich op politiële vertrouwensstrategieën:

> *Onderzoeksvraag 1: In welke mate zijn metingen van vertrouwen van burgers in de politie empirisch vergelijkbaar tussen Europese landen?*
> *Onderzoeksvraag 2: Wat zijn de verschillen tussen Europese landen wat betreft niveaus van vertrouwen van burgers in de politie, en hoe heeft vertrouwen in de politie in Europa zich de afgelopen decennia ontwikkeld?*
> *Onderzoeksvraag 3: Welke factoren op nationaal en individueel niveau verklaren de verschillen tussen landen in het vertrouwen van burgers in de politie?*
>
> *Onderzoeksvraag 4: Wanneer en hoe werd vertrouwen van burgers in de politie in verschillende Europese landen gedefinieerd als een probleem, en hoe heeft dit zich vervolgens ontwikkeld?*

> *Onderzoeksvraag 5: Welke strategieën en 'oplossingen' zijn vanaf dat moment door wie ontwikkeld en toegepast om om te gaan met het probleem van vertrouwen in de politie, en om relaties tussen burgers en de politie in het algemeen te verbeteren? Onderzoeksvraag 6: Hoe kunnen we de verschillen die we aantreffen tussen en binnen landen wat betreft probleemdefinitie en vertrouwensstrategieën verklaren?*

Voordat deze onderzoeksvragen beantwoord konden worden, moesten de sleutelconcepten van deze studie nader gedefinieerd worden: *trust, confidence* en legitimiteit domineren het discours rond de houding van burgers tegenover de politie. *Trust* en *confidence* worden, in Engelstalige publicaties, vaak beschouwd als verschillende concepten. Internationaal gezien echter zijn er weinig tot geen talen die een onderscheid maken tussen de twee—het Nederlands vertaalt ze ook allebei als vertrouwen. Dit maakt dat ik ze beschouw als de facto synoniem. Beide concepten, wanneer we de eigenschappen van de politie in het achterhoofd houden, kunnen gedefinieerd worden als **het geloof en de verwachting dat de politie, als individuen of als institutie, haar taak 'goed' vervult.**

Legitimiteit is een concept dat minstens net zo complex is als *trust* en *confidence* en even populair. Legitimiteit is een kenmerk op institutioneel niveau: de politie als institutie heeft een zekere mate van legitimiteit. Ik onderscheid twee verschillende types: formele en informele legitimiteit. Formele legitimiteit, beïnvloed door het werk van Weber, bestaat uit constellaties van legale en sociale regels en normen op systeemniveau, dus inclusief legaliteit en normconformatie in bredere zin. De meer Durkheimiaanse informele legitimiteit omvat het begrip en de acceptatie van politieel gezag van de kant van burgers, hun medewerking met en gehoorzaamheid aan de politie, en ook *confidence* en *trust*. Alle machtssystemen streven naar een vorm van zelflegitimatie (Beetham, 1991a). In democratische samenlevingen betekent dit, gezien de samenstelling van informele legitimiteit, dat de politie ook vertrouwen zoekt. Behalve deze sleutelconcepten zijn er nog enige concepten van secundair belang voor deze studie: tevredenheid, gezag, en *consent*.

Er zijn drie theoretische paradigma's te onderscheiden op het gebied van denken over vertrouwen in de politie en hoe het te verbeteren. Ik paste deze drie paradigma's toe om vertrouwen te helpen begrijpen, hypothesen te formuleren, en vertrouwensstrategieën van een breder kader te voorzien. Ieder van deze paradigma's heeft verschillende kernassumpties en ze staan ook uiteenlopende strategieën voor: ze veronderstellen dat er bepaalde manieren zijn voor politiemensen en -organisaties om vertrouwen van burgers te winnen.

De eerste is de school van *proximity policing* (in Nederland bekend als gebiedsgebonden politiewerk). Deze beweging kwam op als reactie op de veronderstelde zwaktes van het vroegere professionele model van politiewerk, dat vooral draaide om technologie. *Proximity policing* richt zich op het verbeteren van relaties tussen burgers en politie door de afstand tussen de twee te verminderen. De politie moet benaderbaar en zichtbaar zijn, moet zich bezighouden met een breed scala aan

(sociale) wijkproblemen en onveiligheidsgevoelens, moet samenwerken met partners en proactief zijn in de strijd tegen misdaad en andere problematiek door het
betrekken van burgers. Dit betekent vaak een gedecentraliseerde organisatiestruc-
tuur en veel discretionaire ruimte voor politiemensen. Vanaf de tachtiger jaren is
de populariteit van *proximity policing* in verschillende golven gekomen en gegaan.

Het tweede paradigma is dat van instrumentalisme. Deze school combineert de
focus op effectiviteit van het professionele model met ideeën uit het New Public
Management (NPM) op het gebied van efficiëntie en meetbare output en veronder-
stelt dat deze aspecten vertrouwen en politiële legitimiteit kunnen bevorderen. Om
vertrouwen te winnen moet de politie haar effectiviteit bewijzen, vooral in haar
veronderstelde 'kerntaak': misdaadbestrijding. Dit model van denken over de relatie tussen burgers en politie is sinds de negentiger jaren behoorlijk dominant
geworden in beleid en visie van de belangrijkste actoren—vooral het politiema-
nagement.

De derde school is die van procedurele rechtvaardigheid. Dit paradigma draait
om interacties tussen burgers en politiemensen en benadrukt correcte behandeling
van burgers. Procedureel rechtvaardig politiewerk bevat volgens Tyler (1988) verscheidene elementen: consistentie, onpartijdigheid, kwaliteit van besluitvorming,
bereidheid om besluiten of opvattingen te herzien, ethisch gedrag van de kant van
de politiemensen, en gelegenheid voor burgers om hun zegje te doen. Als politiemensen respect tonen, burgers hun kant van het verhaal laten toelichten, en laten
zien dat ze goed geïnformeerde besluiten willen nemen, wordt verwacht dat burgers de politie vaker gehoorzamen en meer vertrouwen hebben in de politie. Politiële corruptie en gebruik van geweld waar dat niet noodzakelijk is zullen het
omgekeerde effect hebben. Procedurele rechtvaardigheid is vooral een academi-
sche benadering, maar heeft gedurende de afgelopen decennia langzamerhand
aandacht weten te vergaren bij de politie en in beleidskringen.

In **Deel II** beantwoordde ik de eerste drie onderzoeksvragen. Hiervoor moest
een aantal stappen doorlopen worden. Ten eerste was het belangrijk om vast te
stellen in welke mate metingen van vertrouwen van burgers in de politie vergelijk-
baar zijn tussen Europese landen. Hiervoor werden equivalentietoetsen toegepast
op internationale survey data die inmiddels in meerdere jaargangen beschikbaar
zijn: het European Social Survey (ESS) 2002–2014 en de European Values Study
(EVS) 1981–2008. Vervolgens kon de tweede vraag beantwoord worden voor die
landen en jaren waar internationale en longitudinale equivalentie wordt gevonden:
het beschrijven van verschillen tussen en ontwikkelingen in Europese landen wat
betreft niveaus van vertrouwen. Er is een aantal populaire theses rond veronderstelde ontwikkelingen in het vertrouwen in de politie. Als ze waar zouden zijn, zou
dit terug te zien moeten zijn in survey data. Ik heb hier de desacralisatiethese, de
veiligheidsutopiethese, de post-autoritaire paradox these, en het probleem van de
sociaaleconomische crisis onderscheiden. De meeste van deze theses suggereren

negatieve trends: de verwachting, populair in wetenschappelijk, publiek en politiek discours, is dat vertrouwen in de politie over het algemeen aan het afnemen is.

Verschillen tussen landen in niveaus van vertrouwen kunnen vervolgens verklaard worden met internationale survey data van de ESS meting in 2010. Deze
data werden aangevuld met informatie op landniveau. Voor dit deel van de studie
werden de drie theoretische paradigma's ingezet om sets van concurrerende
hypotheses te formuleren. Het *proximity policing* paradigma bracht me tot de verwachting dat burgers meer vertrouwen in de politie hebben in landen die in
hogere mate principes van *proximity policing* toepassen. Het instrumentele paradigma leidde tot de verwachting dat er negatieve relaties zijn tussen criminaliteits-
niveaus in een land (gemeten als moordcijfers en slachtofferschap van inbraak en
(dreiging met) mishandeling) en vertrouwen in de politie. De procedurele
rechtvaardigheidsschool leverde de hypothese dat vertrouwen in de politie lager
zal zijn in landen met hogere niveaus van corruptie. Daarnaast leidde ik uit ieder
paradigma veronderstelde relaties af tussen specifieke individuele percepties van
de politie en vertrouwen in de politie—en tussen de eerdergenoemde landken-
merken en individuele percepties van de politie. Ten slotte voegde ik een aantal
controlevariabelen op individueel en landniveau toe.

De eerste stap in het beantwoorden van de onderzoeksvragen 1 t/m 3 was het
toepassen van *multi-group structural equation modeling* om equivalentie van metingen van vertrouwen in de politie te bepalen, zowel landenvergelijkend als longitu-
dinaal. De resultaten gaven aan dat gemiddelde niveaus van vertrouwen in de EVS
1981–2008 en de ESS 2002–2014 data op valide wijze vergeleken kunnen worden
tussen de meeste meetpunten door de tijd heen, maar niet tussen alle. Daarnaast
vond ik dat gemiddelde niveaus van vertrouwen op valide wijze vergeleken kunnen worden tussen de meeste landen in de ESS meting van 2010, maar niet tussen
alle.

Ik splitste het omschrijven van ontwikkelingen in vertrouwen door de tijd heen
in twee delen: lange termijnontwikkelingen zoals gemeten door de EVS, en middellange tot korte termijnontwikkelingen zoals vervat in de ESS. Op lange termijn
blijkt dat vertrouwen in de politie in grote delen van Europa is toegenomen. Dit
geldt bij uitstek voor de periode tussen 1990 en 2008. Deze toename blijkt echter
niet overal in Europa te gelden; er zijn verscheidene landen die hun vertrouwen in
de politie zagen dalen of het niveau constant hielden. De trends bleken ook niet
geconcentreerd te zijn in specifieke regio's, met één duidelijke uitzondering: de
afname, op lange termijn, van vertrouwen in de politie op de Britse eilanden. De
middellange en korte termijnontwikkelingen van de ESS leverden een gemengd
beeld op: in Europa schommelt het vertrouwen. In een meerderheid van landen
echter blijkt vertrouwen in de politie gemiddeld gezien wel te zijn toegenomen.

Hoewel elk van de vier populaire theses wat betreft ontwikkelingen in het vertrouwen in zekere mate in bepaalde periodes opging voor bepaalde delen van
Europa, blijkt het algemene beeld van trends in vertrouwen zowel op de lange als

op kortere termijn veel positiever dan vaak wordt aangenomen. Een andere relevante bevinding is dat vertrouwen in de meeste andere instituties veel minder positieve trends kent dan vertrouwen in de politie; hoewel vertrouwen in het leger in de EVS data op vergelijkbare wijze toenam als vertrouwen in de politie, was van een algemene toename van vertrouwen in het rechtssysteem en ambtenaren geen sprake. Vertrouwen in politieke instituties blijkt in grote delen van Europa de afgelopen decennia (soms fors) afgenomen te zijn.

Na het schetsen van ontwikkelingen in vertrouwen door de tijd heen, gaf ik aan wat de verschillen tussen landen zijn in het jaar 2010. Vervolgens konden deze verschillen verklaard worden. Vertrouwen was het hoogst in Scandinavische landen, gevolgd door andere West-Europese landen. Zuid-Europese en voormalig communistische landen in Centraal en Oost-Europa hadden over het algemeen lagere niveaus van vertrouwen in de politie. Deze verschillen tussen landen konden verklaard worden in multilevel regressieanalyses. Hoewel er verschillende significante bivariate relaties waren tussen landfactoren en vertrouwen in de politie, bleef na toevoeging van controlevariabelen alleen het negatieve effect van corruptie op vertrouwen op landniveau significant. Na toevoegen van controlevariabelen bleek *proximity policing* niet gerelateerd aan vertrouwen, terwijl criminaliteitscijfers in een land anders dan verwacht (licht) positief samenhingen met vertrouwen in de politie.

Op individueel niveau bleken alle specifieke percepties van de politie (zoals afgeleid van de drie theoretische scholen) significant samen te hangen met vertrouwen in de politie; de sterkste samenhang werd gevonden met de indicatoren van procedurele rechtvaardigheid, gevolgd door die van *proximity policing* en ten slotte die van instrumentalisme. Dit betekende dat de resultaten veel steun opleverden voor hypotheses afgeleid van procedurele rechtvaardigheid, zwakke steun voor *proximity policing*-geïnspireerde hypotheses, en geen steun voor instrumentalisme. Verdere analyses gaven aan dat de effecten van veel individuele controlekenmerken op vertrouwen, zoals die van etniciteit, sterk verschilden tussen landen— ze hingen positief samen met vertrouwen in sommige landen en negatief in andere. Andere determinanten, zoals kerkbezoek, inkomen, en evaluaties van contact met de politie, hadden min of meer vergelijkbare effecten in verschillende landen.

Na het bestuderen van vertrouwen in de politie en daarmee het beantwoorden van de eerste drie onderzoeksvragen, verschoof in **Deel III** van deze studie de aandacht naar de politie zelf als onderzoeksobject; zonder begrip van de belangrijkste actor schiet een onderzoek naar vertrouwen in de politie namelijk tekort. Ik gebruikte elementen van Kingdons (1995) werk op het gebied van probleemdefinities, *policy generation*, en politieke gebeurtenissen om een theoretische benadering te formuleren voor het beantwoorden van onderzoeksvragen 4 t/m 6. Ik paste een *case study* benadering toe op enige landen die in het eerdere deel van dit onderzoek ook waren bestudeerd. Ten eerste wilde ik achterhalen wanneer vertrouwen in de politie voor het eerst als beleidsissue werd gedefinieerd—als een probleem. Ten tweede volgde ik het proces van *policy generation* en de 'uitvinding' van strategieën om vertrouwen mee te bevorderen. Net als in Deel 2 van het boek was hier een prominente rol voor de drie paradigma's in het denken rond vertrouwen—*proximity policing*, instrumentalisme, en procedurele rechtvaardigheid. Deze paradigma's werden hier niet gebruikt om hypothesen mee te formuleren voor het verklaren van vertrouwen, maar om de onderliggende logica van politiële vertrouwensstrategieën bloot te leggen. Ten derde wilde ik met deze analyse de rol van unieke omstandigheden, gebeurtenissen, individuele actoren, en institutionele en culturele context schetsen binnen het proces van *trust-building*: van probleemdefinitie tot evaluatie van vertrouwensstrategieën.

Ik koos drie West-Europese landen, Engeland & Wales, Denemarken, en Nederland. Deze selectie hield verschillende culturele en historische *cases* in, die echter genoeg gemeen hebben om een vergelijking nog betekenisvol te laten zijn (Nelken, 2012). Daarnaast betekende hun relatieve nabijheid dat er waarschijnlijk sprake zou zijn van *policy transfer* en diffusie. Binnen elk land selecteerde ik verschillende locaties voor meer diepgravend onderzoek. De dataverzameling bestond uit semigestructureerde interviews met experts en werknemers in de praktijk, zowel binnen als buiten de politie en van sterk variërende senioriteit.

Engeland & Wales heeft lang bekend gestaan als voorbeeld op het gebied van politiewerk en vertrouwen in de politie, vanwege een bijna mystieke band tussen de politie en burgers (Loader & Mulcahy, 2003), met een centrale rol voor de notie van *democratic accountability*. In de loop van de afgelopen decennia heeft dit beeld echter barsten opgelopen. Een belangrijke periode in de formatie van vertrouwen als beleidsonderwerp, en ook in de formulering van vertrouwensstrategieën, vond plaats in de tachtiger jaren. In deze periode vonden protesten en rellen plaats in de grote steden, waaronder de Brixton riots, die een groeiende spanning tussen de politie en bepaalde minderheden illustreerden. De reacties hierop bestonden uit een eerste golf van *community-oriented policing* (vanuit de politie) en een sterkere nadruk op eerlijke behandeling en democratische verantwoording (vanuit de Home Office). Veel van de energie die werd gestoken in vertrouwensstrategieën verdween echter met de mijnwerkersstaking halverwege het decennium. In de negentiger jaren werd steeds meer nadruk gelegd op het bestrijden van criminaliteit en op *value-for-money* logica—beïnvloed door toenemende criminaliteit en de populariteit van het NPM. Aan het eind van de negentiger jaren kon vertrouwen in de politie volgens de New Labour regering alleen verbeterd worden als de politie aantoonbaar succes kon vieren door het behalen van kwantitatieve doelstellingen: *performance targets*.

In de eerste jaren van de 21ste eeuw was sprake van een zogeheten *reassurance gap*, een discrepantie tussen het succes waarmee de politie haar doelstellingen behaalde en afnemend vertrouwen van burgers in de politie. Dit leidde tot de invoering van *neighbourhood policing*—een nieuwe fase van *proximity policing*. Er werden wijkteams gevormd en een nieuw soort politiemedewerker, de PCSO, werd speciaal aangesteld om de relatie met burgers te verbeteren en veiligheidsgevoelens te bevorderen. Met de economische crisis echter kwam al snel een nieuwe regering aan de macht en een periode van bezuinigingen volgde waarin *neighbourhood policing* het zwaar te verduren kreeg. De nieuwe, door de Conservatieven gedomineerde, regering stond sceptisch tegenover de politie, legde de schuld voor verscheidene schandalen exclusief bij de politie, en stelde dat zij weinig efficiënt was. Een tweezijdig beleid op het gebied van vertrouwensstrategieën volgde. Ten eerste werd de armslag van de politiële inspectiedienst (HMIC) aanzienlijk uitgebreid, met de bedoeling om politiekorpsen betrouwbaarder te maken. Ten tweede werden democratisch gekozen *police and crime commissioners* ingevoerd om democratische controle over de politie te versterken en daarmee vertrouwen te bevorderen.

Denemarken is een *high-trust society* die eigenlijk nooit een serieuze crisis in het vertrouwen in de politie heeft gekend. Kenmerkend voor de relatie tussen burgers en politie in Denemarken is dat het deel is van een breder cultureel complex, waarin de staat gezien wordt als goedaardige actor die veiligheid biedt—of eigenlijk de unieke, harmonieuze notie van *tryghed*. Denemarken is historisch gezien een grotendeels rurale samenleving met een nationale, maar de facto gedecentraliseerde politieorganisatie die goed is ingebed in lokale gemeenschappen. Vertrouwen in de politie werd lange tijd gezien als vanzelfsprekend. Groeiende criminaliteit en demografische veranderingen leidden in de zeventiger jaren tot voorzichtige *proximity policing* hervormingen. Aan het begin van de negentiger jaren stond de politie enigszins onder druk na gewelddadige rellen in de wijk Nørrebro, maar deze werden niet gezien als emblematisch voor een dieper probleem rond vertrouwen.

In de tweede helft van de negentiger jaren vond een nieuwe golf van *proximity policing* experimenten plaats, vooral onder invloed van buitenlandse voorbeelden, gericht op het verder verbeteren van het hoge niveau van vertrouwen. Het leidde tot gemengde resultaten (Holmberg, 2002), en nu twee *proximity policing* golven weinig hadden opgeleverd verschoof de aandacht naar een andere benadering. In een 'vermomde centralisatie' (Holmberg & Balvig, 2013) werd, met als doelstelling meer efficiëntie en effectiviteit, een grootschalige reorganisatie van het politiebestel uitgevoerd. Deze hervorming, in 2007, bracht chaos in de organisatie en plaatste de politie op grotere afstand van burgers. Geschokt door een golf van kritiek ervoer de politie een plotseling probleem met vertrouwen. De problemen rond de reorganisatie en toenemende spanningen tussen politie en etnische minderheden brachten lokale politiedistricten ertoe elementen van *proximity policing* opnieuw in te voeren, deze keer met als expliciet doel om vertrouwen te herstellen. Dat de politie niet langer een institutie is die gevrijwaard is van kritiek werd geïllustreerd door de oprichting van een onafhankelijke politieklachtencommissie in 2012.

Nederland kent historische spanningen tussen burgers en politie. Hoewel vertrouwen in de politie over het algemeen hoog was, werd het gezag van de politie in Nederland eerder uitgedaagd dan in de andere twee landen. De grootschalige straatprotesten en conflicten tussen politie en demonstranten gedurende de zestiger jaren maakten dat de politie een acute legitimiteitscrisis ervoer. Dit inspireerde sommige politiemensen in de daarop volgende decennia tot de ontwikkeling van *proximity policing* strategieën om de verbinding met burgers te zoeken—om nooit meer zo verrast te worden. Het beleidsdocument 'Politie in verandering', geschreven door jonge politiemensen, had hierin een belangrijke rol. Zo werd onder andere de invoering van wijkteams voorgesteld (Heijink et al., 1977).

Wijk- of gebiedsgebonden politiewerk werd de leidende vertrouwensstrategie van de Nederlandse politie na de regionalisering van het daarvoor gefragmenteerde politiebestel in 1993. Deze strategie ontwikkelde zich in de loop van het decennium: individuele politiemensen namen als wijkagenten de rol van wijkteams over, en samenwerking in lokale veiligheidsnetwerken nam toe. Tegelijkertijd echter groeiden de zorgen rond criminaliteit en onveiligheid, en NPM-noties rond efficiëntie begonnen een grotere rol te spelen. Een belangrijk jaar was 2002, toen de moord op Pim Fortuyn een keerpunt betekende in het Nederlandse veiligheidsdenken. De focus van de regering kwam vooral te liggen op effectieve criminaliteitsbestrijding. Geïnspireerd door het Engelse voorbeeld werd de politie een groeiend kader van kwantitatieve doelstellingen opgelegd.

In 2012 vond een revolutie plaats binnen de Nederlandse politie: een nieuwe reorganisatie nationaliseerde het politiebestel. Dit ging samen met een vertrouwensstrategie die primair gefocust was op het verbeteren van tevredenheid en vertrouwen van burgers door het efficiënt verlenen van diensten: het service-model. Het beperkte onderzoek dat hiernaar gedaan is wijst vooral op negatieve bijwerkingen van deze strategie, veroorzaakt door de groeiende afstand tussen burgers en politie.

Na deze drie *case studies* werd het mogelijk om de onderzoeksvragen 4 t/m 6 te beantwoorden. Hoewel vertrouwen in de politie een relevant beleidsonderwerp bleek in ieder land, werd vertrouwen op historisch zeer verschillende momenten gedefinieerd—of 'uitgevonden' (Lee, 2007)—als probleem. Bovendien werd dit probleem vaak begrepen in verschillende termen en concepten en er lagen uiteenlopende probleemdefinities aan ten grondslag. Deze probleemdefinities veranderen ook na verloop van tijd. Ook vertrouwensstrategieën verschillen: verschillende strategieën werden toegepast door uiteenlopende actoren in elk land op verschillende momenten. Vooral interpretaties van *proximity policing* en instrumentalisme hebben lange periodes van populariteit gekend, maar ze werden in elk van de drie landen door verschillende actoren of constellaties van actoren, ieder met uiteenlopende belangen, gestimuleerd. Dit leidt ertoe dat dezelfde strategie, zoals *proximity policing*, in feite heel verschillende interpretaties en implicaties had in de bestudeerde landen.

Zowel de definiëring of uitvinding van vertrouwen als beleidsprobleem en de ontwikkeling van vertrouwensstrategieën zijn sterk afhankelijk van de nationale of zelfs de lokale context—historisch, structureel, of cultureel. Processen van *policy transfer* en diffusie spelen zichtbare of soms minder zichtbare rollen in zowel probleemdefinities als *policy generation*, maar lokale omstandigheden, individuele autonomie en vaak onvoorspelbare gebeurtenissen blijven cruciaal. Dit betekent dat er geen duidelijke trend is naar convergentie van vertrouwensstrategieën in de drie landen die ik bestudeerde. Bij het bestuderen van vertrouwensstrategieën is het belangrijk om rekening te houden met buitenlandse invloeden, door middel van processen als *policy transfer, policy translation*, en diffusie. Maar veel ontwikkelingen—zo niet de meeste—in vertrouwensstrategieën worden in feite gevormd door lokale en nationale factoren, of worden er in ieder geval sterk door gestuurd. Internationale, nationale, en lokale invloeden beconcurreren elkaar in de definitie van het vertrouwensprobleem, in de te formuleren strategieën, en in hoe deze geïmplementeerd worden.

In **Deel IV** reflecteerde ik op een aantal belangrijke conclusies en weerleggingen van populaire ideeën. De veelgehoorde notie van een crisis in vertrouwen in de politie blijkt overtrokken; vertrouwen in de politie neemt over het algemeen eerder toe, terwijl dat in andere instituties juist vaak afneemt. Dit is niet noodzakelijkerwijs goed nieuws, en het ontslaat politieorganisaties ook niet van de verplichting te werken aan vertrouwen. Men heeft hoge verwachtingen van de politie en het is de vraag of zij deze altijd waar kan maken. Een tweede populair idee is dat effectiviteit van de politie de belangrijkste factor is in het bepalen van vertrouwen. Dit blijkt onjuist; hoewel (gepercipieerde) effectiviteit er wel toe doet, blijken belangrijkere factoren procedurele rechtvaardigheid en (in mindere mate) *proximity policing*. Een derde misvatting is dat politiële vertrouwensstrategieën steeds meer op elkaar gaan lijken door processen van diffusie en internationale *policy transfer*. Landen beïnvloeden elkaar inderdaad, maar de manier, intensiteit en frequentie waarmee dit gebeurt is onvoorspelbaar; het nettoresultaat is in ieder geval geen duidelijke convergentie. Dat de lokale en nationale context doorslaggevend blijkt te zijn in het vormgeven van vertrouwensstrategieën beschouw ik overigens als een goede zaak.

Het voorgaande betekent dat het moeilijk is om aan te geven wat goed politiewerk is om vertrouwen mee te winnen. *Slecht* politiewerk is eenvoudiger te definiëren, en het bevorderen van vertrouwen bestaat in mijn optiek dan ook vaak uit het voorkomen van slecht politiewerk. Ik formuleerde enkele ruwe richtlijnen, waarbij de focus lag op het voorkomen van slechte behandeling van burgers, het tegengaan van corruptie, en het goed rekenschap geven van lokale context; het gaat in alle drie de gevallen om het voorkomen van (uiteenlopende) vormen van normoverschrijdend optreden—waarbij een norm breder is dan een wet. Een politieorganisatie kan vertrouwd worden als ze normen deelt met burgers; als er wederzijds overeenstemming is over de spelregels in de publieke ruimte. Zulke overeenstemming blijkt juist vaak afwezig op de plaatsen waar dit het meest van belang is, zoals probleemwijken. Het is daar aan de politie om gedeelde normen met burgers te bereiken.

Na deze aanbevelingen reflecteerde ik op de keuze het onderzoek te richten op zowel burgers als de politie. Ik concludeerde dat deze benadering vruchtbaar is en dat toekomstig onderzoek hier lessen uit kan trekken. Geconstateerd wordt tegelijkertijd dat het moeilijk blijft om *proximity policing*, een sleutelaspect in vertrouwensstrategieën, naar tevredenheid te operationaliseren en bestuderen. Daarnaast was er bewijs voor sterke discrepanties tussen de feitelijke situatie (bijvoorbeeld wat betreft criminaliteitscijfers) en opvattingen van burgers (bijvoorbeeld over de effectiviteit van de politie). Zowel beleid als onderzoek houdt niet genoeg rekening met deze discrepantie. Ik stel voor dat toekomstig onderzoek zich richt op hoe feitelijk politiewerk opvattingen van burgers beïnvloedt. Het zou dat moeten doen op lokaal en regionaal niveau, niet alleen op dat van individuen of landen. Hierbij kunnen kwantitatieve en kwalitatieve benaderingen elkaar aanvullen. De belangrijkste notie blijft echter, wat mij betreft, dat vertrouwen in de politie bepaald wordt door individuele politiemensen in hun dagelijks werk. Dat zij op deze wijze de legitimiteit van de staat vormgeven is een feit waar onderzoekers en beleidsmakers nooit genoeg rekening mee kunnen houden.

References

Ackroyd, S. (1993). A case of arrested development? Some consequences of inadequate management in the British police. *International Journal of Public Sector Management, 6*(2), 5-16.

Adams, R. E., Rohe, W. M., & Arcury, T. A. (2005). Awareness of community-oriented policing and neighborhood perceptions in five small to midsize cities. *Journal of Criminal Justice, 33*(1), 43-54.

AEPC (Association of European Police Colleges) (2001a). *Czech on its way to the EU.* Warnsveld: AEPC.

AEPC (Association of European Police Colleges) (2001b). *Estonia on its way to the EU.* Warnsveld: AEPC.

AEPC (Association of European Police Colleges) (2001c). *Hungary on its way to the EU.* Warnsveld: AEPC.

AEPC (Association of European Police Colleges) (2001d). *Poland on its way to the EU.* Warnsveld: AEPC.

AEPC (Association of European Police Colleges) (2001e). *Slovenia on its way to the EU.* Warnsveld: AEPC.

AEPC (Association of European Police Colleges) (2001f). *Ten candidate member states on their way to the EU.* Warnsveld: AEPC.

AEPC (Association of European Police Colleges) (2001g). *Slovakia on its way to the EU.* Warnsveld: AEPC.

Alalehto, T., & Larsson, D. (2016). Measuring trust in the police by contextual and individual factors. *International Journal of Law, Crime and Justice, 46*, 31-42.

Alderson, J. (1979). *Policing freedom.* Plymouth: MacDonald & Evans.

Algemene Rekenkamer (2011). *ICT bij de politie.* 's-Gravenhage: Sdu Uitgevers.

Amnesty International (1994). *Police ill-treatment in Denmark: A summary of Amnesty International's concerns.* Retrieved September 26, 2017 from https://www.amnesty.org/en/documents/eur18/002/1994/en/

Amnesty International (2008). *Police accountability mechanisms in Denmark.* Retrieved September 26, 2017 from https://www.amnesty.org/en/documents/eur18/002/2008/en/

Amnesty International (2013). *Proactief politieoptreden vormt risico voor mensenrechten. Etnisch profileren onderkennen en aanpakken.* Retrieved September 26, 2017 from https://www.amnesty.nl/actueel/proactief-politieoptreden-leidt-tot-discriminatie-in-nederland

Anderson, C. J., & Tverdova, Y. V. (2003). Corruption, political allegiances, and attitudes toward government in contemporary democracies. *American Journal of Political Science, 47*(1), 91-109.

Andersson, T., & Tengblad, S. (2009). When complexity meets culture: New Public Management and the Swedish police. *Qualitative Research in Accounting & Management, 6*(1/2), 41-56.

Ariel, B., Sutherland, A., Henstock, D., Young, J., Drover, P., Sykes, J., Megicks, S., & Henderson, R. (2016). Wearing body cameras increases assaults against officers and does not reduce police use of force: Results from a global multi-site experiment. *European Journal of Criminology, 13*(6), 744-755.

Ariel, B., Sutherland, A., Henstock, D., Young, J., Drover, P., Sykes, J., Megicks, S., & Henderson, R. (2017). Contagious accountability. A global multisite randomized controlled trial on the effect of police body-worn cameras on citizens' complaints against the police. *Criminal Justice and Behavior, 44*(2), 293-316.

Ashforth, B. E., & Gibbs, B. W. (1990). The double-edge of organizational legitimation. *Organization Science, 1*(2), 177-194.

Baker, B. (2007). Post-war policing by communities in Sierra Leone, Liberia, and Rwanda. *Democracy and Security, 3*(2), 215-236.

Baker, B. (2008). Community policing in Freetown, Sierra Leone: Foreign import or local solution? *Journal of Intervention and Statebuilding, 2*(1), 23-42.

Baker, B. (2009). Introduction: Policing post-conflict societies: Helping out the state. *Policing and Society, 19*(4), 329-332.

Balvig, F. (1990). Fear of crime in Scandinavia—new reality, new theory? In A. Snare (Ed.), *Scandinavian Studies in Criminology. Criminal violence in Scandinavia* (Vol. 11, pp. 89-127). Oslo: Norwegian University Press.

Balvig, F., & Holmberg, L. (2004). *Politi og tryghed. Førsog med nærpoliti i Danmark.* Copenhagen: Jurist- og Økonomforbundets Forlag.

Balvig, F., Holmberg, L., & Nielsen, M. P. H. (2011). *Verdens bedste politi: Politireformen i Danmark 2007-2011.* Copenhagen: Jurist- og Økonomforbundet.

Banton, M. (1964). *The policeman in the community.* London: Tavistock Publications.

Bauman, Z. (2000). *Liquid modernity.* Cambridge, U.K.: Polity Press.

Baumer, E. P., & Lauritsen, J. L. (2010). Reporting crime to the police, 1973-2005: A multivariate analysis of long-term trends in the national crime survey (NCS) and national crime victimization survey (NCVS). *Criminology, 48*(1), 131-184.

Bayerl, P. S., Karlovic, R., Akhgar, B., & Markarian, G. (2017). *Community policing—A European perspective. Strategies, best practices and guidelines.* New York: Springer.

Bayley, D. H. (1979). Police function, structure, and control in Western Europe and North America: Comparative and historical studies. In N. Morris & M. Tonry (Eds.), *Crime and justice: An annual review of research* (Vol. 1, pp. 109-143). Chicago: University of Chicago Press.

Bayley, D. H. (1985). *Patterns of policing. A comparative international analysis.* New Brunswick, NJ: Rutgers University Press.

Bayley, D. H. (2006). *Changing the guard: Developing democratic policing abroad.* New York: Oxford University Press.

Bayley, D. H., & Mendelsohn, H. (1969). *Minorities and the police.* New York: The Free Press.

Bayley, D. H., & Shearing, C. D. (1996). The future of policing. *Law and Society Review, 30*(3), 585-606.

Beck, A. (2005). Reflections on policing in post-Soviet Ukraine: A case study of continuity. *The Journal of Power Institutions in Post-Soviet Societies,* (2). http://pipss.revues.org/294

Beck, A., & Robertson, A. (2009). The challenges to developing democratic policing in post-Soviet societies: The Russian experience. *Police Practice and Research, 10*(4), 285-293.

Beetham, D. (1991a). Max Weber and the legitimacy of the modern state. *Analyse & Kritik, 13,* 34-45.

Beetham, D. (1991b). *The legitimation of power.* Atlantic Highlands, NJ: Humanites Press International.

Benyon, J. (1984). The riots, Lord Scarman and the political agenda. In J. Benyon (Ed.), *Scarman and after. Essays reflecting on Lord Scarman's Report, the riots and their aftermath.* Oxford: Pergamon Press.

Besel, R. (1991). Policing, professionalisation and politics in Weimar Germany. In C. Emsley & B. Weinberger (Eds.), *Policing western Europe* (pp. 187-218). Westport, CT: Greenwood Press.

Biderman, A. D., Johnson, L. A., McIntyre, J., & Weir, A. W. (1967). *Report on a pilot study in the District of Columbia on victimization and attitudes toward law enforcement.* Washington, DC: Government Printing Office.

Biemolt, J., Doeser, A., Glorioso, H. G., Hoogebeen, H. M., Oost, J., & Wansink, O. (2012). *Dienstverleningsconcept nationale politie.* Den Haag: Nationale Politie.

Billiet, J., Philippens, M., Fitzgerald, R., & Stoop, I. (2007). Estimation of nonresponse bias in the European Social Survey: Using information from reluctant respondents. *Journal of Official Statistics, 23*(2), 135-162.

Bittner, E. (1980). *The functions of the police in modern society. A review of background factors, current practices, and possible role models.* Cambridge, MA: Oelgeschlager, Gunn & Hain.

Bittner, E. / Brodeur, J. P. (2007). An encounter with Egon Bittner. *Crime, Law and Social Change, 48*(3-5), 105-132.

Björk, M. (2005). Between frustration and aggression: Legal framing and the policing of public disorder in Sweden and Denmark. *Policing and Society, 15*(3), 305-326.

Blaustein, J. (2015). *Speaking truths to power. Policy ethnography and police reform in Bosnia and Herzegovina.* Oxford: Oxford University Press.

Boateng, F. D. (2017). Police legitimacy in Africa: A multilevel multinational analysis. *Policing and Society*, advance access.

Body-Gendrot, S. (2013). Urban violence in France and England: Comparing Paris (2005) and London (2011). *Policing and Society, 23*(1), 6-25.

Body-Gendrot, S. (2016). Making sense of French urban disorders in 2005. *European Journal of Criminology, 13*(5), 556-572.

Boekhoorn, P., & Tolsma, J. (2016). *De aangifte van delicten bij de multichannelstrategie van de politie*. Amsterdam: Reed Business.

Bottomley, A. K., & Coleman, C. A. (1980). Police effectiveness and the public: The limitations of official crime rates. In R. V. G. Clarke & J. M. Hough (Eds.), *The effectiveness of policing* (pp. 70-97). Aldershot: Gower.

Bottoms, A. E., & Tankebe, J. (2012). Beyond procedural justice: A dialogic approach to legitimacy in criminal justice. *The Journal of Criminal Law and Criminology, 102*(1), 119-170.

Boutellier, H. (2004). *The safety utopia. Contemporary discontent and desire as to crime and punishment*. Dordrecht: Kluwer Academic.

Bradford, B. (2011a). Convergence, not divergence? Trends and trajectories in public contact and confidence in the police. *British Journal of Criminology, 51*(1), 179-200.

Bradford, B. (2011b). Voice, neutrality and respect: Use of Victim Support services, procedural fairness and confidence in the criminal justice system. *Criminology and Criminal Justice, 11*(4), 345-366.

Bradford, B., Huq, A., Jackson, J., & Roberts, B. (2014). What price fairness when security is at stake? Police legitimacy in South Africa. *Regulation & Governance, 8*(2), 246-268.

Bradford, B., & Jackson, J. (2010). Different things to different people? The meaning and measurement of trust and confidence in policing across diverse social groups in London. *Social Science Research Network Working Paper*. Retrieved September 26, 2017 from http://papers.ssrn.com/sol3/papers.cfm?abstract_id=1628546

Bradford, B., Jackson, J., Hough, M., & Farrall, S. (2008). Trust and confidence in criminal justice: A review of the British research literature. Retrieved September 26, 2017 from http://papers.ssrn.com/sol3/papers.cfm?abstract_id=1303567

Bradford, B., Jackson, J., & Stanko, E. A. (2009). Contact and confidence: Revisiting the impact of public encounters with the police. *Policing and Society: An International Journal of Research and Policy, 19*(1), 20-46.

Braga, A. A. (2005). Hot spots policing and crime prevention: A systematic review of randomized controlled trials. *Journal of Experimental Criminology, 1*(3), 317-342.

Braithwaite, J. (1992). Good and bad police services and how to pick them. In P. Moir & H. Eijkman (Eds.), *Policing Australia: Old issues, new perspectives*. Sydney: Macmillan.

Brandl, S. G., Frank, J., Worden, R. E., & Bynum, T. S. (1994). Global and specific attitudes toward the police: Disentangling the relationship. *Justice Quarterly, 11*(1), 119-134.

Braun, M. (2003). Errors in comparative survey research: An overview. In J. A. Harkness, P. P. Mohler, & F. J. R. v. d. Vijver (Eds.), *Cross-cultural survey methods*. Hoboken, NJ: Wiley.

Brodeur, J. P. (1983). High policing and low policing: Remarks about the policing of political activities. *Social Problems, 30*(5), 507-520.

Brodeur, J. P. (2005). Trotsky in blue: Permanent policing reform. *Australian & New Zealand Journal of Criminology, 38*(2), 254-267.

Brodeur, J. P. (2007). High and low policing in post-9/11 times. *Policing. A Journal of Policy and Practice, 1*(1), 25-37.

Brodeur, J. P. (2010). *The policing web*. Oxford: Oxford University Press.

Broekhuizen, J., Van Stokkom, B., Schaap, D., & Maier, D. (2015). *Serieus nemen. Over het vertrouwen van burgers in de Amsterdamse politie*. Amsterdam: Vrije Universiteit.

Broer, W., Schreuder, C. C., & Van der Vijver, C. D. (1987). *Eindbalans organisatieverandering politie Haarlem. Resultaten na drie jaar werken met wijkteams*. Den Haag: Ministerie van Binnenlandse Zaken.

Broer, W., & Van der Vijver, C. D. (1987). Moet de kogel door de kerk? In P. Van Reenen (Ed.), *Het politiebestel* (pp. 331-358). Arnhem: Gouda Quint.

Brogden, M. (1982). *The police: Autonomy and consent*. London: Academic Press.

Brogden, M. (2005). 'Horses for courses' and 'thin blue lines': Community policing in transitional society. *Police Quarterly, 8*(1), 64-98.

Bruinsma, G. (1999). Politie en integrale veiligheid. In C. J. C. F. Fijnaut, E. R. Muller, & U. Rosenthal (Eds.), *Politie. Studies over haar werking en organisatie* (1st ed., pp. 535-548). Alphen aan den Rijn: Samsom.

Button, M. (2007). Assessing the regulation of private security across Europe. *European Journal of Criminology, 4*(1), 109-128.

Cachet, A. (2002). Naar een veiliger samenleving: Het veiligheidsprogramma 2002: Over ambities van een demissionair kabinet, de uitvoerbaarheid van voornemens en het niet leren van ervaring. *Het Tijdschrift voor de Politie, 64*(12), 22-27.

Cachet, A., Muller, E. R., Van der Torre, E. J., Verberk, M. P., Van Sluis, A., & Wolberink, M. M. E. (1994). *Politiebestel in verandering. Verhoudingen tussen politie, bestuur, justitie en gemeenteraad onder de oude en de nieuwe Politiewet.* Arnhem: Gouda Quint.

Cachet, L., & Sey, A. (2009). Nationaal verankerd, lokaal versterkt? Nederland: De ontwikkelingen sinds eind jaren tachtig. In L. Cachet, A. v. Sluis, T. Jochoms, A. Sey, & A. Ringeling (Eds.), *Het betwiste politiebestel. Een vergelijkend onderzoek naar de ontwikkeling van het politiebestel in Nederland, België, Denemarken, Duitsland, Engeland & Wales* (pp. 51-114). Apeldoorn: Politie en Wetenschap; Erasmus Universiteit Rotterdam.

Cain, M. E. (1973). *Society and the policeman's role.* London: Routledge & Kegan Paul.

Cain, M. E. (2000). Orientalism, occidentalism, and the sociology of crime. *British Journal of Criminology, 40*(2), 239-260.

Çankaya, S. (2011). *Buiten veiliger dan binnen: In- en uitsluiting van etnische minderheden binnen de politieorganisatie.* Delft: Eburon.

Çankaya, S. (2015). De politiële surveillance van ras en etniciteit. In L. Gunther Moor, J. Janssen, M. Easton, & A. Verhage (Eds.), *Ethnic profiling en interne diversiteit bij de politie* (pp. 13-33). Antwerpen: Maklu.

Cao, L. (2015). Differentiating confidence in the police, trust in the police, and satisfaction with the police. *Policing: An International Journal of Police Strategies & Management, 38*(2), 239-249.

Cao, L., & Burton, V. S. (2006). Spanning the continents: Assessing the Turkish public confidence in the police. *Policing: An International Journal of Police Strategies & Management, 29*(3), 451-463.

Cao, L., Frank, J., & Cullen, F. T. (1996). Race, community context and confidence in the police. *American Journal of Police, 15*(1), 3-22.

Cao, L., Lai, Y. L., & Zhao, R. (2012). Shades of blue: Confidence in the police in the world. *Journal of Criminal Justice, 40*(1), 40-49.

Cao, L., & Zhao, S. J. (2005). Confidence in the police in Latin America. *Journal of Criminal Justice, 33*(5), 403-412.

Caparini, M., & Marenin, O. (2005). Crime, insecurity and police reform in post-socialist CEE. *The Journal of Power Institutions in Post-Soviet Societies*, (2). Retrieved September 26, 2017 from http://pipss.revues.org/index330.html

Carrier, J. G. (1992). Occidentalism: The world turned upside-down. *American Ethnologist, 19*(2), 195-212.

Cassan, D. (2010). Police socialisation in France and in England: How do they stand towards the community policing model? *Cahier Politiestudies, 16*(3), 243-260.

Catterberg, G., & Moreno, A. (2006). The individual bases of political trust: Trends in new and established democracies *International Journal of Public Opinion Research, 18*(1), 31-48.

Centraal Bureau voor de Statistiek (2006). *Veiligheidsmonitor Rijk 2006. Landelijke rapportage.* Voorburg: Centraal Bureau voor de Statistiek.

Centraal Bureau voor de Statistiek (2013). *Veiligheidsmonitor 2012.* Voorburg: Centraal Bureau voor de Statistiek.

Chambliss, W., & Seidman, R. (1971). *Law, order, and power.* Reading, MA: Addison-Wesley.

Chan, D. (1998). The conceptualization and analysis of change over time: An integrative approach incorporating longitudinal mean and covariance structures analysis (LMACS) and multiple indicator latent growth modeling (MLGM). *Organizational Research Methods, 1*(4), 421-483.

Chanley, V. A., Rudolph, T. J., & Rahn, W. M. (2000). The origins and consequences of public trust in government. A time series analysis. *Public Opinion Quarterly, 64*(3), 239-256.

Charles, J. B., Hofland, H. J. A., & Vrijman, J. (1964). *Slaags met de politie. Een documentaire.* Amsterdam: De Bezige Bij.

Christensen, M. J. (2017). The import/export of police models: Danish 19th century police reform between elites of revolution and reaction. *Journal of Historical Sociology, 30*(4), 845-867.

Cihan, A., Zhang, Y., & Hoover, L. T. (2012). Police response time to in-progress burglary. A multilevel analysis. *Police Quarterly, 15*(3), 308-327.

Clausen, B., Kraay, A., & Nyiri, Z. (2011). Corruption and confidence in public institutions: Evidence from a global survey.*The World Bank Economic Review, 25*(2), 212-249.

Clifton, J. (January 6, 2016). Explaining Trump: Widespread government corruption. Retrieved September 26, 2017 from http://www.gallup.com/opinion/chairman/188000/explaining-%C2%AD%E2%80%90trump-%C2%AD%E2%80%90widespread-%C2%AD%E2%80%90government-%C2%AD%E2%80%90corruption.aspx?g_source=Opinion&g_medium=lead&g_campaign=tiles

CoESS (Confederation of European Security Services) (2011). *Private security services in Europe. CoESS facts & figures.* Wemmel: Confederation of European Security Services.

Crawford, A. (2009). Situating crime prevention policies in comparative perspective: Policy travels, transfer and translation. In A. Crawford (Ed.), *Crime prevention policies in comparative perspective* (pp. 1-37). Cullompton: Willan.

Crow, M. S., O'Connor Shelley, T., Bedard, L. E., & Gertz, M. (2004). Czech police officers: An exploratory study of police attitudes in an emerging democracy. *Policing: An International Journal of Police Strategies & Management, 27*(4), 592-614.

Daalder, H. (1990). *Politiek en historie. Opstellen over Nederlandse politiek en vergelijkende politieke wetenschap.* Amsterdam: Bert Bakker.

Dalton, R. J. (2005). The social transformation of trust in government. *International Review of Sociology, 15*(1), 133-154.

Dammert, L., & Malone, M. F. T. (2006). Does it take a village? Policing strategies and fear of crime in Latin America. *Latin American Politics and Society, 48*(4), 27-51.

Das, D. K., & Robinson, A. L. (2001). The police in Norway: A profile. *Policing. An International Journal of Police Strategies and Management, 24*(3), 330-346.

Davidov, E., Meuleman, B., Cieciuch, J., Schmidt, P., & Billiet, J. (2014). Measurement equivalence in cross-national research. *Annual Review of Sociology, 40*, 55-75.

Davies, M., & Johnson, J. (2016). Navigating the one-on-one model of accountability: Lessons for police and crime commissioners and chief constables through the lens of principal-agent theory. *Policing. A Journal of Policy and Practice, 10*(3), 278-287.,

Davis, R. C., Ortiz, C. W., Gilinskiy, Y., Ylesseva, I., & Briller, V. (2004). A cross-national comparison of citizen perceptions of the police in New York City and St Petersburg, Russia. *Policing: An International Journal of Police Strategies & Management, 27*(1), 22-36.

De Beuckelaer, A., Lievens, F., & Swinnen, G. (2007). Measurement equivalence in the conduct of a global organizational survey across countries in six cultural regions. *Journal of Occupational and Organizational Psychology, 80*(4), 575-600.

De Guzman, M. C., & Kim, M. S. (2017). Community hierarchy of needs and policing models: Toward a new theory of police organizational behavior. *Police Practice and Research, 18*(4), 352-365.

De Kleuver, E. E. (2007). Prestatieafspraken met de politie: Van kritiek naar waardering. In C. J. C. F. Fijnaut, E. R. Muller, U. Rosenthal, & E. J. v. d. Torre (Eds.), *Politie* (2nd ed., pp. 213-234). Deventer: Kluwer.

De Koning, B. (2010). *Operatie Blauw—weg met de bureaucratie bij de Nederlandse politie.* Amsterdam: Balans.

De Maillard, J., Hunold, D., Roché, S., & Oberwittler, D. (2016). Different styles of policing: Discretionary power in street controls by the public police in France and Germany. *Policing and Society,* advance access.

De Maillard, J., & Roché, S. (2016). Studying policing comparatively: Obstacles, preliminary results and promises. *Policing and Society,* advance access.

Devroe, E., & Ponsaers, P. (2013). Reforming the Belgian police system between central and local. In N. R. Fyfe, J. Terpstra, & P. Tops (Eds.), *Centralizing forces? Comparative perspectives on contemporary police reform in Northern and Western Europe* (pp. 77-98). The Hague: Eleven.

Diamond, L. (2015). Facing up to the democratic recession. *Journal of Democracy, 26*(1), 141-155.

Dimovné, É. K. (2004). Hungarian police reform. In M. Caparini & O. Marenin (Eds.), *Transforming police in Central and Eastern Europe: Process and progress*. Geneva: Geneva Centre for the Democratic Control of Armed Forces.

Dixon, B. (2000). Zero tolerance: The hard edge of community policing. *African Security Review, 9*(3), 73-78.

Dodd, V. (2015). Theresa May to launch independent review of deaths in police custody, *The Guardian*, July 23. Retrieved September 26 2017 from http://www.theguardian.com/uk-news/2015/jul/23/theresa-may-independent-review-deaths-police-custody-speech

Donnelly, D. (2013). *Municipal policing in the European Union. Comparative perspectives*. Basingstoke: Palgrave Macmillan.

Donnelly, D., & Scott, K. B. (2002a). Police accountability in Scotland: (1) The new tripartite system. *The Police Journal, 75*(1), 3-14.

Donnelly, D., & Scott, K. B. (2002b). Police accountability in Scotland: (2) New accountabilities. *The Police Journal, 75*(1), 56-66.

Douglas, J. D. (1967). *The social meanings of suicide*. Princeton, NJ: Princeton University Press.

Dunn, K. M., Atie, R., Kennedy, M., Ali, J. A., O'Reilly, J., & Rogerson, L. (2016). Can you use community policing for counter terrorism? Evidence from NSW, Australia. *Police Practice and Research, 17*(3), 196-211.

Dupont, B. (2007). The French police system. Caught between a rock and a hard place—the tension of serving both the state and the public. In M. R. Haberfeld & I. Cerrah (Eds.), *Comparative policing. The struggle for democratization* (pp. 247-276). Thousand Oaks, CA: SAGE Publications.

Durão, S. (2011a). The police community on the move: Hierarchy and management in the daily-lives of Portuguese police officers. *Social Antropology/Antropologie Sociale, 19*(4), 394-408.

Durão, S. (2011b). The social production of street patrol knowledge: Studing local policing in Lisbon (Portugal). In M. Cools, S. De Kimpe, A. Dormaels, M. Easton, F. Enhus, P. Ponsaers, G. Vande Walle, & A. Verhage (Eds.), *Police, policing, policy and the city in Europe* (pp. 79-111). The Hague: Eleven.

Dzhekova, R., Gounev, P., & Bezlov, T. (2013). *Countering police corruption: European perspectives*. Sofia: Center for the Study of Democracy.

Easton, M., & Ponsaers, P. (2010). The view of the police on community policing in Belgian multicultural neighbourhoods. *New Empirical Data, Theories and Analyses on Safety, Societal Problems and Citizens' Perceptions, Governance of Security Research Papers Series, 3*, 161-182.

Easton, M., Ponsaers, P., Demarée, C., Vandevoorde, N., Enhus, E., Elffers, H., Hutsebaut, F., & Gunther Moor, L. (2009). *Multiple community policing: Hoezo?* Gent: Academia Press.

Eck, J. E., & Spelman, W. (1987). *Problem-solving. Problem-oriented policing in Newport News*. Washington, DC: National Institute of Justice.

Economist Intelligence Unit (2010). Democracy index 2010. Democracy in retreat. Retrieved September 26, 2017 from http://graphics.eiu.com/PDF/Democracy_Index_2010_web.pdf

Economist Intelligence Unit (2017). *The economist intelligence unit's democracy index*. Retrieved September 26, 2016 from https://infographics.economist.com/2017/DemocracyIndex/

Eikenaar, T. (2017). *Municipal disorder policing. Dealing with annoyances in public places*. Den Haag: Eleven.

Eisenhardt, K. M. (1989). Building theories from case study research. *Academy of Management Review, 14*(4), 532-550.

Eisenhardt, K. M., & Graebner, M. E. (2007). Theory building from cases: Opportunities and challenges. *Academy of Management Journal, 50*(1), 25-32.

Ellison, G., & Pino, N. W. (2012). *Globalization, police reform and development. Doing it the Western way?* Basingstoke: Palgrave Macmillan.

Ellison, G., Pino, N. W., & Shirlow, P. (2013). Assessing the determinants of public confidence in the police: A case study of a post-conflict community in Northern Ireland. *Criminology and Criminal Justice, 13*(5), 552-576.

Ellison, G., & Smyth, J. (2000). *The crowned harp: Policing Northern Ireland*. London: Pluto Press.

Emsley, C. (1992). The English bobby: An indulgent tradition. In R. Porter (Ed.), *Myths of the English* (pp. 114-135). Cambridge, U.K.: Polity Press.

Emsley, C. (2003). The birth and development of the police. In T. Newburn (Ed.), *Handbook of Policing*. Cullompton: Willan.

Esping-Andersen, G. (1990). *The three worlds of welfare capitalism.* Princeton, NJ: Princeton University Press.

ESS (European Social Survey) (2011). ESS-5 2010 documentation report (1.0 ed.). Bergen: European Social Survey Data Archive.

Eterno, J. A., & Silverman, E. B. (2012). *The crime numbers game. Management by manipulation.* Boca Raton, FL: CRC Press.

EVS (European Values Study) (2011). *European Values Study 1981-2008, longitudinal data file. ZA4804 Data File Version 2.0.0.* Cologne: GESIS Data Archive.

Fan, X., & Sivo, S. A. (2007). Sensitivity of fit indices to model misspecification and model types. *Multivariate Behavioral Research, 42*(3), 509-529.

Fassin, D. (2013). *Enforcing order: An ethnography of urban policing.* Cambridge, U.K.: Polity Press.

Faulkner, D. (2014). *Servant of the crown. A civil servant's story of criminal justice and public service reform.* Sherfield-on-Loddon: Waterside Press.

Feltes, T. (2002). Community-oriented policing in Germany: Training and education. *Policing. An International Journal of Police Strategies and Management, 25*(1), 48-59.

Feltes, T. (2014). Community policing in Germany. In Institute for Peace Research and Security Policy at the University of Hamburg (IFSH) (Ed.), *OSCE yearbook 2013* (pp. 219-230). Baden-Baden: Nomos.

Feltes, T., Marquardt, U., & Schwartz, S. (2013). Policing in Germany: Developments in the last 20 years. In G. Meško, C. B. Fields, B. Lobnikar, & A. Sotlar (Eds.), *Handbook on Policing in Central and Eastern Europe* (pp. 93-113). New York, NY: Springer.

Fielding, N. G. (2005). *The police and social conflict* (2nd ed.). London: Glass House Press.

Fielding, N. G., & Innes, M. (2006). Reassurance policing, community policing and measuring police performance. *Policing and Society, 16*(2), 127-145.

Fijnaut, C. J. C. F. (2007). *De geschiedenis van de Nederlandse politie. Een staatsinstelling in de maalstroom van de geschiedenis.* Amsterdam: Boom.

Fijnaut, C. J. C. F., Meershoek, G., Smeets, J., & Van der Wal, R. (2004). The impact of the occupation on the Dutch police. In C. J. C. F. Fijnaut (Ed.), *The impact of World War II on policing in North-West Europe* (pp. 91-132). Leuven: Leuven University Press.

FitzGerald, M. (2010). A confidence trick? *Policing. A Journal of Policy and Practice, 4*(3), 298-301.

Fleming, J., & McLaughlin, E. (2010). 'The public gets what the public wants?' Interrogating the 'public confidence' agenda. *Policing. A Journal of Policy and Practice, 4*(3), 199-202.

Fleming, J., & McLaughlin, E. (2012). Researching the confidence gap: Theory, method, policy. *Policing and Society, 22*(3), 261-269.

Foa, R. S., & Mounk, Y. (2016). The democratic disconnect. *Journal of Democracy, 27*(3), 5-17.

Foltin, P., Rohál, A., & Šikolová, M. (2013). Policing in the Czech Republic: Evolution and trends. In G. Meško, C. B. Fields, B. Lobnikar, & A. Sotlar (Eds.), *Handbook on policing in Central and Eastern Europe* (pp. 57-80). New York: Springer.

Foster, J. (2003). Police cultures. In T. Newburn (Ed.), *Handbook of policing* (pp. 196-227). Cullompton: Willan.

Frank, J., Smith, B. W., & Novak, K. J. (2005). Exploring the basis of citizens' attitudes toward the police. *Police Quarterly, 8*(2), 206-228.

Freitag, M., & Bauer, P. C. (2013). Testing for measurement equivalence in surveys: Dimensions of social trust across cultural contexts. *Public Opinion Quarterly, 77*(1), 24-44.

Frevel, B., & Kuschewski, P. (2013). The police system of Germany: Police organisation, management and reform in North Rhine-Westphalia. In A. Van Sluis, A. Cachet, T. Jochoms, A. Ringeling, & A. Sey (Eds.), *Contested police systems. Changes in the police systems in Belgium, Denmark, England & Wales, Germany, and the Netherlands* (pp. 119-148). The Hague: Eleven.

Frühling, H. (2007). The impact of international models of policing in Latin America: The case of community policing. *Police Practice and Research, 8*(2), 125-144.

Fyfe, N. R. (2014). Observations on police reform in Scotland. *British Society of Criminology Newsletter, 74,* 8-12.

Fyfe, N. R., & Scott, K. B. (2013). In search of sustainable policing? Creating a national police force in Scotland. In N. R. Fyfe, J. Terpstra, & P. Tops (Eds.), *Centralizing forces? Comparative perspectives on contemporary police reform in Northern and Western Europe* (pp. 119-136). The Hague: Eleven.

Fyfe, N. R., Terpstra, J., & Tops, P. (2013). *Centralizing forces? Comparative perspectives on contemporary police reform in Northern and Western Europe*. The Hague: Eleven.

Gambetta, D. (1988). Can we trust trust? In D. Gambetta (Ed.), *Trust. Making and breaking cooperative relations* (pp. 213-238). Oxford: Basil Blackwell.

Garland, D. (2001). *The culture of control. Crime and social order in contemporary society*. Oxford: Oxford University Press.

Garofalo, J. (1977). *The police and public opinion: An analysis of victimization and attitude data from 13 American cities*. Washington, DC: U.S. Government Printing Office.

Geddes, B. (1990). How the cases you choose affect the answers you get: Selection bias in comparative politics. *Political Analysis, 2*(1), 131-150.

Gerber, T. P., & Mendelson, S. E. (2008). Public experiences of police violence and corruption in contemporary Russia: A case of predatory policing? *Law and Society Review, 42*(1), 1-44.

Gibson, J. L. (2007). The legitimacy of the U.S. Supreme Court in a polarized polity. *Journal of Empirical Legal Studies, 4*(3), 507-538.

Giddens, A. (1990). *The consequences of modernity*. Stanford, CA: Stanford University Press.

Giddens, A. (1991). *Modernity and self-identity. Self and society in the late modern age*. Stanford, CA: Stanford University Press.

Gilinskiy, Y. (2006). Crime in contemporary Russia. *European Journal of Criminology, 3*(3), 259-292.

Gill, C., Weisburd, D. L., Telep, C. W., Vitter, Z., & Bennett, T. (2014). Community-oriented policing to reduce crime, disorder and fear and increase satisfaction and legitimacy among citizens: A systematic review. *Journal of Experimental Criminology, 10*(4), 399-428.

Gilmour, S. (2008). Why we trussed the police: Police governance and the problem of trust. *International Journal of Police Science and Management, 10*(1), 51-64.

Goldsmith, A. J. (2002). Policing weak states: Citizen safety and state responsibility. *Policing and Society, 13*(1), 3-21.

Goldsmith, A. J. (2005). Police reform and the problem of trust. *Theoretical Criminology, 9*(4), 443-470.

Goldsmith, A. J., & Harris, V. (2012). Trust, trustworthiness and trust-building in international policing missions. *Australian & New Zealand Journal of Criminology, 45*(2), 231-254.

Goldstein, H. (1977). *Policing a free society*. Cambridge, MA: Ballinger.

Goldstein, H. (1979). Improving policing: A problem-oriented approach. *Crime and Delinquency, 25*(2), 238-258.

Goldstein, H. (1987). Toward community-oriented policing: Potential, basic requirements, and threshold questions. *Crime and Delinquency, 33*(6), 6-30.

Gooren, W. A. J. (1992). *De organisatie van de reorganisatie. Verslag van een onderzoek naar het project reorganisatie politie*. Tilburg: IVA.

Gooren, W. A. J., & De Zwaan, B. C. (1995). *De reorganisatie; wat een organisatie*. Tilburg: IVA.

Goudriaan, H., Wittebrood, K., & Nieuwbeerta, P. (2006). Neighbourhood characteristics and reporting crime: Effects of social cohesion, confidence in police effectiveness and socio-economic disadvantage. *British Journal of Criminology, 46*(4), 719-742.

Gourley, G. D. (1950). Police discipline. *Journal of Criminal Law and Criminology, 41*(1), 85-100.

Gourley, G. D. (1954). Police public relations. *Annals of the American Academy of Political and Social Sciences, 291*, 135-142.

Green, P. (1990). *The enemy without. Policing and class consciousness in the miners' strike*. Buckingham: Open University Press.

Greenberg, J. (1986). Determinants of perceived fairness of performance evaluations. *Journal of Applied Psychology, 71*(2), 340-342.

Greenberg, J. (1990). Organizational justice: Yesterday, today, and tomorrow. *Journal of Management, 16*(2), 399-432.

Greer, C., & McLaughlin, E. (2017). Theorizing institutional scandal and the regulatory state. *Theoretical Criminology, 21*(2), 112-132.

Grinc, R. M. (1994). 'Angels in marble': Problems in stimulating community involvement in community policing. *Crime and Delinquency, 40*(3), 437-468.

Gruszczynska, B. (2004). Crime in Central and Eastern European countries in the enlarged Europe. *European Journal on Criminal Policy and Research, 10*(2), 123-136.

Gunther Moor, L., Bakker, I., & Brummelkamp, G. (1998). *Evaluatie politiewet 1993. Een breedte-onder-zoek.* 's-Gravenhage: VUGA.

Haberfeld, M. R., & Cerrah, I. (2007). *Comparative policing. The struggle for democratization.* Thousand Oaks, CA: SAGE Publications.

Haberfeld, M. R., Walancik, P., & Uydess, A. M. (2002). Teamwork—not making the dream work. Community policing in Poland. *Policing. An International Journal of Police Strategies and Management, 25*(1), 147-168.

Hakhverdian, A., & Mayne, Q. (2012). Institutional trust, education, and corruption: A micro-macro interactive approach. *The Journal of Politics, 74*(3), 739-750.

Haraholma, K., & Houtsonen, J. (2013). Restructuring the Finnish police administration. In N. R. Fyfe, J. Terpstra, & P. Tops (Eds.), *Centralizing forces? Comparative perspectives on contemporary police reform in Northern and Western Europe* (pp. 59-76). The Hague: Eleven.

Harkness, J. A. (2003). Questionnaire translation. In J. A. Harkness, F. J. R. V. d. Vijver, & P. P. Mohler (Eds.), *Cross-cultural survey methods* (pp. 35-56). Hoboken, NJ: Wiley.

Hawdon, J. (2008). Legitimacy, trust, social capital, and policing styles: A theoretical statement. *Police Quarterly, 11*(2), 182-201.

Heijink, K., Andersson, H., Berkhout, J. T. A. M., Nordholt, E. E., Peters, P. C., Straver, M. A., & Wiarda, J. (1977). Politie in verandering. Een voorlopig theoretisch model: Projectgroep Organisatiestructuren.

Herbert, S. (2006). *Citizens, cops, and power. Recognizing the limits of community.* Chicago: University of Chicago Press.

Heslop, R. (2011). The British police service: Professionalisation or 'McDonaldization'? *International Journal of Police Science and Management, 13*(4), 312-321.

Hetherington, M. J. (1998). The political relevance of political trust. *American Political Science Review, 92*(4), 791-808.

Hilborn, J., & Leps, A. (2005). Crime prevention policy in Estonia, 1991-2005. In E. Marks, A. Meyer, & R. Linssen (Eds.), *Quality in crime prevention* (pp. 156-178). Norderstedt: Books on Demand.

Hinds, L., & Murphy, K. (2007). Public satisfaction with police: Using procedural justice to improve police legitimacy. *The Australian and New Zealand Journal of Criminology, 40*(1), 27-42.

HMIC (2013). Stop and search powers: Are the police using them effectively and fairly? London: HMIC. Retrieved September 26, 2017 from https://www.justiceinspectorates.gov.uk/hmicfrs/publications/stop-and-search-powers-20130709/

HMIC (2014). Crime-recording: Making the victim count. The final report of an inspection of crime data integrity in police forces in England and Wales. London: HMIC. Retrieved September 26, 2017 from https://www.justiceinspectorates.gov.uk/hmicfrs/publications/crime-recording-making-the-victim-count/

Hodgson, J. (2014). De rol van de advocaat tijdens detentie en verhoor op het politiebureau. *Justitiële Verkenningen, 40*(1), 37-49.

Hohl, K., Bradford, B., & Stanko, E. A. (2010). Influencing trust and confidence in the London Metropolitan Police. Results from an experiment testing the effect of leaflet drops on public opinion. *British Journal of Criminology, 50*(3), 491-513.

Holmberg, L. (2000). Discretionary leniency and typological guilt: Results from a Danish study of police discretion. *Journal of Scandinavian Studies in Criminology and Crime Prevention, 1*(2), 179-194.

Holmberg, L. (2002). Personalized policing. Results from a series of experiments with proximity policing in Denmark. *Policing: An International Journal of Police Strategies & Management, 25*(1), 32-47.

Holmberg, L. (2005). Policing and the feeling of safety: The rise (and fall?) of community policing in the Nordic countries. *Journal of Scandinavian Studies in Criminology and Crime Prevention, 5*(2), 205-219.

Holmberg, L. (2014). Scandinavian police reforms: Can you have your cake and eat it, too? *Police Practice and Research, 15*(6), 447-460.

Holmberg, L. (2015). Challenges to Nordic police research. In R. Granér & E. Hellgren (Eds.), *The past, the present and the future of police research. Proceedings from the fifth Nordic police research seminar* (pp. 44-59). Växjö: Linnaeus University.

Holmberg, L., & Balvig, F. (2013). Centralization in disguise—The Danish police reform 2007-2010. In N. R. Fyfe, J. Terpstra, & P. Tops (Eds.), *Centralizing forces? Comparative perspectives on contemporary police reform in Northern and Western Europe* (pp. 41-55). The Hague: Eleven.

Home Office (1962). *Royal Commission on the Police: Final report.* Cmd. 1728. London: HMSO.

Home Office (1993). *Police reform: A police service for the twenty-first century.* Cm. 2281. London: Home Office.

Home Office (2001). *Policing a new century—a blueprint for reform.* Cm. 5326. London: Home Office.

Home Office (2004). *Building communities, beating crime.* Cm. 6360. London: Home Office.

Home Office (2010). *Policing in the 21st century: Reconnecting police and the people.* Cm. 7925. London: Home Office.

Home Office (2015). Police powers and procedures England and Wales year ending 31 March 2015 (Home Office Statistical Bulletin 07/15). London: Home Office.

Home Office. (2016). Police workforce, England and Wales, 31 March 2016 (Home Office Statistical Bulletin 05/16). Retrieved September 26, 2017 from https://www.gov.uk/government/statistics/police-workforce-england-and-wales-31-march-2016

Hood, C. (1991). A public management for all seasons? *Public Administration, 69*(1), 3-19.

Hooper, D., Coughlan, J., & Mullen, M. R. (2008). Structural equation modelling: Guidelines for determining model fit. *Electronic Journal of Business Research Methods, 6*(1), 53-60.

Hoover, L. T. (2005). From police administration to police science: The development of a police academic establishment in the United States. *Police Quarterly, 8*(1), 8-22.

Hoover, L. T. (2010). Rethinking our expectations. *Police Practice and Research, 11*(2), 160-165.

Hörnqvist, M. (2016). Riots in the welfare state: The contours of a modern-day moral economy. *European Journal of Criminology, 13*(5), 573-589.

Hough, J. M., Jackson, J., & Bradford, B. (2013). Legitimacy, trust and compliance: An empirical test of procedural justice theory using the European Social Survey. In J. Tankebe & A. Liebling (Eds.), *Legitimacy and criminal justice: An international exploration* (pp. 326-352). Oxford: Oxford University Press.

Hough, M. (2003). Modernization and public opinion: Some criminal justice paradoxes. *Contemporary Politics, 9*(2), 143-155.

Hough, M. (2007). Policing, New Public Management, and legitimacy in Britain. In T. R. Tyler (Ed.), *Legitimacy and criminal justice* (pp. 63-83). New York: Russell Sage Foundation.

Hough, M. (2012). Researching trust in the police and trust in justice: A UK perspective. *Policing and Society, 22*(3), 332-345.

Hough, M., Jackson, J., Myhill, A., & Quinton, P. (2010). Procedural justice, trust, and institutional legitimacy. *Policing. A Journal of Policy and Practice, 4*(3), 203-210.

House of Commons Home Affairs Committee (2009). *The MacPherson report—ten years on. Twelfth Report of Session 2008-09.* London: House of Commons.

Houston, D. J., Aitalieva, N. R., Morelock, A. L., & Shults, C. A. (2016). Citizen trust in civil servants: A cross-national examination. *International Journal of Public Administration, 39*(14), 1203-1214.

Hox, J. J., & Bechger, T. M. (1998). An introduction to structural equation modeling. *Family Science Review, 11*, 354-373.

Hu, L., & Bentler, P. M. (1998). Fit indices in covariance structure modeling: Sensitivity to underparameterized model misspecification. *Psychological Methods, 3*(4), 424-453.

Hu, L., & Bentler, P. M. (1999). Cutoff criteria for fit indexes in covariance structure analysis: Conventional criteria versus new alternatives. *Structural Equation Modeling, 6*(1), 1-55.

Huq, A. Z., Jackson, J., & Trinkner, R. (2017). Legitimating practices: Revisiting the predicates of police legitimacy *The British Journal of Criminology, 57*(5), 1101-1122.

In 't Veld, R. J., Beemer, F. A., De Haan, W., Mertens, L., Romein, E., & Van Roost, M. A. R. (2001). *Vooruitgang of regendans? Evaluatie beleids- en beheerscyclus politie*: Bestad i.s.m. Berenschot Procesmanagement.

Innes, J. (2011). Public perceptions. In R. Chaplin, J. Flatley, & K. Smith (Eds.), *Crime in England and Wales 2010/11. Findings from the British Crime Survey and police recorded crime* (2nd ed., pp. 83-100). London: Home Office.

Innes, M. (2004). Reinventing tradition? Reassurance, neighbourhood security and policing. *Criminology and Criminal Justice, 4*(2), 151-171.

Innes, M. (2005). Why 'soft' policing is hard: On the curious development of reassurance policing, how it became neighbourhood policing and what this signifies about the politics of police reform. *Journal of Community and Applied Social Psychology, 15*(3), 156-169.

Inspectie Openbare Orde en Veiligheid (2008). *Samenwerkingsafspraken politie 2008*. Den Haag: Ministerie van Binnenlandse Zaken en Koninkrijksrelaties.

Inspectie Openbare Orde en Veiligheid (2010). *Onderzoek samenwerkingsafspraken politie 2008. Stand van zaken 2010*. Den Haag: Ministerie van Binnenlandse Zaken en Koninkrijksrelaties.

Jackson, J., Asif, M., Bradford, B., & Zakar, M. Z. (2014). Corruption and police legitimacy in Lahore, Pakistan. *British Journal of Criminology*, 54(6), 1067-1088.

Jackson, J., & Bradford, B. (2009). Crime, policing and social order: On the expressive nature of public confidence in policing. *The British Journal of Sociology*, 60(3), 493-521.

Jackson, J., & Bradford, B. (2010). What is trust and confidence in the police? *Policing. A Journal of Policy and Practice*, 4(3), 241-248.

Jackson, J., Bradford, B., Hohl, K., & Farrall, S. (2009). Does the fear of crime erode public confidence in policing? *Policing. A Journal of Policy and Practice*, 3(1), 100-111.

Jackson, J., Bradford, B., Hough, J. M., Kuha, J., Stares, S., Widdop, S., Fitzgerald, R., Yordanova, M., & Galev, T. (2010). Trust in justice: Notes on the development of European social indicators. *SSRN research papers*. Retrieved September 26, 2017 from https://papers.ssrn.com/sol3/papers.cfm?abstract_id=1717924

Jackson, J., Bradford, B., Hough, J. M., Myhill, A., Quinton, P., & Tyler, T. R. (2012). Why do people comply with the law? Legitimacy and the influence of legal institutions. *British Journal of Criminology*, 52(6), 1051-1071.

Jackson, J., Bradford, B., Hough, M., Kuha, J., Stares, S., Widdop, S., Fitzgerald, R., Yordanova, M., & Galev, T. (2011). Developing European indicators of trust in justice. *European Journal of Criminology*, 8(4), 267-285.

Jackson, J., Bradford, B., Stanko, E. A., & Hohl, K. (2013). *Just authority? Trust in the police in England and Wales*. Abingdon: Routledge.

Jackson, J., & Sunshine, J. (2007). Public confidence in policing. A neo-Durkheimian perspective. *British Journal of Criminology*, 47(2), 214-233.

Jacob, H. (1971). Black and white perceptions of justice in the city. *Law and Society Review*, 6(1), 69-90.

Jang, H., Joo, H. J., & Zhao, S. J. (2010). Determinants of public confidence in the police: An international perspective. *Journal of Criminal Justice*, 38(1), 57-68.

Jang, H., Lee, J., & Gibbs, J. C. (2015). The influence of the national government on confidence in the police: A focus on corruption. *International Journal of Law, Crime and Justice*, 43(4), 553-568.

Jansson, K. (2008). *British crime survey: Measuring crime over 25 years*. London: Home Office.

Jenks, D. A., Costelloe, M. T., & Krebs, C. P. (2003). After the fall: Czech police in a post-communist era. *International Criminal Justice Review*, 13(1), 90-109.

Jespersen, K. J. V. (2011). *A history of Denmark* (I. Hill & C. Wade, trans., 2nd ed.). Basingstoke: Palgrave Macmillan.

Jochoms, M. P. C. M., Van der Laan, F., Landman, W., Nijmeijer, P. S., & Sey, A. (2006). *Op prestaties gericht. Over de gevolgen van prestatiesturing en prestatieconvenanten voor sturing en uitvoering van het politiewerk*. Den Haag: Elsevier Overheid.

Johansen, A. (2014). The rise and rise of independent police complaints bodies. In J. M. Brown (Ed.), *The future of policing*. Abingdon: Routledge.

Johnson, T. P., & Van de Vijver, F. J. R. (2003). Social desirability in cross-cultural research. In J. A. Harkness, P. P. Mohler, & F. J. R. v. d. Vijver (Eds.), *Cross-cultural survey methods* (pp. 195-204). Hoboken, NJ: Wiley.

Johnston, L. (1992). British policing in the ninetees: Free market and strong state? *International Criminal Justice Review*, 2(1), 1-18.

Johnston, L. (2005). From 'community' to 'neighbourhood' policing: Police community support officers and the 'police extended family' in London. *Journal of Community and Applied Social Psychology*, 15(3), 241-254.

Jonathan, T. (2010). Police involvement in counter-terrorism and public attitudes toward the police in Israel—1998-2007. *British Journal of Criminology*, 50(4), 748-771.

Jones, T., & Newburn, T. (2007). *Policy transfer and criminal justice. Exploring US influence over British crime control policy*. Maidenhead: Open University Press/McGraw-Hill.

Jones, T., Newburn, T., & Smith, D. J. (1996). Policing and the idea of democracy. *British Journal of Criminology*, 36(2), 182-198.

Jöreskog, K. G. (2005). Structural equation modeling with ordinal variables using LISREL. Retrieved September 26, 2017 from www.ssicentral.com/lisrel/techdocs/ordinal.pdf

Jöreskog, K. G., & Sörbom, D. (1996). *LISREL 8 user's guide*. Chicago, IL: Scientific Software.

Jowell, R. (1998). How comparative is comparative research? *The American Behavioral Scientist, 42*(2), 168-177.

Kääriäinen, J. T. (2007). Trust in the police in 16 European countries. A multilevel analysis. *European Journal of Criminology, 4*(4), 409-435.

Kääriäinen, J. T. (2008). Why do the Finns trust the police? *Journal of Scandinavian Studies in Criminology and Crime Prevention, 9*(2), 141-159.

Kääriäinen, J. T., & Sirén, R. (2012). Do the police trust in citizens? European comparisons. *European Journal of Criminology, 9*(3), 276-289.

Karakatsanis, L. (2016). Radicalised citizens vs. radicalised governments? Greece and Turkey in a comparative perspective from the December 2008 uprising to the 2013 Gezi Park protests. *Journal of Contemporary European Studies, 24*(2), 255-279.

Kautt, P. (2011). Public confidence in the British police. Negotiating the signals from Anglo-American research. *International Criminal Justice Review, 21*(4), 353-382.

Kautt, P., & Tankebe, J. (2011). Confidence in the criminal justice system in England and Wales: A test of ethnic effects. *International Criminal Justice Review, 21*(2), 93-117.

Keenan, M. (2009). Please mind the gap: Satisfaction with the police within London. *Policing. A Journal of Policy and Practice, 3*(4), 347-354.

Kelling, G. L., & Bratton, W. J. (1998). Declining crime rates: Insiders' views of the New York City story. *Journal of Criminal Law and Criminology, 88*(4), 1217-1232.

Kelling, G. L., & Moore, M. H. (1988). *The evolving strategy of policing*. Washington, DC: National Institute of Justice.

Kennedy, J. C. (1995). *Nieuw Babylon in aanbouw. Nederland in de jaren zestig*. Amsterdam: Boom.

Kenny, D. A., & McCoach, D. B. (2003). Effect of the number of variables on measures of fit in structural equation modeling. *Structural Equation Modeling, 10*(3), 333-351.

Kerezsi, K., & Lévay, M. (2008). Criminology, crime and criminal justice in Hungary. *European Journal of Criminology, 5*(2), 239-260.

Kingdon, J. W. (1995). *Agendas, alternatives, and public policies*. (2nd ed.). New York: HarperCollins.

Kirby, S. (2013). *Effective policing? Implementation in theory and practice*. Basingstoke: Palgrave Macmillan.

Kline, R. B. (2011). *Principles and practice of structural equation modeling* (3rd ed.). New York: The Guilford Press.

Klockars, C. B. (1988). The rhetoric of community policing. In J. R. Greene & S. D. Mastrofski (Eds.), *Community policing: Rhetoric or reality* (pp. 239-258). New York: Praeger.

Knibbeler, J. M. H. (1966). *De verhouding burgers-politieambtenaren in Nederland in een criminologisch perspectief*. Sittard: Alberts' Drukkerijen.

Koenig, D. J. (1980). The effects of criminal victimization and judicial or police contacts on public attitudes toward local police. *Journal of Criminal Justice, 8*(4), 243-249.

Koopman, J. (2013). Bestuur, justitie en nationale politie in Nederland. In E. Devroe, P. Ponsaers, M. Easton, A. Cachet, & A. J. Meershoek (Eds.), *Schaalveranderingen* (pp. 127-150). Antwerpen: Maklu.

Kort, J., & Terpstra, J. (2015). *'Onnodige' bureaucratie binnen het basispolitiewerk*. Amsterdam: Reed Business.

Koster, N. N. (2017). Victims' perceptions of the police response as a predictor of victim cooperation in the Netherlands: A prospective analysis. *Psychology, Crime & Law, 23*(3), 201-220.

Krajewski, K. (2004). Crime and criminal justice in Poland. *European Journal of Criminology, 1*(3), 377-407.

Krastev, I. (2005). Corruption, anti-corruption sentiments, and the rule of law. In A. Czarnota, M. Krygier, & W. Sadurski (Eds.), *Rethinking the rule of law after communism*. Budapest: Central European University Press.

Kreis, C. (2012). *Community policing in Switzerland's major urban areas. An observational study of the implementation and impact using geospatial data mining*. Lausanne: Université de Lausanne.

Kruize, P., & Jochoms, T. (2009). Naar voltooiing van de nationale politie: Het politiebestel in Denemarken. In A. Cachet, A. Van Sluis, T. Jochoms, A. Sey, & A. Ringeling (Eds.), *Het betwiste politiebestel. Een vergelijkend onderzoek naar de ontwikkeling van het politiebestel in Nederland, België, Denemarken, Duitsland, Engeland & Wales* (pp. 359-411). Amsterdam: Reed Business.

Kruize, P., & Jochoms, T. (2013). The police system in Denmark: Towards a completion of the national police. In A. v. Sluis, L. Cachet, T. Jochoms, A. Ringeling, & A. Sey (Eds.), *Contested police systems. Changes in the police systems in Belgium, Denmark, England & Wales, Germany, and the Netherlands.* The Hague: Eleven.

Kupatadze, A. (2012). Explaining Georgia's anti-corruption drive. *European Security, 21*(1), 16-36.

Kusow, A. M., Wilson, L. C., & Martin, D. E. (1997). Determinants of citizen satisfaction with the police: The effects of residential location. *Policing: An International Journal of Police Strategies & Management, 20*(4), 655-664.

Kutnjak Ivković, S. (2000). Challenges of policing democracies: The Croatian experience. In D. K. Das & O. Marenin (Eds.), *Challenges of Policing Democracies: A World Perspective.* Amsterdam: Gordon & Breach.

Kutnjak Ivković, S. (2005). *Fallen blue knights: Controlling police corruption.* Oxford: Oxford University Press.

Kutnjak Ivković, S. (2008). A comparative study of public support for the police. *International Criminal Justice Review, 18*(4), 406-434.

Kutnjak Ivković, S., & Haberfeld, M. R. (2000). Transformation from militia to police in Croatia and Poland—A comparative perspective. *Policing: An International Journal of Police Strategies & Management, 23*(2), 194-217.

Kyed, H. M. (2009). Community policing in post-war Mozambique. *Policing and Society, 19*(4), 353-371.

Lacey, M. (2014). The hat on the office door. In R. Statham (Ed.), *The golden age of probation. Mission v market.* Sherfield-on-Loddon: Waterside Press.

Lai, K., & Green, S. B. (2016). The problem with having two watches: Assessment of fit when RMSEA and CFI disagree. *Multivariate Behavioral Research, 51*(2-3), 220-239.

Lai, Y. L., Cao, L., & Zhao, J. S. (2010). The impact of political entity on confidence in legal authorities: A comparison between China and Taiwan. *Journal of Criminal Justice, 38*(5), 934-941.

Laitin, D. D. (1998). *Identity in formation. The Russian-speaking populations in the near abroad.* Ithaca, NY: Cornell University Press.

Lambert, E. G., Jiang, S., Khondaker, M. I., Elechi, O. O., Baker, D. N., & Tucker, K. A. (2010). Policing views from around the globe: An exploratory study of the views of college students from Bangladesh, Canada, Nigeria and the United States. *International Criminal Justice Review, 20*(3), 229-247.

Lambropoulou, E. (2004). Citizens' safety, business trust and Greek police. *International Review of Administrative Sciences, 70*(1), 89-110.

Lammers, H. (1964). Nawoord. In J. B. Charles, H. J. A. Hofland, & J. Vrijman (Eds.), *Slaags met de politie. Een documentaire* (pp. 135-143). Amsterdam: De Bezige Bij.

Lammers, J. (2004). *Oordelen over de politie. Een analyse van de invloed van contacten op het oordeel van burgers over het functioneren van de politie.* Enschede: IPIT.

Lappi-Seppälä, T., & Lehti, M. (2014). Cross-comparative perspectives on global homicide trends. *Crime and Justice, 43*(1), 135-230.

Larsson, P. (2010). Ideology as a cover up: Community policing in Norway. *Cahier Politiestudies, 16*(3), 233-241.

Lau, R. W. K. (2004). Community policing in Hong Kong: Transplanting a questionable model. *Criminal Justice, 4*(1), 61-80.

Lee, M. (2007). *Inventing fear of crime. Criminology and the politics of anxiety.* Cullompton: Willan.

Levisen, C. (2012). *Cultural semantics and social cognition. A case study on the Danish universe of meaning.* Berlin: De Gruyter Mouton.

Lewis, P., Newburn, T., Taylor, M., Mcgillivray, C., Greenhill, A., Frayman, H., & Proctor, R. (2011). *Reading the riots: Investigating England's summer of disorder.* London: The London School of Economics and Political Science and The Guardian.

Liedenbaum, C. M. B. (2011). *Politiewerk: Tussen taak en uitvoering. Een vergelijkend onderzoek naar de basispolitiezorg in Nederland en Noordrijn-Westfalen.* Nijmegen: Wolf Legal Publishers.

Liem, M., Ganpat, S., Granath, S., Hagstedt, J., Kivivuori, J., Lehti, M., & Nieuwbeerta, P. (2013). Homicide in Finland, the Netherlands, and Sweden: First findings from the European Homicide Monitor. *Homicide Studies, 17*(1), 75-95.

Light, M. (2014). Police reforms in the Republic of Georgia: The convergence of domestic and foreign policy in an anti-corruption drive. *Policing and Society, 24*(3), 318-345.

Lijphart, A. (1968a). *Verzuiling, pacificatie en kentering in de Nederlandse politiek.* Amsterdam: J. H. de Bussy.

Lijphart, A. (1968b). *The politics of accommodation. Pluralism and democracy in the Netherlands.* Berkeley, CA: University of California Press.

Lind, E. A. (1982). The psychology of courtroom procedure. In N. L. Kerr & R. M. Bray (Eds.), *The psychology of the courtroom.* New York: Academic Press.

Loader, I. (2006). Fall of the 'platonic guardians.' Liberalism, criminology and political responses to crime in England and Wales. *British Journal of Criminology, 46*(4), 561-586.

Loader, I., & Mulcahy, A. (2003). *Policing and the condition of England: Memory, politics and culture.* Oxford: Oxford University Press.

Loader, I., & Walker, N. (2007). *Civilizing security.* Cambridge, U.K.: Cambridge University Press.

Loftus, B. (2009). *Police culture in a changing world.* Oxford: Oxford University Press.

Loftus, B. (2010). Police occupational culture: Classic themes, altered times. *Policing and Society, 20*(1), 1-20.

Loveday, B. (1994). Ducking and diving—Formulating a policy for police and criminal justice in the 1990s. *Public Money & Management, 14*(3), 25-30.

Loveday, B. (1997). Challenge and change: Police authority and chief officer responsibilities under the Police and Magistrates' Courts Act 1994. *Local Government Studies, 23*(1), 76-87.

Loveday, B. (2000). Managing crime: Police use of crime data as an indicator of effectiveness. *International Journal of the Sociology of Law, 28*(3), 215-237.

Loveday, B. (2006). Policing performance: The impact of performance measures and targets on police forces in England and Wales. *International Journal of Police Science and Management, 8*(4), 282-293.

Loveday, B. (2013). Police reform in England and Wales: A new dimension in accountability and service delivery in the 21st century. In N. R. Fyfe, J. Terpstra, & P. Tops (Eds.), *Centralizing forces? Comparative perspectives on contemporary police reform in Northern and Western Europe* (pp. 99-118). The Hague: Eleven.

Loveday, B., & Reid, A. (2003). *Going local. Who should run Britain's police?* London: Policy Exchange.

Luhmann, N. (1979). *Trust and power.* Chichester: Wiley.

Luhmann, N. (1988). Familiarity, confidence, trust: Problems and alternatives. In D. Gambetta (Ed.), *Trust: Making and breaking cooperative relations* (pp. 94-107). Oxford: Basil Blackwell.

Lyman, J. L. (1964). The Metropolitan Police Act of 1829: An analysis of certain events influencing the passage and character of the Metropolitan Police Act in England. *The Journal of Criminal Law, Criminology, and Police Science, 55*(1), 141-154.

Mackenzie, S., & Henry, A. (2009). *Community policing: A review of the evidence.* Edinburgh: Scottish Government Social Research.

Macpherson, W. (1999). The Stephen Lawrence inquiry. Report of an inquiry by Sir William Macpherson of Cluny. London: HMSO.

MacQueen, S., & Bradford, B. (2015). Enhancing public trust and police legitimacy during road traffic encounters: Results from a randomised controlled trial in Scotland. *Journal of Experimental Criminology, 11*(3), 419-443.

Maguire, E. R., Johnson, D., Kuhns, J. B., & Apostolos, R. (2017). The effects of community policing on fear of crime and perceived safety: Findings from a pilot project in Trinidad and Tobago. *Policing and Society,* advance access.

Maguire, M. (2000). Policing by risks and targets: Some dimensions and implications of intelligence-led crime control. *Policing and Society, 9*(4), 315-336.

Makarov, Y. (2013). Police with the regime. *The Ukrainian Week, International Edition,* July 24.

Manning, P. K. (1977). *Police work: The social organization of policing.* Cambridge, MA: The MIT Press.

Manning, P. K. (1984). Community policing. *American Journal of Police, 3*(2), 205-228.

Manning, P. K. (2003). *Policing contingencies.* Chicago: University of Chicago Press.

Manning, P. K. (2005). The study of policing. *Police Quarterly, 8*(1), 23-43.

Manning, P. K. (2008). *The technology of policing. Crime mapping, information technology, and the rationality of crime control.* New York: New York University Press.

Manning, P. K. (2012). Trust and accountability in Ireland: The case of An Garda Síochána. *Policing and Society, 22*(3), 346-361.

Marat, E. (2010). Kyrgyzstan's fragmented police and armed forces. *The Journal of Power Institutions in Post-Soviet Societies*, (11). http://pipss.revues.org/3803#ftn1

Marín, I. (2011). *Community policing in Berlin. Background paper*. Londonderry: International Conflict Research Institute.

Marien, S. (2011). Measuring political trust across time and space. In M. Hooghe & S. Zmerli (Eds.), *Political trust. Why context matters* (pp. 13-46). Colchester: ECPR Press.

Marsh, H. W., Hau, K., & Wen, Z. (2004). In search of golden rules: Comment on hypothesis-testing approaches to setting cutoff values for fit indexes and dangers in overgeneralizing Hu and Bentler's (1999) findings. *Structural Equation Modeling, 11*(3), 320-341.

Mawby, R. C. (2002). *Policing images. Policing, communication and legitimacy*. Cullompton: Willan.

Mawby, R. I. (1992). Comparative police systems: Searching for a continental model. In K. Bottomley, T. Fowles, & R. Reiner (Eds.), *Criminal justice theory and practice* (pp. 108-132). London: British Society of Criminology.

Mawby, R. I. (2003). Models of policing. In T. Newburn (Ed.), *Handbook of policing* (pp. 15-40). Cullompton: Willan.

Mazerolle, L., Antrobus, E., Bennett, S., & Tyler, T. R. (2013a). Shaping citizen perceptions of police legitimacy: A randomized field trial of procedural justice. *Criminology, 51*(1), 33-63.

Mazerolle, L., Bennett, S., Davis, J., Sargeant, E., & Manning, M. (2013b). Procedural justice and police legitimacy: A systematic review of the research evidence. *Journal of Experimental Criminology, 9*(3), 245-274.

McCluskey, J. D. (2003). *Police requests for compliance: Coercive and procedurally just tactics*. New York: LFB Scholarly Publishing.

McLaughlin, E. (2007). *The new policing*. London: SAGE Publications.

Meershoek, A. J. (1999). *Dienaren van het gezag. De Amsterdamse politie tijdens de bezetting*. Amsterdam: Van Gennep.

Meershoek, A. J. (2000). Blauw blauw: Het tanend gezag van de politie. In L. G. Moor & K. v. d. Vijver (Eds.), *Het gezag van de politie* (pp. 81-102). Dordrecht: Stichting Maatschappij, Veiligheid en Politie.

Meershoek, A. J. (2007). *De geschiedenis van de Nederlandse politie. De gemeentepolitie in een veranderende samenleving*. Amsterdam: Boom.

Mendel, J., Fyfe, N. R., & Den Heyer, G. (2017). Does police size matter? A review of the evidence regarding restructuring police organisations. *Police Practice and Research, 18*(1), 3-14.

Meško, G., Fields, C. B., Lobnikar, B., & Sotlar, A. (2013). *Handbook on policing in Central and Eastern Europe*. New York: Springer.

Meško, G., & Klemencic, G. (2007). Rebuilding legitimacy and police professionalism in an emerging democracy: The Slovenian experience. In T. R. Tyler (Ed.), *Legitimacy and criminal justice. International perspectives* (pp. 84-114). New York: Russell Sage Foundation.

Meško, G., & Lobnikar, B. (2005). The contribution of local safety councils to local responsibility in crime prevention and provision of safety. *Policing. An International Journal of Police Strategies and Management, 28*(2), 353-373.

Meško, G., Lobnikar, B., Jere, M., & Sotlar, A. (2013). Recent developments of policing in Slovenia. In G. Meško, C. B. Fields, B. Lobnikar, & A. Sotlar (Eds.), *Handbook on policing in central and eastern Europe* (pp. 263-286). New York: Springer.

Meško, G., Nalla, M., & Sotlar, A. (2005). Cooperation of police and private security officers in crime prevention in Slovenia. In E. Marks, A. Meyer, & R. Linssen (Eds.), *Quality in crime prevention*. Norderstedt: Books on Demand.

Mikkelsen, K. S. (2013). In murky waters: A disentangling of corruption and related concepts. *Crime, Law and Social Change, 60*(4), 357-374.

Millie, A., & Herrington, V. (2004). Reassurance policing in practice: Views from the shop floor. Paper presented at the British Criminology Conference, Portsmouth.

Ministerie van Justitie en Ministerie van Binnenlandse Zaken (1998). *Beleidsplan Nederlandse politie 1999-2002*. 's-Gravenhage: Sdu Uitgevers.

Ministerie van Justitie en Ministerie van Binnenlandse Zaken (2002). *Naar een veiliger samenleving*. 's-Gravenhage: Sdu Uitgevers.

Ministerie van Justitie en Ministerie van Binnenlandse Zaken (2003). Landelijk Kader Nederlandse Politie 2003-2006.

Ministerie van Veiligheid en Justitie (2012a). *Realisatieplan nationale politie*. Den Haag: Ministerie van Veiligheid en Justitie.

Ministerie van Veiligheid en Justitie (2012b). *Inrichtingsplan nationale politie*. Den Haag: Ministerie van Veiligheid en Justitie.

Ministerie van Veiligheid en Justitie (2015). *De kracht van het verschil. Variëteit, gelijkwaardigheid en verbinding*. Den Haag: Ministerie van Veiligheid en Justitie.

Mintrom, M., & Norman, P. (2009). Policy entrepreneurship and policy change. *The Policy Studies Journal, 37*(4), 649-667.

Mishler, W., & Rose, R. (1997). Trust, distrust and skepticism: Popular evaluations of civil and political institutions in post-communist societies. *Journal of Politics, 59*(2), 418-451.

Mishler, W., & Rose, R. (2001). What are the origins of political trust? Testing institutional and cultural theories in post-communist societies. *Comparative Political Studies, 34*(1), 30-62.

Misztal, B. A. (1996). *Trust in modern societies*. Cambridge, U.K.: Polity Press.

Montgomery, K., Jordens, C. F. C., & Little, M. (2008). How vulnerability and trust interact during extreme events. Insights for human service agencies and organizations. *Administration and Society, 40*(6), 621-644.

Morris, C. S. (2015). An international study on public confidence in police. *Police Practice and Research, 16*(5), 416-430.

Mouhanna, C. (2013). Reforms in France: Irreversibly spiralling into (more) centralization. In N. R. Fyfe, J. Terpstra, & P. Tops (Eds.), *Centralizing forces? Comparative perspectives on contemporary police reform in Northern and Western Europe* (pp. 23-40). The Hague: Eleven.

Muir, W. K. (1977). *Police: Streetcorner politicians*. Chicago: University of Chicago Press.

Mulcahy, A. (2007). The governance of crime and security in Ireland (Discussion Paper). Dublin: UCD Geary Institute.

Mulcahy, A., & O'Mahony, E. (2005). Policing and social marginalisation in Ireland. Dublin: Combat Poverty Agency.

Muller, E. R., Zannoni, M., Ammerlaan, K., Schaap, S., Uildriks, N., Van der Varst, L., . . . , Adang, O. (2010). *Ordeverstoringen en groepsgeweld bij evenementen en grootschalige gebeurtenissen. Scherpte en alertheid*. Den Haag: Boom Juridische Uitgevers.

Myhill, A., & Bradford, B. (2012). Can police enhance public confidence by improving quality of service? Results from two surveys in England and Wales. *Policing and Society, 22*(4), 397-425.

Myhill, A., & Quinton, P. (2010). Confidence, neighbourhood policing, and contact: Drawing together the evidence. *Policing. A Journal of Policy and Practice, 4*(3), 273-281.

Nap, J., & Van Os, P. (2006). *Referentiekader gebiedsgebonden politiezorg*. Apeldoorn: Politieacademie.

Neapolitan, J. L. (1999). A comparative analysis of nations with low and high levels of violent crime. *Journal of Criminal Justice, 27*(3), 259-274.

Nelken, D. (1994). Whom can you trust? The future of comparative criminology. In D. Nelken (Ed.), *The futures of criminology*. London: SAGE Publications.

Nelken, D. (2009). Comparative criminal justice: Beyond ethnocentrism and relativism. *European Journal of Criminology, 6*(4), 291-311.

Nelken, D. (2010). *Comparative criminal justice. Making sense of difference*. London: SAGE Publications.

Nelken, D. (2012). Comparing criminal justice. In M. Maguire, R. Morgan, & R. Reiner (Eds.), *The Oxford Handbook of Criminology* (5th ed., pp. 138-158). Oxford: Oxford University Press.

Newburn, T., Diski, R., Cooper, K., Deacon, R., Burch, A., & Grant, M. (2016). 'The biggest gang'? Police and people in the 2011 England riots. *Policing and Society*, advance access.

Newton, K., & Norris, P. (2000). Confidence in public institutions: Faith, culture or performance? In S. Pharr & R. Putnam (Eds.), *Disaffected democracies: What's troubling the trilateral countries?* (pp. 52-73). Princeton, NJ: Princeton University Press.

Norris, P. (2011). *Democratic deficit. Critical citizens revisited*. Cambridge, U.K.: Cambridge University Press.

Oberwittler, D., & Roché, S. (2013). Experience, perceptions and attitudes. Variations of police-adolescents relationships in French and German cities. *Criminology in Europe, 12*(3), 4-13.

Oliver, W. M., & Bartgis, E. (1998). Community policing: A conceptual framework. *Policing: An International Journal of Police Strategies & Management, 21*(3), 490-509.

Olsen, F. Z. (2008). *The use of police firearms in Denmark*. Copenhagen: Rigspolitiet.

O'Neill, O. (2002). *A question of trust*. Cambridge, U.K.: Cambridge University Press.

Osborne, D., & Gaebler, T. (1992). *Reinventing government. How the entrepreneurial spirit is transforming the public sector*. Reading, MA: Addison-Wesley.

Pakes, F. (2010). *Comparative criminal justice* (2nd ed.). Cullompton: Willan.

Papanicolaou, G. (2006). Greece. In T. Jones & T. Newburn (Eds.), *Plural Policing: A Comparative Perspective* (pp. 77-97). London: Routledge.

Payne, B. K., & Gainey, R. R. (2007). Attitudes about the police and neighborhood safety in disadvantaged neighborhoods. The influence of criminal victimization and perceptions of a drug problem. *Criminal Justice Review, 32*(2), 142-155.

Peacock, R., & Cordner, G. (2016). 'Shock therapy' in Ukraine: A radical approach to post-Soviet police reform. *Public Administration and Development, 36*(2), 80-92.

Peterson, A. (2010). From Great Britain to Sweden—the import of reassurance policing. Local police offices in metropolitan Stockholm. *Journal of Scandinavian Studies in Criminology and Crime Prevention, 11*(1), 25-45.

Politikommissionen (2002). *Betaenkning om politiets struktur*. Copenhagen: Statens Information.

Pollitt, C., & Bouckaert, G. (2000). *Public management reform. A comparative perspective*. Oxford: Oxford University Press.

Ponsaers, P., & Easton, M. (2008). Community (oriented) policing reassured: Significance within a Flemish context. In M. Easton, L. Gunther Moor, B. Hoogenboom, P. Ponsaers, & B. Van Stokkom (Eds.), *Reflections on reassurance policing in the low countries* (pp. 31-52). The Hague: BJu Legal Publishers.

Poznyak, D., Meuleman, B., Abts, K., & Bishop, G. F. (2014). Trust in American government: Longitudinal measurement equivalence in the ANES, 1964-2008. *Social Indicators Research, 118*(2), 741-758.

Prick, F. P. M. (1959). Corruptie en politietransactie. *Tijdschrift voor de Politie, 23*(12), 53-56.

Prick, F. P. M. (1961). De honorering der politie in Engeland. Brittannia docet. *Tijdschrift voor de Politie, 23*(7), 197-200.

Pridemore, W. A., & Kim, S. W. (2006). Democratization and political change as threats to collective sentiments: Testing Durkheim in Russia. *The Annals of the American Academy of Political and Social Science, 605*(1), 82-103.

Projectgroep visie op de politiefunctie (2005). *Politie in ontwikkeling. Visie op de politiefunctie*. Den Haag: NPI.

Punch, M. (1985). *Conduct unbecoming: The social construction of police deviance and control*. London: Tavistock.

Punch, M. (2007). *Zero tolerance policing*. Bristol: The Policy Press.

Punch, M. (2009). *Police corruption: Deviance, accountability and reform in policing*. Cullompton: Willan.

Punch, M., Van der Vijver, C. D., & Zoomer, O. (2002). Dutch 'COP:' Developing community policing in the Netherlands. *Policing. An International Journal of Police Strategies and Management, 25*(1), 60-79.

Reiner, R. (1995). From sacred to profane: The thirty years' war of the British police. *Policing and Society, 5*(2), 121-128.

Reiner, R. (2010). *The politics of the police* (4th ed.). Oxford: Oxford University Press.

Reiner, R. (2013). Who governs? Democracy, plutocracy, science and prophecy in policing. *Criminology and Criminal Justice, 13*(2), 161-180.

Reisig, M. D., Bratton, J., & Gertz, M. G. (2007). The construct validity and refinement of process-based policing measures. *Criminal Justice and Behavior, 34*(8), 1005-1028.

Reisig, M. D., & Parks, R. B. (2000). Experience, quality of life, and neighbourhood context: A hierarchical analysis of satisfaction with police. *Justice Quarterly, 17*(3), 607-630.

Reiss, A. J. Jr. (1971). *The police and the public*. London: Yale University Press.

Reuss-Ianni, E. (1983). *The two cultures of policing*. New Brunswick, NJ: Transaction Publishers.

Rigakos, G. S., & Papanicolaou, G. (2003). The political economy of Greek policing: Between neo-liberalism and the sovereign state. *Policing and Society, 13*(3), 271-304.

Rijksen, R. (1946). *Politieorganisatie en voorbereidend onderzoek*. Amsterdam: W. L. Salm & Co.

Ritzer, G. (1983). The McDonaldization of society. *Journal of American Culture, 6*, 100-107.

Ritzer, G. (2008). *The McDonaldization of society*. Thousand Oaks, CA: Pine Forge Press.

Rosenbaum, D. P. (1986). *Community crime prevention. Does it work?* Beverly Hills, CA: SAGE Publications.

Rosenbaum, D. P. (1988). Community crime prevention: A review and synthesis of the literature. *Justice Quarterly, 5*(3), 323-395.

Rosenbaum, D. P. (1996). The changing role of the police: Assessing the current transition to community policing. In J. P. Brodeur (Ed.), *How to recognize good policing. Problems and issues* (pp. 3-29). Thousand Oaks, CA: SAGE Publications.

Rosenthal, U., Bruinsma, G. J. N., Muller, E. R., Van der Torre, E. J., & De Vries, A. W. (1998). *Evaluatie politiewet 1993. Een diepte-onderzoek.* 's-Gravenhage: VUGA.

Roth, F. (2009). The effect of the financial crisis on systemic trust. *Intereconomics, 44*(4), 203-208.

Rother, N. (2005). Measuring attitudes towards immigration across countries with the ESS: Potential problems of equivalence. In J. H. P. Hoffmeyer-Zlotnik, & J. Harkness (Eds.), *Methodological Aspects in Cross-National Research* (pp. 109-126). Mannheim: ZUMA.

Rothstein, B. (2005). *Social traps and the problem of trust.* Cambridge, U.K.: Cambridge University Press.

Rothstein, B., & Stolle, D. (2008). The state and social capital: An institutional theory of generalized trust. *Comparative Politics, 40*(4), 441-459.

Saarikkomäki, E. (2016). Perceptions of procedural justice among young people: Narratives of fair treatment in young people's stories of police and security guard interventions *British Journal of Criminology, 56*(6), 1253-1271.

Sajó, A. (1998). Corruption, clientelism, and the future of the constitutional state in Eastern Europe. *East European Constitutional Review, 7*(1), 37-46.

Sampson, R. J., & Jeglum Bartusch, D. (1998). Legal cynicism and (subcultural?) tolerance of deviance: The neighborhood context of racial differences. *Law and Society Review, 32*(4), 777-804.

Sapsford, R., & Abbott, P. (2006). Trust, confidence and social environment in post-communist societies. *Communist and Post-Communist Studies, 39*(1), 59-71.

Sargeant, E., Antrobus, E., Murphy, K., Bennett, S., & Mazerolle, L. (2016). Social identity and procedural justice in police encounters with the public: Results from a randomised controlled trial. *Policing and Society, 26*(7), 789-803.

Sato, M., Haverkamp, R., & Hough, J. M. (2016). Trust in the German police. *European Police Science and Research Bulletin* (special conference edition).

Savage, S. P. (2007). *Police reform. Forces for change.* Oxford: Oxford University Press.

Scarman, L. G. (1982). *The Scarman report. The Brixton disorders 10-12 April 1981.* Harmondsworth: Penguin.

Schaap, D. (2014). Een vertrouwenscrisis? Ontwikkelingen in het vertrouwen van burgers in de politie in Nederland en Europa. *Het Tijdschrift voor de Politie, 76*(1), 28-31.

Schaap, D., & Scheepers, P. (2014). Comparing citizens' trust in the police across European countries: An assessment of the cross-country measurement equivalence. *International Criminal Justice Review, 24*(1), 82-98.

Schaap, D., Terpstra, J., & Van Stokkom, B. (2017). *Politiebestel in ontwikkeling. Institutionele verandering en onderzoek (1989-2016).* Den Haag: WODC.

Schneider, I. (2017). Can we trust measures of political trust? Assessing measurement equivalence in diverse regime types. *Social Indicators Research, 133*(3), 963-984.

Scott, K. B. (2011). Politics and the police in Scotland: The impact of devolution. *Crime, Law and Social Change, 55*(2-3), 121-132.

SIPR, What Works Scotland & ScotCen (2017). *Evaluation of Police and Fire Reform: Year 2 Report.* Edinburgh: The Scottish Government.

Seagrave, J. (1996). Defining community policing. *American Journal of Police, 15*(2), 1-22.

Seawright, J., & Gerring, J. (2008). Case selection techniques in case study research. *Political Research Quarterly, 61*(2), 294-308.

Seligman, A. B. (1997). *The problem of trust.* Princeton, NJ: Princeton University Press.

Seligman, A. B. (1998). Trust and sociability. On the limits of confidence and role expectations. *The American Journal of Economics and Sociology, 57*(4), 391-404.

Semukhina, O. B. (2016). Public assistance of police during criminal investigations: Russian experience. *Police Practice and Research, 17*(3), 229-248.

Semukhina, O. B., & Reynolds, K. M. (2014). Russian citizens' perceptions of corruption and trust of the police. *Policing and Society, 24*(2), 158-188.

Sharp, D., & Atherton, S. (2007). To serve and protect? The experiences of policing in the community of young people from black and other ethnic minority groups. *British Journal of Criminology, 47*(5), 746-763.

Sharp, E. B., & Johnson, P. E. (2009). Accounting for variation in distrust of local police. *Justice Quarterly, 26*(1), 157-182.

Sherman, L. W. (1983). Patrol strategies for police. In J. Q. Wilson (Ed.), *Crime and public policy* (pp. 145-164). San Francisco, CA: ICS Press.

Sherman, L. W., & Weisburd, D. L. (1995). General deterrent effects of police patrol in crime 'hot spots': A randomized, controlled trial. *Justice Quarterly, 12*(4), 625-648.

Shevlin, M. & Miles, J. N. V. (1998). Effects of sample size, model specification and factor loadings on the GFI in confirmatory factor analysis. *Personality and Individual Differences, 25*(1), 85-90.

Shlapentokh, V. (2006). Trust in public institutions in Russia: The lowest in the world. *Communist and Post-Communist Studies, 39*(2), 153-174.

Simiti, M. (2016). Rage and protest: The case of the Greek indignant movement. *Contention: The Multidisciplinary Journal of Social Protest, 3*(2), 33-50.

Sindall, K., & Sturgis, P. (2013). Austerity policing: Is visibility more important than absolute numbers in determining public confidence in the police? *European Journal of Criminology, 10*(2), 137-153.

Sindall, K., Sturgis, P., & Jennings, W. (2012). Public confidence in the police. A time-series analysis. *British Journal of Criminology, 52*(4), 744-764.

Singer, J. D. & Willett, J. B. (2003). *Applied longitudinal data analysis. Modeling change and event occurrence.* Oxford: Oxford University Press.

Six, F. (2004). *Trust and trouble. Building interpersonal trust within organizations.* Rotterdam: Erasmus Research Institute of Management.

Sklansky, D. A. (2008). *Democracy and the police.* Stanford, CA: Stanford University Press.

Skogan, W. G. (1978). Citizen satisfaction with police services: Individual and contextual effects. *Policy Studies Journal, 7*(1), 469-479.

Skogan, W. G. (1990). *Disorder and decline.* New York: The Free Press.

Skogan, W. G. (2006a). Asymmetry in the impact of encounters with police. *Policing and Society, 16*(2), 99-126.

Skogan, W. G. (2006b). *Police and community in Chicago: A tale of three cities.* Oxford: Oxford University Press.

Skogan, W. G. (2009). Concern about crime and confidence in the police: Reassurance or accountability? *Police Quarterly, 12*(3), 301-318.

Skogan, W. G., & Hartnett, S. M. (1997). *Community policing, Chicago style.* New York: Oxford University Press.

Skolnick, J. H. (1966). *Justice without trial. Law enforcement in democratic society.* New York: Wiley.

Skolnick, J. H., & Bayley, D. H. (1988). Theme and variation in community policing. In M. Tonry & N. Morris (Eds.), *Crime and Justice: A Review of Research* (Vol. 10, pp. 1-37). Chicago: University of Chicago Press.

Smit, P. R., De Jong, R., & Bijleveld, C. C. J. H. (2011). Homicide data in Europe: Definitions, sources and statistics. In M. Liem & W. A. Pridemore (Eds.), *Handbook of European homicide research* (pp. 5-24). New York: Springer.

Smith, D. J. (2007). The foundations of legitimacy. In T. R. Tyler (Ed.), *Legitimacy and criminal justice* (pp. 30-58). New York: Russell Sage Foundation.

Smith, P. E., & Hawkins, R. O. (1973). Victimization, types of citizen-police contacts, and attitudes toward the police. *Law and Society Review, 8*(1), 135-152.

Smith, P. T. (1985). *Policing Victorian London: Political policing, public order, and the London Metropolitan Police.* Westport, CT: Greenwood Press.

Sparks, J. R., & Bottoms, A. E. (1995). Legitimacy and order in prisons. *The British Journal of Sociology, 46*(1), 45-62.

Spelman, W., & Brown, D. K. (1984). *Calling the police—Citizen reporting of serious crime.* Rockville, MD: National Institute of Justice.

Stack, S., Cao, L., & Adamzyck, A. (2007). Crime volume and law and order culture. *Justice Quarterly, 24*(2), 291-308.

Stamatel, J. P. (2006). An overview of publicly available quantitative cross-national crime data. *IASSIST Quarterly, 30,* 16-20.

Stanko, E. A., & Bradford, B. (2009). Beyond measuring 'how good a job' police are doing: The MPS model of confidence in policing. *Policing. A Journal of Policy and Practice, 3*(4), 322-330.

Steiger, J. H. (2007). Understanding the limitations of global fit assessment in structural equation modeling. *Personality and Individual Differences, 42*(5), 893-898.

Steinberg, J. (2011). Crime prevention goes abroad: Policy transfer and policing in post-apartheid South Africa. *Theoretical Criminology, 15*(4), 349-364.

Steinberg, J. (2012). Establishing police authority and civilian compliance in post-apartheid Johannesburg: An argument from the work of Egon Bittner. *Policing and Society, 22*(4), 481-495.

Stevnsborg, H. (2010). *Politi 1682-2007.* Frederiksberg: Samfundslitteratur.

Stone, C., & Travis, J. (2011). Toward a new professionalism in policing. *New Perspectives in Policing,* March, 1-26. Washington, DC: National Institute of Justice.

Straver, M. A. (2006). Onveiligheid en de legitimiteit van de politie. In C. D. V. d. Vijver & F. Vlek (Eds.), *De legitimiteit van de politie onder druk? Beschouwingen over grondslagen en ontwikkelingen van legitimiteit en legitimiteitstoekenning* (pp. 187-226). Den Haag: Elsevier Overheid.

Suchman, M. C. (1995). Managing legitimacy: Strategic and institutional approaches. *The Academy of Management Review, 20*(3), 571-610.

Sung, H. E. (2006). Police effectiveness and democracy: Shape and direction of the relationship. *Policing: An International Journal of Police Strategies & Management, 29*(2), 347-367.

Sunshine, J., & Tyler, T. R. (2003). The role of procedural justice and legitimacy in shaping public support for policing. *Law and Society Review, 37*(3), 513-547.

Szikinger, I. (1993). Community policing in Hungary: Perspectives and realities. In D. Dölling & T. Feltes (Eds.), *Community policing: Comparative aspects of community oriented police work.* Holzkirchen: Felix.

Sztompka, P. (1999). *Trust. A sociological theory.* Cambridge, U.K.: Cambridge University Press.

Tankebe, J. (2008). Police effectiveness and police trustworthiness in Ghana: An empirical appraisal. *Criminology and Criminal Justice, 8*(2), 185-202.

Tankebe, J. (2010). Public confidence in the police. Testing the effects of public experiences of police corruption in Ghana. *British Journal of Criminology, 50*(2), 296-319.

Tansey, O. (2007). Process tracing and elite interviewing: A case for non-probability sampling. *Political Science and Politics, 40*(4), 765-772.

Tarling, R., & Morris, M. (2010). Reporting crime to the police. *British Journal of Criminology, 50*(3), 474-490.

Terpstra, J. (2002). *Sturing van politie en politiewerk. Een verkennend onderzoek tegen de achtergrond van een veranderende sturingscontext en sturingsstijl.* Enschede: IPIT.

Terpstra, J. (2004). Lokale inbedding van de Nederlandse politie: Stand van zaken en overzicht. In F. Vlek, K. Bangma, K. Loef, & E. Muller (Eds.), *Uit balans: Politie en bestel in de knel* (pp. 59-80). Zeist: Kerckebosch.

Terpstra, J. (2008). *Wijkagenten en hun dagelijks werk. Een onderzoek naar de uitvoering van gebiedsgebonden politiewerk.* Den Haag: Reed Business.

Terpstra, J. (2010). Community policing in practice: Ambitions and realization. *Policing. A Journal of Policy and Practice, 4*(1), 64-72.

Terpstra, J. (2011). Two theories on the police—The relevance of Max Weber and Emile Durkheim to the study of the police. *International Journal of Law, Crime and Justice, 39*(1), 1-11.

Terpstra, J. (2013). Towards a national police in the Netherlands: Background of a radical police reform. In N. R. Fyfe, J. Terpstra, & P. Tops (Eds.), *Centralizing forces? Comparative perspectives on contemporary police reform in northern and western Europe* (pp. 137-156). The Hague: Eleven.

Terpstra, J., Foekens, P., & Van Stokkom, B. (2015). *Burgemeesters over hun nationale politie. Een onderzoek naar de opvattingen van burgemeesters over hoe zij hun rol als gezagsdrager onder het regime van de nationale politie kunnen waarmaken.* Den Haag: Stichting Maatschappij en Veiligheid.

Terpstra, J., & Fyfe, N. R. (2013). Introduction: A 'transformative moment in policing.' In N. R. Fyfe, J. Terpstra, & P. Tops (Eds.), *Centralizing forces? Comparative perspectives on contemporary police reform in Northern and Western Europe* (pp. 1-22). The Hague: Eleven.

Terpstra, J., & Fyfe, N. R. (2014). Policy processes and police reform: Examining similarities and differences between Scotland and the Netherlands. *International Journal of Law, Crime and Justice, 42*(4), 366-383.

Terpstra, J., Gunther Moor, L., & Van Stokkom, B. (2010). De kerntakendiscussie in Nederland. Retoriek en realiteit. In B. v. Stokkom, J. Terpstra, & L. G. Moor (Eds.), *De politie en haar opdracht: De kerntakendiscussie voorbij* (pp. 25-50). Apeldoorn-Antwerpen: Maklu.

Terpstra, J., & Schaap, D. (2011). Politiecultuur. Een empirische verkenning in de Nederlandse context. *Proces, 90*(4), 183-196.

Terpstra, J., & Schaap, D. (2013). Police culture, stress conditions and working styles. *European Journal of Criminology, 10*(1), 59-73.

Terpstra, J., & Trommel, W. (2006). *Het nieuwe bedrijfsmatig denken bij de politie. Analyse van een culturele formatie in ontwikkeling.* Enschede: IPIT.

Terpstra, J., & Trommel, W. (2009). Police, managerialization and presentational strategies. *Policing: An International Journal of Police Strategies & Management, 32*(1), 128-143.

Terpstra, J., & Van der Vijver, C. D. (2005). Het Nederlandse politiebestel en de druk tot centralisatie. *Tijdschrift voor Criminologie, 47*(4), 335-344.

Terpstra, J., & Van der Vijver, C. D. (2006). The police, changing security arrangements and late modernity: The case of The Netherlands. *German Policy Studies, 3*(1), 80-111.

Terpstra, J., Van Duijneveldt, I., Eikenaar, T., Havinga, T., & Van Stokkom, B. (2016). *Basisteams in de nationale politie. Organisatie, taakuitvoering en gebiedsgebonden werk.* Amsterdam: Reed Business.

Terpstra, J., & Van Stokkom, B. (2014). Toezichthouders op straat. Een internationaal vergelijkende benadering. *Tijdschrift voor Toezicht, 5*(4), 6-23.

Terpstra, J., Van Stokkom, B., & Spreeuwers, R. (2013). *Who patrols the streets? An international comparative study of plural policing.* The Hague: Eleven.

Thibaut, J., & Walker, L. (1975). *Procedural justice: A psychological analysis.* Hillsdale, NJ: Erlbaum.

Thomassen, G. (2013). Corruption and trust in the police: A cross-country study. *European Journal of Policing Studies, 1*(2), 152-168.

Tilley, N. (2003). Community policing, problem-oriented policing and intelligence-led policing. In T. Newburn (Ed.), *Handbook of policing.* Cullompton: Willan.

Torcal, M. (2014). The decline of political trust in Spain and Portugal. Economic performance or political responsiveness? *American Behavioral Scientist, 58*(12), 1542-1567.

Transparency International (2010a). Corruption perceptions index 2010. Retrieved September 26, 2017 from http://www.transparency.org/content/download/55725/890310/CPI_report_ForWeb.pdf

Transparency International (2010b). Corruption perceptions index 2010. Long methodological brief. Retrieved September 26, 2017 from http://www.transparency.org/content/download/55903/892623/CPI2010_long_methodology_En.pdf

Trinkner, R., Tyler, T. R., & Goff, P. A. (2016). Justice from within: The relations between a procedurally just organizational climate and police organizational efficiency, endorsement of democratic policing, and officer well-being. *Psychology, Public Policy, and Law, 22*(2), 158-172.

Trojanowicz, R. C., & Bucqueroux, B. (1990). *Community policing: A contemporary perspective.* Cincinnati, OH: Anderson.

Tuffin, R., Morris, J., & Poole, A. (2006). *An evaluation of the impact of the National Reassurance Policing Programme.* London: Home Office Research, Development and Statistics Directorate.

Twenge, J. M., Campbell, W. K., & Carter, N. T. (2014). Declines in trust in others and confidence in institutions among American adults and late adolescents, 1972-2012. *Psychological Science, 25*(10), 1914-1923.

Twining, W. (2004). Diffusion of law: A global perspective. *Journal of Legal Pluralism and Unofficial Law, 49*, 1-46.

Tyler, T. R. (1988). What is procedural justice? Criteria used by citizens to assess the fairness of legal procedures. *Law and Society Review, 22*(1), 103-136.

Tyler, T. R. (1990). *Why people obey the law.* New Haven, CT: Yale University Press.

Tyler, T. R. (2001). Public trust and confidence in legal authorities: What do majority and minority group members want from the law and legal institutions? *Behavioral Sciences & the Law, 19*(2), 215-235.

Tyler, T. R. (2004). Enhancing police legitimacy. *The Annals of the American Academy of Political and Social Science, 593*(1), 84-99.

Tyler, T. R., & Huo, Y. J. (2002). *Trust in the law. Encouraging public cooperation with the police and courts.* New York: Russell Sage Foundation.

Tyler, T. R., & Jackson, J. (2014). Popular legitimacy and the exercise of legal authority: Motivating compliance, cooperation, and engagement. *Psychology, Public Policy, and Law, 20*(1), 78-95.

UNU-WIDER (2011a). UNU-WIDER world income inequality database version 2.0c. Retrieved September 26, 2017 from UNU-WIDER https://www.wider.unu.edu/download/wiid-v30a

UNU-WIDER (2011b). World income inequality database. User guide and data sources. Retrieved September 26, 2017 from UNU-WIDER http://62.237.131.23/wiid/WIID2c.pdf

Uslaner, E. M. (2011). Corruption, the inequality trap and trust in government. In S. Zmerli & M. Hooghe (Eds.), *Political trust. Why context matters* (pp. 141-162). Colchester: ECPR Press.

Van Craen, M. (2013). Explaining majority and minority trust in the police. *Justice Quarterly, 30*(6), 1042-1067.

Van Damme, A. (2017). The impact of police contact on trust and police legitimacy in Belgium. *Policing and Society: An International Journal of Research and Policy, 27*(2), 205-228.

Van de Vijver, F. J. R. (2003). Bias and equivalence: Cross-cultural perspectives. In J. Harkness, F. J. R. van de Vijver, & P. P. Mohler (Eds.), *Cross-cultural survey methods* (pp. 143-156). Hoboken, NJ: Wiley.

Van de Walle, S. (2011). NPM: Restoring the public trust through creating distrust? In T. Christensen & P. Lægreid (Eds.), *The Ashgate research companion to New Public Management* (pp. 309-320). Farnham: Ashgate.

Van de Walle, S., Van Roosbroek, S. & Bouckaert, G. (2008). Trust in the public sector: Is there any evidence for a long-term decline? *International Review of Administrative Sciences, 74*(1), 47-74.

Van der Meer, T., & Dekker, P. (2011). Trustworthy states, trusting citizens? A multilevel study into objective and subjective determinants of political trust. In S. Zmerli & M. Hooghe (Eds.), *Political trust. Why context matters* (pp. 95-116). Colchester: ECPR Press.

Van der Spuy, E. (2000). Foreign donor assistance and policing reform in South Africa. *Policing and Society, 10*(4), 343-366.

Van der Torre, E. J., Gieling, M., Holvast, R., Vlek, G. C. K., & Lanza, R. (2015). *De lokale positie van de nationale politie. Een eerste verkenning.* Apeldoorn: Politieacademie.

Van der Torre, E. J., & Van Harmelen, E. (1999). Basispolitiezorg en hulpverlening. In C. J. C. F. Fijnaut, E. R. Muller, & U. Rosenthal (Eds.), *Politie. Studies over haar werking en organisatie* (pp. 399-422). Alphen aan den Rijn: Samsom.

Van der Veld, W. M., & Saris, W. E. (2011). Causes of generalized social trust. In E. Davidov, P. Schmidt, & J. Billiet (Eds.), *Cross-cultural analysis. Methods and applications.* (pp. 207-248). New York: Routledge.

Van der Veld, W. M., Saris, W. E., & Satorra, A. (2008). Judgment Rule Aid for structural equation models version 3.0.4.

Van der Vijver, C. D. (1993). *De burger en de zin van strafrecht.* Lelystad: Koninklijke Vermande.

Van der Vijver, C. D. (2004). Kerntaken, sturing en professionaliteit. In B. v. Stokkom & L. G. Moor (Eds.), *Onoprechte handhaving? Prestatiecontracten, beleidsvrijheid en politie-ethiek* (pp. 35-55). Dordrecht: SMVP.

Van der Vijver, C. D. (2006). Legitimiteit, gezag en politie. Een verkenning van de hedendaagse dynamiek. In C. D. van der Vijver & F. Vlek (Eds.), *De legitimiteit van de politie onder druk? Beschouwingen over grondslagen en ontwikkelingen van legitimiteit en legitimiteitstoekenning.* (pp. 15-132). Den Haag: Elsevier Overheid.

Van Dijk, J. (2001). Attitudes of victims and repeat victims toward the police: Results of the International Crime Victims Survey. In G. Farrell & K. Pease (Eds.), *Repeat victimization. Crime prevention studies, Volume 12* (pp. 27-52). Monsey, NY: Criminal Justice Press.

Van Duyn, R. (1985). *Provo. De geschiedenis van de provotarische beweging 1965-1967.* Amsterdam: Meulenhoff.

Van Reenen, P. (1993). Het zwevende politiebestel. *Justitiële Verkenningen, 19*(4), 7-36.

Van Reenen, P. (2006). Politiële legitimiteit, paradigma's en problemen. In C. D. Van der Vijver & F. Vlek (Eds.), *De legitimiteit van de politie onder druk? Beschouwingen over grondslagen en ontwikkelingen van legitimiteit en legitimiteitstoekenning.* Den Haag: Elsevier Overheid.

Van Reenen, P., & Verton, P. C. (1974). Over de legitimiteit van het hedendaagse politie-optreden. *Mens en Maatschappij, 49*(1), 72-87.

Van Sluis, A., Cachet, A., De Jong, L., Nieuwenhuyzen, C., & Ringeling, A. (2006). *Cijfers en stakeholders. Prestatiesturing en de gevolgen voor de maatschappelijke en politiek-bestuurlijke relaties van de politie*. Den Haag: Elsevier Overheid.

Van Sluis, A., Cachet, A., Jochoms, T., Ringeling, A., & Sey, A. (2013). *Contested police systems. Changes in the police systems in Belgium, Denmark, England & Wales, Germany, and the Netherlands*. The Hague: Eleven.

Van Sluis, A., Cachet, A., & Ringeling, A. (2005). Results-based agreements for the police in The Netherlands. *Policing: An International Journal of Police Strategies & Management, 31*(3), 415-434.

Van Steden, R., & Sarre, R. (2007). The growth of private security: Trends in the European Union. *Security Journal, 20*, 222-235.

Vandenberg, R. J., & Lance, C. E. (2000). A review and synthesis of the measurement invariance literature: Suggestions, practices, and recommendations for organizational research. *Organizational Research Methods, 3*(1), 4-70.

Visionsudvalget. (2005). *Fremtidens politi*. Copenhagen.

Visser, M., Scholte, M., & Scheepers, P. (2013). Fear of crime and feelings of unsafety in European countries: Macro and micro explanations in cross-national perspective. *The Sociological Quarterly, 54*(2), 278-301.

Vuorensyrjä, M. (2014). Organizational reform in a hierarchical frontline organization: Tracking changes in stress and turnover intention during the Finnish police reform years. *Policing: An International Journal of Police Strategies & Management*.

Waddington, D. P. (1992). *Contemporary issues in public disorder. A comparative and historical approach*. London: Routledge.

Waddington, P. A. J. (1999). *Policing citizens: Authority and rights*. London: UCL Press.

Walker, S. (1984). 'Broken Windows' and fractured history: The use and misuse of history in recent police patrol analysis. *Justice Quarterly, 1*(1), 75-90.

Wallace, C., & Latcheva, R. (2006). Economic transformation outside the law: Corruption, trust in public institutions and the informal economy in transition countries of Central and Eastern Europe. *Europe-Asia Studies, 58*(1), 81-102.

Walsh, D. P. J. (2009). Tightening the noose of central government control over policing in Ireland: Innovations in the Garda Síochána Act 2005. *Northern Ireland Legal Quarterly, 60*(2), 163-180.

Weatherford, M. S. (1992). Measuring political legitimacy. *American Political Science Review, 86*(1), 149-166.

Weber, M. (1980). *Wirtschaft und Gesellschaft: Grundriss der verstehenden Soziologie* (5th ed.). Tübingen: Mohr.

Weitzer, R. (1985). Policing a divided society: Obstacles to normalization in Northern Ireland. *Social Problems, 33*(1), 41-55.

Weitzer, R. (2014). The puzzling neglect of Hispanic Americans in research on police-citizen relations. *Ethnic and Racial Studies, 37*(11), 1995-2013.

Weitzer, R., & Tuch, S. A. (2005). Determinants of public satisfaction with the police. *Police Quarterly, 8*(3), 279-297.

Wells, L. E., & Falcone, D. N. (2005). Policing in the United States: Developing a comprehensive empirical model: Illinois State University.

Wennström, B. (2013). Police reform in Sweden: How to make a perfect cup of espresso. In N. R. Fyfe, J. Terpstra, & P. Tops (Eds.), *Centralizing forces? Comparative perspectives on contemporary police reform in Northern and Western Europe* (pp. 157-172). The Hague: Eleven.

Westley, W. A. (1970). *Violence and the police*. Cambridge, MA: The MIT Press.

White, A. (2014). Post-crisis policing and public-private partnerships: The case of Lincolnshire Police and G4S *British Journal of Criminology, 54*(6), 1002-1022.

WHO (World Health Organization Regional Office for Europe) (2017). European mortality database. Retrieved September 26, 2017 from http://data.euro.who.int/hfamdb/

Wiley, M. G., & Hudik, T. L. (1974). Police-citizen encounters: A field test of exchange theory. *Social Problems, 22*(1), 119-127.

Wilkes, R. (2015). We trust in government, just not in yours: Race, partisanship, and political trust, 1958-2012. *Social Science Research, 49*, 356-371.

Wilson, J. Q., & Kelling, G. L. (1982). Broken windows: The police and neighborhood safety. *The Atlantic Monthly* (March), 29-38.

Wilson, O. W. (1950). *Police administration*. New York: McGraw-Hill.

Wisler, D. (2008). Interview with Dr Monica Bonfanti, chief of the Geneva cantonal police. *Police Practice and Research, 9*(3), 251-259.

Wolfe, S. E., Nix, J., Kaminski, R., & Rojek, J. (2016). Is the effect of procedural justice on police legitimacy invariant? Testing the generality of procedural justice and competing antecedents of legitimacy. *Journal of Quantitative Criminology, 32*(2), 253-282.

Worden, R. E., & McLean, S. J. (2017). *Mirage of police reform. Procedural justice and police legitimacy*. Oakland, CA: University of California Press.

Wu, Y., Lake, R., & Cao, L. (2015). Race, social bonds, and juvenile attitudes toward the police. *Justice Quarterly, 32*(3), 445-470.

Xenakis, S. & Cheliotis, L. K. (2016). 'Glocal' disorder: Causes, conduct and consequences of the 2008 Greek unrest. *European Journal of Criminology, 13*(5), 639-656.

Yin, R. K. (2009). *Case study research: Design and methods* (4th ed.). Thousand Oaks, CA: SAGE Publications.

Zernova, M. (2012). Coping with the failure of the police in post-Soviet Russia: Findings from one empirical study. *Police Practice and Research, 13*(6), 474-486.

Zhao, J. S., He, N., & Lovrich, N. P. (2003). Community policing: Did it change the basic functions of policing in the 1990s? A national follow-up study. *Justice Quarterly, 20*(4), 697-724.

Zhao, J. S., Lovrich, N. P., & Thurman, Q. (1999). The status of community policing in American cities. Facilitators and impediments revisited. *Policing: An International Journal of Police Strategies & Management, 22*(1), 74-92.

Appendix A

There are multiple ways to go about assessing structural equation models and each
of those methods has its drawbacks. This makes structural equation models fundamentally different from statistical approaches that often have more or less commonly accepted criteria for accepting or rejecting a hypothesis. The assessment of
structural equation models is a more elaborate process where different criteria
should be taken into consideration. This is somewhat challenging, as measurement
equivalence tests demand acceptance or rejection of a multi-group structural equation model.

Several experts have argued against applying so-called 'golden rules' in terms
of when to accept and when to reject a model in SEM (Hu & Bentler, 1999; Lai &
Green, 2016; Marsh, Hau, & Wen, 2004). Fit indices, while useful and commonly
applied, never yield hard cutoff points and all have different weaknesses and sensitivities. The choice of whether to accept or reject a model should hence be well
argued and should rest on solid empirical evidence. This means that merely reporting a single global fit indicator is out of the question (Hooper et al., 2008; Hu &
Bentler, 1999; Steiger, 2007; Vandenberg & Lance, 2000). A balanced approach
toward judging a model requires a careful procedure to diagnose potential issues.
In order to do so, I apply a strategy that I will refer to as a stepwise diagnostics
procedure. While most researchers of measurement equivalence tend to rely either
on indicators of model fit (Hu & Bentler, 1998; Vandenberg & Lance, 2000) or on
evidence of misspecifications (Van der Veld & Saris, 2011), the stepwise diagnostics
procedure aims to reach a model that is both well-fitting and correctly specified. It
aims to avoid both accepting faulty models and rejecting correct ones. Misspecifications—empirical deviations from the theoretical model—can be tolerated if they
are minute ánd combined with good or very good overall model fit. Similarly, a
mediocre fit can be acceptable if there are no overt misspecifications in the model.
The stepwise procedure is strict enough to ensure that reasonably fitting models
featuring considerable misspecifications are not blindly accepted. On the other
hand, it will be lenient to trivially misspecified models that nevertheless have

excellent overall fit. This avoids the pitfalls of relying either merely on measures of global fit or on the diagnosis of misspecifications.

The stepwise diagnostics approach borrows from multiple research traditions in testing structural equation models. These influences result in a four-step procedure, which will be followed for each of the three levels of invariance we require in order to ascertain we can validly compare trust across different points of measurement (countries or years). These levels are configural invariance, metric invariance, and scalar invariance (Vandenberg & Lance, 2000).

The first step for each of these three tests is that we should know whether the observed data fit the full model well. Through the statistical package LISREL 8.80 (Jöreskog & Sörbom, 1996), the model as a whole will be scrutinized. This step, **Step 1**, is based on the values of two well-reputed indicators designed to measure full model fit from different angles, the RMSEA and the CFI (Lai & Green, 2016).

If neither of these indicators gives any ground for concern, meaning that they yield better values than those usually deemed to indicate good or excellent model fit, that is encouraging, but insufficient. We should, as a precaution, also assess the individual groups (years or countries of measurement) involved in our multi-group analysis: it is possible that data from a single year or country included fit poorly, yet are compensated for by excellent fit in other points of measurement, yielding overall highly satisfactory fit measures. This is why in **Step 2**, the model fit in every specific group will also be assessed, again with two different indicators: the GFI and the SRMR.

If none of these four often-used (Hooper et al., 2008) indicators gives any cause for concern and they all yield values that are universally deemed good or excellent, invariance will be established: the model fit is so good that any potential model misspecifications must be so minor as to be irrelevant. In this case, our stepwise diagnostics procedure will include only the minimal amount of steps: two.

However, the procedure become more challenging when there is no perfect or near-perfect model fit in either Step 1 or Step 2. This is where the classical debate surrounding 'golden rules' becomes relevant. While authors usually agree on which values of fit indices are excellent and which ones are disastrous, they differ on what values are acceptable or satisfactory (Hooper et al., 2008; Marsh et al., 2004). There is considerable variation, often depending on the type and complexity of the model and on the nature and quantity of the data involved, in when an indicator is supposed to signal acceptable fit. My proposal is that the theoretical 'gray zone,' indicator values that are acceptable to some authors but problematic to others, reflects potential issues with the model. If values on one or more of these four indicators fall within that gray zone, I consider it cause for further investigation. This investigation will take the form of a search for model misspecifications.

Following the procedure recommended by Van der Veld and Saris (2011), **Step 3** commences with a search for misspecifications on the level of indicators and individual factor loadings, rather than that of the full model or groups of measurement. This will be done through the statistical program J-rule (Van der Veld, Saris, & Satorra, 2008), which is especially designed for finding model misspecifications. The misspecifications that we will focus on are different for each type of invariance test: the configural invariance test concentrates on correlated error terms and other issues that touch on the basic structure of the model; the metric invariance test concentrates on possibly misspecified factor loadings; and the scalar invariance test focuses on misspecified intercepts. If after observing 'gray zone' values on one or more fit indicators we find no misspecifications in Step 3, we will conclude that there is insufficient evidence of noninvariance, meaning that measurement equivalence is provisionally established: the model fit may not be perfect, but empirical deviations from the theoretical structure are insignificant.

If we do find misspecifications in Step 3, we shall proceed to the final step, **Step 4**. It is here that we shall get the opportunity to adjust a nonfitting, misspecified model until we achieve a model that chimes with the data. By definition, changing the model structure in a single group eliminates measurement equivalence: if the model structures are not equivalent, they cannot be validly compared. However, an important note here is that we are not necessarily interested in the model as a whole, but merely in the position of trust or confidence in the police specifically: one indicator within the model. If the misspecifications (and the ensuing adjustments to make the model well-fitting) are present in an indicator not directly related to trust in the police, even a changed structure in a single group can still result in equivalent measures of trust in the police over time or across countries. So, while going through Step 4 will often result in partial noninvariance and hence nonequivalence, measurement equivalence is still at least a theoretical option if the changes to the model do not affect trust in the police in any way. The stepwise diagnostics procedure is displayed in Table A.1, including the 'gray zone' of indicator values that may or may not signal equivalence issues.[1]

---

1.   The GFI as a measure of model fit is flawed because of sensitivity to sample size (Hooper et al., 2008; Hu & Bentler, 1999; Shevlin & Miles, 1998). However, I consider it to be a useful auxiliary indicator to the more reliable SRMR: as most groups included in our examinations have similar sample sizes, a deviant GFI value is still informative.

Table A.1   The stepwise diagnostics procedure for establishing cross-group measurement equivalence

	Configural invariance	Metric invariance	Scalar invariance
What is being tested?	Does the factor structure hold across groups?	Are factor loadings invariant across groups?	Are intercepts invariant across groups?
What does it mean?	Do people in different groups have similar frames of reference concerning what institutional trust entails?	Do institutions have the same weight to people in different groups in constituting institutional trust?	Is the measurement scale identical across countries?
What are the implications?	Common frame of reference means that concepts are comparable across groups	Common metric means that relationships between concepts are comparable across groups	Common measurement scale implies that means are comparable across groups
By what criteria?	Global fit indices: RMSEA and CFI	Global fit indices: RMSEA and CFI Group-level indices: GFI and SRMR Misspecifications: as indicated in J-rule	Global fit indices: RMSEA and CFI Group-level indices: GFI and SRMR Misspecifications: as indicated in J-rule
Stepwise procedure, **Step 1**: Assessing whole model	RMSEA > .099: refute configural invariance RMSEA > .059 < .1: **proceed to Steps 2 & 3** CFI < .95: refute configural invariance CFI > .97 > .94: **proceed to Steps 2 & 3** Else: accept configural invariance	RMSEA > .099: refute metric invariance RMSEA > .059 < .1: **proceed to Steps 2 & 3** CFI < .95: refute metric invariance CFI > .97 > .94: **proceed to Steps 2 & 3** Else: **proceed to Step 2**	RMSEA > .099: refute scalar invariance RMSEA > .059 < .1: **proceed to Steps 2 & 3** CFI < .95: refute scalar invariance CFI > .97 > .94: **proceed to Steps 2 & 3** Else: **proceed to Step 2**

	Configural invariance	Metric invariance	Scalar invariance
Stepwise procedure, **Step 2**: Assessing model by group	GFI < .95: refute configural invariance GFI < .98 > .94: **proceed to Step 3** SRMR > .09: refute configural invariance SRMR > .06 < .10: **proceed to Step 3** Else: accept configural invariance	GFI < .95: refute metric invariance GFI < .98 > .94: **proceed to Step 3** SRMR > .09: refute metric invariance SRMR > .06 < .10: **proceed to Step 3** Else: accept metric invariance	GFI < .95: refute scalar invariance GFI < .98 > .94: **proceed to Step 3** SRMR > .09: refute scalar invariance SRMR > .06 < .10: **proceed to Step 3** Else: accept scalar invariance
Stepwise procedure, **Step 3**: Assessing model by indicator	Misspecifications in error terms: **proceed to Step 4** Else: accept configural invariance	Misspecifications in factor loadings: **proceed to Step 4** Else: accept metric invariance	Misspecifications in indicator intercepts: **proceed to Step 4** Else: accept scalar invariance
Stepwise procedure, **Step 4**: Establishing partial invariance	Aim for partial configural invariance by releasing constraints on misspecified error terms Repeat stepwise procedure	Aim for partial metric invariance by releasing constraints on misspecified factor loadings Repeat stepwise procedure	Aim for partial scalar invariance by releasing constraints on misspecified intercepts Repeat stepwise procedure

Appendix B

Results of longitudinal equivalence tests on the European Values Studies, 1981–2008

B.1   Basic model structure

Germany was split into 'East' and 'West,' as designed in the data. In the case of the U.K., the preferable choice would be to split the data in England & Wales, Scotland, and Northern Ireland (so three cases) because of the three different police systems. The EVS data have included two cases here: Great Britain and Northern Ireland. Scotland, unfortunately, has too few respondents to be split from England & Wales. I have retained Great Britain as a unit of analysis, including Scotland. This leaves us with a total of 28 countries for the analyses.

The reference year was 2008. The factor structure consisted of a single factor with five indicators of institutional trust: confidence in the army, police, parliament, civil servants, and justice agencies. However, preliminary analyses indicated that in order for the model to accurately reflect reality, two correlated error terms needed to be added: between confidence in the army and the police on the one hand, and between parliament and civil servants on the other. This indicated that within the factor structure of institutional trust, some institutions were more closely related. The factor loading for confidence in the justice system was fixed to one to set a scale for the factor loadings. In the three Baltic states, the factor structure was different, as only three indicators were included in the questionnaire: confidence in the army, the police, and the justice system. This led to a simpler factor structure with all three indicators loading on one construct, without correlated error terms. Again, confidence in the justice system had its factor loading set to one.

Figure B.1   Basic model structure, EVS

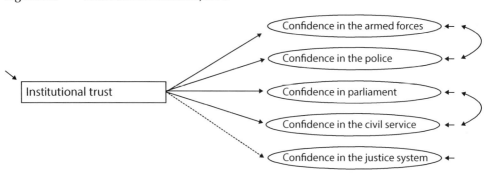

B.2   Longitudinal equivalence tests, EVS 1981–2008

This factor structure held across all years, meaning that configural invariance was established: respondents in different years of measurement within the same country had similar frames of reference regarding the constitution of institutional trust. This included confidence in the police.

The results of the metric and scalar invariance tests for each country are displayed in Table B.1. Contained are the χ-square value, the degrees of freedom of the model, and four fit indices (RMSEA, CFI, lowest GFI value, and highest SRMR value). If any of these four fit indices have values in the 'gray zone' (see Appendix A) or values that are clear indications of a <u>poorly fitting model</u> (again, see Appendix A), tests with J-rule were conducted to check for misspecifications in the model. In case of misspecifications, attempts were made to reach partial (metric or scalar) invariance by adjusting the model (see Table B.2). If partial invariance was reached and adjusting the model did not affect the indicator confidence in the police, measurements of confidence in the police in that country were still equivalent over time. If, however, partial invariance was reached only by adjusting the indicator confidence in the police in the model, measurements of confidence in the police were not equivalent over time: there is a likelihood that values of confidence in the police in that country cannot be validly compared over time. In this latter event, it is indicated in Table B.1 by emboldening and underlining the **<u>misspecification</u>**.

Based on the results presented in Tables B.1 and B.2, confidence in the police shows evidence of nonequivalence in Bulgaria (1990), Finland (1990), East Germany (1990), Malta (1981), and Poland (1990). In all other countries, levels of confidence in the police can validly be compared across different moments in time.

Table B.1   Results of longitudinal measurement equivalence tests, EVS 1981–2008

	Austria		Belgium		Bulgaria		Czech Republic		Denmark		Finland		France	
	Metric	Scalar	Metric	Scalar	Metric	Scalar	Metric	Scalar	Metric	Scalar	Metric	Scalar	Metric	Scalar
χ-square	25.01	107.98	72.66	274.92	63.36	305.72	22.95	342.03	37.96	292.65	52.43	47.22	53.85	191.19
df	17	25	24	36	17	23	17	25	24	36	17	14	24	36
RMSEA	0.019	0.049	0.034	**0.062**	0.053	**0.112**	0.014	**0.083**	0.023	**0.080**	0.050	0.049	0.032	**0.060**
CFI	1.00	0.99	1.00	0.98	0.99	**0.97**	1.00	0.98	1.00	**0.96**	0.99	0.99	1.00	0.98
Min GFI	0.99	0.99	0.99	0.99	**0.97**	**0.97**	1.00	1.00	0.99	0.99	**0.97**	0.99	0.98	**0.97**
Max SRMR	0.03	0.03	0.03	0.04	0.06	**0.08**	0.02	0.03	0.03	0.05	**0.07**	0.04	0.06	0.06
	no		no		1 missp	**2**	1 missp		no		**2**		no	
	missp		missp			**missp**		missp		missp		**missp**		missp

	East Germany		West Germany		Great Britain		Hungary		Iceland		Ireland		Italy	
	Metric	Scalar	Metric	Scalar	Metric	Scalar	Metric	Scalar	Metric	Scalar	Metric	Scalar	Metric	Scalar
χ-square	91.32	519.07	79.89	256.47	91.85	410.34	43.12	167.90	45.37	294.96	62.28	316.56	117.40	453.44
df	17	25	24	34	24	36	17	25	17	25	24	36	24	36
RMSEA	**0.066**	**0.127**	0.042	**0.070**	0.049	**0.093**	0.037	**0.072**	0.047	**0.118**	0.040	**0.089**	0.049	**0.084**
CFI	0.99	**0.92**	1.00	0.98	0.99	**0.95**	1.00	0.98	0.99	**0.91**	1.00	**0.97**	0.99	**0.97**
Min GFI	**0.97**	**0.95**	**0.97**	0.98	0.98	**0.97**	0.99	0.98	0.98	**0.97**	**0.97**	**0.97**	0.98	0.98
Max SRMR	0.06	**0.10**	**0.07**	0.06	0.06	**0.07**	0.04	0.04	0.05	0.05	0.05	0.05	**0.07**	**0.07**
	no	**1**	no		1 missp	**2**	no		1 missp		no	1 missp	no	
	missp	**missp**	missp			**missp**	missp		missp		missp		missp	

	Malta		Netherlands		Northern Ireland		Norway		Poland		Portugal		Romania	
	Metric	Scalar	Metric	Scalar	Metric	Scalar	Metric	Scalar	Metric	Scalar	Metric	Scalar	Metric	Scalar
x-square	62.47	168.01	36.32	159.34	31.37	78.77	34.43	72.26	48.63	603.48	31.13	212.22	42.16	169.19
df	24	25	24	36	24	36	17	25	17	25	17	25	17	25
RMSEA	0.047	**0.082**	0.021	0.055	0.026	0.051	0.030	0.041	0.043	**0.151**	0.028	**0.083**	0.036	**0.071**
CFI	1.00	0.98	1.00	0.98	1.00	0.99	1.00	0.99	1.00	**0.91**	1.00	0.98	1.00	0.98
Min GFI	**0.93**	0.99	0.99	0.99	0.98	**0.97**	0.99	0.99	0.98	**0.92**	0.99	0.99	0.98	0.98
Max SRMR	**0.13**	0.04	0.04	0.05	0.06	**0.07**	0.04	0.04	0.05	**0.08**	0.04	0.05	0.04	0.05
missp	**2 missp**		**1 missp**		no missp				**2 missp**		no missp		no missp	

	Slovakia		Slovenia		Spain		Sweden	
	Metric	Scalar	Metric	Scalar	Metric	Scalar	Metric	Scalar
x-square	18.36	211.05	19.97	107.14	132.91	418.90	38.34	97.26
df	17	24	17	24	24	36	24	36
RMSEA	0.008	**0.080**	0.013	0.054	0.051	**0.078**	0.026	0.044
CFI	1.00	0.98	1.00	0.99	0.99	0.98	1.00	0.99
Min GFI	0.99	0.99	0.99	0.99	0.98	0.98	0.99	0.98
Max SRMR	0.03	0.03	0.04	0.05	0.04	0.03	0.06	0.06
missp	1 missp				no missp			

Table B.2   Partial invariance tests on misspecified models, EVS 1981–2008

	Bulgaria	Bulgaria	Czech Republic	Finland	East Germany	West Germany	Great Britain	Iceland	Ireland	Malta	Poland	Slovakia
	Metric2	Scalar2	Scalar2	Metric2	Scalar2	Metric2	Scalar2	Scalar2	Scalar2	Metric2	Scalar2	Scalar2
Year adjusted	1990	1990	1990	1990	1990	2008	2008	2008	1999	1981	1990	1990
Action	LY 4 1	removed	TY 3	removed	TY 1	ref 1990, LY 3 1	ref 1999, TY 1	ref 1999, TY 3	TY 3	removed	removed	TY 5
X-square	52.83	128.75	129.48	26.84	278.29	58.25	255.54	157.32	229.61	21.83	95.44	94.82
df	16	14	24	10	29	23	35	24	35	17	14	24
RMSEA	0.048	**0.092**	0.049	0.041	**0.092**	0.034	**0.072**	**0.085**	**0.075**	0.018	0.072	0.051
CFI	1.00	0.98	0.99	1.00	**0.95**	1.00	**0.97**	**0.96**	0.98	1.00	0.98	0.99
Min GFI	0.98	0.98	0.99	0.99	**0.95**	0.98	0.98	0.98	**0.97**	0.99	0.98	0.99
Max SRMR	0.05	0.04	0.03	0.04	**0.09**	0.06	0.06	0.05	0.05	0.03	0.03	0.03

B.3   Longitudinal equivalence tests, EVS 1981–2008, on the Baltic states

Figure B.2   Basic model structure, EVS, for the Baltic states

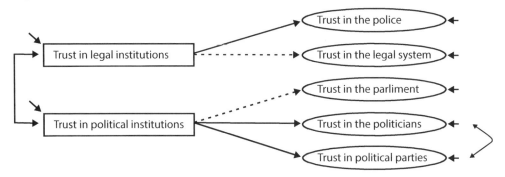

The results displayed in Table B.3 show that while there were indications of poor model fit, and even several misspecifications in each country, these did not affect confidence in the police. Measurement equivalence of confidence in the police is hence reached for these three countries.

Table B.3   Results of longitudinal measurement equivalence tests, EVS 1981–2008, Baltic states

	Estonia		Latvia		Lithuania	
	Metric	Scalar	Metric	Scalar	Metric	Scalar
χ-square	8.71	200.50	18.31	307.97	5.98	268
df	4	8	4	7	4	8
RMSEA	*0.033*	***0.149***	***0.060***	***0.186***	*0.023*	***0.183***
CFI	*1.00*	***0.90***	*0.99*	***0.87***	*1.00*	***0.85***
Min GFI	*0.99*	*0.98*	*0.99*	*0.99*	*1.00*	*0.99*
Max SRMR	*0.03*	*0.06*	*0.06*	*0.06*	*0.04*	*0.05*
		2 misspecs	1 misspec	2 misspecs		2 misspecs

Table B.4   **Partial invariance tests on misspecified models, EVS 1981–2008, Baltic states**

	Estonia	Latvia	Latvia	Lithuania
	scalar2	metric2	scalar2	scalar2
Year adjusted	1990; 2008	1990	1990	1990
Action	ref 1999, TY3; TY1	TE 1 3	TY1; TY3	TY1; TY3
χ-square	60.79	2.95	35.46	7.27
df	6	3	5	6
RMSEA	***0.092***	*0.000*	***0.078***	*0.015*
CFI	*0.97*	*1.00*	*0.98*	*1.00*
Min GFI	*0.99*	*1.00*	*1.00*	*1.00*
Max SRMR	*0.04*	*0.02*	*0.04*	*0.04*

B.4   *Cross-national EVS measurement equivalence results*

I conducted measurement equivalence tests on EVS data cross-nationally as well, to see to what extent we can compare mean levels of confidence in the police in different countries at the same moment in time. I included 25 countries (without the three Baltic states, due to the different factor structure). 13 were included in 1981 (Belgium was the reference country for configural and metric invariance, the Netherlands for scalar), 25 in 1990, 24 in 1999, and 25 in 2008. In the latter three waves, Austria was the reference country. I have not included the number of misspecifications that were found in each year, since this number was simply too high.

Table B.5   Results of cross-nationally comparative measurement equivalence tests, EVS 1981–2008

	1981			1990			1999			2008		
	Configu-ral	Metric	Scalar	Configu-ral	Metric	Scalar	Configu-ral	Metric	Scalar	Configu-ral	Metric	Scalar
X-square	138.41	367.82	1613.94	173.10	548.76	4723.05	178.68	529.23	3405.43	169.85	568.90	3455.42
df	39	87	121	75	171	249	72	164	244	75	171	251
RMSEA	0.049	0.055	**0.108**	0.033	0.043	**0.122**	0.037	0.046	**0.110**	0.032	0.044	**0.103**
CFI	1.00	0.99	**0.96**	1.00	0.99	**0.93**	1.00	0.99	**0.94**	1.00	0.99	**0.95**
Min GFI	**0.96**	**0.91**	**0.93**	0.98	**0.96**	**0.89**	0.97	**0.96**	**0.94**	0.98	**0.96**	0.97
Max SRMR	0.04	**0.15**	**0.07**	0.03	**0.10**	**0.09**	0.04	**0.11**	**0.08**	0.03	**0.10**	0.06

Table B.6 features the countries that show evidence of noninvariance in a comparative equivalence test for each wave included in the EVS, either in the stage of metric invariance (Me) or scalar invariance (Sc). Bold and underlined type mean that confidence in the police is nonequivalent—or confidence in the army, which has correlated error terms with confidence in the police. Those entries that are not bold and underlined are countries where noninvariance does not affect confidence in the police. Clearly, a large number of countries in each wave (between a third and half) show evidence of noninvariance. This makes cross-national comparisons of mean levels of confidence based on EVS data run high risks of being invalid.

Table B.6   Noninvariant countries in cross-nationally comparative measurement equivalence tests, EVS 1981–2008

1981	1990	1999	2008
Denmark (Me)	Bulgaria (Me, Sc)	East Germany (Me)	East Germany (Me)
Great Britain (Sc)	Denmark (Sc)	Finland (Sc)	West Germany (Me)
Malta (Me, Sc)	East Germany (Sc)	Great Britain (Sc)	Finland (Me)
Norway (Me, Sc)	Finland (Me)	Iceland (Me)	Great Britain (Me, Sc)
Sweden (Me)	Great Britain (Sc)	Ireland (Sc)	Iceland (Sc)
	Iceland (Sc)	Northern Ireland (Me)	Malta (Me, Sc)
	Ireland (Sc)	Romania (Sc)	Portugal (Me, Sc)
	Italy (Sc)	Slovakia (Sc)	Romania (Me)
	Malta (Me)	Slovenia (Me)	Slovakia (Sc)
	Northern Ireland (Me)		Sweden (Sc)
	Norway (Me)		
	Poland (Sc)		
	Romania (Sc)		

Appendix C

Results of longitudinal equivalence tests on the European Social Survey, 2004–2014

The same approach was followed as for the longitudinal equivalence tests on the EVS data (see Appendix B), applying the general methodology explained in Appendix A. Twenty-nine countries were analyzed. The U.K. is included as a single case in the original data; I have split Scotland from the rest and removed all respondents from Northern Ireland: this is because of the vastly different history and structure of the police there. Equivalence tests could only be conducted for 2004–2014: I had to exclude 2002 because the question about trust in political parties was not asked at that time. The same factor structure was hence not present in that year. As a result, we have no information on the validity of comparisons between 2002 and other years. The reference year was selected as 2014. If not available, the most recent year was used as the reference year. The most applicable structural equation model was a two-factor structure, with the police and the legal system forming trust in legal institutions, and parliament, politicians, and political parties forming trust in political institutions. There are correlated error terms between the latter two indicators.

Figure C.1   Basic model structure, ESS

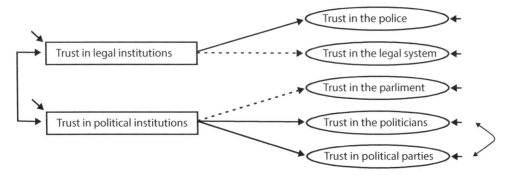

The same procedure was followed as in Appendix B. The results of the metric and scalar invariance tests for each country are displayed in Table C.1. Contained are the χ-square value, the degrees of freedom of the model, and four fit indices (RMSEA, CFI, lowest GFI value, and highest SRMR value). If any of these four fit indices have values in the 'gray zone' (see Appendix A) or values that are clear indications of a poorly fitting model (again, see Appendix A), tests with J-rule were conducted to check for misspecifications in the model. In case of misspecifications, attempts were made to reach partial (metric or scalar) invariance by adjusting the model (see Table C.2). If partial invariance was reached and adjusting the model did not affect the indicator trust in the police, measurements of trust in the police in that country were still equivalent over time. If, however, partial invariance was reached only by adjusting the indicator trust in the police in the model, measurements of trust in the police were not equivalent over time: there is a likelihood that values of trust in the police in that country cannot be validly compared over time. In this latter event, this is indicated in Table C.1 by emboldening and underlining the **misspecification**.

Based on the results presented in Tables C.1 and C.2, trust in the police shows evidence of nonequivalence in Slovenia (2004, 2006, 2008, 2012), Spain (2006), and Ukraine (2004). In all other countries, levels of trust in the police can validly be compared across different moments in time. Spain was an exceptional case in that its violation of invariance in 2004 could be found in the configural invariance stage, rather than the more stringent metric or scalar phases. Results from the configural invariance tests are otherwise not displayed in the tables as, with this sole exception, their results tend to be quite satisfactory.

Table C.1   Results of longitudinal equivalence tests, ESS 2004–2014

	Austria		Belgium		Bulgaria		Cyprus		Czech Rep.		Denmark		England & Wales	
	Metric	Scalar	Metric	Scalar	Metric	Scalar	Metric	Scalar	Metric	Scalar	Metric	Scalar	Metric	Scalar
X-square	78.07	231.37	118.25	188.19	81.01	136.03	116.80	187.94	129.41	409.98	113.41	222.44	131.74	183.23
df	15	21	33	48	21	30	21	30	27	39	33	48	33	48
RMSEA	0.046	**0.070**	0.038	0.041	0.039	0.043	**0.067**	**0.072**	0.041	**0.066**	0.040	0.049	0.040	0.039
CFI	1.00	0.99	1.00	1.00	1.00	1.00	0.99	0.99	1.00	0.99	1.00	0.99	1.00	1.00
Min. GFI	0.99	0.99	0.99	0.99	0.99	0.99	0.98	0.98	0.99	0.99	0.99	0.99	0.99	0.99
Max. SRMR	0.03	0.03	0.03	0.03	0.04	0.04	0.03	0.04	0.04	0.04	0.02	0.02	0.03	0.03
	no	missp					no	missp	no	missp				

	Estonia		Finland		France		East Germany		West Germany		Greece		Hungary	
	Metric	Scalar	Metric	Scalar	Metric	Scalar	Metric	Scalar	Metric	Scalar	Metric	Scalar	Metric	Scalar
X-square	113.16	304.48	78.30	106.83	145.95	251.97	66.62	105.69	79.98	136.88	116.75	300.43	193.41	310.30
df	33	48	33	48	33	48	33	48	33	48	15	21	33	48
RMSEA	0.038	0.056	0.026	0.025	0.043	0.048	0.032	0.035	0.028	0.032	0.054	**0.075**	0.056	**0.060**
CFI	1.00	0.99	1.00	1.00	1.00	0.99	1.00	1.00	1.00	1.00	1.00	0.99	1.00	0.99
Min. GFI	0.99	0.99	0.99	0.99	0.99	0.99	0.99	0.99	1.00	1.00	0.99	1.00	0.99	0.99
Max. SRMR	0.03	0.03	0.02	0.02	0.03	0.03	0.03	0.03	0.02	0.02	0.05	0.02	0.05	0.05
	no	missp									no	missp	no	missp

	Ireland		Israel		Lithuania		Netherlands		Norway		Poland		Portugal	
	Metric	Scalar	Metric	Scalar	Metric	Scalar	Metric	Scalar	Metric	Scalar	Metric	Scalar	Metric	Scalar
X-square	167.77	349.52	304.80	381.37	130.28	251.53	155.00	291.47	130.86	320.90	80.78	137.89	115.02	474.33
df	33	48	21	30	21	30	33	48	33	48	33	48	33	48
RMSEA	0.044	0.055	**0.077**	**0.072**	0.053	**0.063**	0.045	0.053	0.043	**0.060**	0.030	0.034	0.036	**0.069**
CFI	1.00	0.99	0.99	0.99	1.00	0.99	1.00	0.99	1.00	0.99	1.00	1.00	1.00	0.99
Min. GFI	0.99	0.99	0.98	0.98	0.99	0.98	0.99	0.99	0.99	0.99	1.00	1.00	0.99	0.99
Max. SRMR	0.04	0.04	0.03	0.03	0.03	0.03	0.02	0.02	0.03	0.04	0.02	0.03	0.04	0.04
SRMR			no missp		no missp				no missp				no missp	

	Russia		Scotland		Slovakia		Slovenia		Spain		Sweden		Switzerland	
	Metric	Scalar	Metric	Scalar	Metric	Scalar	Metric	Scalar	Metric	Scalar	Metric	Scalar	Metric	Scalar
X-square	278.31	351.36	40.15	78.77	140.23	199.94	113.07	629.07	120.36	428.10	119.98	138.64	113.04	153.13
df	21	30	33	48	27	39	33	48	33	48	33	48	33	48
RMSEA	**0.075**	**0.071**	0.033	0.057	0.050	0.050	0.044	**0.099**	0.038	**0.066**	0.039	0.033	0.039	0.037
CFI	0.99	0.99	1.00	0.99	1.00	1.00	1.00	0.98	1.00	0.99	1.00	1.00	1.00	1.00
Min. GFI	0.98	0.98	**0.97**	**0.97**	0.99	0.99	0.99	0.99	0.99	0.99	0.99	0.99	0.99	0.99
Max. SRMR	0.02	0.02	0.03	0.03	0.03	0.03	0.04	0.05	0.04	0.05	0.02	0.02	0.03	0.02
SRMR	no missp		no missp				**missp**		missp					

	Ukraine	
	Metric	Scalar
χ-square	225.20	319.07
df	27	37
RMSEA	**0.065**	**0.066**
CFI	0.99	0.99
Min. GFI	**0.97**	0.98
Max. SRMR	0.05	0.03
	missp	no missp

Table C.2   **Partial invariance tests on misspecified models, ESS 2004–2014**

	Slovenia	Spain	Ukraine
	Scalar2	Configural2	Metric2
Year adjusted	2004, 2006, 2008, 2012	2006	2004
Action	**TY 2**	**TY 2**	**LY 3 2**
χ-square	174.24	330.98	194.59
df	44	47	26
RMSEA	0.049	0.058	**0.061**
CFI	1.00	0.99	1.00
Min. GFI	0.99	0.99	0.98
Max. SRMR	0.05	0.05	0.03
			no missp

APPENDIX D

Results of cross-national equivalence tests, ESS 2010

This appendix displays the results of cross-national measurement equivalence tests, conducted on 28 countries in the 2010 data wave. Belgium was selected as the reference country. The factor structure was the same as in the longitudinal ESS measurement equivalence tests (see Figure C.1): a two-factor structure, with the police and the legal system forming trust in legal institutions, and parliament, politicians, and political parties forming trust in political institutions. There are correlated error terms between the latter two indicators.

The same procedure was followed as in Appendices B and C. The results of the metric and scalar invariance tests for each country are displayed in Table D.1. Contained are the χ-square value, the degrees of freedom of the model, and four fit indices (RMSEA, CFI, lowest GFI value, and highest SRMR value). If any of these four fit indices have values in the 'gray zone' (see Appendix A) or values that are clear indications of a poorly fitting model (again, see Appendix A), tests with J-rule were conducted to check for misspecifications in the model. In case of misspecifications, attempts were made to reach partial (metric or scalar) invariance by adjusting the model (see Table D.2). If partial invariance was reached and adjusting the model did not affect the indicator trust in the police, the measurement of trust in the police was still equivalent for that country. If, however, partial invariance was reached only by adjusting the indicator trust in the police in the model, measurements of trust in the police were not equivalent for that country.

As is shown in Table D.2, measurement equivalence was not reached for a limited number of countries. Metric invariance was not reached for Bulgaria, Cyprus, Finland, Russia, and Ukraine (in all cases, the misspecification in the model was trust in the police). Scalar invariance was not reached for Spain and Israel (trust in the police was again misspecified). In the Netherlands, trust in parliament was noninvariant. As this did not affect trust in the police, measurements of trust in the police are still equivalent for the Netherlands. In all other countries, the results of these measurement equivalence tests on the ESS 2010 wave indicated that trust in the police can be compared validly.

Table D.1   Results of cross-national equivalence tests, ESS 2010

	Configural	Metric	Scalar
χ-square	538.15	1315.32	4537.85
df	84	165	236
RMSEA	0.056	**0.064**	**0.104**
CFI	1.00	0.99	**0.97**
Min. GFI	**0.97**	**0.96**	**0.96**
Max. SRMR	0.02	**0.07**	0.06
	no missp	**missp**	**missp**

Table D.2   Partial invariance tests on misspecified models, ESS 2010

	Metric2	Scalar2
Countries adjusted	BG, CY, FI, RU, UA	ES, IL, NL
Action	LY 1 1 (all)	TY 1 (ES, IL), TY 3 (ES, NL)
χ-square	932.56	2879.51
df	160	232
RMSEA	0.053	**0.082**
CFI	1.00	0.98
Min GFI	**0.97**	**0.96**
Max SRMR	0.06	0.06
	no missp	no missp

Appendix E

Developments in levels of trust in different institutions, EVS and ESS

Table E.1   Trends in levels of confidence, EVS 1990-2008. Countries with nonequivalent years marked bold

	Strong increase, ≥ .30	Weak increase, .10 to .30	About equal, .10 to -.10	Weak decrease, -.10 to -.30	Strong decrease, ≤ -.30
Armed forces	*Latvia (1.00)*	Spain (.28)		Sweden (-.13)	Northern Ireland (-.35)
	Estonia (.90)	Slovenia (.26)		Norway (-.14)	*Bulgaria (-.59)*
	Malta (.80)	Slovakia (.17)		Poland (-.18)	
	East Germany (.78)	Austria (.16)		Romania (-.19)	
	Lithuania (.67)	Ireland (.14)		Czech Republic (-.20)	
	Italy (.58)			Hungary (-.27)	
	Iceland (.53)*				
	Finland (.42)				
	Portugal (.37)				
	France (.36)				
	Netherlands (.36)				
	Belgium (.35)				
	Denmark (.35)				
	West Germany (.33)				
	Great Britain (.30)				
Police	*Estonia (.87)*	Belgium (.26)	Slovenia (.09)	Great Britain (-.14)	Ireland (-.40)
	Latvia (.58)	Italy (.20)	Denmark (-.02)		*Bulgaria (-.41)*
	Malta (.58)	Spain (.20)	Austria (-.04)		Northern Ireland (-.45)
	Finland (.56)	France (.19)	Hungary (-.04);		
	Portugal (.49)	Romania (.14)	Norway (-.04)		
	East Germany (.35)	Lithuania (.12)	Sweden (-.04)		
	Iceland (.34)	Slovakia (.11)	Netherlands (-.06)		
	Poland (.30)	West Germany (.11)	Czech Republic (-.07)		

	Strong increase, ≥ .30	Weak increase, .10 to .30	About equal, .10 to -.10	Weak decrease, -.10 to -.30	Strong decrease, ≤ -.30
Parliament†	Denmark (.39)	Malta (.26)	*Finland (.09)*	*East Germany (-.12)*	*West Germany (-.30)*
		Slovakia (.26)	Spain (.09)	*Ireland (-.13)*	Northern Ireland (-.32)
		Romania (.12)	Slovenia (.08)	*Iceland (-.18)*	Hungary (-.38)
		Sweden (.11)	France (.07)	Austria (-.24)	Great Britain (-.44)
			Italy (.07)		*Czech Republic (-.57)*
			Netherlands (.05)		*Poland (-1.02)*
			Norway (.04)		*Bulgaria (-1.11)*
			Portugal (.00)		
			Belgium (-.02)		
Civil service†		Malta (.29)	Portugal (.07)	Netherlands (-.10)	*Bulgaria (-.31)*
		Italy (.28)	Slovenia (.06)	Great Britain (-.11)	
		East Germany (.20)	Sweden (.03)	Czech Republic (-.12)	
		Denmark (.18)	Romania (.02)	Northern Ireland (-.13)	
		France (.18)	Ireland (-.05)	Hungary (-.14)	
		Slovakia (.18)	Austria (-.08)	Poland (-.20)	
		Belgium (.17)	West Germany (-.08)		
		Iceland (.17)			
		Norway (.13)			
		Spain (.12)			
		Finland (.10)			

	Strong increase, ≥ .30	Weak increase, .10 to .30	About equal, .10 to -.10	Weak decrease, -.10 to -.30	Strong decrease, ≤ -.30
Justice system		*Estonia (.28)*	Italy (.09)	Ireland (-.10)	*Slovakia (-.31)*
		Denmark (.10)	*Finland (.08)*	West Germany (-.11)	Czech Republic (-.33)
		Sweden (.10)	Great Britain (.08)	Netherlands (-.16)	*Poland (-.34)*
			Belgium (.06)	Slovenia (-.19)	Hungary (-.39)
			Latvia (.06)	Romania (-.24)	Northern Ireland (-.39)
			Austria (.05)	*Lithuania (-.25)*	*Bulgaria (-.86)*
			Iceland (.05)		
			France (.00)		
			Norway (-.01)		
			Malta (-.02)		
			East Germany (-.03)		
			Portugal (-.07)		
			Spain (-.08)		

*Curiously, Iceland has no armed forces.

† Questions about trust in parliament and the civil service were not asked in the three Baltic countries

Table E.2   Trends in levels of trust, ESS 2002–2014 (0–10 scale). Countries with nonequivalent years marked bold

	Strong increase, ≥ .40	Weak increase, .15 to .40	About equal .15 to -.15	Weak decrease, -.15 tc -.40	Strong decrease, ≤ -.40
Police	Lithuania (1.19) ***Spain (.90)*** Czech Republic (.69) Portugal (.66) ***Slovenia (.63)*** Netherlands (.60) Hungary (.42)	Estonia (.43) Belgium (.38) Norway (.37) Switzerland (.35) England & Wales (.23) France (.22) Poland (.21) Russia (.17)	East Germany (.13) Sweden (.11) Austria (.08) Scotland (.06) West Germany (.04) Finland (-.05)	Slovakia (-.16) Denmark (-.21) Bulgaria (-.24) Ireland (-.27)	Cyprus (-.62) ***Ukraine (-1.11)*** Israel (-1.41) Greece (-1.77)
Parliament	Norway (1.04) Lithuania (.95) West Germany (.63) East Germany (.58) Switzerland (.46)	Sweden (.32) Czech Republic (.25) Estonia (.24)	Slovakia (.12) Russia (.08) Netherlands (.01) Bulgaria (-.06)	Belgium (-.15) Finland (-.23) Denmark (-.26) England & Wales (-.26)	Austria (-.48) France (-.49) Israel (-.54) Ireland (-.66) Poland (-.68) Spain (-.97) Scotland (-1.03) Portugal (-1.15) Hungary (-1.16) Slovenia (-1.29) Cyprus (-2.29) Ukraine (-2.46) Greece (-2.76)
Politicians	Lithuania (.97) Norway (.67) West Germany (.40)	East Germany (.36) Switzerland (.35) Sweden (.28)	Russia (.08) Czech Republic (.06) Netherlands (.01)	England & Wales (-.27) Israel (-.31)	Ireland (-.43) Denmark (-.53) Poland (-.68)

	Strong increase, ≥ .40	Weak increase, .15 to .40	About equal .15 to -.15	Weak decrease, -.15 to -.40	Strong decrease, ≤ -.40
		Slovakia (.23) Estonia (.22)	Bulgaria (-.01) Austria (-.08) Belgium (-.14)		Scotland (-.76) Portugal (-.78) Hungary (-.92) Spain (-1.11) Slovenia (-1.16) Ukraine (-1.68) Cyprus (-1.76) Greece (-2.05)
Legal system	Lithuania (1.10) Czech Republic (.88) Norway (.86) Belgium (.63) Netherlands (.57) England & Wales (.53) Switzerland (.42)	Estonia (.35) Scotland (.33) Sweden (.32) France (.29) Denmark (.28) East Germany (.18)	Ireland (.11) West Germany (.10) Finland (.01) Poland (-.12)	Russia (-.16) ***Spain (-.16)*** Bulgaria (-.21) Slovakia (-.33)	Austria (-.47) Hungary (-.47) Portugal (-.57) Israel (-1.12) ***Slovenia (-1.16)*** Cyprus (-1.33) ***Ukraine (-1.75)*** Greece (-2.49)

Appendix F

The proximity policing index: Development and robustness checks

F.1   Questionnaire development

Eighty requests were sent to experts in 24 countries between April and June 2013. It is noteworthy that several informants did not consider themselves to be well enough acquainted with the state of affairs to complete the questionnaire; most of these were kind enough to suggest a colleague instead. I received 46 completed questionnaires, which, discounting those who forwarded the request to someone else, meant a 69% response rate.[1]

The introductory text to the survey was clear that the inquiry concerned the situation in about 2010, which is when the survey data on the comparative study were collected. Hence, the analysis concerned the degree to which countries adhered to proximity policing principles in the same year as when our main data were collected. Questions were phrased in terms of community policing since, internationally, that is the more recognized term.

To avoid bias, I gave preference to informants not currently part of the police organization or a branch of government. With three exceptions (Portugal, Slovakia, and Switzerland), this resulted in two or more completed surveys per country. Completed questionnaires were compared to existing scientific literature on the subject in that country (if available) and with other completed questionnaires for the same country (also if available). In the case of strong discrepancies, additional queries were sent through e-mail to find out what caused the differences in assessments. This led to the removal of one completed questionnaire, as the informant— employed at a Ministry of Internal Affairs—indicated in informal personal communication that the results were in reality far less positive in terms of proximity policing than the formal record of the survey suggested. In some other cases—for instance, where the literature clearly aligned with one informant against another from the same country—this meant that I followed the score of one of the experts

---

1.   Due to equivalence issues surfacing after initial data collection, the 24 initial countries were reduced to 21.

for that particular indicator, discounting the other. In most cases, however, I interpreted the (usually small) differences in scores between experts in the same country as genuine differences in assessment, and used the mean score of the different informants as final score.

In one country, Slovakia, I managed to receive only one completed questionnaire, which was from an internal police source. Unlike the other two countries that yielded only a single questionnaire, Portugal and Switzerland, I had no scientific literature with which to compare it. Moreover, results from other countries had indicated that government or police officials often evaluated proximity policing in their country more positively than experts from the scientific community. Taking this into consideration, I imputed the proximity policing score for Slovakia with the mean of the other neighboring Visegrád countries (the Czech Republic, Hungary, and Poland).

The questionnaire is included below.

Proximity policing questions:
1. **To what extent do you consider the police in your country to adhere to the principles of community-oriented policing?**
   To a large extent
   To some extent
   To little extent
   To virtually no extent
2. **To what extent is the police organization in your country centralized?**
   Centralized refers to a lot of central management and little autonomy for regions and municipalities.
   A great deal
   Somewhat
   Not so much
   Not at all
3. **To what extent are there police officers and/or units in your country whose main focus is on the needs of local communities or neighborhoods?**
   To a large extent
   To some extent
   To little extent
   To virtually no extent
4. **Do individual street-level police officers in your country have a large discretionary autonomy, or do they mostly have to adhere to standardized procedures and rules?**
   Large autonomy
   Some autonomy
   Not so much autonomy
   Hardly any autonomy

5. **Do neighborhoods and local communities in your country usually have their own police station or (part-time) office?**
    Almost always
    Often
    Sometimes
    Never or almost never
6. **To what extent do the local police in your country concentrate on a broad range of local problems besides crime, such as nuisances, social disorder, and feelings of insecurity among citizens?**
    A great deal
    Somewhat
    Not so much
    Not at all
7. **To what extent do the local police in your country consider it important to focus on preventing crime and disorder rather than merely reacting to them?**
    A great deal
    Somewhat
    Not so much
    Not at all
8. **To what extent do the police in your country cooperate with public and private agencies in dealing with crime and disorder at the level of local communities?**
    A great deal
    Somewhat
    Not so much
    Not at all
9. **To what extent do the police in your country have a policy of promoting citizen involvement in reducing crime and disorder in their local communities?**
    A great deal
    Somewhat
    Not so much
    Not at all
10. **To what extent do you consider the police in your country to be responsive to citizen demands and sensitive to their complaints or feedback?**
    A great deal
    Somewhat
    Not so much
    Not at all

These indicators cover the core elements of proximity policing. Indicator 1 is a general, global assessment of community policing. Indicators 2-5 probe to what extent the organizational and legal structure is conducive to proximity policing practice.

Of those organizational indicators, items 3 and 5 correspond to Terpstra's (2010) first core principle of community policing, which entails that the police concentrate on the level of communities and neighborhoods and do so by being approachable and visible, operating in close proximity to citizens.

Indicators 6-9 offer operationalizations of the other four core principles outlined by Terpstra (2010): focusing on a broad range of problems, emphasizing preventive strategies, cooperating with public and private agencies, and working with citizens as well as promoting citizen involvement, respectively. Indicator 10 is again a more global assessment testing a core assumption of proximity policing models: taking citizens' demands as central to policing.

Table F.1 contains the scores on the proximity policing index. The original 1-4 scale was recoded to a 0-3 scale. This composite index of proximity policing consists of the mean of all indicators. The values of all but the second indicator were reversed, so that a higher score implied greater adherence to proximity policing principles.

Table F.1   Countries' scores on the proximity policing index, 2010

Country	Score
Belgium	2.15
Croatia	1.90
Czech Rep.	1.50
Denmark	1.75
England & Wales	2.25
Estonia	1.80
France	.89
East Germany	1.43
West Germany	1.60
Greece	1.18
Hungary	.40
Ireland	1.87
Netherlands	1.90
Norway	1.95
Poland	1.70
Portugal	1.50
Scotland	2.55
Slovakia	1.20
Slovenia	1.93
Sweden	1.95
Switzerland	1.60

The findings from the survey were compared to existing literature on the subject, as displayed in Table F.2. In most cases, this did not result in any adjustment to the proximity index score, but in some cases it did.

Table F.2   The proximity policing literature used per country

Country	References
Belgium	Devroe & Ponsaers, 2013; Easton et al., 2009, Easton & Ponsaers, 2010; Ponsaers & Easton, 2008
Croatia	Kutnjak Ivković, 2000; Kutnjak Ivković,& Haberfeld, 2000
Czech Republic	AEPC, 2001a; Crow et al., 2004; Foltin et al., 2013; Jenks et al., 2003
Denmark	Balvig et al., 2011; Holmberg, 2002, 2005; Kruize & Jochoms, 2009
England & Wales	Cassan, 2010; Innes, 2005; Millie & Herrington, 2004; Myhill & Quinton, 2010; Tuffin et al., 2006
Estonia	AEPC, 2001b; Hilborn & Leps, 2005
France	Cassan, 2010; Dupont, 2007; Fassin, 2013; Mouhanna, 2013
East Germany	Feltes, 2002, 2014; Feltes et al., 2013; Marín, 2011
West Germany	Feltes, 2002, 2014; Feltes et al., 2013; Frevel & Kuschewski, 2013; Liedenbaum, 2011
Greece	Lambropoulou, 2004; Papanicolaou, 2006; Rigakos & Papanicolaou, 2003
Hungary	AEPC, 2001c; Dimovné, 2004; Kerezsi & Lévay, 2008
Ireland	Ellison & Smyth, 2000; Mulcahy, 2007; Mulcahy & O'Mahony, 2005; Walsh, 2009
Netherlands	Fijnaut, 2007; Liedenbaum, 2011; Punch et al., 2002; Terpstra, 2004, 2008, 2010
Norway	Das & Robinson, 2001; Holmberg, 2005; Larsson, 2010
Poland	AEPC, 2001d; Haberfeld et al., 2002; Krajewski, 2004; Kutnjak Ivković & Haberfeld, 2000
Portugal	Durão, 2011a,b
Scotland	Donnelly & Scott, 2002a,b; Fyfe & Scott, 2013; Mackenzie & Henry, 2009; Scott, 2011
Slovakia	AEPC, 2001g
Slovenia	AEPC, 2001e; Meško & Lobnikar, 2005; Meško et al., 2005, 2013
Sweden	Andersson & Tengblad, 2009; Björk, 2005; Holmberg, 2005; Peterson, 2010
Switzerland	Kreis, 2012; Wisler, 2008

F.2   Robustness checks in the analyses

Robustness checks of the effects of the different indicators comprising the proximity policing index were conducted: first, to observe whether some indicators had different effects from others; and, second, to test the extent to which removal of clusters of countries affected the general effects of the index. Neither of the two gave cause for concern.

Table F.3   Robustness checks for the proximity policing indicators and their relation-
               ship with trust

N = 34,622	Model Prox-a		Model Prox-b		Model Prox-c		Model Prox-d	
	B	s.e.	B	s.e.	B	s.e.	B	s.e.
Proximity police index	.35	*.17*	-.05	*.07*	-.07	*.07*	-.11*	*.05*
Prox1	.31	*.28*	-.13	*.11*	-.15	*.11*	-.16*	*.08*
Prox2	.46*	*.20*	.14*	*.07*	.16*	*.07*	.06	*.06*
Prox3	.10	*.28*	-.05	*.10*	-.10	*.10*	-.11	*.07*
Prox4	.43*	*.24*	-.15	*.11*	-.16	*.11*	-.15*	*.08*
Prox5	-.15	*.27*	-.15*	*.10*	-.22*	*.09*	-.15*	*.07*
Prox6	.33	*.34*	-.02	*.13*	-.04	*.13*	-.11	*.09*
Prox7	.38	*.31*	.03	*.12*	-.02	*.12*	-.08	*.08*
Prox8	.35	*.37*	-.06	*.14*	-.07	*.14*	-.20*	*.09*
Prox9	.29	*.27*	-.14	*.10*	-.15	*.10*	-.18**	*.06*
Prox10	.44	*.27*	-.10	*.12*	-.14	*.12*	-.20*	*.08*

a: only proximity policing indicator as determinant
b: all country-level indicators as determinants
c: background individual characteristics included
d: full model

Table F.4   Robustness checks for the proximity policing index and different clusters
               of countries

Proximity police index	Model Prox-d	
N = 34,622	B	s.e.
Without continental Western Europe	-.13**	*.05*
Without British Isles	-.14*	*.06*
Without Eastern Europe	-.10	*.07*
Without former Yugoslav states	-.10*	*.05*
Without Nordic countries	-.12**	*.05*
Without Mediterranean countries	-.11*	*.05*

Appendix G

1. What does career of informant look like? To what extent personally involved in trust-building or the study of trust?
2. When have subjects such as legitimacy or trust first made it to the societal agenda?
   a. When on the police agenda?
   b. When on the governmental agenda?
3. Do the police have the feeling there is a lack of trust and/or legitimacy?
   a. In what words and concepts is this problem described?
   b. What is perceived to be the cause of this?
   c. Is the idea that the police themselves should address this issue?
4. What 'milestones,' defining moments, can we find regarding thinking about trust?
   a. Are these formulated as crises?
   b. Are they more gradual developments?
   c. Have they been coupled with political changes?
   d. What were these milestones?
   e. Who were the core actors involved?
5. Is there a dominant strategy to gain public trust? What developments have we seen in this respect over recent decades?
   a. What is the role of proximity policing in fostering trust and legitimacy?
   b. What is the role of quantitative targets and indicators?
   c. If both are employed, is there a tension between them?
   d. Is fostering trust and legitimacy perceived to be something that needs to be done through individual interactions, or rather on the system-level?
6. To what extent are there policies to make the police, in their interaction with citizens, act according to procedural justice principles such as fairness, impartiality, respectfulness, explaining their actions, and letting citizens state their views?
   a. Have police behaviour in this sense, and policies addressing this, changed over recent decades?

7. How prolific are police violence and (corruption) scandals, and to what extent are they perceived to influence police–public relationships?
8. To what extent do approaches toward trust and legitimacy per region, district, or area?
9. How do the police attempt to shape their relationship with citizens in problematic neighborhoods?
10. To what extent do the police import models from foreign countries? What developments have taken place in these processes?
11. Do the police have the idea that their legitimacy and trust are connected with that of government or the state?
    a. If so, how is this connection phrased?
12. Who are the most important partners for the police? How is their relationship, and how does cooperation work?
13. What should be done to improve public trust in the police?

Case-specific modules:

England & Wales:

E1.   Recent decades have also seen the rise of police-community partnerships such as neighbourhood watch and crime and disorder reduction partnerships. What is the extent of this cooperative venture and how did such partnerships affect the way the police deal with the public?

E2.   How do PCCs affect policing and the way the police deal with the public?
          How diverse are they in their approach and how influential are they really?

E3.   An important recent addition to the 'police family' is that of PCSOs. What was the rationale behind introducing PCSOs?
          How has the rise of PCSOs altered the relationship between the police and the public?

E4.   What is the impact of the coalition government's budget cuts on police–public relationships and trust-building?

E5.   My analysis of developments in citizens' trust in the police in England & Wales shows stable values between about 1999 and 2006, and increasing rates of trust after that up to 2012. How does this relate to the London riots in 2011? What problems and issues do these surveys appear to miss?

E6.   What is the importance of civilian control and police accountability to the public in police–public relationships?

E7.   Recent decades have witnessed a trend to privatize at least part of the police function. To what extent are these processes of privatization still ongoing and how do they affect the way the police deal with the public?

Denmark:

D1.   What, historically, is the role of the Danish police?
          What do people think is their role?
          Do citizens care about policing and crime?

D2.   What have been the motivations for the 2007 police reform?
          What were the roles, if any, of trust, confidence, and legitimacy?
          How has the reform affected police–public relationships?

D3.   What are *resultatkontrakten*, how do they work, how long have they been
       around, and what were the reasons for their implementation?
           How have performance targets influenced police behaviour and police–
       public relationships over recent decades?

D4.   There has been an independent complaints commission since 2012. Why has
       it been instituted and what was the situation before?

D5.   What is the relationship between local police districts and the National
       Police?

Netherlands:

N1.   What have been the motivations for the regionalization of the police in 1993?
           What were the roles, if any, of trust, confidence, and legitimacy?
           How has the reform affected police–public relationships?

N2.   What have been the motivations for the nationalization of the police in 2013?
           What were the roles, if any, of trust, confidence and legitimacy?
           How has the reform affected police–public relationships?

N3.   How does the rise of other public and private actors in public safety matters
       affect police thinking about trust?
           Does it imply a more distant relationship with citizens?
           If that is the case, is that considered a problem?

N4.   What is the position of neighborhood police officers in the organization?
       How has this role changed over time?

Curriculum Vitae

Dorian Schaap was born in Roden, the Netherlands, on June 13, 1988. He obtained his Bachelor's degree in Sociology at Radboud University Nijmegen (2011) and then obtained a Research Master's degree in Social and Cultural Science (2012) at the same university. He worked as a research assistant at the Department of Criminal Law and Criminology between 2010 and 2012 and as a teaching assistant at the Department of Sociology between 2011 and 2012. He conducted Ph.D. research at the Department of Criminal Law and Criminology on a Netherlands Organization for Scientific Research (NWO) Talent Grant—again at Radboud University. He worked as a Ph.D. candidate between September 2012 and December 2017. During this time, he also served a two-year term in the University Works Council and spent six months working on a grant from the Ministry of Justice and Security participating in the evaluation of the Police Act 2012. As of 2018, he continued working as a researcher at the Department of Criminal Law and Criminology at Radboud University.